T0374466

2/1 Game Force A Modern Approach

-Third Edition

With Chapters on Precision for
Beginning and Intermediate Players

NEIL H. TIMM, PH. D.

TRAFFORD
PUBLISHING™

Order this book online at www.trafford.com
or email orders@trafford.com

Most Trafford titles are also available at major online book retailers.

Printed in the United States of America.

ISBN: 978-1-4669-4384-1 (sc)
ISBN: 978-1-4669-4383-4 (e)

Trafford rev. 06/26/2012

 www.trafford.com

North America & international
toll-free: 1 888 232 4444 (USA & Canada)
phone: 250 383 6864 ♦ fax: 812 355 4082

Contents

Acknowledgements

Acknowledgments to the first edition

I first must thank my bridge partner, Lucy Tillman, who suggested I write this book.

Without her encouragement, it would not have been written. I must also thank my other partners, Ed Schusler, Dave Stentz, Mary Belle Thimgan, Bob Ellis, and Donna Ziemann, for their critical reviews and comments which helped with the presentation and organization of the material.

Finally, I must thank my wife, Verena, who supported me as I sat for many hours in front of my computer typing the material for the book and Marielle Marne for proof reading. However, I am responsible for any errors.

The book, to a large extent, reflects our approach to playing the 2/1 Game Force System. I hope the methods I have presented helps to improve your game.

Sincerely,

Neil H. Timm, Ph.D.

timm@pitt.edu (please e-mail comments and corrections)

Web Page: www.pitt.edu/~timm
December 2009

Acknowledgements for the second edition

I have had the good fortune of having responses from numerous proof-readers. Many read the first edition and provided me with invaluable feedback. I have tried to incorporate all of their suggestions and corrections into this second edition. Thank you all for your constructive and informative input. I want to extend special thanks to Brendon Conlon who provided me with numerous detail suggestions for this second edition.

Changes for the second edition

In this second edition, I have included additional Bridge Rules, expanded and added material in several sections and included many more conventions common to the 2/1 Game Force System. This edition includes the Montreal club and diamond relay bids, the Kennedy club, the Kaplan interchange bid, the Ekren 2♦ convention, picture bids, the forcing pass, masked mini splinters, the Ingberman and Ping Pong conventions, and the Marvin two spades convention, among others.

Finally, a new chapter on Precision called Simplified Precision has been added.

Acknowledgements for the third edition

I have had the good fortune of again having responses from several proof-readers. Thank you for bringing to my attention some of the remaining errors in the text. I have incorporated their suggestions and corrections into this third and final edition. Thank you all for your constructive and informative input. I want to extend special thanks to Charlene Young, Bev McMullen, and Ed Schusler who provided me with numerous detail suggestions for this third edition.

Changes in the third edition

I have made corrections brought to my attention by several readers. The Chapter on Slam bidding has been expanded to include asking for aces and king's simultaneouly, the Baron 4NT convention, and more. New material on Roman Jump overcalls, the Mc Cabe Adjunct and the Reverse Mc Cabe Adjunct, Bergen's Jacoby 2NT bids, Meckwell major suit bids and Meckwell responses to minor suit openings, more on interference over strong notrump, minor suit Stayman, Kokish Relays and several other conventions have been added to this latest edition.

Finally, new Chapters on Transfer Precision, the Meckwell Precision (Meckwell Lite) Bids are also included in this issue. The Meckwell Lite material (Chapter 18) was developed by a **Luke Gillespie & Jim Streisand** and is included in the book with their kind permission.

Introduction

The 2/1 Game Force bidding system is an improvement over the Standard American System that has been in effect and played by bridge players for many years. The advantage of the 2/1 system is that it allows the partnership to know that game is possible with only a single bid. In this book, I have tried to present the fundamental aspects of the bidding structure for playing a "pure" Two-Over-One Game Force system of bidding.

While many players "claim" they play 2/1, this is not the case. They have allowed the bidding structure of Standard American to prevail, like bidding suits up-the-line or ignoring the Walsh club.

In this book, I have tried to change behavior by presenting a series of bids geared toward the 2/1 bidding structure that includes Bergen, Reverse Bergen, and Combined Bergen Raises, inverted minor suit raises with crisscross and flip-flop, cuebidding, modified scroll bids, and many more methods not used in Standard American or Precision.

This is not a book on conventions, it is a book about bridge that incorporates conventions that allow the partnership to reach game or slam. In this regard, I have incorporated modern methods for hand evaluation developed by Marty Bergen. New bidding conventions like SARS (Shape Asking Relays after Stayman), Quest transfers, and an overview of "Bridge Rules and Laws" that I hope will improve your approach to the bidding structure you may use today.

My goal in writing this book is to provide a careful organization of topics so that one may easily follow the concepts unique to the 2/1 game force bidding system.

The material is divided into chapters that illustrate bids by the opener, responder, and rebids by both. In addition, numerous bidding schedules are provided that summarizes standard responses and rebids with or without interference.

While many conventions are presented, those selected were chosen because they are designed to form a basic bidding structure that enhances the 2/1 Game Force Bidding System.

Bridge is a complicated game. I hope the approach I have taken is useful in the improvement of your game whether you play Standard American, Precision, or the 2/1 Game Force bidding system. To further promote your understanding of bridge, Chapters on Precison have been added.

Some of the following material appeared in my monthly newsletter "Bridge News" which is available on my site: www.pitt.edu/~timm. To access newsletters on my Web page, click on

BRIDGE NEWS. I have also posted on my Web page corrections to my books when informed by readers. Corrections are in the files called Errata and may be accessed by clicking on Bridge News also.

Chapter 1
Hand Evaluation, Opening Bids, and Rebids

Hand Evaluation—Starter Points

The standard deck of cards for the game of bridge contains fifty-two cards. The cards are organized into suits—spades (♠), hearts (♥), diamonds (♦), and clubs (♣). The sequence spades, hearts, diamonds, and clubs represent the rank order of the suits within the deck. Thus, spades is higher ranking than hearts; hearts is higher ranking than diamonds, etc. The major suits are spades and hearts and the minor suits are diamonds and clubs.

Each suit contains thirteen cards as follows:

A K Q J 10 9 8 7 6 5 4 3 2

The Ace (A), King (K), Queen (Q), Jack (J), and 10 are called honor cards.

A bridge hand is created by dealing the fifty-two cards to four players, one at a time, so that each player has a total of thirteen cards. Partnerships at the game are the two persons sitting North-South and those sitting East-West. To evaluate the value of your hand, independent of rank, the standard/traditional method promoted by Charles Goren in the late 1940s is to assign values to the honor cards:

Honor	Value
Ace	4
King	3
Queen	2
Jack	1
Ten	0
	10

The evaluation method is referred to as 4-3-2-1-0 point count system. Using this method, one observes that a bridge deck contains a total of 40 High Card Points (HCP). Hence, an "average" hand consists of 10 HCP. While the method of assignment is accurate, a computer analysis of bridge hands shows that the point count system (4-3-2-1-0) tends to undervalue aces and tens and to overvalue queens and jacks. Only kings are correctly valued. Using only HCP, a hand with at least 12 HCP is usually opened. More later!

To compensate for the over and under valuation using the "standard/traditional" method, Marty Bergen, ten-time national champion, developed the ADJUST-3 Method. His 2008 book, "Slam Bidding Made Easier" published by Bergen Books, devotes the 100 pages to his proposed method. Why adjust three? Because the accuracy of the HCP in a hand depends on the difference of overvalued and undervalued honors by the value of three.

Let's see how the process works. With a dealt hand, one goes through six simple steps to employ the Adjust-3 Method:

Step 1: Add up your HCP using the table presented earlier
Step 2: Count the number of aces and 10s (undervalued honors).
Step 3: Count the number of queens and jacks (overvalued honors).
Step 4: Subtract the smaller number from the larger number.
Step 5: Evaluate the difference:
   If between 0-2, make no adjustment
   If within the range 3-5, adjust by 1 point
   If 6+ (rare), adjust by 2 points
Step 6: If the number of aces and 10s is more, add;
   If the number of queens and jacks is more, subtract

We next apply the method to a few examples.

Hand 1	Hand 2	Hand 3	Hand 4	Hand 5
♠AKQ105	♠AK10	♠A67	♠A104	♠K78
♥10982	♥KJ3	♥KQ54	♥10543	♥AQ9852
♦6	♦J105	♦Q7	♦KJ67	♦A109
♣J67	♣567	♦J68	♣K10	♣A

Hand 1: 10 HCP
   3 (undervalued) 10A10; 2 (overvalued) honors QJ
   3-2=1; no adjustment
   The adjusted total for the hand is 10
Hand 2: 12 HCP
   3 aces and 10s (undervalued); 2 Js (overvalued)
   3-2= 1 no adjustment, but skewed in undervalued honors
   The adjusted total for the hand is 12
Hand 3: 12 HCP
   3 queens and jacks (overvalued); 1 ace (undervalued)
   3-1=2 no adjustment, but skewed in overvalued honors
   The adjusted total for the hand is 12
Hand 4: 11 HCP
   4 undervalued honors; 1 overvalued honor
   4-1=3; add 1 HCP; more overvalued honors
   The adjusted total for the hand is 12

Hand 5: 17 HCP
4 undervalued honors; 1 overvalued honor
4-1=3; add 1 HCP; more undervalued honors
The adjusted total for the hand is 18

Using the Adjust-3 method of hand evaluation, one would consider opening hands two-five. However, is there more to the story? Yes. Clearly, if a suit includes AKxxx and another suit contains Axxx, one may take two tricks with the first and only one with the second. Thus, in addition to HCP, one must consider suit length.

After the Adjust-3 process, you must apply the following rule to modify your points for suit length:

ADD FOR SUIT LENGTH

1 additional point for a 5-card suit
2 additional points for a 6-card suit
3 additional points for a 7-card suit, etc.

In summary, add one additional point for each card in a suit over four.

However, in addition to suit length, one has to consider dubious honors since they are OVER VALUED.

Subtract ONE point for hands with the following doubletons or singleton honors

DOUBLETONS: AJ, KQ, KJ, QJ, Qx, Jx
SINGLETONS: K, Q, J

Lastly, you must adjust for QUALITY SUITS—a suit with 3+ of the top five honor cards.

ADD ONE ADDITIONAL POINT FOR EACH QUALITY SUIT.

In summary, one proceeds through the following steps to obtain the total value of a hand.

Step 1: HCP
Step 2: Adjust-3 (add or subtract)
Step 3: Suit Length (add for length)
Step 4: Dubious Honors (subtract)
Step 5: Suit Quality (add)
Step 6: Total Starting Points

Completing steps 1-4, one has what Mr. Bergen calls "starting points." **To open the bidding in the game of bridge (one of a suit), a hand is opened if it has at least twelve starting points in the first seat.** There is more to a hand than simply high card points (HCP).

One final comment, in a suit contract, if your shape is 4-3-3-3, 5-3-3-2, or 6-3-2-2, or 7-2-2-2, you should downgrade your hand one point for "flatness."

Returning to Hands 1-5, we apply the process outlined above.

Hand 1	Hand 2	Hand 3	Hand 4	Hand 5
♠AKQ105	♠AK10	♠A67	♠A104	♠K78
♥10982	♥KJ3	♥KQ54	♥10543	♥AQ9852
♦6	♦J105	♦Q7	♦KJ67	♦A109
♣J67	♣567	♦J68	♣K10	♣A

Hand 1:	HCP	10
	Adjust -3	0
	Suit Length	add 1
	Dubious Honors	none
	Suit Quality	add 1
	Starting points	**12**

Hand 2:	HCP	12
	Adjust -3	0
	Suit Length	none
	Dubious Honors	none
	Suit Quality	none
	Starting points	**12**

Hand 3:	HCP	12
	Adjust -3	0
	Suit Length	none
	Dubious Honors	subtract 1
	Suit Quality	none
	Starting points	**11**

Hand 4:	HCP	11
	Adjust -3	1
	Suit Length	none
	Dubious Honors	none
	Suit Quality	none
	Starting points	**12**

Hand 5:	HCP	17

Adjust -3	1
Suit Length add	2
Dubious Honors	none
Suit Quality	none
Starting points	**20**

Counting only HCP, one would have opened hands 2, 3, and 5; however, using Bergen's "starting points" method, open hands 1, 2, 4, and 5. Also observe that these hands have at least TWO QUICK TRICKS.

BASIC RULE: Open a bridge hand one of a suit with at least 12-21 starting points and two quick tricks (in the first or second seat).

The first step at the bridge table is that all players evaluate their hands; the process begins by the person designated DEALER. The person with twelve starting points opens the auction by bidding (there are exceptions called pre-emptive bids and strong two-level bids to be discussed later). As the auction progresses, the value of your hand may increase or decrease depending upon what you learn from your partner and your opponents. To keep the process simple at this juncture, suppose one person has a sufficient number of "starter points" to open a hand one of a suit with no interference.

Another facet of the game one must consider when bidding is vulnerability. In general, there are four situations. The two pairs are non-vulnerable, two pairs are vulnerable, one pair is vulnerable, and the other pair is non-vulnerable. The value of tricks (won or lost) depends upon the vulnerability of your pair. More on this later!

Opening Notrump Bids

Having sufficient starting points to open, the first goal is to describe your hand to your partner. When you open, you may have a balanced hand, an unbalanced hand, or a semi-balanced hand. A hand with a singleton or a void is by definition unbalanced (35.7%). The patterns that do not contain a singleton or a void are 4-4-3-2, 5-3-3-2, and 4-3-3-3 (47.6%) and are called balanced hands; semi-balanced hands are hands with the following patterns: 5-4-2-2, 6-3-2-2, and 7-2-2-2 (16.7%). A frequency table of hand patterns follows.

Common Hand Patterns Arranged in Order of Frequency*

Pattern	Percentage
4 - 4 - 3 - 2	21.55
5 - 3 - 3 - 2	15.52
5 - 4 - 3 - 1	12.93
5 - 4 - 2 - 2	10.58
4 - 3 - 3 - 3	10.54

6 - 3 - 2 - 2	5.64
6 - 4 - 2 - 1	4.70
6 - 3 - 3 - 1	3.45
5 - 5 - 2 - 1	3.17
4 - 4 - 4 - 1	2.99
7 - 3 - 2 - 1	1.88
6 - 4 - 3 - 0	1.33
5 - 4 - 4 - 0	1.24
5 - 5 - 3 - 0	0.90
6 - 5 - 1 - 1	0.71
6 - 5 - 2 - 0	0.65
7 - 2 - 2 - 2	0.51
7 - 4 - 1 - 1	0.39
7 - 4 - 2 - 0	0.36
7 - 3 - 3 - 0	0.27
All Others	0.69

* Observe that over 33% of the hand patterns contain a singleton or a void so do not be surprised.

When you open the bidding, you first want to communicate to you partner whether you have a balanced or non-balanced (unbalanced or semi-balanced) hand. However, if the semi-balanced hand has honor cards (AKQJ) in two of its doubletons, it may be considered balanced. When hands are balanced, one usually opens the hand with an opening notrump (NT) bid. Because roughly 50 percent of the hands dealt are balanced, many hands are opened using the notrump bidding scheme. In addition, it is used to describe rebids by an opener when bidding one of a suit. When bidding notrump you are saying to your partner, I have a balanced hand; suit bids convey non-balanced hands.

Playing bridge the 2/1 way, the notrump ranges for NT bids and rebids follow.

Opening Notrump Bids	**Opener Notrump Rebids**
1NT = 14/15-17 starter points	1NT = 12-14 starter points
2NT = 20-21 starter points	2NT = 18-19 starter points

Opener may make an artificial and forcing opening bid of two clubs and then rebid notrump with 22+ starting points; more on this in Chapter 4. Interference is common over 1NT openings; bidding strategies are discussed in Chapter 9.

While some will open 3NT with 25-27 starting points, this will not be the case in this book. We will use the Gambling 3NT bid. Playing 2/1 the Gambling 3NT bid shows a solid seven-card suit and denies holding an ace or a king (in the third or fourth seat it may include an outside ace honor); more on opening 2♣ and 3NT in Chapter 4.

An opening bid of 1NT usually shows stoppers in at least three suits where a minimum stopper is defined as Qxx.

Opening 2NT, you should have all suits stopped; however, some may open it with an honor doubleton hoping his partner has the suit stopped. To reach game in a notrump contract, the bid is 3NT (for example, the bidding sequence may be simply 1NT-2NT-3NT), both hands combined usually require twenty-six starting points; however, with long suits and points balanced between the two hands, only twenty-four starting points may be needed. To make a game in notrump, you must take a minimum of NINE TRICKS out of thirteen totals.

If you take twelve tricks (the bid is 6NT), you have made what is known as a slam. To make a (small) slam usually requires thirty-three starting points in the two hands. And, if you take all thirteen tricks (the bid is 7NT), you have taken all of the tricks, a grand slam; to make a grand slam normally requires approximately thirty-seven starting points. The goal of a partnership when bidding is to determine whether or not one has enough points for a partial notrump contract, a game notrump contract, a small, or grand slam contract.

Let's apply our methodology (yes, it applies when opening a major or notrump).

    Step 1: HCP
    Step 2: Adjust-3
    Step 3: Add for suit length
    Step 4: Subtract for dubious honor doubletons/singletons
    Step 5: Add for suit quality
    Step 6: Total starting points

A few more examples:

Example N1	Example N2	Example N3	Example N4
♠KJ	♠KJ6	♠K9	♠98
♥AQ4	♥A104	♥AQ5	♥AKJ2
♦A108	♦AQ8	♦K8	♦102
♣Q10854	♣AQ96	♦K109874	♣AKJ42

Example N1

    Step 1: 16HCP
    Step 2: [Undervalued Honors = 4—Overvalued Honors = 3] = 1; no adjustment
    Step 3: Add 1 for suit length
    Step 4: Subtract 1 for dubious doubleton
    Step 5: Add 0 for suit quality

Step 6:   Total: 16 starting points

Open the bidding 1NT (balanced 5-3-3-2)

Example N2
Step 1:   20 HCP
Step 2:   [Undervalued Honors = 4—Overvalued Honors = 3] = 1; no adjustment
Step 3:   Add 0 for suit length
Step 4:   No dubious doubletons
Step 5:   Add 0 for suit quality
Step 6:   Total: 20 starting points

Open the bidding 2NT (balanced 4-3-3-3)

Example N3
Step 1:   15 HCP
Step 2:   [Undervalued Honors = 2—Overvalued Honors = 1] = 1; no adjustment
Step 3:   Add 2 for suit length
Step 4:   No dubious doubletons
Step 5:   Add 0 for suit quality
Step 6:   Total: 17 starting points

Open the bidding 1NT (semi-balanced 6-3-2-2)

Example N4
Step 1:   16 HCP
Step 2:   [Undervalued Honors = 3—Overvalued Honors = 2] = 1; no adjustment
Step 3:   Add 1 for suit length
Step 4:   Subtract 0 for dubious doubletons
Step 5:   Add 2 for suit quality (hearts and clubs)
Step 6:   Total: 19 starting points

With nineteen starting points, you should not open the bidding 1NT (if partner is a passed hand; some may open 1NT with eighteen starting point in the fourth seat**). With twenty points, you would not open the hand 2NT when holding two worthless doubletons and good suits. You must open the bidding one of a suit.**

Before discussing suit bids, one needs to understand what it means to "take tricks" in notrump. To set our ideas, suppose you open 1NT and all other players at the table pass.

You have won the contract (1NT), and to succeed, you must take seven tricks. The first six tricks are called your book; hence to make a 1NT contract you must take book plus one trick. Similarly, for a contract of 3NT, you must take book plus three tricks or nine tricks.

To capture tricks in notrump, each card in a suit is of decreasing value from the ace down to the 2 (A K Q J 10 9 8 7 6 5 4 3 2). However, the values are only meaningful for the suit led. If you lead, for example a club, only clubs are played and four cards constitute a trick. The highest valued card in the suit is the ♣A. When you are unable to follow suit, you may discard any card in your hand; however, if you get in the lead later, you must be careful when discarding. One generally discards cards in other suits with low value.

Because there are no trumps in "notrump contracts," they are the most difficult contracts to make. Tricks are only won with a suit led. To establish tricks in notrump, you want to take advantage of long suits since these are the source of tricks.

Let's look at an example. You have the following hand: ♠KQ ♥A10 ♦AKQ10753 ♣KQ and your contract is 3NT. In this hand, you have one spade trick, one heart trick, seven diamond tricks, and one club trick or ten tricks (ten potential tricks without a heart lead); hence you can make 4NT. Bidding only 3NT you can make your contract plus an overtrick. In duplicate bridge, 3NT is worth 400 points if your side is non-vulnerable and 600 points if your side is vulnerable. Each overtrick is worth a score of thirty so that you have made either 430 or 630 points for the contract.

If you fail to make your contract, the value of a trick lost depends on vulnerability. Fifty points if you lose a trick non-vulnerable and 100 points if you lose a trick vulnerable. And, if the opponents do not think you can make a contract, it may be doubled. This doubles the values of tricks lost. Hence, when bidding a partial (1NT = score of 90 or 2NT = score of 120) game or slam contract, one must consider the "risk" of not making the contract. Conversely, if you make a doubled contract, it also has a higher value when doubled and made. And, a contract may be re-doubled; even more points if made. When bidding, you must consider vulnerability.

Opening One of a Suit (Major or Minor)

When opening one of a suit (one club, diamond, heart, or spade), one needs a minimum of twelve starting points. Even though notrump bidding was discussed first, the first priority in bidding is to find a fit in a major suit. A fit is defined as at least eight cards for the partnership; the best fit between two hands is 5-3, or 4-4; however, a 6-2 fit also works. In general, it is usually better to play in a 4-4 fit than a 5-3 fit. Contracts may be played in a major suit, notrumps, and a minor suit. Because of its simplicity, we considered notrumps bidding first. A game in notrump only requires taking nine tricks. A major suit game (four spades or four hearts) requires making ten tricks. A minor suit game (five clubs and five diamonds) requires making eleven tricks, book plus five; almost, the same as a small slam.

The number of total points required for a major suit game is the same as that for 3NT, from 24-26 points; while the points required for a minor suit game is twenty-nine points. The value of each game vulnerable is respectively 600 points for notrump, 620 points for a major suit game, and 600 points for a minor suit game. With this knowledge, the first priority is to reach a game contract in a major, notrump, and lastly a minor.

What about tricks in suit contracts? Again, four cards played constitute a trick; however, the values of the cards change with suit contracts. Now, the boss suit is the trump suit, spades, hearts, diamonds, or clubs. If spades is the trump suit, and let's say one leads the ace in another suit (say the ♣A), it may not win a trick since it may be trumped with ♠2, if a person is void in clubs. Thus when playing in a trump contract losers, low valued cards in a non trump suit, may be trumped to win tricks. **In trump contracts, 4-4 fits in the major suit allow one to trump in either hand, it is superior to 5-3 fits. You have less ruffing value with only three trumps.**

Playing the 2/1 game force method, with a five-card or longer five-card major suit and 12-21 starting points, one should bid one of a major (with a non-balanced hand). If one has two five-card majors, the higher ranking major (spades) is opened, not hearts. Ideal hand patterns for major suit opening are hands with the patterns 5-5-x-x, 5-4-x-x, and 5-3-3-2.

A problem hand frequently encountered is the balanced hand with a 5-3-3-2 pattern when one has sufficient values for opening 1NT and you are 5-3 in the majors. Do you open it with one of a major or with sufficient values 1NT? While there are special circumstances when opening, 1NT is better; in general, one would always prefer to open the hand one of a major. However, you may not always get a top score. Making four notrump is better than making four of a major since 430/630 is better than 420/620. In team games using IMPS there is no difference. Generally, you will score better by playing a 4-3-3-3 hand pattern opposite a 4-3-3-3 in notrump than in a 4-4 major suit fit. A 3-3-3-4 pattern opposite a 5-3-3-2 pattern is better in notrump and not the 5-3 major suit fit! To find these hand patterns require advanced bidding methods. For now, my advice is to always open the hand one of a major given the choice.

A similar problem occurs when you are 5-4-2-2. Do you communicate values or shape? For example, suppose the distribution was as follows: ♠AK92 ♥AKJ42 ♦102 ♣98. Do you open the hand 1NT or 1♥? Again, there is no clear cut answer. Some would open the hand 1♠ and others may open the hand 1NT. The risk when your partner is weak is that if you open it 1NT you may miss your major suit fit.

Alternatively, one may use the Flannery Convention or the Extra Shape Flannery Convention. And if you are 4-4-4-1, you might consider the Mini Roman Convention. These distributional hands are reviewed in Chapter 2.

Not having a five-card major, one must bid a minor suit (clubs and diamonds) with 12-21 starting points.

(1) With two minors of unequal length, open the bidding with the longer minor, regardless of strength. Here, one must be careful if one is 5-4 in clubs and diamonds. Depending

on the strength of your hand, less than seventeen starter points, one may open one diamond to avoid a reverse rebid. This will be discussed more fully shortly (briefly, bidding one club, followed by a rebid say two diamonds, partner cannot return to your first bid suit at the two-level called a reverse; this is not the case if you bid one diamond followed by two clubs).

(2) With two three-card minors, open the bidding with the stronger minor. If approximately equal, open the bidding with 1♣. For example, if you hold ♦AKQ and ♣564, open the hand 1♦.

(3) With two four-card minors, one opens one diamond. However, if clubs are significantly stronger, some will open one club.

(4) When one is 5-5 in the minors or 6-5 (clubs-diamonds), a difficult decision presents itself. Open the higher ranking minor if 5-5 or 6-5 (diamonds-clubs). When you are 6-5 (club-diamonds), open the bidding 1♦ unless you have seventeen starting points.

With hand patterns [4-3-3-3, 4-4-3-2, and 3-2-3-5 (♠-♥-♦-♣)] one three-card minor or a five-card minor, always open the hand one of a minor, unless of course the hand evaluation process suggests notrump. A few examples:

M1 ♠AK43	♥J876	♦A1082	♣K
M2 ♠A1054	♥A897	♦A5	♣Q75
M3 ♠A98	♥K54	♦A103	♣Q754
M4 ♠A98	♥K5	♦QJ103	♣QJ43
M5 ♠8	♥987	♦AQ105	♣AQ987
M6 ♠KJ98	♥AQ976	♦J2	♣Q2

For hand M1, you have fourteen starting points (15 HCP + no adjustment-1 dubious king) and no five-card major, open 1♦.

For hand M2, you have fifteen starting points [14 HCP+ 1 adjustments (4 aces and 10s-1 queen=3 so add 1)]. Open 1NT.

For hand M3, you have thirteen starting points, open the hand 1♣.

For hand M4, you have two four-card minors; open the higher ranking minor (1♦) with thirteen starting points (13HCP+1 for quality suit).

For hand M5, clubs are longer than diamonds and you have only fourteen starting points (12 HCP+1 long suit+1 quality suit). Hence, open the hand 1♦. You have not told the truth about your shape, but you will not mislead your partner regarding hand strength by reversing—do not open 1♣.

For hand M6, you are 5-4 in the majors with twelve starting points; open the hand 1♥.

Playing Extra shape Flannery if partner bids 2NT*, respond 3♥* to show a heart minimum opening. Partner will pass or bid game. Playing Flannery, you would also open 2♦*, again bidding 3♥* to show shape and values (see Chapter 2).

Hand Evaluation—Dummy Points

When partner opens one of a major and you have three-card support, you have found a fit in the major. If you win the major suit contract, you will become Dummy and partner will play the hand. When you have a short-suit or two, you must reevaluate your hand.

The dummy hand reevaluation process is used when partner opens a major; it does not apply to minor suit or notrump openings. Conversely, if opener opens a minor and partner (responder) bids a major, opener must reevaluate his starting points with a major suit fit. Thus, the reevaluation process may be done by responder when opener opens a major and a fit is found or by opener when opening a minor and partner bids a major (with 4+ cards) and opener has a four-card major, a fit has also been found. The "dummy" reevaluation process may be employed by opener or responder.

The short-suit Dummy Points are evaluated as follows:

Doubleton	1 point each, always
Singleton	2 points each, **but 3 each with 4+ trump**
Void	equal to the value of the number of trumps in hand

When considering starting points, short-suit points are not counted (except for dubious honor doubletons/singletons). Remember, shortness is not helpful in notrump contracts, and you do not know if your partnership will find a major suit fit. Thus, never count for shortness when you open the bidding. Except for dubious doubletons or singletons, you must ignore suit shortness when calculating starting points. However, with a fit in a major suit, this is not the case.

Dummy Points = Starter Points + Short-suit Points

Let's look at a few examples, when your partner opens 1♠ and you hold the following hands.

Hand A: ♠ AJ62 ♥ 6542 ♦ void ♣ AK987
Hand B: ♠ AQ67 ♥ 678 ♦ AK10432 ♣ void
Hand C: ♠ KQJ32 ♥ 1098 ♦ 7 ♣ J987
Hand D: ♠ 9876 ♥ AK ♦ 75 ♣ AQ1084
Hand E: ♠ 10986 ♥ K ♦ 753 ♣ Q9432
Hand F: ♠ 102 ♥ J64 ♦ KQJ ♣ KQ1098

First, you must calculate starter points. After calculating starting points, add to the total Dummy Points. The analysis for the five hands follows.

Hand A: ♠ AJ62 ♥ 6542 ♦ void ♣ AK987

Hand A: 12 HCP + [Undervalued Honors = 2—Overvalued Honors = 1] = 1; no adjustment + 1 for suit length, no dubious doubletons, no points for suit quality; hence, the total number of starter points = 13. To establish Dummy Points, add four points for the void. There are no singletons or doubletons. Thus in Hand (A) now has seventeen Dummy Points.

Hand B: ♠ AQ67 ♥ 678 ♦ AK10432 ♣ void

Hand B: 13 HCP + [Undervalued Honors = 3—Overvalued Honors = 1] =2; no adjustment+ 2 for suit length, no dubious doubleton, 1 point for suit quality; hence, the total number of starter points = 16. However, you have one doubleton (1more point) and a void (3 more points). Thus, for Hand (B) we now have twenty Dummy Points.

Hand C: ♠ KQJ32 ♥ 1098 ♦7 ♣ J987

Hand C: 7 HCP + [Undervalued Honors = 1—Overvalued Honors =3] =—2; no adjustment + 1 for length + 0 for dubious doubleton honors + 1 for quality suits. Hand (C) has nine starter points. With five trumps, the singleton is worth three points; the hand has twelve Dummy Points.

Hand D: ♠ 9876 ♥ AK ♦ 75 ♣AQ1084

Hand D: 13HCP + [Undervalued Honors = 3—Overvalued Honors =1] = 2; no adjustment + 1 length points + 0 for dubious doubletons (note that the AK does not qualify) + 1 for suit quality. Total starter points = 15. Hand (D) has two doubletons, add 2 points. The total for the hand, Dummy Points = 16.

Hand E: ♠ 10986 ♥ K ♦ 753 ♣ Q9432

Hand E: 5 HCP + [Undervalued Honors = 1—Overvalued Honors = 1] = 0; no adjustment + 1 length point—1 for the dubious king singleton + no quality; total of five starter points. With the singleton king and four trumps, add 3. Dummy Points = 5 + 3 = 8.

Hand F: ♠ 102 ♥ J64 ♦ KQJ ♣ KQ1098

Hand F: 12 HCP + [Undervalued Honors = 2—Overvalued Honors = 4] =-2; no adjustment + 1 length point—0 dubious honor doubleton + 1 quality suits. Total starting points = 14. Do not add 1 point for the doubleton spade—you do not have a fit. The total number of Dummy Points = 15. In review:

Hand A = 13 starter points + 4 shortness points = 17 Dummy Points
Hand B = 16 starter points + 4 shortness points = 20 Dummy Points
Hand C = 9 starter points + 3 shortness points = 12 Dummy Points
Hand D = 15 starter points + 1 shortness points = 16 Dummy Points
Hand E = 05 starter points + 3 shortness points = 08 Dummy Points
Hand F = 14 starter points + 1 shortness points = 14 Dummy Points

When responding to your partner, you always must reevaluate your starter points and convert them to DUMMY POINTS with a fit.

Minor suit Dummy Points

With a minor suit opening (one club or one diamond), the reevaluation process is considerably different. When partner opens in a minor suit, you do not know if the length of the suit is 5+, 4, or 3. Furthermore, game in a minor is often difficult to make. You do not in general support a minor suit opening with only four cards. Instead, you should show a four-card major suit. Remember, your goal is to discover a major suit game which may happen if you and partner are 4-4 in the majors. When partner opens a minor or notrump, **dummy points=starting points.**

The bidding goals have a hierarchy: (1) Major suit fit, (2) Notrump, and (3) Minor suit. **Never reevaluate your hand with a minor suit opening or notrump. Shortness does not count until a fit is established in a suit (major or minor).**

Responses to one-level major suit bids

Game forcing Responses

When responding to a major suit opening, remember that 24-26 points will produce a major suit game, your first priority. When partner opens a major, partner has at least twelve starting points. If you have a fit (often exactly three cards) and upon reevaluation of your hand have at least **thirteen Dummy Points,** you have a game in the major. Your goal with 13+ points is to show a fit with a 2/1 game forcing response. The game force bid forces partner (opener) to bid; it is an absolute force to game for the partnership.

A game forcing response by responder is accomplished by showing a new suit at the two—level without jumping or skipping a bidding level. After a major suit opening, and the OPPONENTS HAVE PASSED and YOU ARE NOT A PASSED HAND, the 2/1 game force bids are:

Opening bid	2/1 Game Forcing Responses
1♠	2♣/2♦ (4+cards), 2♥ (5+cards)
1♥	2♣/ 2♦ (4+cards)

Note that the bid of 2♠ as a response to an opening bid of a heart is not a 2/1 game forcing response. This is because the bid of two spades skips a level of bidding (as we will see later, it denotes a weak hand). In addition, the response of 1♠ to 1♥ is not a 2/1 game force bid. The response of 1♠ over the bid of 1♥ shows a hand with at least four spades and 5+ starting points. The true value of the responders hand is only known through subsequent rebids by the responder.

The game forcing bid is always made in a suit that has at least four cards and is **forcing** for one round of bidding. The opener may not pass (unless the opponents interfere); the pass made by the opener is called a forcing pass since your side has established a game force bidding sequence. These problems will be discussed in Chapter 5.

Let's look at an example using Hands 5 and F above for opener and responder, respectively.

Opener   Hand 5: ♠K78 ♥AQ9852 ♦A109 ♣A
Responder   Hand F: ♠ 102 ♥ J64 ♦ KQJ ♣ KQ1098

Because Hand 5 has a six-card major and twenty starting points, one opens 1♥.

Hearing the heart bid, responder has a fit and fourteen starting points; however, upon reevaluation of his hand, has fifteen Dummy Points, enough for a 2/1 game force bid. With five clubs, the game force bid is 2♣ (note that we are in the slam range).

In the previous example, responder has three-card support and fifteen Dummy Points, a balanced hand and the 5-5-3-2 hand pattern. At this point, the opener does not know about the heart fit. All he knows is that the partnership has a game somewhere. Rebids by opener are needed to establish where the game will be played, usually in the major suit or in notrump.

With exactly three-card support and a balanced hand, is there an alternative bid that would set the game contract with one bid? The answer is yes, it is part of the Bergen Raise system of bids. With a balanced hand and exactly three-card trump support (some may use this bid with only two-card support; in general this is not a good idea since it makes it difficult for partner to decide between a suit contract and notrump), bid 3NT*. Partner now knows you have an upper limit for your bid and three-card support. His rebid depends on the structure of his hand. He will either pass 3NT* or bid 4♥. Given your (worthless) spade doubleton, the safer contract is 4♥, but it may not yield the best result. Because of the nature of the bid, 3NT* must be alerted (hence the asterisk *). If the opponents ask, you must explain the bid "exactly three-card support and 13-15 points."

In some cases, you may want to play in notrump, even though you have a 5-3 major suit fit.

We look at an example from Ron Klinger (2003), "100 Winning Duplicate Tips" published by Orion Press. In this example, south is dealer and with thirteen starting points (HCP + quality + 2 long suits) and opens the bidding 1♥.

North having three-card support and sixteen Dummy points (15 starting points + 1 shortness point) partner bids 3NT*. The hand patterns for south are 2-5-5-1 and north are 4-3-2-4, clear patterns for a suit contract, right?

Dealer East N-S vulnerable.

		♠	KQ106		
		♥	1074		
		♦	Q4		
		♣	AK106		
♠	987	**N**		♠	AJ52
♥	65			♥	J98
♦	K986	**W**	**E**	♦	A3
♣	QJ852	**S**		♣	9742
		♠	43		
		♥	AKQ32		
		♦	J10752		
		♣	3		

Playing hearts, with a diamond lead by west or a spade lead followed by a diamond switch will beat four hearts if the defense finds the diamond ruff. With any other lead, declarer can succeed in four hearts, but the winning sequence is not straightforward. Try it! A three notrump contract is cold and made easily. With better than two stoppers in the black suits by north, 3NT is the better contract even though you have the 5-3 major suit fit. The notrump contract succeeds due to the double minor suit fits in the hands.

In general, when one finds a major suit fit, do not play in notrump unless you have fast tricks and solid suits. Slow tricks favor a trump contract.

Let's consider another example using Hands 1 and F.

Opener	Hand 1: ♠ AKQ105 ♥ 10987♦ 6 ♣ J67
Responder	Hand F: ♠ 102 ♥ J64 ♦ KQJ ♣ KQ1098

Hand 1 from our analysis has twelve starting points (10 HCP + 1 length + 1 quality suit) and so would be opened 1♠. However, south has only two spades, but fourteen Dummy Points and bids 2♣. Again, the opener does not know whether the contract will be in a major or notrumps. Only that they have a game contract. Where the contract is played depends on the opener's rebid. With a singleton, he would prefer a suit contract.

Jacoby 2NT (forcing to game, with perhaps slam interest)

Playing 2/1 game force, we imposed the restriction that one have 13+ Dummy Points and exactly three trumps and a non-balanced hand. With exactly three trumps and a balanced hand, one bids 3NT*. What happens if you have four-card support and 13+ points?

In this case, the bid becomes 2NT*, called the (Oswald) Jacoby's 2NT bid. There are many versions and modifications of the Jacoby 2NT bid. Thus, one should always explain to the opponents the meaning of the bid; and it must always be alerted.

The bid of 2NT* in response to partner's opening bid of one of a major most often shows four trumps and 13+ Dummy Points.

It is not a bid to suggest notrump; you almost always want to play in the major.

Let's look at an example using Hands 1 and D.

Opener   Hand 1: ♠ AKQ105 ♥ 10982♦ 6 ♣ J67
Responder   Hand D: ♠ 9876 ♥ AK ♦ 75 ♣AQ1084

With a five-card major and twelve starting points, opener bids 1♠. Partner (Hand D) has sixteen Dummy Points and four cards in the major. He must bid 2NT*. The two hands have twenty-eight points between them; hence, game in the major is certain. However, is it close to slam!

We will continue the analysis later after introducing the reevaluation of opener's hand called "Bergen Points" and then explain rebids by responder.

In this book, we have said that 2/1 game forcing bids to a major suit opening require exactly three-card support. Some relax this requirement by partnership agreement to include 3/4+ cards support.

Why make this adjustment? Because we already know that a 2/1 bid is a game force bid, and it ensures a major suit game. Why waste the Jacoby 2NT bid to restate that you have game? Use the bid to investigate slam. Hence, you may increase the point requirements for the Jacoby 2NT* bid and use it for slam investigation. **The bid would still require four-card support for the major, but with 15/16+ Dummy Points.** As you develop your game, you may want to consider this change in strategy. You should discuss this change with your partner, since most players (the masses) still use the original version with 13+ Dummy Points, even when using the 2/1 game force system (some even use only 12 HCP). It is advisable to discuss Jacoby 2NT with your partner.

Splinter Bids

The 2/1 game force bids and the Jacoby 2NT bid are two bidding tools used to reach a game contract in a major and to investigate slam. Another type of bid used to investigate game and perhaps slams are splinter bids. Splinter bids show two important things, a fit in the major (four trumps) and shortness (a singleton or void) in a non-trump, side suit. To employ a splinter bid, you again must have 13+ Dummy Points. With shortness, a game in a major suit may be realized with as few as twenty-two points and a slam with as few as twenty-eight points. Thus, they are powerful tools in reaching a game or slam.

There are two kinds of splinter bids (1) direct splinters that are used by the masses and the newer version called (2) concealed/ambiguous splinters that are yet another aspect of Bergen Raises and the 2/1 system supported in this book. Both will be discussed.

Direct Splinters are shown by a **DOUBLE JUMP** in the shortness suit other than partner's major. It is a game forcing raise in the major suit and shows shortness (singleton/void). The Direct Splinter bids are defined as follows:

1♥ - double jump to 3♠/ 4♣ / 4♦ shows SHORTNESS in spades, clubs, and diamonds.

The corresponding jump bids for the opening of one spade are:

1♠ - double jump to 4♥/ 4♣ / 4♦ shows SHORTNESS in hearts, clubs, and diamonds.

While shortness is important, it only has value when the information conveyed to the opener allows the opener to evaluate how well the two hands fit, knowing exactly where the shortness resides. An example will help to clarify this point. Consider the two hands:

| Opener | ♠ AKJ83 | ♥ KQ104 | ♦ 567 | ♣ 7 |
| Responder | ♠ Q762 | ♥ 7 | ♦ AJ42 | ♣ A567 |

With spades as trump, opener must lose one heart and one or two diamonds, depending on the lie of the cards. But, suppose we switch the red suits in responder's hand (dummy) and observe the difference

| Switched Dummy | ♠ Q762 | ♥ AJ42 | ♦ 7 | ♣ A567 |

In the first case, opener's heart honors are duplicated by responder's singleton; both parties prevent two heart losers. In the second case, the defenders hold the diamond honors AKQ of diamonds, but only the ace is useful to the opponents. What can one conclude from this example?

(1) If a singleton or void is opposite high card concentrations, it has less value.

(2) If a singleton or void is opposite partner's low, losing cards, with high values more usefully placed, it has effective value.

Rule: An effective holding is an asset while duplicated holdings are a liability. Or, more importantly, you want your losers opposite shortness to allow losers to be trumped.

While shortness knowledge may help you to reach game (when of value), it also tells your opponents exactly where your weakness resides. Sophisticated defenders love splinters! They will lead the suit and try to off-set your tempo for making the hand. However, many times it is not shortness, **but the degree of fit, that is most important**.

Let's look at two examples where opener again opens 1♠.

Opener (1)	♠ Q9874	♥ KJ2	♦ K107	♣ A6
Opener (2)	♠KQ1062	♥AK52	♦AK72	♣ void

With either hand, opener has no weakness, and if partner splinters, it has little value; a direct splinter bid by his partner will only help the opponents. Is there a better approach to the direct splinter? Yes, and it is called the concealed/ambiguous splinter bids, part of the System of Bergen Raises, and they work as follows:

1♠ - pass - 3♥* **is a single jump** and 1♥ - pass - 3♠* a **double jump in the other major!**

The bid must be alerted; it indicates a singleton or void "somewhere" with 13+ Dummy Points and four-card trumps support.

The advantage of the bid is clear; the opponents only know that shortness exists, but not where. Depending on the nature of opener's hand, opener may not need the shortness information to proceed to game or slam.

When the opener has a need to know about shortness, he uses the relay asking bids: 3NT*, after the bid of 3♠* and the relay bid of 3♠* after 3♥*, the next sequential bid. **The sequential asking bids are called scroll asking bids.** They are asking: where is your singleton or void?

The scroll asking bid and responses follow. If the bidding goes: 1♥ - 3♠*, 3NT* is the scroll ask or 1♠ - 3♥*, 3♠* is the scroll ask. The responses after the 3NT* scroll asks are: 4♣*, 4♦*, 4♥* which shows singletons in clubs, diamonds, or spades, respectively; and the corresponding responses after bidding 3♠* are: 3NT*=♣, 4♣*=♦, and 4♦*=♥, the suit below the singleton (submarine-like bids).

If you do not like the "submarine" bids, one may instead use the bids: 3NT=♠, 4♣=♣, and 4♦=♦; this makes the two options more consistent where clubs and diamonds are directly bid and the remaining bids show the other major singleton!

All the asking bids and responses must be alerted (*). We will subsequently have more examples when we discuss what I have called modified **scroll bids,** used by responders after opener responds to Jacoby 2NT to investigate slam.

We have shown how one may use 2/1 game force bids, Jacoby 2NT, and Splinters to move toward game in a major. All these techniques are tools to force one to reach the goal of a game or slam in a major suit. The next concept is called Swiss Bids.

Swiss Bids

When opening one of a major, forcing 2/1 bids, Jacoby 2NT, concealed/ ambiguous splinters, and 3NT* are used. Playing concealed/ambiguous splinters, the bids 4♣ and 4♦ may now be used to describe responder's hand when other bids fall short.

It often happens that responder has support for the major with four trumps and a balanced hand (4-3-3-3) or a hand with five trumps and invitational values. To describe these types of hands, one may now employ the bids 4♣ and 4♦, called Swiss Bids. The "Swiss Convention" comes in many flavors. There is Trump Swiss, Fruit Machine Swiss, Keycard Swiss, Singleton Swiss, and Super Swiss, among others, with all types of extensions and modifications.

In the duplicate bridge, many prefer some form of Swiss bids to Jacoby 2NT, others prefer Jacoby, and still others combine the two. So which approach should you use? The Swiss Convention is a jump to 4♣ or 4♦ over partner's 1♥/1♠ opening to show different types of sound raises with 3-5 card support. Last century, the most popular form of Swiss was "Fruit Machine Swiss" whereby a bid of 4♣/4♦ over partner's 1♥/1♠ opening showed 12+ points with the 4♣ bid promising two aces and a feature; the feature being either a third ace, the king of trumps, or a singleton. The 4♦ shows the same strength hand without two aces and a feature. This works fine and some have updated it to incorporate the concepts of slam bidding. While this may work for some, we recommend a simpler approach and use a Modified Swiss Convention recommended by Max Hardy.

Now, 4♣* shows three-card support for the major and 16+ HCP with a balanced hand (4-3-3-3) since one may not bid 3NT*. And, 4♦* shows only an invitational hand with five—card support and 13-15 Dummy Points, balanced or semi-balanced. We recommend using the Max Hardy Swiss bids with Jacoby:

16+	starter points	4♣* with a balanced hand and three exactly card support for the major
12/13-15	starter points	4♦* with and balanced or semi-balanced hand and at least five card support.

Both bids must be alerted (*).

The bid of four clubs fills a gap. 3NT* =13-15 balanced with three, and 4♣* shows a 16+ hand with three-card support and balanced. The bid of 4♦*shows a fit with length, balanced or semi-balanced.

Let's look at some examples after one opens 1♠.

Hand SA:	♠KQ9	♥ A752	♦ A104	♣ K96
Hand SB:	♠AQ932	♥ KQ5	♦ 74	♣ AQ7
Hand SC:	♠ AK93	♥ Q52	♦ 74	♣ AQ74

With hand SA, you have three-card support, you cannot bid 3NT* so you bid 4♣* showing 16+ Dummy Points and a fit. With hand SB, you have five-card support and a doubleton so you cannot use the concealed/ambiguous bid. You have five trumps so you should not bid Jacoby; instead, you must bid 4♦*. With hand SC, one would use the Jacoby 2NT bid.

We conclude this section with one more example that is not geared toward game but only a partial score (a contract less than game).

Opener	♠ AKQ105 ♥ 10982 ♦ 6 ♣ J67
Responder	♠ 9864 ♥ A ♦ 753 ♣ K9432

With a five-card major and twelve starting points, opener bids 1♠ (the 10 HCP have been upgraded to 12 because of suit length and quality).

Responder has four-card support but only eleven Dummy Points. He cannot make a 2/1 game force bid. He has to make a one-round forcing bid. These bids are discussed next.

Semi—Forcing Responses

1NT (semi-forcing)

The 2/1 bid by responder is forcing to a game contract. However, suppose you have less than thirteen starting points, you hold 5-12 starting points. To address this situation playing the 2/1 game force system, responder makes the bid of 1NT which IS ANNOUNCED as semi-forcing for one round (it is blue on your convention card). The bid of 1NT does not promise a rebid by responder. To use the bid, responder is either a passed or an unpassed hand, and there is no interference by the opponents. The bid usually says the following:

1. Denies a hand strong enough to force to game.
2. May have a balanced or non-balanced distribution.
3. Denies four-card support for opener's major (may have three-card support, a singleton, two-card support, or a void).
4. In response to 1♥, it denies four spades.

An example follows.

Opener   ♠ AQ987 ♥ K87♦ KJ2 ♣ 56
Responder   ♠ K2 ♥ Q65 ♦ 964 ♣ J10753

Opener and responder first calculate their starting points. Opener = 14 (13 HCP + 1 length point) and Responder = 6 HCP +1 length point = 7 starting points. Opener would bid 1♠. Because responder only has shortness in spades, no short-suit adjustments are made, so responder has only seven starting points and must therefore bid 1NT (most often announced as forcing when playing the 2/1 game force system). In this example, responder has only two-card support for the major.

Let's modify the above hand slightly.

Opener   ♠ Q9876 ♥ KJ2♦ 789 ♣ AK
Responder   ♠ K23 ♥ Q65 ♦ 96 ♣ J10753

Again, one would open the hand 1♠ and after hearing 1NT, dealer **would like to pass**. In this example, responder has only three-card support for the major. Opener is unable to differentiate between the two (two—or three-card support). Furthermore, in this example, opener has no nice rebid. You are stuck, especially if the opponents interfere. If, instead of announcing 1NT as forcing, even if you play 2/1, you can have your cake and eat it, too.

We recommend that the bid of 1NT be announced not as forcing but as semi-forcing. In 90 percent of the cases, opener will bid again.

With 0-2 (sometimes 3) trumps and 5-12 starting points, the bid of 1NT is announced as semi-forcing (also in blue on the convention card).

Why semi-forcing and not forcing? When you announce the bid as forcing, the opponents tend to take a "free" bid. In a semi-forcing auction, they are not sure if the opponents will bid again so they may not risk a call.

Constructive Raises (non-forcing fit bid—invitational)

With 8-10 HCP and three-card trump support, one has a "constructive" hand and would support the major suit bid at the two-level (1♥-2♥* or 1♠-2♠*). This is called a constructive raise over a one-level bid of the major and must be alerted since it guarantees exactly three-card support when playing the Bergen System of raises. For example, suppose partner opens 1♥ and you hold the following hand.

Hand F*: ♠ J2 ♥ 1076 ♦ KJ34 ♣ KQ76

This hand has ten Dummy Points (9 starting + 1 short-suit point). You would bid 2♥* (constructive). Suppose, however, your partner did not open 1♥, but 1♠. Now, you would bid 1NT.

If hand F* was more balanced say (4-3-3-3) with 10-12 starting points with three-card support, one would instead prefer to bid 1NT followed by the bid of 3♠, a limit raise in spades, playing Bergen Raises.

If you do not play Bergen Raises, a constructive raise may have four-card support. Persons who play constructive raises and allow for 4+ card support for the major should **not alert their two-level bid**.

Let's consider an example.

Opener   ♠ AKQ95 ♥ 10982♦ 6 ♣ J67
Responder   ♠ 10986 ♥ A ♦ 753 ♣ Q9432

After the bid of 1♠, one cannot make a constructive bid of 2♠ because one has a weak hand and four-card support. The Bergen Raise of 3♣* is made showing 7-9 Dummy Points, considered next.

Non-forcing responses (with a fit)

There are only two major suit opening bids: 1♥/1♠. When responder has four spades, and the opener bids one heart, he must show the spades. Opener may have five hearts and four spades, and as advised before, a 4-4 fit is better than a 5-3 fit. The bid of 1♠ over 1♥ only requires 5+ starting points and is non-forcing. Rebids by opener and responder will clarify the situation.

When one opens 1♠ and responder has 0-3 card support in spades, and four hearts, and only 5-7 starting points, one must bid 1NT (with 8-10 HCP and 3card support, one would make a constructive raise). You cannot show your four-card heart suit. In general, the bid of 1NT usually signifies LACK OF FIT!

If one opens a major and responder has four-card support with between 5-12 Dummy Points, use Bergen Raises to show the nature of the support.

Bergen Raises and Combined Bergen Raises

Suppose partner opens with 1♥/1♠ and you have **four-card support for the major,** then the bids of:

3♣*   shows 7-9 Dummy Points with four-card support
3♦*   shows 10-12 Dummy Points with four card support (called a limit raise)

If one reverses these two bids, the two bids are called Reverse Bergen Raises. **The primary advantage of Reverse Bergen over Bergen is that one may now employ the bid of three diamonds as an invitational ask since 3♣= 10-12 Dummy Points.** The bid of 3♦ is used to ask, do you have 12 points; if so, bid game. Otherwise, sign off at the three level of the agreed upon major.

Because Bergen bids are made at the three-level, they may be played when the opponents interfere with a double. They are free bids; however, many pairs play that Bergen Raises are off. Others use the system called BROMAD (Bergen Raise over Major Suit Double) recommened by Mr. Marty Bergen.

In general, the concept is to indicate the length of the support by the responder as well as the limited number of points. The general guidelines to show this difference is as follows:

1.	A redouble denies in prinicple a 3-card support.
2.	A first response of 2♣ is a constructive raise with 8-9 points and at least a 3-card support.
3.	The bid of 2♦ shows a limit raise with a 3-card support.
4.	A one level raise is preemptive in nature.
5.	Jump raises are normal Bergen/Combined/Reverse Bergen raises withat least 4-card support.
6.	A first response of 2 No Trump can be employed to show a preempt in either Minor suit.

However, consistent with Bergen/Combined raises, one may employ the following club and dimond bids over a **double** of a major to show a limit raise:

2♣*   shows 10-12 Dummy Points with three-card support
2♦*   shows 10-12 Dummy Points with four-card support

Again the bids are to be alerted.

Another modification is:

2♣*   7-9 points and at least 3-card support
2♦*   10-12 and at least 3-card support
2M   0-6 and at least 3-card support
2NT   a weak hand with a long minor, Opener is forced to bid 3♣
3♣*   10-12 with 4-card support

3♦* 10-12 with 4-card support

Finally, yet another option is to using the following bids:

XX   A redouble is not part of BROMAD per se, but is worth mentioning. It shows 10+ points and denies 3+ card support.

2♣   A 3-card "Constructive" raise, showing 7-10 points and exactly 3-card trump support.

2♦   A 3-card Limit Raise or better, showing 10-12 points and exactly 3-card trump support.

2♥/♠   A 3-card "Preemptive" raise, showing 0-6 points and exactly 3-card trump support.

2NT   A preempt in clubs or diamonds (i.e. a hand that would normally make a 3♣ or 3♦ weak jump shift).

3♣   A 4-card "Constructive" raise, showing 7-10 points and exactly 4-card trump support.

3♦   A 4-card Litim Raise showing 10-12 points and exactly 4-card trump support.

3♥/♠   A 4-card "Preemptive" raise, showing 0-6 points and exactly 4-card trump support.

BROMAD assumes that the partnership plays 5-card majors. The theory is to reach the correct level of bidding in accordance with the Law of total tricks.

Note that the preemptive direct raises (i.e. 1♠ : 2/3♠) are based on the principle of fast arrival. They are designed rob the opponents of bidding space as quickly as possible.

While many play that Bergen is always off over any interference, I believe this is too extreme. Why do you allow the opponents to interfere with your bidding sequences?

I also recommend they be played on over two-level bids when both sides are non-vulnerable or when the opponents are vulnerable and you are not. For example, if the bidding goes 1♠ - 2♥—there is room for the three-level bids, make it. If the overcall is a minor suit bid of say 2♣, then 3♣ (a cuebid) only ensures 3+ card support for the major suit bid of 1♠. **Finally, they are always on over a double!**

Another system that has become popular is called "Combined Bergen" Raises, developed by Pat Peterson from Hernando, Florida. I like the convention. It works like this.

3♣* shows 7-12 Dummy Points (note that we have combined the Bergen point range for this bid; hence the name Combined Bergen) with four-card support. If opener wants to know whether or not you are at the lower end (7-9) points or higher end (10-12) points, opener bids 3♦*.The response 3♥* shows the lower range and the response 3♠* shows the upper range.

3♦* shows 10-12 Dummy Points with three-card support (a limit raise).

Thus, you do not have to bid 1NT (semi-forcing) and make a jump rebid in the major with 10-12 Dummy Points. One normally has 0-2 card trump support for the bid major.

Let's consider our prior example.

Opener   ♠ AKQ95 ♥ 10982♦ 6 ♣ J67
Responder   ♠ 10986 ♥ A ♦ 753 ♣ Q9432

With a five-card major and twelve starting points, opener bids 1♠ (10 HCP have been upgraded to twelve starting points because of suit length and quality).

Using the Bergen Raises, responder would bid 3♦* showing a limit raise in support of the spade opening bid.

Using Combined Bergen Raises, one bids 3♣*, and opener would ask the range by bidding 3♦*, now you would respond 3♠* (10-12 Dummy Points).

A minor problem occurs when playing Combined Bergen and partner opens 1♥ and partner responds 3♣*. If you now ask using the bid of 3♦* and partner responds 3♠*, you are committed to game in hearts. Instead, one merely invites game by bidding 3♥. Alternatively, some use Bergen Raises for hearts and Combined Bergen for spades.

Combined Bergen with a Spade Gadget

When opening the bidding one heart and responding 1NT, what do you do after hearing the bid of two hearts with two card support with a top honor, A/K/Q-x?

Let's look at two bidding sequences.

(1)Partner	You	(2)	Partner You
1♥	1NT	1♥	1NT
2♥	??	3♥	??

Because you have not bid one spade, in the two examples you may make the impossible 2♠ and 3♠ spade bids, respectively.

Each of the bids tells partner that you have at least a top high honor doubleton in hearts. In example (2) partner can decide between passing, bid a major suit game, or 3NT.

However, in (1) the opening bidder has more flexibility. You may make a help suit game try in the major by bidding a suit at the three level (Help Suit Game Try, usually alerted) asking partner to bid game with help or you may make the bid of 2NT (tell me about your hand, alert). The 2NT bid may be used to ask for shortness, allowing partner to bid 3NT or 4♥. However, it may also be used to show your worst side suit fragment with 3 or 4 losers by bidding the suit or 3♥ to show neither. The approach you use after the bid of 2NT is by partnership agreement. I prefer shortness.

When opening 1♠, what do you do with the bidding sequence 1♠-1NT-2♠—? As opener you might have the following hand:

♠K76542 ♥ Q53 ♦ KJ ♣ AK

Now the bid of 2NT by partner shows a doubleton honor in spades and 10-12 dummy points with stoppers in other suits, invitational to game in notrump.

A rebid of 3♠ is invitational to game, with two card support, all other suits not stopped.

With opener's rebid is 3♠, showing 16-17 points, partner may either pass, bid 3NT or 4♠.

When opening one spade, it is often difficult to find a 5-3 fit in hearts. To find the fit in hearts, many advanced players use the Bart or Lisa Conventions. I prefer Lisa which is discussed shortly.

Preemptive Bids

With only 0-6 Dummy Points and four-card support, for hearts or spades, one makes a preemptive three-level bid of three hearts (3♥*) or three spades (3♠*), and if you have five trumps, bid GAME. Why? This has become known as the adjunct to the LAW OF TOTAL TRICKS that states "bid to the level equal to the combined number of trumps held by your side". For example, with eight trumps bid to the two-level, with nine trumps, bid to the three-level, with ten trumps, bid to the four-level. Again, both bids must be alerted, and if asked, described as weak.

We will discuss the LAW of TOTAL tricks later in the book (Chapter 10), following Larry Cohen (1972), "To Bid or Not to Bid" by Natco Press. Do not apply the law blindly; it does not work with unbalanced hands.

With only 0-6 starting points and five trumps, one should bid game (4♥/4♠), you have ten trumps.

Before discussing responses to minor suit openings, the following chart summarizes Bergen (responses) and the Combined Bergen (responses) with no interference when opening a major suit (1♠/1♥). Also included are the Swiss bids and Concealed or Ambiguous splinter bids. It is important to realize that not all persons will play the structure below that I have suggested. You can pick and choose. The "Bergen" system you play must be discussed. Some bridge players do not play Bergen, but instead they prefer fit bids where, for example, one of a major followed by a three-level jump in the major shows a fit with 10-12 Dummy Points (an invitational bid and non-forcing). This approach is more consistent with Standard American and not the 2/1 System.

OVERVIEW COMBINED BERGEN AND BERGEN RAISES
Max Hardy Swiss Bids and Concealed/Ambiguous Splinters

Combined Bergen Raises Bergen Raises

Dummy Points	Responder Bid	Dummy Points	Responder Bids
	2 Trumps		
5-9 Pts	*1NT then 2 Major	5-9 Pts	*1NT then 2 Major
	3 Trumps		
5-9 Pts	*1NT then 2 Major	5-9 Pts	*1NT then 2 Major
8-10(bad) Pts	@2Major (Constructive)	8-10(bad) Pts	@2Major Constructive)
10-12 Pts	**3 ♦	10-12 Pts	*1NT then 3 of Major
13-15 Pts	*3NT	13-15	*3NT
13+	2 Over 1 Bids	13+	2 Over 1 Bids
16+ Pts Balanced	@4♣ (Swiss)	16+ Pts Bal	@4♣ (Swiss)
	4 Trumps		
0-6 Pts	@3 Major (Weak)	0-6 Pts	@3 Major (Weak)
7-12 Pts	@3 ♣ Bid 3 Diamonds to Ask 3♥=7-9, 3♠=10-12	7-9 Pts	**3♣ (Weak)
		10-12	**3♦ (Invitational)
13+ Singleton (Concealed Splinter)	@3 Other Major then Step Bids	13+ Singleton (Concealed)	@3 Other Major then Step Bids
13+ No Singleton	2/1 Bid or Jacoby 2NT	13+ No Singleton	Jacoby 2NT

15/16+ Pts   @Jacoby 2NT

5 Trumps

| 0-11 Pts | Bid Game | 0-11 Pts | Bid Game |
| 12-15 Pts | @4 ♦ (Swiss) | 12-15 Pts | @4♦ (Swiss) |

Note: With 5 HCP and three-card trump support, pass, unless holding either a singleton or at least one trump honor with all other HCP in one side suit. *=Semi-Forcing, **Forcing, and @=Alert

If you play Reverse Bergen Raises, you merely switch the meaning of the 3♣ and 3♦ bids.

The advantage of this approach is that a preemptive bid forces the opponents to a higher level and the after the bid of 3♣, one may use the bid of 3♦ to ask if you have 12 Dummy Points.

Walsh Bidding System

Some final remarks follow on the **Walsh Bidding System** developed by Richard Walsh, John Swanson, and Paul Soloway in the 1960's and is commonly ignored today because of Bergen Raises and Swiss bids.

From the previous table using Bergen Raises, one shows a limit raise with 10-12 Dummy Points and four-card support is signified by bidding 3♦*, a good limit raise. With 10-12 Dummy Points and three-card support, one bids one notrump and then bids three of the major, a bad limit raise usually with no singleton or void. Using Combined Bergen Raises, one bids 3♣* with four-card support (7-12 Dummy Points) and after the asking bid of 3♦*, a good limit raise by bidding 3♠*, 10-12 Dummy Points. Or, one bids 3♦* directly to show three-card support and 10-12 Dummy Points, a bad limit raise.

However, suppose the bid is 1♥ and the responder has three hearts and four spades and only 10-12 Dummy Points but ruffing values (a singleton or void). Since the responder has less than thirteen starting points and only three-card support, he cannot use the Concealed/ Ambiguous Splinter major bid of three spades. A jump bid of three hearts shows 0-6 starting points and four-card support. And, one notrump followed by three hearts does not show ruffing values. One uses the Walsh Bid; **the Walsh bid is one spade followed by a bid of three hearts, a good limit raise with three-card support, and ruffing values**. Consider the hand after a one heart opening bid.

♠ 9854   ♥ Q107   ♦ 9   ♣ AK1062

One has three-card support for hearts, but only twelve Dummy Points and cannot bid two hearts constructive. While one may bid one notrump followed by three hearts, this does not show the ruffing values in diamonds. Thus, one makes the Walsh bid of 1♠ followed by 3♥, a good limit raise in hearts.

What do you do if one opens the bidding with one spade and you want to distinguish between a good limit raise with three-card support and ruffing values from a bad limit raise with no ruffing value? Consider responder's hand after one opens one spade.

♠ J85   ♥J1074   ♦9   ♣AK1062

Here, one bids one notrump (semi-forcing). After the rebid of two clubs or two diamonds, responder would jump to four spades. Do not bid three spades, a bad limit raise since you have ruffing values in diamonds.

Review of some of 2/1 bids and Bergen Responses when opening 1♥/1♠

1♠ (over 1♥)	4+ spades and 5+ Dummy Points
1NT	(0-2) card support 5-12 Dummy Points
2♣	4+ clubs and 13+ Dummy Points (2/1 game force)
2♦	4+ diamonds and 13+ Dummy Points (2/1 game force)
2♥/2♠ (over 1♠/1♥)	5+ cards in major and 13+ Dummy Points (2/1 game force)
2♥*/2♠* (over 1♥/1♠)	3-card support with 8-10 Dummy Points (constructive)
2NT*	13+ starting points with 4-card support
3♣*	Bergen Raise 4+ card support of major
3♦*	Bergen Raise 4+ card support of major
3♥*/3♠* (over 1♥/1♠)	4-card support 0-6 starting points
3♠*/3♥* (over 1♥/1♠)	13+ starting points ambiguous/concealed splinter
3NT*	13-15 starting points and 3-card support (balanced)
4♣*	16+ with 3-card support and a balanced hand
4♦*	12-15 starting points and 5-card support
4♥*/4♠* (over 1♥/1♠)	0-11 starting points and 5+ trumps
*Alert bids	

Responses to one-level minor suit bids

Opening one of a minor, there is no 2/1 game forcing suit bid when one opens 1♣; however, if one opens 1♦, the bid of 2♣ is forcing to game. This is also the recommendation of Max Hardy. **However, if one rebids the club suit, the game force is off** (mark this on your convention card).

The bid of two clubs over one diamond is not considered forcing to game by all who play the 2/1game force system; some experts like Mike Lawrence, Audrey Grant, and Eric Rodwell suggest that the bid should only be forcing for one round, not to game. We do not support this approach since we recommend using crisscross for an invitational game in diamonds. More later on crisscross.

Opening bid	2/1 Bids
1♣	**Walsh Responses (may or may not be forcing to game)**
1♦	**2♣ (4/5+ cards) (forcing to game)**

Non-Forcing Responses

Walsh Responses to the one club (1♣) opening

Recall that the opening bid of one club shows hands with 3-5+ clubs and denies a five-card major.

Even when you open a minor, the goal is to find a major suit fit. Using the Walsh approach (which is quite different from the "Standard American" convention), your goal is to show strength and shape as soon as possible. You bypass a four, five, or even a six-card diamond suit to bid a four-card major with minimum to invitational values (5-12 starting points) and bid your four-card major (usually with non-balanced hands).

With two five-card major suits, bid the higher ranking suit (spades). With a five-card suit and a four-card suit, bid the longer suit first. With two four-card majors, you bid them up-the-line, first hearts and then spades.

Examples:

♠AK432 ♥ 109876 ♦ 78 ♣ 7	bid 1♠ the higher ranking (5-5)
♠109876 ♥ AK43 ♦ 789 ♣ 7	bid 1♠ (5-4)
♠10987 ♥ AK43 ♦ 789 ♣ 76	bid 1♥ (4-4)

On your convention card you must mark "Frequently bypass 4+diamonds." If you have invitational starting values (10-12), you may rebid your major suit. For example, the bidding may go 1♣ - 1♥ - 2♣ - 2♥. Or, if instead you bid 2♠, this has a special meaning called fourth suit forcing and will be discussed later.

With a five-card major and 13+ starting points, one may use the New Minor Forcing Convention as a forcing bid to explore game (to be discussed later).With a balanced hand and 8-10 starting points, you bid 1NT; 2NT =11-12, and 3NT=13-15; these bids are used to show balanced hands and values and deny a four-card major.

The response bid of 1♦ is used as a waiting bid showing **no four-card major** and 4+ diamonds (responder has 6-12 starting points); opener may respond two clubs (6+ card suit with 12-16 starting points or with a singleton may bid a major, again with 12-16 starting points. The opener's bid of 1NT (and 12-14 starting points) shows a balanced hand since you have denied a major suit bid; more on responses by opener later.

The bid of 1♦ is also used with a stronger hand; after the bid of 1NT, you may now bid your major suit (up-the-line) a **reverse by responder** to show your four-cards major. The reverse bid shows 13+ starting points and a four-card major (forcing to game).

Let's look at a few examples.

1. ♠ KQ65   ♥Q874   ♦Q1042   ♣8

2. ♠ QJ84   ♥53   ♦KJ954   ♣92

3. ♠ Q104   ♥KJ5   ♦J6543   ♣Q6

4. ♠ AK54   ♥A6   ♦K8743   ♣93

5. ♠ Q104   ♥K105   ♦KJ654   ♣Q9

(1)   Bid 1♥, bypassing the bid of one diamond to bid four-card majors up-the-line with a minimal hand.

(2)   Bid 1♠, bypassing diamonds with minimum hand, bid the major.

(3)   Bid 1♦, too weak to bid 1NT; you want the strong hand to play contract.

(4)   Bid 1♦, strong enough to reverse, diamonds then spades.

(5)   Bid 2NT, you have 12 starting points.

In summary, 2/1 "Walsh" bidders show a four-card major immediately with a weak hand and use one diamond as a waiting bid. With a strong (13+ starting points) hand, the bid of 1♦ is followed by a bid of a four-card major, a reverse bid. For Walsh bidders, the bid of 1NT is semi-forcing showing 8-10 starting points and denying a four-card major.

With no four-card major and 13+ starting points, one bids 2♣* (called the inverted minor bid) or 2♦* (called crisscross), a limit raise in clubs (10-12 starting points) in clubs with 5+ clubs and is the non-forcing bid. More on these two bids later.

Note: The bidding sequence 1♣ - 1♦ - 1♥ (opener) - 1♠ is forcing to game playing Walsh style bids since with a weak hand responder would have bid spades and not diamonds (a fourth suit forcing auction playing Walsh and show a suit, 5-4 in hearts and spades); more on fourth suit forcing soon.

Weak Jump Shifts (Preemptive Bid)

The bid of 2♥/2♠ over a one club or one diamond opening is a weak Jump Shift in the major showing 6/7+ cards and a very weak hand, 2-5 starting points. With six starting points (6+), you bid one of the majors.

To show a preemptive raise in clubs, one jumps to the four-level (4♣).

Forcing Responses

The bid of 2♣ over 1♦ (game force)

Recall that the opening bid of 1♦, denies a five-card major by opener and shows 3-5+ diamonds.

With an opening bid of one diamond, as when one opened one club, the first objective of the responder is to show a major suit. With 5+ starting points and a four or five-card major, bid the major.

With at least five clubs and 13+ starting points, one bids 2♣. This bid is forcing to game. However, some partnerships use the bid to show a weak hand with clubs!

With a balanced hand and 6-10 starting points, bid 1NT; 2NT =11-12, and 3NT=13-15; these bids are used to show balanced hands and values and deny a four-card major. Note that over a one diamond opening, the 1NT range is not the same as for a one club opening. You do not have a relay bid to allow the stronger hand to play 1NT; either hand may play the notrump contract.

After the opener bids, a new suit at the two-level, the rebid of 3♣ by responder shows the opener that the force to game is off and will allow one to be in a contract short of game.

For example, the bidding may go: 1♦ - 2♣ - 2♥ - 3♣ showing less than 5-12 starting points and long clubs. If instead the bidding goes 1♦ - 2♣ - 2♥ - 2♠, you are showing all the suits and you are at the two-level. This is a fourth suit forcing sequence; however, the fourth suit may or may not be real (and can be played forcing for one round only or to game).

To appreciate why we recommend that the bidding sequence 1♦ - 2♣ as a game force sequence, consider the following:

Opener   ♠876   ♥AQ   ♦A652   ♣K875

Responder   ♠AKJ   ♥KJ4   ♦743   ♣QJ92

Clearly, one would open 1♦ and responder would bid 2♣ (forcing to game). Not playing two clubs forcing to game you may respond 1♥ and opener may bid 1NT. What next?

Perhaps 2♠ by responder and the contract may stop in 2NT. You missed not only your club game, but a club slam!

If responder instead had the hand: ♠7 ♥A103 ♦678 ♣AQJ952.

One would again respond 2♣; however, after the bid of 2♥, one would bid 3♣ (game force off).

Let's look at another example. Suppose partner opens 1♦ and you hold the hand:

♠K32 ♥56 ♦AQ5 ♣KJ742

You would clearly make a forcing raise of 2♦. However, suppose opener bids 1♣. You have no four-card major and may temporize with a bid of 1♦; hoping opener would perhaps bid hearts. Is there a better approach? Yes, one may use the forcing inverted minor bid discussed next.

Inverted Minors and Crisscross (game forcing and invitational bids)

Using inverted minors, one bids 1♣ followed by 2♣* or 1♦ followed by 2♦*, when bidding one club or one diamond, respectively. The bid denies a four-card major and shows a hand with 13+ points and at least four-card support for the bid minor. The bids are forcing to game (and alerted); there is no upper limit for the inverted minor raise. Again, we assume no interference. **Over a double** and playing **flip-flop** inverted minor raises are on; for those who do not play flip-flop, inverted minor bids are off over a double. More on this later!

Using crisscross, responder bids are 2♦* over the bid of 1♣, and 3♣* over the bid of 1♦, when opening one club and one diamond, respectively. These bids are a Jump Shifts (J/S) in the other minor (and alerted); the bids show a limit raise (10-12 starting points) and at least four-card support for the bid minor and deny a four-card major. These bids are invitational to game. On the convention card you must mark "J/S in other minor" in red.

To show a weak hand (between 5-9 starting points), one employs double jump bids in the minor bid suits: 1♣ - 3♣* and 1♦ and 3♦*. These bid require 5+ card support and again and may be used with or without interference.

Returning to our example, suppose opener bids 1♣ and you again hold the hand:

♠K32 ♥56 ♦AQ5 ♣KJ742

You would respond 2♣*, 13+ starting points and 5+ clubs.

Note: Not all partnerships play inverted minors and crisscross as explained previously. Instead, some REVERSE the bids. This is called reverse inverted with crisscross.

The reason for the reverse is that many feel the jump to the three-level is too extreme with only 10-12 starting points. Be careful when sitting down with a new partner.

Playing inverted minors with crisscross, one gives up the Weak Jump shift bid in the other minor or the mini-splinter bid which may be played with the 10+ inverted minor raise approach, played by the masses (better ask your partners what they play). With either approach (inverted minors or inverted minor raises with crisscross), a weak hand (nine or less points) is shown by a preemptive double raise in the minor (alerted), again denying a four-card major.

Rebids by Opener [(following a single raise (13+) or a J/S response].

A rebid of 2NT by opener shows a hand in the 12-14 point range with both majors stopped. This bid may not be used after the 3♣ bid, instead one must bid 3NT!

A jump rebid of 3NT by opener shows 18-19 HCP with stoppers in both majors, only after a 2-level bid. This is not used with criss cross after the 3♣ bid, it is given up.

Opener's rebid of a new suit (after a single raise) at the 3-level (a mini-splinter over a single raise) shows more than a minimum, at least 14 HCP, usually distributional and forcing.

After an inverted minor raise, opener rebids show "stoppers up the line". Opener must not by pass any suit containing a stopper, for single raises this is identical to the 10+ inverted minor raise bids.

Note: With criss cross (a J/S response), a 3-level minor suit bid (3♣ after 2♦) shows a minor two suiter (5-4+) and a minimum hand (12-13hcps). The bids 2♥ and 3♦ (after 1♣ - 2♦) show stoppers. A clear disadvantage of criss cross J/S limit raises is that they take up bidding room, especially when one bids 3♣ after 1♦. Now it is more difficult to show stoppers since one must use 3-level bids. For this reason, some play criss cross only after a 1♣ bid, and **do not use it over the 1D bid.** This is sometimes referred to as partial Criss Cross bids.

Rebids by responder

With game forcing values, the responder may also bid stoppers to try to get to NT after a single forcing raise. With a J/S limit raise, no call should again be made that takes the auction beyond the three level.

Minor Suit Splinter Bids

When opening one club (diamond), a double jump in diamond (clubs), hearts, or spades, is a splinter bid. The bid shows 5+ cards for the minor bid and 13+ starting points with a singleton or void in the suit bid. It is forcing to game in the minor.

In our discussion when opening one of a major or one of a minor, there have been several times we have found a fit in a major or in a minor. After finding a fit in a major, the responder added starting points to short-suit points to create Dummy Points. With a fit in a minor using inverted minors or crisscross, one again finds a fit. Now, the original value of opener's starting point's increases in value. So opener must again reevaluate his hand.

This reevaluation process is again due to Marty Bergen to create "Bergen Points."

Review of responses to minor suit opening of (1♣)

1♦	4+ diamonds and no 4-card major 5+starting points
1♥/1♠	4+card major 5+ starting points
1NT	8-10 starting points and no 4-card major
2♣*	13+ starting points and 4+clubs (inverted)
2♦*	10-12 starting points (crisscross) with 4+ clubs
2♥/2♠	Weak Jump Shift in hearts/spades
2NT	10-12 starting points balanced
3♣*	5-9 starting points (weak) and 4+ clubs
3♦*/3♥*/3♠*	13+ starting points, splinter bids in support of clubs
3NT	13-15 starting points and a balanced hand
4♣	Preemptive, 7+ clubs
4♥/4♠	to play in hearts/spades

Review of responses to minor suit opening of (1♦)

1♥/1♠	4+card major 5+ starting points
1NT	6-10 starting points and no 4-card major
2♣	weak hand with 6+ clubs 5-12 starting points
2♦*	13+ starting points (inverted) with 4+ clubs
2♥/2♠	Weak Jump shifts in hearts/spades
2NT	10-12 starting points balanced
3♣*	10-12 starting points (crisscross) with 4+ diamonds
3♣*/3♥*/3♠*	13+ starting points, splinter bids in support of diamonds
3NT	13-15 starting points and a balanced hand
4♦	Preemptive, 7+ diamonds
4♥/4♠	to play in hearts/spades

Meckwell 2NT Response to Minors Suit Openings

As an alternative to inverted minors, Jeff MECKstroth and Eric RodWELL use the bid of 2NT as a response to a minor suit opening to show game forcing values and a hand that may contain one or both four card majors. Opener rebids are:

Over 1♦, 3♣ asks partner for a four card major. If opened 1♣, showing 5+ clubs, and an unbalanced hand, with mild slam interest, responder mayy choose to try for a club game/ slam, bid 3NT, or rebid a four card major with additional values.

Over 1♣, 3♦ asks partner for a four card major. If opened 1♦, showing 5+ diamonds and an unbalanced hand, with mild slam interest, responder may choose to try for a diamond game/ slam, bid 3NT, or rebid a four card major with additional values.

3♥ = showing a heart control and asking partner to bid 3NT with a spade control.
3♠ = showing a spade control and asking partner to bid 3NT with a heart control.
3NT = signinf off in game
4♣ = Either a 6+ clubs suit with slam interest if opened 1♣, 5+ clubs if opened 1♦, or Gerber, depending upon partnership agreement.
4♦ = 6+ diamond suit if opened 1D, 5+ diamonds if opened 1C
4♥ = 6/5 minor/hearts.
4♠ = 6/5 minor/spades.

Hand Evaluation—Bergen Points

When you have a fit, a major, minor, or notrump, the value of your hand will often increase.

Recall that as opener, you only considered your starting points that EXCLUDED short-suit points. And, while you did account for suit length, you may have additional value for the extra trump length. And finally, while you accounted for quality suits, the value of these may also increase when finding a fit.

These observations suggest that your Starting Points must be modified with a fit. It works as follows.

Bergen Points (the final hand evaluation)

Step 1: **Extra Trump Length (with 6+ trumps, add 1 for each trump after 5)**

Add   1 Point 6 card suit
       2 Points 7 card suit, etc.

Step 2: **Side Suits (for a 4-card or 5-card suit)**

Add   1 point for each

Step 3: **Short-Suit Points (Used with suit contracts only NOT notrump)**

Add   1 extra point for 2 or 3 doubletons, **not each** (Note this is not the same as Dummy short-suit point procedure)
2 extra points for a singleton
4 extra points for a void

Adding the above aspects of your hand to your starting points, your total points are called Bergen Points. This total is now used to determine if you have twenty-six points (Bergen Points + Dummy Points) for game in a major, twenty-six points for notrump [Bergen Points (steps 1 and 2) + Partner's Starting Points), twenty-nine points for game in a minor (Bergen Points + Partner's Starting Points), or thirty-three points for a slam (notrump or suit).

In notrump, you cannot count shortness; hence, only steps 1 and 2 above are used to count Bergen Points.

Let's apply the process to Hands 1, 2, and 5 with 12, 12, and 19 starting points, respectively.

Hand 1	Hand 2	Hand 5
♠AKQ105	♠AK10	♠K78
♥10982	♥KJ3	♥AQ9852
♦6	♦J105	♦A109
♣J67	♣567	♣A

And, suppose we have found a fit in spades, for hands 1 and 2 and hearts for hand 3.

To calculate Bergen Points for hand 1, you add 2 points for the singleton. Thus, hand 1 has 12 starting + 2 short-suit points = 14.

Because hand 2 is balanced, there is no adjustment Starting Point= Bergen Points.

For hand 5, you add 1 more point for 6 trumps and 1 more point for the ace singleton. Hence, Bergen Points = 19 + 2 = 21.

Suppose you hold the following hand and partner responds 3♣* and you know he has 7-12 Dummy Points playing Combined Bergen Raises or only 7-9 Dummy Points playing Bergen Raises.

♠AK42 ♥ KQ632 ♦ AK109 ♣ void

19 HCP
Adjust-3 no adjustment (3 overvalues; 1 under value)
Length points: Add 1
Quality Suit: Add 1
Starting Points: 21

However, finding a fit in hearts, you must reevaluate
Short-suit: Add 4 points for void
Side Suits: Add 1 point (4-card diamond suit)
Bergen Points Total= 26 points

Because your partner bids three clubs, you now know, upon reevaluation, that you may have a slam in hearts. Without the reevaluation, you may have only bid game!

Suppose you have the following hand: ♠A598 ♥ KJ87 ♦ AQ ♣ 1085.

With two four-card majors and thirteen starting points (14 HCP—1 dubious doubleton), you open 1 ♣. Partner with the following hand ♠K32 ♥ 56 ♦ KJ5 ♣ AJ742 with thirteen starting points, bids 2♣*. With the diamond doubleton, notrump is of no interest. You have a club fit. You now reevaluate your hand, using the Bergen Method. You add two points for the doubleton and two points for the two four-card suits. You have seventeen Bergen points. Adding this to partner's minimum 13 starting points = 30 points and you confidently bid 5♣, a minor suit game.

Overview of Forcing and Semi-Forcing Rebids by Opener

We have discussed opening one-level bids for majors and minors and corresponding responses by your partner to both bids. Before discussing rebids by the opening bidder, after a one-level bid of a suit, recall that the point range when opening at the one-level may be starting points, Dummy Points, or Bergen points, depending upon the bidding sequence.

Playing the 2/1 Game Force System, one divides the strength of the opener's hand into three categories:

Minimum Strength	12-15 points
Medium Strength	16-18 points
Maximum Strength	19+ points

The minimum (most frequent) range for a one-level bid is between 12-15 points, above this range, the opener is said to have a strong or forcing hand. Thus, special bids by the opener have been created to show invitational hands, game forcing hands, and hands with slam interest. To show a strong hand, opener must make a "jump" bid.

Strong Jump Shift

A strong jump shift is a skip bid into a new suit (one level higher than necessary) showing 19+ points (or a hand with no more than 5 losers by LTC). The suit of the opener's jump bid is a **single rank higher** than either opener's original bid suit or responder's bid suit. While it is usually made into a suit of length four, at times you may have to jump into a three-card suit. Example sequences of Jump Shift bids follow.

1♣ - 1♦ - 2♥	two hearts is single rank higher than clubs or diamonds
1♣ - 1♥ - 2♠	two spades is a single rank higher rank than clubs or hearts
1♦ - 1♥ - 2♠	two spades is a single rank higher than diamonds or hearts
1♦ - 1♥/1♠ - 3♣	three clubs is a single rank higher than hearts or spades
1♥ - 1♠ - 3♣/3♦	three-level bids are required to be a rank higher than spades
1♥ - 1NT - 3♣/3♦	over notrumps must make three-levels bid
1♠ - 1NT - 3♣/3♦/3♥	over notrumps must make three-levels bid

When opener makes a strong jump shift bid, it is forcing to game.

Reverses

The opener's second bid is called a reverse **bid** when responder cannot return to opener's first bid suit at the same level (opener's second suit is higher ranking than his first bid suit) and shows 17+ points. Responder is unable to return to opener's first suit at the two—level. Reverse auctions show distributions in the first and second suits that are at least 5-4 where the first bid suit is longer than the second and higher ranking. **In addition, your partner should have bypassed your second suit with his bid**. Examples of reverse sequences follow.

1♣ - 1♥ - 2♦	5+ clubs and 4+ diamonds
1♣ - 1♠ - 2♦/2♥	5+ clubs and 4+ diamonds/hearts
1♦ - 1♠ - 2♥	5+ diamonds and 4+ hearts
1♥ - 1NT - 2♠	5+ hearts and 4+ spades
1♥ - 2♣/2♦ - 2♠	Playing 2/1, this is not a reverse but shows 5+♥ and 4+♠

An important note one must remember when playing the 2/1game force system is that a jump three-level bid for example (1♠ - 2♥ - 3♦) is not a reverse but natural. The suit is of lower rank than your first bid suit and usually shows 5-5 distribution.

Any time opener makes a reverse bid, responder is forced to bid. Partner cannot pass. Reverses do not apply after a 2/1 game force bid.

A reverse is forcing for one round of bidding. Responder may (1) support partner's first suit with four-card support, (2) raise partner's first suit bid with 3+ card support, (3) jump in partner's first bid suit showing slam interest, (4) rebid his own long suit with 6+ cards and no fit in partner's bid suits, (5) bid notrump, or (6) bid a fourth suit (called fourth suit forcing) or (7) use new minor forcing bids; more on each of these options later when we review rebids by responder.

Jump Reverses (Mini Splinters)

Jump reverses, also called Mini splinters, are used when opener bids a minor and responder bids a major at the one-level (e.g., 1♣/1♦ - 1♥/1♠). Opener makes a jump bid one level higher than a reverse (a jump) to show a singleton or void in the suit bid and four-card supports for the major. The jump reverse shows 16+ points. Examples of jump reverse sequences follow.

1♣ - 1♥ - 3♦	shows 4 hearts and a singleton/void in diamonds (2♦ would be a reverse)
1♣ - 1♠ - 3♦	shows 4 spades and a singleton/void in diamonds (2♦ would be a reverse)
1♣ - 1♠ - 3♥	shows 4 spades and a singleton/void in hearts (2♥ would be a reverse)
1♦ - 1♠ - 3♥	shows 4 spades and a singleton/void in hearts (2♥ would be a reverse)

All bids by the opener are one level above the reverse bid (a jump reverse). **The bids allow responder to sign off at the three levels (3♥ or 3♠) or with enough points to bid game.**

Jump Rebids into opening suit bid

To show a hand of with 6+ cards and only 16-17 points and a hand of medium strength, opener may make a jump bid in his opening bid suit. For example:

1♣ to 3♣	1♦ to 3♦	1♥ to 3♥	1♠ to 3♠

A jump bid by opener may be passed, it is not forcing.

Full Splinters or reverse jump shifts

A Full Splinter is a jump bid in a suit in which a non-jump bid would have been either a strong jump shift, reverse, or a jump reverse (mini splinter). The Full Splinter is always a rank above responder's bid and shows 4+ card support for responder's suit and a singleton or void in the suit bid; the bid shows 18/19+ points and a fit in responder's suit.

1♣ - 1♦ - 3♥/3♠	4+ diamonds and a singleton/void in hearts/spades
	(Note that 2♥/2♠ would have been a Strong Jump Shift)

1♣/1♦ - 1♥ - 3♠	4+ hearts and a singleton/void in spades (Note 2♠ would have been a Strong Jump Shift)
1♣/1♦ - 1♠ - 4♥	4+ spades and a singleton/void in hearts (Note 2♥ would be a reverse and 3♥ a jump reverse)
1♠ - 1NT - 4♣/4♦/4♥	5+ spades singleton/void in clubs/diamonds/hearts

A Full Splinter bid is usually forcing to game in responder's bid suit: diamonds, hearts, or spades.

Fit Bids (Jump Minor Suit Support Splinters)

When opening a minor suit, responder will frequently bid a major. To show four-card supports for the major bid (hearts or spades), one may jump to the four-level in the bid minor (4♣/4♦) which also shows a strong club/diamond suit. These are support splinters or Fit Bids showing a good 5+ cards in the bid minor and support for the major bid. The bids show 17-19 points and are invitational to at least game with slam interest. These bids are used if you do not play Swiss bids. In addition, if you are a passed hand they may be used to show 10-12 points with a fit in a major and a solid side suit.

Jumps into Notrump

A jump into 2NT by opener shows 18-19 points and a balanced hand with stoppers in all suits except perhaps the one bid by responder. A jump into 3NT shows 20-21 points, a balanced hand, and stoppers in all suits.

Rebids by Opener after Major opening bids

The responder may bid 1NT semi-forcing, make a 2/1 game force bid, and use a series of Bergen bids either invitational or forcing. For each of these responses, we shall consider bids available to the opening bidder, again without interference.

After 1NT (semi-forcing)

Recall that the bid of 1NT by responder shows 5-12 starting points and no fit. **The only forcing bid that opener may make as a game force is a jump shift bid into a suit.** The jump shift bid shows 19+ starting points.

Suppose one opens 1♠ and partner bids 1NT, an overview of bids by the opener follows.

Rebids by Opener	Suit Length	Starting Points
2♣/2♦	3+ cards	12-15

2♥	4+ cards	12-15
2♠	6+ cards	12-15
2NT (non-forcing)	(5-3-3-2)	16/17-18
3♣/3♦/3♥	4+ cards	19+ (strong jump shift)
3♠	6+ cards	16-17 (jump rebid in bid suit)
3NT	5-3-3-2	19+
4♠	7+ spades/8+spades	14+/12+

After the major suit bid of 1♥, the schedule is similar. However, the jump in hearts shows 16-17 points, and the jump shift may be made into a minor or spades. There is one additional bid available to the opener when opening the bidding with the bid of 1♥. It is the **reverse** bid. **Recall that the definition of a reverse is that responder must go to the next higher level to return to the opening bidder's first suit, in this case 1♥.** The reverse bid is:

2♠	4 cards	17+

Using the above schedule as a guideline, consider your rebid on each of the following hands. In each example, we indicate the bidding sequence.

(1) 1♠ - 1NT ♠AK876 ♥KQ432 ♦J10 ♣7

Clearly, your rebid is 2♥ showing 4+ cards.

(2) 1♥ - 1NT ♠AK87 ♥AKJ32 ♦7 ♣K54

You have enough to reverse, bid 2♠.

(3) 1♥ - 1NT ♠KQJ5 ♥AK832 ♦J92 ♣7

You cannot reverse; hence your only rebid is 2♦.

(4) 1♠ - 1NT ♠AK8765 ♥KQ43 ♦J10 ♣7

Show your six spades, but make a jump bid, bid 3♠.

(5) 1♥ - 1NT ♠A6 ♥Q10432 ♦AJ2 ♣AQ9

Your rebid is clearly 2NT, an invitational bid, partner may pass.

(6) 1♥ - 1NT ♠A6 ♥A109432 ♦7 ♣AQ109

Your heart suit is weak, your rebid is 2♣.

(7) 1♥ - 1NT ♠AQ6 ♥A109432 ♦AJ10 ♣7

Your hearts are not good enough to bid 3♥, and the hand is too good for 2♥, hence you must bid 2♦. Partner may have four diamonds and pass or bid hearts.

(8) 1♠ - 1NT ♠AK456 ♥89 ♦KQJ ♣AJ7

You only have three diamonds, not four, do not jump-shift into 3♦; instead, bid 3NT.

(9) 1♠ - 1NT ♠KQJ98762 ♥89 ♦ void ♣AQ7

With long spades, partner has 0-2 card support and 5+ points, bid 4♠.

When opening one spade, it is normally not difficult to find a heart fit after partner bids 1NT when you have four hearts; however, if responder has only three hearts and a weak hand, the fit may be more difficult to find after opener bids of 2♣/2♦. Partner with five hearts and a weak hand may pass.

For example, suppose partner has the hand: ♠7 ♥KJ752 ♦ 5672 ♣AJ7. Partner may pass the bid of a minor! You may have missed a 3-5 heart fit. Partner cannot bid 2♥ since it shows a six-card suit.

When responder has a stronger hand, for example: ♠J ♥KJ752 ♦ 567 ♣AK75, he will certainly bid his hearts after a minor suit bid.

When opener bids 2♦, there is no way to force your partner to bid when opening one heart. However, if you bid 2♣, showing 3+ clubs, there is hope of finding a heart fit playing either the Bart Convention, developed by the bridge expert Les Bart, or the Lisa Convention, developed by Jamie Radcliffe and Pete Whipple, in the October 2007 issue of "The Bridge World."

Using the Bart Convention, after the bidding sequence: 1♠ - pass 1NT - pass - 2♣ - pass -?, the responder bids 2♦* as an artificial forcing bid (alert). This sequence is used to show opener one of the following hands:

1. Five hearts and two spades. Responder plans to pass opener's rebid (hopefully two hearts).
2. A doubleton spade honor with 9-11 HCP. Responder plans to correct two hearts to two spades, pass a rebid of two spades, or raise two notrump to three notrump.
3. A weak/invitational hand with a good diamond suit. Responder plans to bid three diamonds.

4. A favorable hand with a club raise. Responder plans to bid three clubs over partner's rebid.
5. A raise of two notrump with four clubs. Responder plans to bid two notrump.

Aside from giving up the "natural" two diamond bid, Bart has two serious drawbacks. When opener has extra values but fewer than two hearts, the partnership might miss a game when responder is unable to show a strong simple preference; and when opener has good heart support, he cannot safely bid past two hearts, because responder might not have heart length. WHAT DO YOU DO?

You may replace the Bart Convention with the **LISA CONVENTION,** Bart's smarter little sister.

Basic Lisa

Bidding sequence 1♠ - pass - 1NT - pass - 2♣ - pass -?

2♦*   artificial (alert); usually six-plus hearts or weak spade preference
2♥   exactly two spades and five hearts
2♠   exactly two spades; strong simple preference
2NT   invitational; fewer than four clubs
3♣   invitational; five-plus clubs
3♦   invitational; six-plus-card suit
3♥   invitational; six-plus-card suit

Bidding sequence 1♠ - pass - 1NT - pass - 2♣ - pass - 2♦* - pass - Opener bids 2♥

Pass   weak; six-plus-card suit
2♠   weak simple preference
2NT   invitational; exactly four clubs
3♣   moderate values; five-plus clubs
3♦   weak; six-plus-card suit

Bidding sequence 1♠ - pass - 1NT - pass - 2♣ - pass - 2♦* - pass - Opener bids 2♠

Pass   weak suit preference
2NT   invitational; exactly four clubs
3♣   moderate values; five-plus clubs
3♦   weak; six-plus-card suit
3♥   signoff
4♦   transfer to hearts

The Basic Lisa Convention does not have Bart's shortcomings, and compared to other methods, the only significant disadvantage is the loss of the natural two-level diamond rebid.

In addition, the basic Lisa bids are easily extended to non-Bart situations using, for example, Extended Lisa and Fourth-suit Lisa as discussed in the "The Bridge World" article.

Responder's Rebids without Basic Lisa

When the bidding goes **1M—1NT—2m/2M—?**

(1) Responder may pass opener's bid with 5-8 starting points.
(2) With two-card support for opener's bid suit and less than eleven starting points, return to the major (M) at the two-level.
(3) With less than two-card support and 10-12 starting points, bid 2NT.
(4) Raise partner's minor (m) with 5+ card support and 10+ starting points.
(5) With 10-12 starting points, playing Bergen Raises, jump to the three levels in opener's major. Playing Combined Bergen, you would not bid 1NT, but 3♦*.
(6) Bid your own suit with 5-9 starting points and a 6+ card suit.
(7) Bid your own suit at the three-level, without jumping, with 6+ cards in the suit and 5-12 starting points.
(8) Bid your own suit at the four-level, by jumping, with 6+ card and 10-12 starting values.

Let's consider a few examples.

(a) The bidding goes: 1♠—1NT—2♦ and you hold ♠2 ♥A106543 ♦J756 ♣Q104

You cannot support diamonds since opener may have only three, bid 2♥.

With the hand ♠J7 ♥KQ2 ♦Q987 ♣K1042, you would bid 2NT.

(b) The bidding goes 1♥—1NT—2♦ and you hold ♠K987 ♥Q6 ♦K43 ♣K965

Even though you have only two hearts, you should support hearts by bidding 2♠. Do not bid 2NT.

(c) The bidding goes 1♠—1NT—2♣ and you hold ♠J98 ♥A86 ♦AK43 ♣965

Playing Bergen Raises, bid 3♠ to show limit raise in spades. Playing Combined Bergen, you would not bid 1NT, but bid 3♦ to show a limit raise with three trump.

(d) The bidding goes 1♠—1NT—2♦ and you hold ♠2 ♥A1065 ♦K10543 ♣A43

You would support diamonds by bidding 3♦.

(e) The bidding goes 1♠—1NT—2NT and you hold ♠2 ♥AK98765 ♦105 ♣Q87

Your partner is showing 16-18 starting points with five spades, bid 4♥.

(f) The bidding goes 1♥—1NT-2♠ and you hold ♠987 ♥K9 ♦10875 ♣AQ92

Your partner has reversed showing 17+ points, bid 3♥. You cannot pass.

If the opener raises your 1NT bid to 2NT, it is non-forcing; you may pass with 5-8 starting points. This is also the case if opener makes a jump rebid in his bid major. However, all jump shift bids are forcing to game.

If opener bids 1♥ and partner bids 1NT, it always denies four spades. If opener bids 2♣/2♦/2♥ and now you bid 2♠* (it is called the impossible two spades bid), it requests opener to bid 2NT* (a relay bid) so responder can sign off in a minor at the three-level. If opener makes a jump bid in hearts, after you have bid 1NT, you may use the impossible 3♠* bid. Opener will bid 3NT or pursue game in the minor, knowing you probably have neither hearts nor spades and less than twelve starting points.

Gazilli Convention

For those who do not use Lisa, another option is to employ the Gazilli (sometimes spelled Gazzilli) converntion; it is a conventional method of rebidding by opener employing a low level forcing rebid of 2♣. The base auction for this convention is 1♠-1NT-2♣. The 2♣ rebid shows either clubs or various strong hands. With a weak hand responder rebids either 2♠ (preference) or 2♥ (natural, 5+ suit). With a better hand (8+ HCP) responder usually relays with 2♦, over which opener rebids 2♥ (minimum 5532 hand) or 2♠ (unbalanced, 4+ clubs). Opener's higher rebids (2NT thru 3NT) show hands in the 16-18 HCP and are game forcing over the 2♦ rebid.

Using Gazilli opener has two ways to rebid beyond 2♠, either directly over 1NT, or indirectly via 2♣. This allows opener to show 54, 55, 64 and 63 hand patterns of 16 or more points. There are many versions of Gazilli, and they vary mostly in the meaning of these high direct and indirect rebids.

Gazilli may be used after 1♥-1NT, 1♥-1♠ and 1♦ - 1M also; where the 1♠ response uses the Kaplan Interchange (Inversion), Chapter 15.

After 2/1 game force bids

Recall that after opening one of a major, playing the 2/1 game force system; the following bids are absolute forcing to game.

1♠	2♣/2♦ (4+cards), 2♥ (5+cards)
1♥	2♣/ 2♦ (4+cards)

The goal of the partnership is to find a game or a slam in a major suit. Although sometimes one may play in notrumps. The last priority is to play in a minor suit game. When responding to your partner's 2/1 bid, opener has several avenues to pursue: (1) he can support partner's suit to allow partner to bid notrump, (2) he can show his own second suit, (3) he can rebid his major, and (4) he can bid notrump.

(1a) Opener may support the 2/1 suit bid by responder (♣ or ♦) at the three-level showing 4+ card support and 12-15 Bergen Points. With 16+ points and support for the 2/1 bid suit, and a singleton not in the 2/1 bid suit, opener may jump (**splinter**) to the four-level in a suit that neither he nor partner bid. Note: The bid of 1♥ - 2♣/2♦ - 2♠ shows 5-4 distribution and is **not a reverse** (alternatively playing the Flannery Convention, one would open an artificial 2♦* that shows 5♥-4♠ and 11-15 starting points; more on this soon).

(1b) After the bid of 1♠ - 2♥, with 3/4+ hearts and 12-15 points bid 4♥ (the principle of fast arrival); however, with 3+ hearts and 16+ bid 3♥ shows slam interest.

(2a) Opener may bid his own higher ranking suit at the two-level, usually showing 4+ cards with 5-4 distribution.

(2b) Opener may bid a lower ranking suit at the three-level showing 15+ points, usually showing 5-5 distribution.

(3) Opener may rebid his major suit typically showing 6+ cards in the major. On occasion, it may also be his only rebid, having only five cards.

(4) With a balanced hand, pattern (5-3-3-2), and at least three-card support in the 2/1 suit bid, and stoppers in the unbid suits, he will bid 2NT (12-15 Bergen Points) or 3NT (16+ Bergen Points).

Let's look at a few examples of the prior guidelines.

The bidding goes 1♠ - 2♥. What would you respond as opener?

| ♠AK843 | ♥K62 | ♦J4 | ♣AQ3 |

You have a strong hand, eighteen Dummy Points (17 starting + 1 Shortness); bid 3♥ (slam interest)

| ♠AK843 | ♥K62 | ♦54 | ♣Q32 |

You have a weak hand, fourteen Dummy Points (13 starting + 1 shortness); bid 4♥ (fast arrival to game)

| ♠AK843 | ♥K1062 | ♦7 | ♣AQ3 |

You have four-card supports for hearts twenty Dummy Points (17 starting + 3 shortness); bid 4♦ (splinter)

♠AKJ84   ♥75   ♦A97   ♣J32

You have only two hearts and weak clubs, rebid spades with only 5 (bid 2♠), you should not bid notrump; even with fifteen Dummy Points.

♠AK984   ♥75   ♦AJ8   ♣KJ6

You have a balanced hand with stoppers in all suits and eighteen Dummy Points, bid 3NT; changing the A♦ to a Q, bid 2NT.

♠AQ984   ♥7   ♦A8   ♣K10862

You have a nice club suit and 5-5 distribution, bid 3♣. You have eighteen Dummy Points (14 starting + 4 shortness points).

Next, we consider examples where the bidding is 1♥/1♠ - 2♣/2♦; because the responses are similar, we assume one opens 1♥ - 2♣. What would you respond as opener?

♠984   ♥KQ875   ♦AQJ2   ♣7

You have four diamonds, bid 2♦. Shows 4-4 distribution and you have twelve Dummy Points.

♠Q107   ♥KQ875   ♦AJ2   ♣J7

You have a balanced hand, bid 2NT with thirteen starting points.

♠7   ♥AK875   ♦A92   ♣KQJ7

You have a very strong hand, splinter by bidding 3♠ in support of clubs. You have twenty Bergen points (assume a club fit).

♠AJ3   ♥KQ875   ♦1092   ♣K6

Even with only five hearts, you must rebid them. You have no other bid due to your diamond holdings.

These examples should help to clarify opener's rebids when opening a major and partner makes a 2/1 bids. Remember, we want to get to game. Rebids by responder and subsequent bids by the opener will be covered later in the book.

When responding with a 2/1 bid to a major, we have said that the partnership may not stop short of game. This is also the case with the forcing Bergen Raise of 2NT* and Concealed/ Ambiguous Splinter bids. These are game force bids with serious interest in slam.

After Jacoby 2NT*

Rebids by Opener	Suit Length	Bergen Points
3 (new suit)*	Singleton/Void	12+

3 (major suit opened)*	5/6+ in major	18+
3NT*	(5-3-3-2) balanced	15-17
4 (new suit)*	4+ card suit	12+ to 16
4 (major suit opened)	5+ major	12+ to 14

A jump to the four levels after 2NT* is clearly invitational to slam. When showing a singleton after 2NT*, the trump suit should contain at least two of the top three honors. Do not show a singleton with a weak trump suit or if the singleton is an ACE.

Furthermore, a new suit at the four-level should contain two of the top three honors in the suit bid. **All rebids by opener must be alerted and explained in detail if asked.**

Examples Responses to Jacoby 2NT

The bidding goes 1♠ - 2NT*. What do you bid?

(1) ♠AKJ84   ♥7   ♦K10987 ♣A2
Show your singleton, bid 3♥. You have nineteen Bergen points.

(2) ♠AKJ84   ♥107   ♦54   ♣AQ108
You have a nice four-card suit, bid 4♣ with seventeen Bergen points. You are too unbalanced to bid notrump.

(3) ♠AKJ84   ♥K107   ♦KJ4   ♣76
You have a balanced hand, bid 3NT with sixteen Bergen points.

(4) ♠AKJ84   ♥J107   ♦QJ4   ♣76
You have a weak hand, using Fast Arrival, bid 4♠.

(5) ♠AKQ842   ♥ void   ♦AQ42   ♣J76
You have a great hand, bid 3♥ to show shortness. Count your Bergen Points. Are you interested in slam?

Following is a summary of descriptive bids following 2NT*.

After 1♥ - 2NT*
3♣ = ♣ shortage
3♦ = ♦ shortage
3♥ = good hand with no shortage
3♠ = ♠ shortage
3NT = better hand with no shortage

After 1♠ - 2NT*
3♣ = ♣ shortage
3♦ = ♦ shortage
3♥ = ♥ shortage
3♠ = good hand with no shortage
3NT = better hand with no shortage

4♣	= a 4+card ♣ suit		4♣	= a 4+card ♣ suit	
4♦	= a 4+card ♦ suit		4♦	= a 4+card ♦ suit	
4♥	= poor hand with no shortage (Fast arrival)		4♥	= a 4+card ♥ suit	
			4♠	= poor hand with no shortage (Fast arrival)	

After Concealed/Ambiguous Splinters

Recall that a double jump in the major not bid (3♠*/3♥*), after the bid of 1♥ and 1♠, respectively, shows shortness somewhere. The decision the opener must make is whether or not he needs to ask about the singleton/void since it provides information to the opponents. If one needs to locate the singleton/void, one employs the scroll bids 3NT* and 3♠*, respectively, after 3♠* and 3♥*. As a general guideline, one should not employ the scroll asking bids if not interested in slam. In general, you need about 18+ Bergen points after hearing the jump major bid by your partner. Let's look at an example.

Opener
♠AQJ762
♥3
♦9872
♣KQ

Responder
♠K984
♥AQ92
♦void
♣A7632

Let's evaluate starting points for the two hands. Opener has (12 HCP—1 dubious honor doubleton + 2 length points + 0 for adjust-3) thirteen starting points. Responder has fourteen starting points; however, upon hearing the bid of 1♠, reevaluates his hand for the void (four points) and has eighteen Dummy Points. And, opener upon hearing the bid of 3♥* calculates Bergen points. Thus, he adds for extra trump length (one point), the void (two points), and for the side suit (one point) eighteen Bergen Points. Thus, he makes the asking bid 3♠*, and with a diamond void, responder bids 4♣*.

We have provided the entire bidding sequence below but will wait to explain the modified scroll bids and their responses in Chapter 3 on Slam Bidding.

Opener
1♠
3♠* (shortage asking bid)
4♦* (modified scroll ask)
6♠ (if you have 3 bid 7)

Responder
3♥* (shortness somewhere)
4♣* (submarine bid—singleton/void in diamonds)
4NT (void in diamonds with 0 or 3 keycards)
7♠

After Swiss bid of 4♣

4♥/4♠ says weak hand 12-15 Dummy Points with strong and long trump suit.
4♦/ (4 of other Major) show a singleton or void with slam interest.
4NT shows slam interest with 16+ points (Roman Keycard Blackwood; more on this later).

5♣ shows (5-5) hand with major and clubs, with slam interest with double fit.

After Swiss bid of 4♦

4♥/4♠ says weak hand, 12-15 Dummy Points with strong and long trump suit.
4♣/ (4 of other Major) show a singleton or void with slam interest.
4NT shows slam interest with 16+ points (Roman Keycard Blackwood; more on this later).
5♦ shows (5-5) hand with major and clubs, with slam interest with double fit.

After Constructive Raises (support at the two-level)

Recall that a constructive raise shows three-card support and only 8-10 Dummy Points.

Hence, to reach game, opener may need help in either a side suit or trumps to reach a game contract.

Help Suit Game Try Bids

There are many game try conventions available to investigate game or to settle on a part score. The Long Suit Game Try (LSGT) is probably the oldest method employed. This is an attempt by opener to tell responder more about his hand. He shows a second suit with the understanding that as responder revalues his hand, he should give extra weight to honors in this suit. However, over the years the LSGT has given way to the Help Suit Game Try (HSGT). The major difference is that the opening bidder may hold fewer than four cards in that suit and usually a good 15 HCP or perhaps less if he is 5-5 in two suits, the major and another suit. Let's look at an example when used by opener, with no interference:

1♥-2♥

3♣/3♦/3♠ needs help in the suit bid with help (ace or king) bid game

1♠-2♠

3♣/3♦/2NT needs help in clubs, diamonds, or hearts (ace or king) bid game

The method may also be used by responder in the auction 1♣-1♥; 2♥—(Help suit bid). For responder to use the bid, he should have 10 Dummy Points.

Some prefer the Short Suit Game Try. Using the Short Suit Try (SSGT) approach, a new bid by the opener shows a **singleton**. For responder this means that the ace is probably the only honor in the short suit that will help opener. Of course, this means that honors in the OTHER suits will be what opener needs. Alternatively, one may combine the HSGT and the SSGT bids by using the 2-Way Game Try method. How does this work?

Two-Way Game Try Bids

Instead of using the HSGT method, opener bids the next suit up to tell responder that we are going into "Short Suit Mode". Opener initiates the short suit try with the bids of 2♠ and 2NT, respectively, after hearts and spades. Responder acknowledges the short suit try with relay bids of 2NT and 3♣, respectively.

1♥-2♥-2♠ (going into shortness mode)—responder next bids 2NT (as a relay)

- 3♣ = shows shortness in clubs
- 3♦ = shows shortness in diamonds
- 3♥ = shows shortness in spades

1♠-2♠-2NT (going into shortness mode)—responder next bids 3♣ (as a relay)

- 3♦ = shows shortness in diamonds
- 3♥ = shows shortness in hearts
- 3♠ = shows shortness in clubs

Shortness is always 1 or 0 cards in the suit.

Reponder again has few values, but not in the short suit. If they are, he stops at the three level; otherwise he bids game at four level of the agreed upon major suit.

To inquire about help, one may employ with an asking bid or a telling bid called respectively "help asking" or "telling."

Short Suit Game Try Bids

An alternative to the two-way try is to use the Short Suit Game Try (SSGT). Opener again initiates the short suit try with the bids of 2♠ and 2NT, respectively, after hearts and spades. However now responder acknowledges the short suit try by bidding short suits:

1♥-2♥-2♠

- 3♣ = shows shortness in clubs
- 3♦ = shows shortness in diamonds
- 2NT = shows shortness in spades
- 3♥ = 4333 Minimum (8/9 dummy points)
- 3NT = 4333 Maximum (10 Dummy points)
- 3♠ = 4333 Maximum with four spades
- 4m = 5+ to KQ in minor bid with Maximum
- 4♥ = Stiff other major with Maximum

1♠-2♠-2NT

- 3♣ = shows shortness in clubs
- 3♦ = shows shortness in diamonds
- 3♥ = shows shortness in hearts
- 3♠ = 4333 Minimum (8/9 dummy points)
- 3NT = 4333 Maximum (10 Dummy points)
- 4m = 5+ to KQ in minor bid with Maximum
- 4♠ = Stiff other major with Maximum

Shortness is always 1 or 0 cards in the suit.

Reponder again has few values, but not in the short suit. If they are, he stops at the three level; otherwise he bids game at four level of the agreed upon major suit.

If opener bids at the three level, he is showing shortness in the bid suit by not using the relay bids.

Help "Asking" vs. Game Try "Telling" Bids

When using the asking bids, opener is asking for help in the suit bid, traditionally first or second round control due to losers in the suit. Except for the Long Suit Game Try bid which is a natural bid, the other asking bids must be **alerted by agreement,** a red flag to the opponents. Another problem with the asking bids is that it is often difficult to figure out the "help suit." Instead of using the help suit type asks, one may instead make an Artificial bid of 2NT* which is played either as a relay bid or asks the responder to tell him something more about his hand; in particular, shortness. While this also communicates information to the opponents, it is less damaging. Thus, the sequence one of a major, followed by a simple raise, and the bid of 2NT becomes a relay bid or an artificial game try bid! If used as a relay bid, partner bids three clubs and the opener tells the responder about shortness. Then the Responder is captain of the sequence. Alternatively, when opener bids the Artificial 2NT* not as a relay, but as "telling" bid, it asks responder to tell the opener where he has shortness. I prefer the responder to tell, not the opener; hence, we shall illustrate the "telling" sequence.

Let's compare the two approaches (Help Suit Game Try and Artificial 2NT "telling"), and you decide which is best for your partnership agreement. If you play help suit asks, how do you know where to ask for help with the following hands when your partner supports you by bidding 2♠, constructive?

Hand (1)	♠ AKJ54	♥ 86	♦ 97	♣ AQJ7
Hand (2)	♠ AKJ972	♥ QJ4	♦ QJ3	♣ 9
Hand (3)	♠ KQJT6	♥ AQ7	♦ K965	♣ 8
Hand (4)	♠ KQT87	♥ 86	♦ AKT5	♣ K6

| Hand (5) | ♠ AKJ74 | ♥ AKQ | ♦ 942 | ♣ 63 |
| Hand (6) | ♠ AKJ742 | ♥ AJ | ♦ J53 | ♣ 92 |

When opener prefers to make a short-suit game try, as in (2) and (3), or a long-suit try, as in (1) and (4), he is in trouble. On (5) and (6), he'd like to make a general game try of 3♠, but this is commonly played as a game try asking for extra help in trumps.

Opener could bid 3♦ on the last two hands and hope for the best. The fact is there are lots of players who might bid 3♦ on all six hands! Partner must figure out what is the right diamond holding for the game try. A small doubleton would be helpful opposite K-9-6-5, A-K-10-5, or 9-4-2, but would be wasted opposite 9-7 or Q-J-3. Even the worth of K-8-6 would be unclear. It would be a good holding opposite Q-J-3 but doubtful opposite 9-4-2 or J-5-3.

So, using the help suit approach, one frequently does not know in which suit to ask for help, and often partner does not know when to accept. Instead, one may use the artificial 2NT* Game Try "telling" (not the relay) approaches. In each of the above examples, one employs the bidding sequence: one simple bids 1♠-2♠-2NT*.

Responder's first obligation is to bid his lowest ranking doubleton, even if he has a singleton. This tells partner he may have to cover two losers. However, with the "right" doubleton (say Ax), he may bid four of the major. But, if "turned off" by a doubleton, he might just bid three of the major. With a balanced hand (4-3-3-3), bid three of a major with a minimum (8-10 Dummy Points) and 3NT (11-13 Dummy Points), a maximum. Or, you may choose to bid a new suit to preserve all options.

Let's consider a few examples.

Opener	Responder
♠KQJ74	♠A63
♥AK8	♥974
♦J73	♦8654
♣K9	♣AJ5

In this example, the bidding would go: 1♠-2♠-2NT-3NT-pass. Three notrump is easier than four of a major as long as responder has at least three diamonds. Using the help suit bid of 3♦, responder may bid three of a major and opener might pass, missing game!

Next, consider the hand:

Opener	Responder
♠KQT87	♠A63
♥86	♥J754
♦AKT5	♦93
♣K9	♣QJ75

Now, the bidding goes:

Opener	Responder
1♠	2♠
2NT	3♦
4♠	Pass

Using the Help Suit bid, opener may bid 2♥, and responder may bid 3♠ (no help), again missing a game contract.

If in the above hand you held three hearts and three diamonds (3-3-3-4 distribution), you would bid 3♠ to show a minimum hand. With a stronger club suit, you may bid 3♣ called a counter try/trial rebid showing good holdings in clubs and maximum points.

Questions:

(1) How do you respond to 2NT holding a singleton or a void? A jump to four of the trump promises 0 or 1 in the other major. With fewer than two cards in a minor, bid the minor at the three-level just as you would a doubleton. Don't sit for 3NT if partner bids it—a rebid of your minor suit shows fewer than two cards.
(2) Is 2NT still on in competition? Yes, as long as your partner has raised the major, you must ignore the competition from either side.
(3) If opener does not bid 2NT, he may make a short-suit game try with a minimum bid showing shortness in the suit (0 or 1) and interest in game!

For more information on the Game Try Bids, consult Marty Bergen's (1985) "Better Bidding with Bergen, Volume One, Uncontested Auctions" by Devyn Press, page 148. This discussion is based upon his book.

After 3♣* and 3♦* (Bergen Raises)

Playing Bergen Raises recall that the jump bids of 3♣* and 3♦* show a trump fit but only 7-9 Dummy Points and 10-12 Dummy Points, respectively. To reach game with the bid of three clubs, opener needs at least 17-19 Bergen Points. Hence, he will bid game or invite game. Similarly, after the limit raise bid of 3♦, opener may either invite with between 14-16 Bergen Points or use the 2NT* Game Try bid as mentioned above.

After 3♣* and 3♦* (Combined Bergen Raises)

Recall that 3♣* shows four-card support and 5-12 Dummy Points, the bid of 3♦* shows only three-card support and a limit raise (10-12 Dummy Points). When opening a major and responding 3♣*, recall that 3♦* asks whether you are at the lower end of the range (3♥* shows the lower end and 3♠* indicates the upper end). After the bid of 3♥, you can bid 3♠/4♠ and after 3♠ you can pass or bid 4♠. This is not the case if/when you open 1♥, now an ask bid may commit you to game in hearts when you hear the response 3♠. Thus, it is best not to ask by bidding 3♦; now one invites by bidding 3♥, do not ask by bidding 3♦.

Rebids by Opener after Minor opening bids (1♣/1♦)

If the opening bid is the Walsh club bid, the first priority of the responder is to bid a four-card major, not notrump. This is also the case if one opens one diamond.

Opener's first priority is to support the major suit bid with 3/4 cards (YOU HAVE FOUND A MAJOR SUIT FIT). Now what? Do you have game or slam? As responder, all you know is that opener has between 12-21 Dummy Points.

After 1♣-1♥

Opener rebids

1♠	4 spades, denies 4 hearts
1NT	12-14 starter points, balanced hand, denies a 4-card major
2♣	12-17 starting points, 5+ clubs, denies a 4-card major
2♦	**Reverse bid showing 17+ starting points (5-4)**
2♥	3+ card support, 12-16+ Dummy Points
2♠	**Jump Shift 19+, game force bid**
2NT	18-19 starting points, balanced hand, may have a 4-card major
3♣	16-17 starting points **jump rebid** with good suit and 6+ clubs
3♦	**Jump Reverse** 4+clubs, singleton/void in diamonds 16+ points
3♥	17-19 starter points, four hearts, invitational to game
3♠	**Full Splinter** 4 hearts, singleton/void in spades 18+ slam interest
3NT	Solid club suit, with stopper in side suits, to play
4♣	**Fit bid** showing strong clubs and spades 17-19 points
4♥	20+ Dummy Points
4NT	Roman Keycard Blackwood (Chapter 3)

After 1♣—1♠

Opener rebids

1NT	12-14 starter points, balanced hand, denies a 4-card major
2♣	12-17 starting points, 5+ clubs, denies a 4-card major
2♦	**Reverse bid showing 17+ starting points (5-4)**

2♠	3+ card support, 12-16+ Dummy Points
2NT	18-19 starting points, may have a 4-card major
3♣	16-17 starting points **jump rebid** with good suit and 6+ clubs
3♦	**Jump Reverse** 4 spades, singleton/void in diamonds 16+ points
3♥	**Jump Reverse** 4 spades, singleton/void in hearts 16+ points
3♠	17-19 starter points, four hearts, invitational to game
3NT	Solid club suit, with stopper in side suit, to play
4♣	**Fit bid** showing strong clubs and hearts 17-19 points
4♠	20+ Dummy Points
4NT	Roman Keycard Blackwood (Chapter 3)

After 1♦—1♥

Opener rebids

1♠	4 spades, denies 4 hearts
1NT	12-14 starter points, balanced hand, denies a 4-card major
2♣	12 - 17 starting points, 5+ clubs, denies a 4-card major
2♦	12 - 17 starting points, 5+ diamonds, denies a 4-card major
2♥	3+ card support, 12-16+ Dummy Points
2♠	**Jump Shift 19+, game force bid**
2NT	18-19 starting points, balanced hand, may have a 4-card major
3♣	**Jump Shift 19+, game force bid**
3♦	16-17 starting points **jump rebid** with good suit and 6+ clubs
3♥	17-19 starter points, four hearts, invitational to game
3♠	**Full Splinter** 4+diamonds, singleton/void in spades18+ slam interest
3NT	Solid club suit, with stopper in side suits, to play
4♦	**Fit bid** showing strong diamonds and spades 17-19 points
4♥	20+ Dummy Points
4NT	Roman Keycard Blackwood (Chapter 3)

After 1♦—1♠

Opener rebids

1NT	12-14 starter points, balanced hand, denies a 4-card major
2♣	12-17 starting points, 5-4 diamonds and clubs, no 4-card major
2♦	12-17 starting points, 5+ diamonds, denies spades
2♠	3+ card support, 12-16+ Dummy Points
2NT	18-19 starting points, may have a 4-card major
3♣	**Jump Shift 19+, game force bid**
3♦	16-17 starting points **jump rebid** with good suit and 6+ clubs
3♥	**Jump Reverse** 4 spades, singleton/void in hearts 16+ points
3♠	17-19 starter points, 4 hearts, invitational to game
3NT	Solid club suit, with stopper in side suit, to play
4♦	**Fit bid** showing strong diamonds and hearts 17-19 points

4♠   20+ Dummy Points
4NT   Roman Keycard Blackwood (Chapter 3)

3344 Convention

When opening a minor and partner responds a major, Eric Rodwell developed a sophisticated game try convention called the Rodwell Game Try Convention. I will not try to go into the complexities here (it is for experts), but I will use a subset of the Rodwell Convention called the **3344 Convention;** the name was suggested by Joe Sacco of The Villages Duplicate Bridge Club.

After hearing support for the major at the two-level (2♥/2♠), responder needs to know whether major support is three or four cards and whether the opening points are a **minimum** (12-15) or a **maximum** (16-21). To investigate, responder bids 2NT*. The responses by the opening bidder are:

3♣* shows **three-card (3)** support and a **minimum** opening hand
3♦* shows **three-card (3)** support and a **maximum** opening hand
3♥* shows **four-card (4)** support and a **minimum** opening hand
3♠* shows **four-card (4)** support and a **maximum** opening hand

Val Covalciuc recommends in her September 2007 issues of the ACBL "Bridge Bulletin" (page 39) article that there are two requirements for the opener when raising partner's major: opener should have some decent values in his three-card major suit and he should have ruffing values in his hand.

Let's consider an example.
Opener   ♠ K 10 9 ♥ Q J 8 4 ♦ Q J 6 5 ♣ A 10 9 8
Responder   ♠ 8 7 ♥ A K 3 2 ♦ A K 4 3 2 ♣ K 5 4

With no five-card major, opener opens the bidding with 1♣ (Walsh) and responder would bid 1♥, bypassing his five-card diamond suit. A MAJOR fit is found. Observe that responder has eighteen Starter Points. Next, responder bids 2NT*. How good is your hand and what is its shape?

Opener has fourteen Dummy Points and bids 3♥. With a minimum and four hearts, responder has no interest in slam and signs off in the heart game by bidding 4♥.

Without a four-card major, opener has several rebids options depending on the structure of his hand:

(a) With 12-17 starting points, opener's rebid is 1NT showing a weak hand.

(b) With a balanced (5-3-3-2) and 18+ starting points, his bid is 2NT.

Point Count Game Try Convention (PCGT)

Some may not need the 3344 convention since they may always support a major with four cards. However, to evaluate whether or not your have game going values, you may next employ the Point Count Game try Converntion.

The convention is used after the sequences 1♣/1♦ - 1♥/1♠ followed by a two level rebid in the major; 2♥ and 2♠ respectively.

Next the responder bids either 2♠/2NT over 2♥ and 2♠, respectively. Then the next three level bids show dummy points:

For Spades ask = 2NT	For Hearts ask = 2♠
3♣* = 16+ Dummy Points	15 Dummy Points
3♦* = 15 Dummy Points	14 Dummy Points
3♥* = 14 Dummy Points	12/13 Dummy Points
3♠* = 12/13 Dummy Points	2NT= 16+ Dummy Points

The more values, the lower the bid; this allows one to investigate slam or to reach game in the major. The minimum bid is a simple raise of the major suit, 3♠ or 3♥. Over the maximum bid of 4♣ one asks for points in the trump suit. Then steps show 0,1,2, or 3.

After 1NT

When opening a minor and responder does not bid a major but bids 1NT, the opener sees little hope in a major suit game. Responder does not have a four-card major. Recall that partner has either 8-10 starting points after the bid of 1♣ or 6-9 starting points after opening bid of 1♦ and no four-card major. Opener's rebids are:

Rebids by Opener	Suit Length	Starting Points
2♣/2♦	5+ cards	12-15
2NT	5-3-3-2	16-18
3♣/3♦	5+ cards	16-17 (jump in bid suit)
3♥/3♠	4 cards	19+ (jump shift)

3NT 5-3-3-2 19+

Another option is to employ the "Puppet Checkback" over a 1NT rebid as described by Ron Kinger. Max Hardy calls the bid Modified Two-Way Stayman (however, the two are not the same). Here is how Klinger's version works.

A puppet bid simply asks partner to make the cheapest bid, whatever his holding. It is a like a transfer, except that a transfer promises a holding in the suit being transferred to, whereas a puppet does not promise a holding in the requested suit.

The purpose of a puppet bid is to create an alternate pathway to some higher bid, so that a later bid can be assigned a different meaning if made via the puppet to the meaning it has if bid without travelling via the puppet. For example, in Puppet Checkback, we use 1♣, 1♥; 1NT, 2♥ as a sign-off, but (with a puppet 2♣, 2♦ inserted) 1♣, 1♥; 1NT, 2♣; 2♦, 2♥ becomes a game-invitation.

A puppet bid can also be used as an escape to the puppet suit, like a transfer. But, unlike a transfer, if the puppet bidder then continues the auction he does **not** promise any holding in the puppet suit.

The Puppet Checkback system over a 1NT rebid is:

- 2♣: Forces opener to bid 2♦, which responder can pass to play, if that is his wish. If responder bids again, his bid is natural and game-invitational.
- 2♦: An artificial game force, asking for help in uncovering the best fit.

Opener is asked to bid an unbid 4-card suit or to give 3-card support to responder, and failing that to bid NT or perhaps a good minor suit.

- 2♥: Natural and weak. To play, if a repeat of the suit. Offering opener a choice between responder's 5-card spade suit and 4-card heart suit if spades was bid first.
- 2♠: Natural and weak if a repeat of the suit. Natural and game-forcing if a reverse.
- 2NT: Forces opener to bid 3♣, which responder can pass to play, if that is his wish. If responder bids again, he shows a strong 6-card suit in his original major, including two of the top three honours. If he repeats his major suit he shows no singleton or void. If he bids a suit (even if it is opener's suit) it is a splinter. If he bids 3NT or 4♣ it is a splinter in clubs. Opener can bid or pass 3NT if he expects that to be the best contract (if, for example, he has K Q x x or similar in responder's splinter suit).

Three level suit bids are natural, strong and distributional: 5-5 or better if a second suit is bid by responder, a 6-card suit or longer if a repeat of responder's suit.

In Max Hardy's "Modified Two-Way Stayman" is very similar to Puppet Checkback but with one significant difference. He plays responder's 2NT as a natural invitational raise but denying 4-card support for opener's suit. The bid of 2NT via the 2♣, 2♦ puppet sequence promises 4-card support for opener's suit, allowing opener to convert to three of his suit if he doesn't wish to accept the invitation. That is useful variation, but may be forgotten. And it has the serious disadvantge that responder's 3♣ must now be a natural weak takeout, rather than strong and forcing.

After weak minor suit responses

Playing inverted minor suit raises, recall that responder shows five-card support with a jump to the three-level bid of 3♣*/3♦* after an opening bid of 1♣/1♦, respectively. These are both weak bids showing 5-9 points. The primary goal of the bid is to require the opponents to enter the bidding at the three-level. If the opener has a balanced hand and 19+ points, he may bid 3NT. And, with a strong minor suit unbalanced hand, he may invite game in the bid minor.

After the opening of one club, responder would bid 3♣ with the hand:

♠ 8 7 ♥ A 2 ♦ K 4 3 ♣ Q 10 6 5 4

However, suppose opener had the hand: ♠AJ62 ♥654 ♦ void ♣ AK987, a minor suit game is possible. With a more balanced hand, opener may bid notrump.

After inverted minor and crisscross

Inverted minor   (1♣/1♦ - 2♣*/2♦*)

Recall that the sequence 1♣ - 2♣* or 1♦ - 2♦* shows 13+ starting points and is forcing to game.

After an inverted minor suit raise, opener rebids show "stoppers up-the-line." Opener should not bypass any suit containing a stopper. Responder next bids a stopper where the goal is to reach a notrump contract. The search for stoppers is geared toward major suit stoppers; this is because the responder has already denied a four-card major and there is an increased likelihood that the opponents will initially attack the major suits in a notrump contract.

The bidding sequences follow when opening 1♣ (diamonds follow similarly).

1♣ - 2♣* - 2♥ promises a full stopper in hearts but denies a full stopper in spades

> Responder must now continue cuebidding in search of notrump:

2♠	shows a spade stopper
2NT	spades stopped and 15+ starting points
3♣	no spade stopper
3♦	no spade stopper A or K of diamonds
3♥	cuebid showing A or K
3♠	spade singleton/void and 15+ starting points
3NT	spades and diamonds stopped

1♣ - 2♣* - 2♠ promises a full stopper in spades but denies a full stopper in hearts

Responder must now continue cuebidding in search of notrump:

2NT	hearts stopped and 15+ starting points
3♣	no spade stopper
3♦	no heart stopper A or K of diamonds
3♥	heart singleton/void and 15+ starting points
3♠	no heart stopper A or K of spades
3NT	spades and diamonds stopped

1♣ - 2♣* - 2NT promises a full stopper in both majors

Responder now usually bids 3NT

1♣ - 2♣* - 2♦ promises a full stopper in diamonds

Cuebidding usually continues to find notrump

1♣ - 2♣* - 3♣ suggests a minimal hand with 5+ clubs and little interest in playing NT

1♣ - 2♣* - 3NT promises a full stopper in both majors and a hand with slam possibilities with a balanced hand and 16-21 starting points.

Opener's rebid of a **new** suit at the three-level, a jump reverse (mini splinter), shows 16+ points and a very distributional hand with a singleton or void in the bid suit. The goal is to play in a minor suit game and little slam interest.

For example, after one bids 1♣ - 2♣* with the hand: ♠ A K 9 7 ♥ 7 ♦ Q 4 3 ♣ A K J 9 5, one would bid 3♥ to show 16+ points and shortness in hearts.

Slam investigation after inverted minor bid

Opener may also investigate slam with a Jump Raise in the minor bid suit. The bids for slam investigation are:

1♣ - 2♣* - 4♣ (or)
1♦ - 2♦* - 4♦

When opening one club and one diamond, respectively, the four-level bid shows 19+ points with no interest in notrump. The bid is Minorwood Roman Keycard Blackwood and will be discussed later (Chapter 3).

Crisscross (1♣ - 2♦* or 1♦ - 3♣*)

Recall that the bidding has gone 1♣ - 2♦* or 1♦ - 3♣* and indicates that responder has only 10-12 starting points and 5+ cards in the minor suit.

With the crisscross bid, one continues with the bidding procedure outlined for the inverted response; however, game in a minor or notrump is less likely.

What is Flip-Flop?

Playing inverted minor raises at the 13+ level, inverted minor raises are off in competition. However, there is an exception. The exception is over a double when playing Flip-Flop.

Over a double and playing **flip-flop** inverted minor raises are on. Then, a bid of 2NT* (an alert) shows a preemptive raise of the opener's minor suit bid and the 3♣*/3♦* bids are reversed (Flip-flopped) showing a minor suit limit (10-12 starting points) raise (an alert). To show a hand with 13+, one uses a redouble.

What about slam bidding when playing Inverted Minor Raises (13+) in 2/1, with Crisscross and Flip-Flop?

These bids are identical to those summarized using inverted minor raises.

After 2/1 game force bid (1♦ - 2♣)

Hearing the response of two clubs to a one diamond opening, the first priority of the opener is to show the length of the diamond suit. Recall that is/may be 3-5+. A rebid of diamonds indicates a 5+ card suit.

A rebid of 2NT over 2♣ shows a balanced hand and does not deny a four-card major. It shows stopper in all suits and tenaces and a desire to play in notrump. Opener may have two types of hands: minimal strength (12-15 starting points) or maximum strength (19-21 points). With 15-17 points and a balanced hand, one would have opened 1NT. A jump to 3NT is stronger, showing 19-21 starting points and a balanced hand with all suits stopped.

A raise in clubs (3♣) shows 12-15 starting point, a minimum hand, and at least four clubs.

A jump to a new suit (diamond, hearts, or spades) is a splinter in support of clubs.

A summary of opener's bid follows.

Rebids by Opener	Suit Length	Starting Points
2♦	5+ cards	12-15

2♥	4 cards with 4 diamonds	12-15
2♠	4 cards with 4 diamonds	12-15
2NT	(5-3-3-2)	12-15 or 19-21
3♣	4+ clubs	12-15
3♦	6+ diamonds	16-18
3♥/3♠	singleton/void	16+
3NT	5-3-3-2	18/19-21

After the bid of 2NT, responder can next bid 3NT with no interest in slam, show a four-card major, or rebid clubs to show 6+ clubs with perhaps interest in a club slam. Recall that slam requires thirty-three points. **However, if responder rebids clubs, the game force is off.**

Returning to our previous example, the bidding would go 1♦ - 2♣, invitational to game in diamonds or notrump.

Opener   ♠876 ♥ AQ ♦ A652 ♣ K875
Responder   ♠AKJ4 ♥ KJ43 ♦ 7 ♣ QJ92

Clearly, one would open 1♦ and responder would bid 2♣ (game force). Next, opener would bid 2NT showing a balanced minimal hand. Even with a singleton, responder may next bid 3NT knowing partner has a balanced hand. (It is better to use Stayman Convention to ask whether opener has a four-card major by bidding 3♣. The convention will be discussed shortly.) Let's look at another example.

Opener   ♠9876 ♥ AQ ♦ A652 ♣ K87
Responder   ♥ Q3 ♥KJ102 ♦ 7 ♣ AQ10765

Here, responder would again bid 2♣ (game force); however, after the bid of 2♠ by opener, not having four spades, responder would bid 3♣ to remove the game force auction.

Golady Convention

Many pairs playing 2/1, play that 1♦ - 2♣ is a 2/1 game force except if clubs is rebid. However, one may use a modification of the Golady Convention to establish a major fit at the two-level. Playing the Golady Convention 2♣* is alerted (may not have clubs). The convention follows.

2♦*	four-card heart suit (as if you bid 2♥)
2♥*	four-card spade suit (as if you bid 2♠)
2♠*	long diamonds
2NT	balanced hand

3♣   long clubs game force off

*These bids must be alerted since they are transfers and not natural.

The major advantage of the convention is to allow the partnership to reach a major suit (GF) fit at the two-level. And then one can begin using cuebids to investigate slam discussed later in this book and also by Ken Rexford (2006) in "Cuebidding at Bridge: A Modern Approach," published by Master Point Press, Toronto.

Responses to 1NT opening bid

When opening 1NT, opener has 14/15-17 starting points. Recall that a game in a major or notrump requires between 24-26 starting points. Thus, we can conclude that partner should think about the following as soon as partner bids 1NT.

Responder Starting Points*   **Goal**

    Min 14 / Min15

(1)	0-8	0-7	Pass or play in two of a suit holding 5+ cards.
(2)	9-10	8-9	Invite game in notrump or a suit with a fit.
(3)	11-16	10-15	Bid a game in notrump or a suit with a fit.
(4)	17-18	16-17	Invitational to slam in suit or notrump.
(5)	19-22	18-21	Bid a slam in notrump or a suit with a fit.
(6)	23+	22+	Bid a grand slam.

*Both ranges are noted depending upon the notrump range you prefer, 14-17 or 15-17. More and more players are lowering the range for the strong notrump.

Over 80 percent of games reached in duplicate bridge involve a major and the most used bid is the strong (14/15-17) 1NT opening. It conveys points and shape to your partner with one bid. Most players will not open a hand 1NT with a five-card major. However, a common practice is to open a hand 1NT when you are 5-3 in the majors. Some will even open a hand using the strong 1NT bid with two doubletons.

To decide, one may use the following rule: **given a strong NT 14/15-17 range, if the five-card suit is higher ranking than the four-card suit, open the five-card suit and rebid the four card suit. If the four card suit is higher ranking with 14-16 points, less than the maximum, then open the hand 1NT.**

Even when you open the bidding 1NT, the first goal is to find a 4-4 major suit fit. A convention designed for this purpose is the Stayman Convention first published by Samuel M. Stayman in "The Bridge World" (1945) but actually invented by J.C.H. Marx, a British bridge player in 1939.

Stayman Convention

After the bid of 1NT, the Stayman Convention uses the asking bid of 2♣ as an artificial bid to inquire whether or not partner has a four-card major. The convention is so engrained in bridge that it need not be alerted. Opener's responses are:

2♦   no 4-card major
2♥   denotes a 4-card heart suit, but may have 4 spades
2♠   denotes a 4-card spade suit

The original Stayman Convention incorporated a 2NT response to show a maximum hand with both majors. Higher bids like 2NT should not be used. To quote Marty Bergen, "Never, never, never, respond 2NT to Stayman." This approach is unsound because it precludes the use of "Garbage Stayman," a convention that allows one to find a major suit fit with only 0-8 points (see below). If you insist on showing a maximum, one may employ the Stayman Super-accept convention.

Stayman with Super-accepts

After the bid of 2♣ by responder, opener responses are:

2NT   5 diamonds and a 4-card major
3♣   5 clubs and a 4-card major
3♦*   both majors and exactly 17 starting points (a maximum)
3♥   5 hearts and a maximum
3♠   5 spades and a maximum

Playing Stayman with super-accepts, after 3♦, responder's next bids are:

3♥   to play
3♠   to play
3NT   to play
4♣   Gerber (later in this chapter) or Roman Keycard Gerber (Chapter 3)
4♦   transfer to hearts with 5
4♥   transfer to spades with 5

Stayman with Super-accepts requires that the opener has 17 starting points and is 4-4 in the majors. Another approach is to use 3-level bids to show shape or doubletons with 17 starting points. Then the bids are:

3♣*   minor two suiter, at least 4-4
3♦*   doubleton in clubs or diamonds
3♥*   doubleton in hearts
3♠*   doubleton in spades

After the 3♦* response showing a soubleton in either minor, opener now bids 3♥* to ask which minor. Responder's bid of 3♠* shows clubs and 3NT* shows diamonds.

Garbage Stayman Convention

Garbage Stayman is used when responder has the exact distributions: 4=4=4=1 or 4=4=5=0 and you have 0-6 starting points. Responder will pass whatever opener bids; some refer to this as "Drop Dead Stayman."

But, suppose you are 4-4 in the majors, then what? Now, opener may bid 2♦; playing Garbage Stayman, the bid of 2♥ becomes a relay bid, partner must pass with three or bid 2♠ with three; you want to find the best 4-3 fit. As you can see, the optimal distribution for Garbage Stayman is when you are 5-5 in the majors and very weak since you will end up in a 5-3 major fit. Garbage Stayman is sometimes called **Crawling or Creeping Stayman.**

Puppet Stayman

Many partnerships use the bid of 2♣ for puppet Stayman instead of Stayman. It is needed when one bids 1NT with a five card major. As with Stayman responder should have at least eight starter points. A summary of the bids are as follows.

Opener	Responder	Meaning
1 NT	2 ♣	Asking for a 5-card Major suit. Promises at least 8 points in valuation.
2 ♦		This first response by the opener denies a 5-card Major suit and is a Relay bid.
	2♥	Shows a 4-card Spade suit, fewer than 4 Hearts.
	2♠	Shows a 4-card Heart suit, fewer than 4 Spades.
	2 NT	Shows a 4-card Spade suit and a 4-card Heart suit. This bid is invitational. Opener may pass with minimum.
	3♥	Shows a 4-card Heart suit, a 4 - or 5-card Spade suit. Game-forcing.
	3 ♠	Shows a 4-card Spade suit, a 4 - or 5-card Hearts suit. Game-forcing.
	3 NT	Shows no 4-card Major suit and game values.
	4 NT	This response is slam invitational and is accepted by the opener only if holding maximum values.

In the following auction, the responder shows a 4-card Heart suit, and the opener can show either minimum or maximum values:

Opener	Responder	Meaning
1 NT	2♣	Asking for a 5-card Major suit. Promises at least 8 points in valuation.
2♦		This first response by the opener denies a 5-card Major suit and is a Relay bid.
	2♠	Shows a 4-card Heart suit, fewer than 4 Spades.
2 NT		Shows no fit for the Heart suit and minimum values.
3♥		Shows a 4-card Heart suit and minimum values.
3 NT		Shows no fit for the Heart suit and maximum values.
4♥		Shows a 4-card Heart suit and maximum values.

The puppet Stayman convention is used most often when partnerships bid 1NT with a 5-card majopr.

Raising 1NT, 2NT, 3NT, and beyond

The Stayman convention is used when responder has at least one four-card major and should always be used even when your distribution is 4=3-3-3 or 3=4-3-3, very balanced hands.

However, suppose your hand is semi-balanced and you have only 9-10 (8-9 playing 15-17 range), you may raise to 2NT which is invitational to game. Note, as we will see later, we recommend playing four-way transfers and so we will use 2NT as a transfer to diamonds. Hence, we will have to bid 2♣* via Stayman and the bid 2NT. Stayman must now be alerted immediately with four-way transfers and if asked, one responds that partner may not have a four-card major. With more points and balanced hand, what do you do?

With 11-16 points, bid 3NT. With 17-18, bid 4NT this is a quantitative bid. It asks partner to bid 6NT with a maximum. Finally, with 19-21, bid 5NT, a grand slam force, with a maximum partner will bid 7NT and with less sign off in 6NT; more on quantitative bids in Chapter 3.

Jacoby Transfers four-way

Jacoby Transfers may be employed with a variety of hands. Responder may have a one—suited, two-suited, or even a three-suited hand. The transfer can involve the minors or the majors. They are used with weak, invitational, or strong hands. There is no point counts required to use transfers. Responders will clarify the nature of his hand with subsequent bidding.

After the bid of 1NT, responder makes the following bids, promising at least 5+ cards in the transfer suit.

2♦   transfer to hearts (♥)
2♥   transfer to spades (♠)
2♠   transfer to clubs (♣)

2NT transfer to diamonds (♦)

The bids are announced as a transfer. While some may prefer to use the bid 2♠ as minor suit Stayman and 2NT as an ambiguous transfer to a minor with slam interest, we recommend instead **Shape Asking Relays after Stayman (SARS)** to be discussed later.

For each of the requested transfers, the 1NT bidder must respond by bidding the requested suit, for the majors; however, for the minors, this is not the case. With at least Qxx in a minor transfer suit, he may substitute **super acceptance bids** by bidding 2NT (the bid below) instead to 3♣, and 3♣ (the bid below) instead of 3♦ to encourage 3NT. Without at least three-card supports with an A, K, or Q, opener will again merely accept the transfer by bidding 3♣ and 3♦ as requested. Playing four-way transfers, most players use the "super accept bid." However, you should review this with your partner.

With a very weak hand (0-8 points), it is better to transfer to a five-card suit, since partner will have at least two-card support. Playing in a suit will usually be better than notrump.

However, suppose you are weak and 5-4 in the majors.

Help Suit Game Try after a Jacoby Transfer

When using the Jacoby Transfer, one may not be sure of game in a major. In this case, responder may use the bid of 2NT as a Help Suit Game Try 2NT. After a Jacoby Transfer, responder bids 2NT, opener's responses follow.

Transfer to hearts

After 1NT - 2♦ - 2♥ - 2NT* (ASK)
Pass—minimum and normally denies 3♥s
3♣ = is a ♣ help suit game try
3♦ = is a ♦ help suit game try
3♥ = sign off
3♠ = is looking for a 5-3 ♠ fit (else 3NT)
3NT normally denies 5 ♠ or 3 ♥s

Transfer to spades

After 1NT - 2♥ - 2♠ - 2NT* (ASK)
Pass—minimum and normally denies 3♠s
3♣ = is a ♣ help suit game try
3♦ = is a ♦ help suit game try
3♥ = is looking for 5-3 ♥ fit (else 3NT)
3♠ = sign off
3NT normally denies 5♥ or 3 ♠s

Let's consider an example.

Opener	Responder	Opener	Responder	Comments
♠ AJ9	♠ KQ876	1NT	2♥ (1)	(1) transfer
♥ AQ104	♥ J3	2♠ (2)	2NT* (3)	(2) normal accept
♦ 85	♦ Q104	3♣ (4)	3♠ (5)	(3) invitational with 5♠

♣ KJ72	♣ 964	pass	(4) can you help in clubs
			(5) No

Smolen Transfers

If one has a five-card major and is weak, one will use a Jacoby Transfer bid to transfer into the major and if 5-4 and weak, one can use Garbage Stayman; however, when 5-4 in the majors and with 11+ points (10+ playing 15-17 NT), one may play Smolen. Playing Smolen, one again bids 2♣; as Stayman (alerted if you are playing four-way transfers). If partner bids a major, you have found a fit, raise to game. What if the bid is 2♦? Not playing Smolen, you would bid three of your five-card suit (game forcing) and allow partner to choose between four of the major or 3NT. However, playing Smolen you bid:

3♥*   shows 5 spades and 4 hearts and is forcing to game
3♠*   shows 5 hearts and 4 spades and is forcing to game

You bid three of the shorter four-card suit (partner knows you are 5-4). Opener may pass or complete the Smolen Transfer to game in a major, although 3NT is allowed. By bidding the game in the 4-4 or 5-3 major fit, opener denies interest in slam.

If the sequence goes:

1NT - 2♣ - 2♦ - 3♥* (5-4) What would the bids 3♠, 4♣/4♦/4♥ mean?

Or

1NT - 2♣ - 2♦ - 3♠* (5-4) What would the bid 4♣/4♦ mean?

These are called **Smolen Super-accept cuebids** and have the following meaning:

After 1NT - 2♣ - 2♦ - 3♥* and after 1NT - 2♣ - 2♦ - 3♠*

3♠*	3 spades and ♥A		4♣*	3 hearts and ♣A	
4♣*	3 spades and ♣A		4♦*	3 hearts and ♦A	(#)
4♦*	3 spades and ♦A		4♥*	Smolen Transfer	
4♥*	slam interest, but no ace to cue (#)				
4♠	Smolen Transfer				

(#)With no further interest in slam, responder may bid game in the five-card major.

Quest Transfers

Jacoby Transfers are usually used with weak hands. Smolen Transfers are game forcing transfers. What do you do with invitational values 9-10 points (8-9 points playing 15-17 NT)? An option is to use Quest Transfers which are again initiated by bidding 2♣. But, after the response of 2♦, responder now bids 3♦* as a transfer to hearts and 3♥* as a transfer to spades. Thus, we have a simple invitational sequence. The Quest bids may be invitational or better. To review,

After 1NT - 2♣ - 2♦,

3♦*   transfer to hearts (5-4 in hearts and spades)
3♥*   transfer to spades (5-4 in spades and hearts)

Using Quest Transfers, the normal accept bids show a minimal hand with two-card support or perhaps three. As with Smolen, these bids must be alerted.

We also have **Quest Super-accept cuebids:**

After 1NT - 2♣ - 2♦ - 3♦*   and after   1NT - 2♣ - 2♦ - 3♥*

3♥	Quest Transfer		3♠	Quest Transfer
3NT*	natural, non-minimum		3NT*	natural, non-minimum
	normally 3-2 in the majors			normally 2-3 in the majors
4♣*	3 hearts and ♣A		4♣*	3 spades and ♣A
4♦*	3 hearts and ♦A		4♥*	3 spades and ♥A
4♥*	3 hearts, but no ace to cue		4♠*	3 spades, but no ace to cue

Many players may not be familiar with Quest Transfers; if you do not currently play Smolen, you should consider them.

Texas Transfers (4♦ and ♥)

After opener bids 1NT, suppose you have a six-card major with game going values and no interest in slam. Using the principle of fast arrival, one employs the four-level bids of:

4♦*   transfer to hearts
4♥*   transfer to spades
* Alert

Instead of using Texas Transfers, some use South African Transfers. Then 4♣* is a transfer to hearts and 4♦* is a transfer to spades. A disadvantage of these bids is that one now may not use Gerber (four clubs to ask for aces).

Two-suited Hands (Mini-Maxi Convention)

When partner opens 1NT, you often find that you are either 5-5 in the minors or 5-5 in the majors. A simple and straightforward convention to address this distribution is the Mini-Maxi. After the bid of 1NT, one bids:

3♣*   5-5 in the minors and less than 11 starting points
3♦*   5-5 in the minors and 11+ starting points
3♥*   5-5 in the majors and less than 11 starting points
3♠*   5-5 in the majors and 11+ starting points

If you prefer the 15-17 notrump range, eleven may be replaced with ten.

Because playing in a minor is not usually a goal, some may prefer to replace the minor suit three-level bids with Broken Suit Slam Try bids (since the goal is to play in a major). If you prefer this approach, then one would replace the three-level minor suit bids with the following.

1NT - 3♣*   transfer to hearts 5/6+, indicates a broken heart suit with slam interest and shortage somewhere
1NT - 3♦*   transfer to spades 5/6+, indicates a broken spade suit with slam interest and shortage somewhere

Of course, there are many more options; readers may define their own preferences.

Extended Texas Transfers when 6-4 in the Majors

We can combine the Stayman Convention with Texas Transfers when one is 6-4 in the majors. After 1NT - 2♣ - 2♦/2♥/2♠, one next bids

4♦*   transfer to hearts with 6 and 4 spades
4♥*   transfer to spades with 6 and 4 hearts

If you are 6-5 in the majors, since we are using Mini-Maxi Convention when 5-5 in the majors, we can use Jacoby Transfers to show the long six-card suit and next bid the other major to show the five-card suit. After 1NT

2♦   transfer to hearts (♥)
2♥   transfer to spades (♠)

After opener's bid of 2♥   responder bids 4♠* to show 6 hearts and 5 spades
                      2♠   responder bids 4♥* to show 6 spades and 5 hearts

Thus, you simply transfer to the six-card suit and bid the other major at the four levels (the shorter following Smolen) to show 6-5. Other bridge authors have devised more complicated systems using Quest/Smolen Transfers with super-accepts, but they are more complex. I have tried to keep it simple.

Minor Suit Stayman

This convention, devised by Oswald Jacoby, is used by the responder when partner has opened the bidding with 1NT. It is used when partner has a long minor suit and, generally, very little values or very strong values indicating a strong interest in a possible slam contract in a minor suit.

The Minor Suit Stayman convention is applied as follows. Even with an overcall by the immediate opponent on the two level will have no bearing on the functionality of this concept since any overcall on the two level will not affect the concept. If the overcall is 2 Spades, then the partner of the No Trump bidder simply doubles to initiate this conventional method.

Opener	Responder	Meaning
1 NT	2 ♠	Responder wishes to inquire about the holding in the Minor suits.
3 ♣		Opener has a 4-card Club suit.
3 ♦		Opener has a 4-card Diamond suit.
3 ♥		Opener has both 4-card Minor suits and shows a control in Hearts.
3 ♠		Opener has both 4-card Minor suits and shows a control in Spades.
2 NT		Opener indicates interest in a possible Minor suit slam.
3 NT		Opener indicates no interest in a Minor suit slam.
	3 ♥ or 4 ♥	Responder shows a singleton in Hearts; the level is dependent.
	3 ♠ or 4 ♠	Responder shows a singleton in Spades; the level is dependent.

The Minor Suit Stayman convention was devised for specifically three types of holdings held by the responder, and which will be determined during the ensuing auction:

1.	A holding with a 6-card plus Diamond suit and weak values.
2.	A 5-5 distribution in both Minor suits and weak values.
3.	A 5-4 distribution in both Minor suits and possible slam values.

Note: Some parnership understandings have the agreement that, **after the auction shows slam interest**, any rebid by the responder at the lowest possible level of No Trump promises a distribution containing doubletons in both Major suits.

When playing Minor Suit Stayman, the bid of 2NT is also often also revised. Instead of being used with 8-9 dummy points as an invitational bid to 3NT, it is used as a puppet relay to 3♣

which responder can pass with a club bust. Or it is used to show a game forcing three suited hand, either 4-4-4-1 or 4-4-5-0 with a 5-card minor. With a strong hand, responder bids his singleton/void. And with short clubs, either bids 3NT, non-forcing or bids 4♣ with slam interest to force opener to bid.

Examples: after 1NT-2NT-3♣-?

1. Pass (x xxx Kxx QT9xxxx)
2. 3♥ (AJxx x AKxx Qxxx)
3. 3NT (AJxx AKxx Qxxx x)
4. 4♣ (AJxx AKxx AQxx x)

After the strong shortness showing bids, opener picks a suit or rebids in NT with the short suit well-stopped (and hence wasted values for a suit slam). Over a suit agreement, 4NT is RKC (Chapter 3). Over 3NT, 4NT by responder is natural and invitational.

When playing a direct 2NT to 1NT as artificial, one must start with 2♣ **Stayman** to invite game in NT.

1. Opener with both **hearts** and **spades** bids 2♥
2. The sequence 1NT-2♣-2♥-2♠ shows exactly 4 **spades** and is invitational to game. Opener may pass, bid 2NT, 3NT, or 4♠
3. The sequence 1NT-2♣-2♥-2NT is invitational to game and denies 4 **spades**
4. Other sequences that start 1NT-2♣-2any-2NT do not promise or deny a 4 card **major**. This should be explained at the time of the 2NT rebid (an alert).

Shape Asking Relay after Stayman (SARS)

We have spent most of our discussion around the major suits. After using all of our conventions and hearing 2♦, we know that the opener does not have a four-card major. And when responder is 4-3 in the majors, he needs to know something about opener's shape in the minors to consider notrump or game/slam in a minor. This is accomplished using the bid of 3♣* after the opener's bid of 2♦, called the Shape Asking Relay after Stayman (SARS). SARS provides more information than Minor Suit Stayman and is an alternative to Minor Suit Stayman. The bidding sequence follows.

After 1NT - 2♣ - 2♦, **3♣* second ask**
Opener's responses about shape in the minors

3♦*   5 card minor (either clubs or diamonds), no 4 card major
3♥*   4 clubs (3=3=3=4)
3♠*   4 diamonds (3=3=4=3)
3NT*   4 clubs and 4 diamonds (2=3=4=4) or (3=2=4=4)
4♣*   5 clubs and 4 diamonds (2=2=4=5)

4♦*   5 diamonds and 4 clubs (2=2=5=4)

Next, after the response of 3♦*, the bid **3♥* asks** which minor has five cards.

3♠*   5 clubs
3NT*   5 diamonds

After minor suit shapes ask, the bid of four of the minor always sets the minor trump suit.

The Gerber Convention

After the bid of notrump 1NT, 2NT, or 3NT, the bid of 4♣ is known as the Gerber Convention. It was devised by John Gerber of Houston, Texas in 1938. It asks partner about the number of aces and subsequently about the number of kings. When using Gerber, remember that you should not use the convention if (1) you have a void, (2) you have worthless doubletons (e.g., Qx, Jx, xx) in an unbid suit, and (3) you need to know if partner has controls in a specific suit, discussed in Chapter 3.

The responses to the 4♣ Gerber ask are:

4♦   shows 0 aces or 4 aces
4♥   shows 1 ace
4♠   shows 2 aces
4NT   shows 3 aces

Having all the aces, you may next ask for the number of kings by bidding 5NT. The responses are:

5♦   shows 0 kings or 4 kings
5♥   shows 1 king
5♠   shows 2 king
5NT   shows 3 king

If you have a void, it is not an ace. Ignore the void when responding to Gerber. As we will see in Chapter 3, to handle voids you must use Roman Keycard Gerber.

Splinters after Stayman (with fit and slam interest)

When opening a major, recall that concealed/ambiguous splinter bids of 3♠* after 1♥, and 3♥* after 1♠ showed a heart and spade fit, respectively, and a singleton or void somewhere. The same scheme may be used after Stayman when opening 1NT. The bidding sequences would be as follows.

After 1NT - 2♣ - 2♥ - 3♠* and after 1NT - 2♣ - 2♠ - 3♥*

The jump bids of three spades and three hearts are a concealed/ambiguous splinter showing a heart fit and a spade fit, respectively. One again uses scroll bids to ask about shortness, if needed:

3NT* asks		3♠* asks	
4♣*	club singleton/void	3NT*	ambiguous void
4♦*	diamond singleton/void	4♣*	club singleton
4♥*	spades singleton/void	4♦*	diamond singleton
		4♥*	heart singleton

With a heart fit, one cannot ask about voids without passing game or bidding too high. This is not the case with a spade fit, one merely bids 4♣*. The entire bidding sequence becomes:

1NT - 2♣ - 2♠ - 3♥* - 3NT* - 4♣* (ask) where 4♦* shows a diamond void

4♥* shows a heart void

4♠* shows a club void

Because 4♣ in the above sequence denotes a splinter, it is not Gerber. Hence, if after 3NT you want to ask about aces, you must use the bid of 5♣ called **Super Gerber** (or you may use Roman Keycard Blackwood with the bid of 4NT, discussed in Chapter 3).

The responses to the 5♣ (Super Gerber) ace ask is:

5♦	shows 0 aces or 4 aces
5♥	shows 1 ace
5♠	shows 2 aces
5NT	shows 3 aces

Overview of Responses to 1NT (14-17) and Examples

Starting Points	Bids	Meaning
0-8	2♣	Stayman
(Weak)	2♦/2♥	Jacoby Major Suit Transfer
	3♠/2NT	Jacoby Minor Suit Transfer
	Pass	
9-11	2♣ then 2NT	Invite game
(Invitational)	2♣ then 2♦/3♥	Quest Transfer (if played)
	2♦/2♥	Jacoby Major Suit Transfer
	3♠/2NT	Jacoby Minor Suit Transfer
12-16	2♣	Quest or Smolen
(Game)	2♣ next 3♣*	SARS

	2♦/2♥	Jacoby Major Suit Transfer
	3♣/2NT	Jacoby Minor Suit Transfer
	3NT	semi-balanced no 4-card major
	4♦*/4♥*	Texas Transfer
17-18	2♣	Stayman
(Slam	2♦/2♥	Jacoby Major Suit Transfer
Invitational)	3♣/2NT	Jacoby Minor Suit Transfer
	3♦*/3♥*	Mini-Maxi
	4NT	Quantitative Bid
19+	4♣	Gerber
(Slam)	5NT	Quantitative (Slam/Grand Slam)

We have covered a lot of material, basic, intermediate, and advanced, when responding to the bid of 1NT. To review the concepts discussed, we next consider several examples.

Your partner opens 1NT, what is your bid with the following hands?

(1) ♠QJ84 ♥10786 ♦8543 ♣A

You have only six starting points, bid 2♣ and pass any two-level bid made by partner (Drop Dead Stayman). What if partner bids 3♦ (17 starting points and both majors—Super accept Stayman)? He has the majors, bid 4♥, your weakest major since he should have strength in hearts.

(2) ♠AKJ8 ♥10764 ♦54 ♣98   or   (3) ♠J10987 ♥109876 ♦54 ♣7

Hands are weak, one is 4-4 in the majors and the other is 5-5, again bid 2♣.

If partner bids a major, pass; otherwise, with both hands bid 2♥, asking partner to pass or bid 2♠ (Garbage Stayman).

(4) ♠AKJ8 ♥J764 ♦54 ♣J8   or   (5) ♠K1098 ♥A95 ♦Q2 ♣K987

Hands (4) and (5) are invitational. With both, one again bids Stayman. If in hand (4) partner bids 2♥ or 2♠, we would raise either to game in the major. Without the support of either major, the bid of 2♦, you would bid 3NT. However, hand (5) is different; after the bid of 2♥, you would bid 3NT; he will pass or correct to four spades if he has four.

(6) ♠KJ85 ♥K764 ♦AQ ♣AJ8   or   (7) ♠AQ4 ♥KQ76 ♦Q4 ♣KQ67

Hand (6) is very strong. Bid 4NT as quantitative. With hand (7), bid 2♣. If partner bids either 2♦ or 2♠, one would bid Gerber to investigate a club slam.

(8) ♠Q10987 ♥76 ♦7810 ♣432   or   (9) ♠AQ6542 ♥KQ7 ♦Q4 ♣67

With the hand (8), bid 2♥ (Jacoby) and pass partner's bid. This is also the case with hand (9); however, next bid 3NT. Do not invite, partner may pass.

(10) ♠542 ♥Q7 ♦KQ9876 ♣67   (11) ♠542 ♥97 ♦J109876 ♣67

With hand (10), bid 2NT and after partner's response of 3♦, pass. What if he responds 3♣, the super-accept bid? Next bid 3NT. For hand (11), again use the transfer bid of 2NT; however, with a super-accept, bid 3♦. If partner bids 3♦, then pass.

As to the next hand, let's look at a complete example. North is the dealer and opens 1NT. South bids 2♦ and north announces the bid as a transfer. After bidding 2♥, south next shows his diamond suit and bids 3♦. North has a tough choice, notrump or hearts.
He bids 4♥.

		♠ KQ106	
		♥ 1074	
		♦ Q4	
		♣ AK106	
♠ 987		N	♠ AJ52
♥ 65			♥ J98
♦ K986	W	E	♦ A3
♣ QJ852		S	♣ 9742
		♠ 43	
		♥ AKQ32	
		♦ J10752	
		♣ 3	

With a diamond lead, the contract is down one due to the diamond ruff. However, with a club lead, the contract is bid and made.

Partner bids 1NT. What are your responses with each of the following hands?

(12) ♠KQ97 ♥Q10876 ♦AQ ♣Q9   (13) ♠KQ976 ♥K10975 ♦ 7 ♣A6

With hand (12), you would bid Stayman. Upon hearing the bid of 2♦, playing Smolen you would bid 3♠* to show your 4-5 distribution. Partner must now bid 4♥ with three. However, playing Quest transfers, you would bid 3♦* as a transfer to hearts, an invitational bid. Now, partner can either pass or bid 4♥.

With hand (13), after 1NT, you would bid 3♠*, 5-5 in the majors (Mini-Maxi). After the bid, partner is the captain to bid a major game, notrump, or investigate slam.

(14) ♠KQJ972 ♥Q106 ♦56 ♣Q2   (15) ♠KQJ972 ♥AQ72 ♦ J7 ♣A

Hand (14) has a six-card spade suit, bid 4♥* (Texas transfer), and pass 4♠. Partner knows you have six spades and game values. If he likes spades, he will go on.

With hand (15) would bid 2♣. If partner now bids 2♦, you would bid 4♦ (Extended Texas Transfer) to show that you are 6-4 in the majors (hearts and spades).

For our last example, we consider two hands:

Opener   ♠KQ2 ♥A106 ♦A756 ♣K104
Responder   ♠AJ107 ♥Q72 ♦KQJ2 ♣Q2

Again, one would open 1NT. And, responder would bid 2♦ (deny a four-card major). Now, responder would bid 3♣* (SARS). Opener would bid 3♠* (showing four diamonds). East next bids 6♦.

We again consider two hands where opener bids 1NT.

Opener   ♠AJ56 ♥J98 ♦AK4 ♣KJ4
Responder   ♠KQ975 ♥ void ♦Q65 ♣AQ762

In this hand, you have several options: transfer to the minor and then bid spades or bid 2♣ Stayman to find a major suit fit. Playing Broken Suit Slam tries, bid 3♣* to show shortage somewhere and good spades. We will bid 2♣ Stayman. Opener would next bid 2♠. Playing concealed/ambiguous splinters over Stayman, we would next jump and bid 3♥* (singleton or void somewhere). Opener next uses the relay bid of 3♠* (to ask). Responding 3NT* (it is a void). Now, 4♣* is bid to ask where. And partner bids 4♥ (heart void). Opener would next bid 4NT as Roman Keycard Blackwood (responding 5NT—two keycards with a void, see Chapter 3). The grand slam of 7♠ may be reached.

Five-card Major Suit Stayman

Some partnerships that play the 2/1 force system open the bidding 1NT with a five-card major with at least three cards in the other major where the pattern is 5-3-x-x or 3-5-x-x. On the convention card the box "five-card Major common" is marked. The 1NT bid has the advantage of showing points immediately, and if one transfers into the other major, it guarantees a 3-5 fit. However, playing Stayman, if partner bids 2♣, one usually jumps to the three-level in the major to show five. This takes up valuable bidding space. If you do open 1NT when 5-3 in the majors, there are at least two bidding conventions you may use to find a major fit: Puppet Stayman and Five-Card Stayman. The Puppet Stayman bid is often initiated with the bid of 3♣* (a better approach is to use Modified Puppet Stayman to be explained in some detail later). This would replace the Mini-Maxi bid of three clubs showing 5-5 in the minors with a weak hand, if you play Puppet. It is a popular bid when you open 2NT. Another option is to play five-card Major Suit Stayman as a replacement for Stayman. Playing the Five-Card Stayman one again bids: 1NT pass 2♣?

However, opener's responses are: 2♥/2♠ minimum hand (14-16) with a 5-card major

                                        3♥/3♠ maximum hand (17) with a 5-card major

To deny a five-card major, opener's responses are:

                        2♦ minimum hand with no 5-card major

                        3♦ maximum hand no 5-card major

With enough for game interest, to find a 4-4 major suit fit, responder merely repeats the inquiry by bidding 3♣. Note that responder may also bid either 3♥*/3♠* which are Smolen bids showing **four** cards in the bid major suit and **five** cards in the other suit (alert). Smolen does not interfere with the five-card Major Suit Stayman bids. This is also the case if you are playing Quest Transfers.

After the 3♣ bid by responder, opener can show a four-card major by bidding 3♥, the cheapest major suit, identical to the 2♣ response using Stayman.

Without game interest and hearing opener's two diamond minimum response, responder does not bid three clubs, but 2♥ = four hearts, 2♠ = four spades, or 2NT= no 4-card major.

Notes: Using non-forcing Puppet Stayman, you bid 2♣ for Puppet Stayman and respond by bidding 2♦ (no five-card major), then responder bids the major suit at the **two-level** that he DOES NOT HAVE. This allows the opener to become declarer if there is a 4-4 fit. If the responder is 4-4 in the majors, he bids 2NT (in five-card Major Stayman this signifies no four-card major). If the responder has shown one four-card major, the opener bids 2NT to deny holding four cards in the responder's major. Both methods allow you to find 5-3 and 4-4 fits in the major suits. If the responder bids at the three—level and not the two-level, this is again Smolen or Quest Transfers.

For forcing Puppet Stayman with 1NT, one uses the same structure for Puppet Stayman after opening 2NT. The bid is 3♣*, forcing Puppet Stayman. With this approach, 3NT* by opener denies a four-card or five-card major and 3♦* denies a five-card major, but, promises one or two four-card majors. Responder then bids at the three-level the major he does not have (this is not Smolen). If instead, responder bids four clubs after a three diamond bid by opener, this shows both majors. A bid of four diamonds by responder is a transfer to hearts and a bid of four hearts is a transfer to spades.

Overview of Several Responder Rebids

We have reviewed major, minor, and notrump opening bids, responses by partner, and rebids by the opening bidder. In this section, we review several significant rebids by the responder.

New Minor Forcing (NMF)

In this chapter, we have stressed the importance of finding a major suit fit. With a three—or four-card major, playing 2/1 game force, one opens a minor suit. After the bid of a minor, partner will often bid a four-card major. With a minimum hand (12-15 starting points), opener may support the major with only three-card support and a semi-balanced hand. Using the 3344 Convention, responder would bid 2NT* to investigate opener's shape and strength. However, suppose opener bids 1NT instead with a balanced hand. Because any new suit bid by partner or a rebid of the major is non-forcing, a forcing bid at a low level is needed to facilitate the investigation of a major suit fit.

After responder has bid a major suit and has heard opener's rebid of one notrump, responder with 10+ starting points makes the auction forcing and seeks additional information by bidding a minor suit that is new to the auction. Introduction of the second minor is called New Minor Forcing (NMF). Because this is not a natural bid, it must be **alerted**; the bid is forcing and is asking the opener if he has three-card support for the bid major. When playing NMF, the bid after one notrump cannot be passed; it is artificial and forcing.

Alternatively, one may open a diamond, responder bids one heart and opener bids one spade. Again, two clubs is NMF by responder and starts an invitational auction. Or, suppose you open one club, and partner responds one spade and you bid one notrump. A bid of two hearts by responder shows 5-4 in the majors and a weak hand asking partner to pass or bid two spades if he prefers the suit. To show invitational values or better, bid three diamonds, NMF, to force (even with a singleton). This will allow you to find an eight-card fit in either major. If partner has three spades, he will bid two spades and you may bid three spades to invite. If he has two spades and three hearts, he will bid two hearts and you can invite a heart game by bidding three hearts.

Several NMF sequences follow.

(1) 1♦ - 1♠, 1NT - 2♣*   (2) 1♣ - 1♥, 1NT - 2♦*

(3) 1♥ - 1♠, 1NT - 2♣*   (4) 1♣ - 1♠, 1NT - 2♦*

The New Minor Forcing bid asks opener to show major suit support and strength. With four in the opposite major, responder first bids the other major. He may show three-card support for support for the major later. Without four cards in the other major, he supports responder's major at the two-level (10-12 starting points, minimum values) or three-level (13-15 starting points, maximum values) with three-card support. Without support, the bids of 2NT and 3NT are available. Opener's responses must also be alerted.

In summary, Responder's bids are:

Responder Starting Points	Bids
5-9	Pass
10-12	2 level of the other major with 4 cards in the suit
	2 level of responder's major with 3-card support
	2 notrump without support maximum hand
13-15	3 level of the other major with 4 cards in the suit
	3 level of responder's major with 3-card support
	3 notrump without support maximum hand

More specifically, we consider a few bidding sequences:

Opener	Responder	Opener	Responder
1♣	1♥	1♣	1♠
1NT	2♦*	1NT	2♦*

2♠ four spades no support hearts
2NT—no support, good hand

2♥ four hearts, but may have spades
2♠ three spade support, invitational
2NT no support, invitational
3♥ four hearts, game force
3♠ three spades, game force
3♦/3♣/3NT no support, game force

The convention may also be played with a major suit opening; one heart by opener followed by a bid of one spade by responder. If opener bids one notrump, the bid of a minor by responder is again NMF. It may also be used in the sequence: opener bids one diamond, you bid one heart, and opener rebids one spade. To begin an invitational auction and check on partner's heart length, bid two clubs, NMF. In most situations, NMF is used by the responder. However, it can be used by the opener in the sequence: 1♣-1♥, 1♠-1NT, 2♦* (NMF). In this case, the bid is asking responder if he has three-card support for hearts. We next consider a few examples.

Opener   ♠K2   ♥K432   ♦K7   ♣K10789
Responder ♠Q107653 ♥J3   ♦Q65 ♣A7

The bidding would be:

1♣	1♠
1NT	2♦*
2♥	2♠
Pass	

The bid of two diamonds is NMF. Opener bids hearts to show four, and responder signs off in a partial, two spades.

Opener   ♠K2   ♥A542   ♦K7   ♣KQ789
Responder ♠QJ97 ♥7   ♦AQ6 ♣J10654

The bidding would be:

1♣	1♠
1NT	2♦*
2♥	3♣

The bid of 3♣ is forcing. With a weaker hand, one would bypass NMF and jump to three clubs after the bid of 1NT.

Opener   ♠K89   ♥K52   ♦7   ♣AKQ789
Responder ♠A2   ♥AQ987 ♦5643 ♣106

The bidding would be:

1♣	1♥
1NT	2♦*
2♣	3♥
4♥	

Using the NMF Convention, you easily reach your heart game.

Two-Way New Minor Forcing (game force NMF)

A disadvantage of NMF is that the opener cannot tell whether or not the responder has invitational or game going values until the responder's rebid. To overcome this problem, one may use the Two-way NMF convention. This tool is based upon a relay and using both minors effectively. The club suit signals all invitational hands (10-11 starting points) and the diamond suit a game going hand (12-13+ starting points).

Bidding sequences follows:

(1) 1♦/1♣ - 1♥/1♠, 1NT -2♣   Invitational Values

(2) 1♦/1♣ - 1♥/1♠, 1NT -2♦   Game Forcing Values

Now, two clubs is used by an invitational hand (whether one opens one club or one diamond) to seek three-card support for the major bid or an unbid four-card major. Lacking these, opener bids two diamonds. Now, any bid by responder may be passed.

Thus, with the hand ♠7 ♥K7432 ♦Q65 ♣AQ32, a bid of three clubs may be passed by opener. Or, suppose opener bids one diamond and you have an invitational hand: ♠AJT32 ♥KQT4 ♦654 ♣7 and bid one spade. After the bid of 1NT, you bid two clubs, suppose you hear the bid of two diamonds. You now bid two hearts to describe a 5-4 card hand with invitational values. With game forcing values and 5-4 or 5-5, you would bid two diamonds. At this time, a 2NT bid by opener is not needed. Instead, the bid of 2NT* (called the Wolff sign-off relay bid) is used as a relay. Partner wants you to bid three clubs which he will pass with a long weak club hand, or if he bids another suit, it is forcing to game.

As another example, suppose you hold ♠AJ432 ♥AJT43 ♦65 ♣7 and partner opens one diamond. You respond one spade and partner bids 1NT. With only invitational values, you bid two clubs, partner bids two diamonds, and you bid three hearts. Holding the hand: ♠AKJ432 ♥7 ♦6 ♣AQT56, if partner opens one diamond, you again bid one spade. Now, with game forcing values after a bid of 1NT, you bid 2♦, having a game forcing bid early keeps the bidding low and permits one to investigate slam.

Two-Way NMF with Checkback Stayman after 1NT

The Checkback Stayman Convention is used with the bidding sequence 1m-1M-1NT (with 12-14 minimum and 15-17 maximum points with a non-balanced hand). Again, with invitational values, one needs a forcing sequence. Playing Two-Way New Minor forcing as a game force bid, we can redefine the bid of 2♣ as an invitational game force bid. The bids follow.

2♣ as Checkback Stayman

1m-1M
1NT-2♣ (Checkback)

2♦	No 4-card major or 3-card support for the major
2♥/2♠	Min and shows either the other 4-card majors or 3-card support for responders Major
3♥/3♠	Max and show either the other 4-card major or 4-card support for respondes Major

After the bid of two diamonds, responder may rebid his six-card major suit to the two—level with a weak hand. With a six-card major and a weak hand, responder may raise his major suit; if 5-4 in spades and hearts, one may show the other major. However, if responder bids hearts, to show spades, a reverse by responder, shows 13+ starting points and is game forcing.

New Minor Forcing vs. Checkback Stayman

Having reviewed both which system should you play? The major disadvantage for NMF is that one cannot show invitational values and the bidding process takes up too much bidding space. In addition you can not show a weak 5-5 major minor hand. Finally, NMF takes up too much bidding space. Recommendation, use Checkback Stayman by bidding 2♣ (invitational values) and NMF by bidding 2♦ (game going values).

X-Y-Z Convention

Much like the Two-Way NMF Convention, after a bid of 1NT, the X-Y-Z Convention may be employed to one's advantage over any one-level rebid by opener.

Playing the 2/1 game force system, it is only used with two auctions: 1♣-pass-1♥-pass, 1♠; 1♦-pass-1♥-pass, 1♠; since playing Walsh responses after a one club opening and a one diamond response, one will usually bid one notrump, **not a major!**

Following the format for Two-Way NMF, we have the following bids.

Two clubs = invitational values (10-11 starting points) and is used as a relay bid to two diamonds

Two diamonds = game forcing values (12-13+ starting points)
Three Clubs = to play

All other 3 level bids = strong suits and suggest slam possibilities (16+ starting points).

The X-Y-Z Convention makes all jump bids strong (except three clubs which is weak). The convention is always off in competition or by a passed hand. For additional detail for those interested, consult Max Hardy's (2002) "Advanced Bridge Bidding for the 21st Century," New York: SQueeZe Books.

Wolff Sign-off with Checkback Stayman

What do you do when you respond to partner's one-level bid with five or a bad six starting points HCP and your partner then bids Two Notrump?

For example:

Hand 1)   ♠ K 7 6 4 2   Hand 2)   ♠ Q 10 9 5
                 ♥ K 9 6 5 4   ♥ 6 3
                 ♦ 5 2   ♦ K 9 8 7 4 3
                 ♣ 6   ♣ 6

In both hands, your partner opens one club and you respond one spade and now your partner bids 2NT (showing a balanced hand with 18-19 starting points). Your hands are very distributional; pass is not an acceptable bid and any suit continuation is forcing to game. You do not want to encourage to game. How can you stop the auction at the three levels? To solve this problem, Bobby Wolff proposed the Wolff sign-off bid.

Responder must bid 3♣* (an alert) as an artificial relay to 3♦. Opener is asked to go no higher. This permits the opener to get to any suit except clubs and stop at the three-level.

With the first hand, bid three clubs, and after opener's bid of three diamonds, you bid three hearts. Opener knows to either pass or correct to three spades.

With the second hand, you pass the three diamond bid by the opener. If responder bids three notrump after the relay bid of three diamonds, this shows **mild** interest in slam in the opener's minor suit.

What if you have a strong hand with clubs? For example, suppose you have the hand:

Hand 3)   ♠ A K 6 3
                 ♥ Q 4
                 ♦ 8 4
                 ♣ A 9 8 6 5

After the relay bid of three clubs, you would bid 5♣ showing no interest in slam (principle of fast arrival). With a stronger hand (15+ starting points), bid four clubs instead. This suggests **strong** interest in a minor suit club slam.

With a balanced hand and 7-10 starting points, bid 3NT after 2NT as a sign-off.

Major Suit Checkback Stayman (with 9+ starting points)

Because three clubs is always the Wolff Sign-off, 3♦* is used as a Checkback for major suit fits. Responder is usually seeking three-card support for a five-card major already bid, four cards in the major not bid, or if holding five spades and four hearts either a 4-4 fit in hearts (preferred) or a 5-3 fit in spades.

If responder's first bid was in hearts, opener shows four spades after the Checkback bid. If responder's first suit was spades, opener's first priority is to show four hearts after the Checkback.

The goal of the Checkback sequence is to first find a 4-4 fit in the majors and if not a 5-3 fit. A bid of 3NT by the opener, after Checkback, denies a major suit fit.

In the auction 1m-1♥, 2NT - 3♦*, opener knows that partner is seeking a 5-3 heart fit. The bid of 3♠ shows four spades. If responder bids 3NT, opener will correct to four hearts holding three hearts or will pass with a heart doubleton.

In the auction 1m-pass-1♠ - 2NT, 3♦*, opener knows that partner is seeking a fit in the majors holding five spades and four hearts. The goal is to reach game in hearts or a heart slam. With four hearts, partner will bid 3♥, finding a heart fit, the partnership will be in a heart game or investigate slam. With three spades, he would bid 3♠ and a 5-3 spade fit would be found. With a spade doubleton or with only three hearts, opener would bid 3NT.

What if responder is 5-3 in the majors? And the bidding goes 1m-1♠, 2NT-3♦* - ?

Checkback is asking for a spade fit. If opener bids 3♥ to show four, responder would bid 3NT. Opener now realizes the Checkback bid was to find a 5-3 spade fit. Opener would correct to 4♠ holding three.

There are many ways to play Checkback Stayman. The version provided here follows that recommended by Max Hardy.

Fourth Suit Forcing

Fourth Suit Forcing is used to allow responder to create a forcing auction at his second turn to bid. The convention may be used by responder as a one round force or a game force. If you play it as a one round force, responder should have 10-12 starting points. If you play it as a game force bid, responder should have 13+ starting points (both are on the convention card in red so the bid must be alerted). It usually implies that one has no good bid, but values, and allows the partnership to search for the best contract. While the fourth suit bid is usually made by the responder, it may also be made by the opening bidder. The convention was developed by Norman Squire from England.

Playing the Walsh club, the sequence 1♣ - 1♦ - 1♥ - 1♠ was a one-round forcing auction; however, the bid of one spade is usually natural.

However, a more typical sequence may be 1♣-1♥-1♠-2♦* or 1♦-1♠-2♣-2♥*, among others. After the fourth suit bid, opener may:

1. Raise responder's first bid suit with three-card support and a minimum hand.
2. Jump in responder's first bid suit with three-card support and a maximum.
3. Bid 2NT with the fourth suit stopped without three-card supports in the first bid suit of responder and even a doubleton.
4. Raise the fourth suit with four-card support.

2/1 Game Force a Modern Approach - Third Edition

5. A jump in the fourth suit shows 5-5 distribution.
6. Make a more natural rebid by rebidding his first bid suit.

To illustrate, the above steps:

1♥ - 1♠ - 2♣ - 2♦* - 2♠	shows **3-card** spade support.
2NT	shows a **diamond stopper**.
2♥	shows **6 hearts** (or 5 good ones).
3♣	shows **5 clubs**.
3♦	shows **4-card** diamond support.
3♠, 3NT, 3♥, 4♣	extra strength

Let's look at an example. Suppose as responder you hold the following hand.

Responder   ♠AJ567   ♥987   ♦Q7   ♣AK5

And the bidding goes: 1♦-1♠-2♣ - (?) What do you bid? Clearly, you have sufficient points for game (14 starting points) somewhere.

After the bid of two clubs, responder sees sufficient values for game. A rebid of spades shows a weak hand and responder is not strong enough to jump to three spades. He cannot support either minor since the opener is probably 5-4 in the minors. Without a heart stopper, he cannot bid 2NT. The only forcing bid that responder may make is 2♥*, fourth suit forcing to show values (to game or for one round, depending on the agreement). Partner with a heart stopper may bid notrump or rebid clubs to show 5-5 distribution in the minors. Responder will then bid 5♣.

Let's consider another example when you hold the following hand.

♠Q 10 7 ♥A K 8 7 4 ♦J 10 4 ♣A 7

And the bidding goes: 1♦-1♥-2♣ - (?)

Clearly, you would bid 2♠* (fourth suit forcing) to see if partner has three hearts. If he does not and rebids diamonds, you would bid 3NT.

As responder, you hold the following hand ♠A963 ♥A K 6 5 ♦Q 8 4 ♣A 7
And the bidding goes: 1♦ - 1♥ - 2♣ - (?) What do you bid? Clearly, bid 3NT, do not use fourth suit forcing.

As opener and responder, you have the following hands.

Opener	♠AQJ56	♥KJ98	♦K4	♣J4
Responder	♠75	♥ AQ	♦9865	♣AQ762

The bidding may go: 1♠ - 2♣ (game force) - 2♥ - 3♦ (natural) - 3NT. The bid of three diamonds is not fourth suit forcing after a 2/1 bid.

Failure to use the fourth suit as a forcing bid always limits responder's hand. If, for example, the bidding were to go:

1♦ - 1♥
1♠ - 3♠ (the 3♠ bid is non-forcing)

While fourth suit forcing is most often used by responder, it may also be employed by the opening bidder. For example, with the following hands:

Opener	♠7	♥987	♦AK84	♣AKQ98
Responder	♠AJ9876	♥A2	♦Q7	♣762

The bidding sequence may go as follows.

1♣	1♠
2♦	2♠
3♥*	3NT (I have a heart stopper)

Opening Bids and Rebids—Some additional examples

(1) Your partner opens 1♠ and you hold the following hand.

Responder   ♠1095   ♥A1032   ♦A106   ♣Q98

You have ten starting points. Playing Combined Bergen, bid 3♦* (three pieces with three trumps). If you play Bergen Raises, bid 1NT and jump to 3♠ to show a limit raise in spades. If you do not play Bergen, you would have to bid a minor suit fragment. You cannot bid 2♥ because you hold only four cards.

(2) Your partner opens 1♣ and you hold the hand.

Responder   ♠K93   ♥K7   ♦A1094   ♣Q1075

You have eleven starting points (12 HCP—1 for dubious doubleton) and bid 1♦. Partner bids 2♥ (a reverse showing 17+ points). You are near slam so you should show your four—card club suit, bid 3♣. Partner is the captain and will bid on.

(3) Your partner opens 1♠ and you hold:

Responder ♠AQJ762 ♥7 ♦AK983 ♣5

You have great spade support and seventeen starting points, bid Jacoby 2NT.

(4) You hold the following hand.

Opener ♠AQJ106 ♥A8 ♦QJ7 ♣K98

You have seventeen starting points. You have five spades and only three hearts, bid 1♠ and then jump into notrump to 2NT for your next bid, over a one level suit bid.

(5) You hold ♠A2 ♥AJ984 ♦AK852 ♣7

and your partner opens 1♣. What do you bid? You have eighteen starting points and two five-card suits. Bid 1♥ (new suit forcing). Partner now responds 1♠. If you bid 2♦* (fourth suit forcing), your hand is limited to 10-12 points not playing it as a game force. You are too strong; you should jump to 3♦ to show your values.

(6) You hold ♠AKJ93 ♥AK96 ♦7 ♣KJ8. What do you open?

You have twenty-one starting points, with an unbalanced hand. Open 1♠. Partner bids 2NT* (Jacoby). You next show your singleton, bid 3♦*. You have to move toward slam. Tools for your continued responses are discussed in Chapter 3.

(7) You hold ♠AJ7 ♥1075 ♦KQJ6 ♣A85

Partner opens 1♣; you have a balanced hand with fifteen starting points. To show your values, bid 3NT.

(8) You hold ♠76 ♥Q1075 ♦QJ62 ♣J98

Partner opens 1♣; what do you bid? You have four hearts and four diamonds and only six starting points. Show your major and bid 1♥, bypassing diamonds. Partner next bids 2♠, a reverse showing 17+ points. To show your stopper in diamonds, bid 2NT.

(9) You hold ♠Q9 ♥AK10752 ♦Q ♣KJ98

You open 1♥ and partner responds 1NT. What is your rebid?
Here you must decide whether or not to show your club suit or rebid your hearts. You have fifteen starting points; your hand is in the minimum range. Rebid hearts; with 16+ points, you would show your club suit.

(10) You hold ♠9843 ♥A75 ♦78 ♣AKJ8

You open the hand 1♣ and partner responds 1♦. What is your rebid?

Your choices are to show your four-card spade suit or bid 1NT. Even with those spades, you must show your four-card major. With a more balanced hand, one less club and one more diamond card, some may then bid 1NT.

(11) You hold ♠AQJ984 ♥75 ♦QJ1078 ♣Void

You have 10 HCP and 3 length points or 13 starting points. Open the hand 1♠.

Jacoby 2NT (Modified by the Experts)

Many established partnerships play a modified version of the Jacoby 2NT bid. It is a game force bid promising 4-card support for the major suit bid with an opening hand, 13+ dummy points. However, it better describes hand shape and values and does not require the use of scroll bids.

After the opening bid of a major and a 2NT response by partner, opener's responses are now:

4 of the major	a very bad hand always 5-3-3-2
3♣	any other minimum hand even 5-3-3-2, but with redeeming value
3♦	non-minimum, with a side singleton/void somewhere
3♥	non-minimum, any 5-4-2-2 distrbution
3♠	non-minimum, 6+ trumps (no singleton/void)
3NT	non-minimum, 5-3-3-2
4 of a new suit	a 5+ card suit with an ace/king

After the above responses, if responder (parnter) jumps to game in the bid major, it is a sign-off bid with no slam interest.

With slam interest, responder may ask for additional information.

After opener's 3♣:
Responde bids 3♦ to ask for more information which is similar to the original responses by the opener:

4 of other major	a bad hand always 5-3-3-2
3♥	minimum, with a side singleton/void
3♠	minimum, any 5-4-2-2 distribution
3NT	minimum with 6+ trumps and no singleton/void
4 of a new suit	minimum, 5+ card suit with ace/king

(After opener's 3♥ or 3♠ answer to 3♦, the next steps use the same schedule of responses as below)

After opener's 3♦:

Responder bid 3♥ to ask for more information, then

Step 1	a void somewhere
Step 2	singleton in the lowest side suit (clubs)
Step 3	singleton in next side suit (diamonds)
Step 4	singleton in highest side suit (other major)

After Step 1 (void), the next bids asks where, and the first step is clubs, second step is diamonds and the third step is the other major.

After opener's 3♥; responder bids 3♠ to ask for more information, then

Step 1	singleton in the lowest side suit (clubs)
Step 2	singleton in next side suit (diamonds)
Step 3	singleton in highest side suit (other major)

Playing the Modified (expert) 2NT convention, it is never on if the opponent's interfere.

However, to cope with interference over the bid of 2NT, the following set of bids is employed.

Double by opener	shortness in opponets bid suit
New suit	natural or a control
3NT	balanced maximum (ace/king in their suit)
Pass	flat hand 5-3-3-2—if partner next double it for penalty Jump to 4
other M	minimum hand with 6+ in original major

If the opponents double as asking bid, redouble= business, pass= Step 1, etc. If the opponents bid after and asking bid, double= penalty, pass=Step 1, etc. (except when the double-shortness, as above).

Another version of Jacoby 2NT has been suggested by Marty Bergen. His version summarized by Don Varvel (varvel@cs.utexas.edu) follows.

Bergen's Jacoby 2NT

The convention is explained using the bid 1♥-2NT. The bids for 1♥-2Nt are similar.

Opener's rebids:

3♣ = Non-minimums with singletons OR big balanced or semi-balanced hands.
3♦ = Non-minimum two-suiters OR *any* good hand that is anxious to learn more about responder's distribution.

3♥ = All hands with voids.
3♠ = All minimums with singletons.
3NT = Good hands with a 6-card suit.
4m = Decent minimums, identifying cheaper ace or king.
4♥ = Decent minimums with no control in a minor suit.
4♠ = Signoff.

"Decent" tends to center around 13 HCP. 5-4 qualifies as a 2-suiter when there are 13 HCP. Big balanced is 17+, big semibalanced is 15+.

Over 3♣ or 3♥ opener will usually relay; over 3S, sometimes. The relay suit is the next higher. Opener shows his shortness in steps, in the order ♣, ♦, OM. Over 3♣-3♦, with the big balanced or semi-balanced hand opener bids the cheaper minor-suit control. Non-relay bids are asking bids, again in steps. That is, over 3♣, 3♥ is an asking bid in clubs. Responses are in steps, showing control of the suit asked: 1st step shows no control, 2nd shows Q or XX, 3rd shows K or X, 4th shows ace.

Over 3♦ responder shows shortness: 3♥ = doubleton club, 3♠ = doubleton diamond, 3NT = doubleton heart, 4♣ = non-minimum 4x3, 4♦ and 4♥ show singleton club and diamond respectively and a hand too strong to splinter, and 4♠ shows a minimum 4x3. (Bergen's splinters are limited to 12 HCP at most.)After all of this, cuebids and kickback follow.

Chapter 2
Opening Two-, Three-, and Four-Level Bids

When opening one of a suit, one has between 12-21 starting points. In this chapter, we review opening bids with more than nineteen starting points, distributional hands, and weak hands, less than eleven starting points.

The Flannery Convention

For the Flannery Convention, one uses the bid of 2♦* to show five hearts and four spades and 11-15 starting points. It was devised by William L. Flannery from McKees Rocks, Pennsylvania.

When playing Flannery, a response of one spade ensures five (not four) spades (and must be alerted) when one opens one heart.

With less than invitational values (0-9 Dummy Points), the responses are:

2♥/2♠ is signoff; play in two hearts/spades.
3♥/3♠ is a limit raise, inviting opener to bid game with a maximum.
3♣/3♦ shows a long six-card minor with 10-13 Dummy Points (defined shortly) and no major. Opener may pass or bid 3NT.
3NT balanced hand with 16-18 Dummy Points; slam invitational.
4♣ is by agreement the ace asking Gerber Convention (more on this later).

2NT* is a one-round force with a good hand (10+ Dummy Points), asking opener to describe his distribution. Responder may have support. Opener's rebids after 2NT are:

3♣*	shows 4=5=1=3 distribution
3♦*	shows 4=5=3=1
3♥*	shows 4=5=2=2 and 11-13 starting points
3♠*	shows 4=5=2=2 and 14-15 starting points
3NT*	shows 4=5=2=2, 14-15 starting points and concentrated minor strength
4♣*	shows 4=5=0=4
4♦*	shows 4=5=4=0

Responder sets the contract or seeks slam (note that we have used = signs to show hand patterns, this represents an exact pattern whereas a dash [-] means any pattern). **All of the Flannery bids in response to 2NT* must be alerted.**

In the defense against Flannery, a suit overcall at the two-level shows a three-suited hand on which the overcall suit is the shortest. Suit overcalls at the three levels are natural. A double indicates a hand with strong notrump values. And a bid of 2NT shows the minors.

Mini Roman Three-suited hands

The origin of the Mini Roman bid is unknown, although it is widely played. When playing Mini Roman, one gives up the weak two diamonds bid (more on weak bids later). There is **no standard way to play** Mini Roman. We review two commonly employed approaches. However, the first question you may ask is why play it? (1) It is preemptive and allows partnerships to steal part-score hands, (2) you are aware of the hand distribution quickly, and (3) it allows the opener to bid three four-card suits with one bid!

Mini Roman with four spades

Mini Roman uses the bid of 2♦* to describe a hand with any 4-4-4-1distribution and 11-15 starting points and four spades (some players who want to play Flannery and Mini Roman will use the bid of 2♥* for Flannery, giving up the weak two heart bid). With a weak hand (0-9 Dummy Points) and 3+ spades, partner bids two spades, to play. With invitational values (10+ Dummy Points), responder bids 2NT* to ask for the singleton suit. After the suit with the singleton is bid, responder places the contract or asks for the number of aces with slam interest or perhaps a cuebidding sequence.

Mini Roman with four spades "submarine" singleton bid

Here, the opener again has four spades, but instead of bidding the singleton after the 2NT* bid, the suit below the singleton is bid: clubs for diamonds, diamonds for hearts, and hearts for clubs. Now, a cuebid of the singleton suit (diamonds, hearts, or clubs) by the responder asks for more information. The opener's responses are the following:

Steps	short ♦	short ♥	short ♣
1	4-4-4-1 min	4-4-4-1 min	4-4-4-1 min
2	4-4-4-1 max	4-4-4-1 max	4-4-4-1 max

For example, after the response 3♦, one may bid 3♥. Then, the steps are 3♠ or 3NT; showing 4-4-4-1 with min (11-13 starting points) and 4-4-4-1 with a max (14-15 starting points), respectively. After a response of 3♥, one bids 4♣. Then the min and max bids are 4♦ and 4♥, respectively.

We now look at an example. Opener has fourteen starting points and is 4-4-4-1 and opens the bidding 2♦*.

Opener	♠AK78	♥QJ87	♦J	♣A1098
Responder	♠5432	♥K1095	♦A1078	♣K5

The bidding sequence would be:

2♦*	2NT*
3♣* (singleton diamond)	3♦* (cue asking bid)
3NT (max)	4♠
Pass	

Some will also use the Mini Roman bid with a void in a minor suit (4=4-5-0/4=4-0-5). Again, the opener bids the suit below to show shortness; three clubs shows diamonds, three diamonds shows hearts, three hearts shows spades, 3♠ shows 4=4=5=0, and 3NT shows exactly 4=4=4=1. Cuebids of the singleton suit are again used to obtain more information. The Mini Roman convention may also be played with hand patterns that may or may not include four spades [(e.g., (4-4-4-1/4-4-5-0/4-4-0-5)]. If interested in Mini Roman, consult the book by Robert Munger (1998), "The Roman Two Diamond Opening and Variations," by Devyn Press, for an advanced treatment of the bids.

The best defense against Mini Roman is to lead trump in a suit contract since these cut down on ruffing values.

The Extra-Shape Flannery Convention

Many partnerships do not play the Mini Roman 2♦* bid to show 4-4-4-1 or the Flannery (2♦*) Convention to show four spades and five hearts (4=5-x-x) since they feel too much information is conveyed to the opponents. Those who like both conventions do not like to substitute the weak 2♥* bid for Flannery in order to play both. If you fit into either of these categories, you may like the **Extra-Shape Flannery Convention that uses the 2♦* bid** to describe either a two-suiter with four spades and five hearts (4=5-x-x) or three-suited hands (4=4=4=1), with exactly one club. Again, the opener has 11-15 starting points.

With this convention, the artificial 2NT* bid is forcing to game or the start of slam investigation and is used to ask the opener about his distribution. The opener's bids after a 2NT* ask are:

3♣* shows 4=5 in spades and hearts and 3-1 in the minors; a relay 3♦ bid by responder asks the opener to identify his singleton.

Opener uses step responses:

3♥* = singleton diamond and 3♠* = singleton club

3♦*	shows 4=4=4=1
3♥*	shows 4=5-2-2 with minimum 11-12 starting points strength
3♠*	shows 4=5-2-2 with maximum 14-15 starting point strength
3NT*	shows 4=5=4=0, void in clubs (submarine bid)
4♣*	shows 4=5=0=4, void in diamonds (submarine bid)

If the responder is not interested in finding out about the opener's distribution, the following non-forcing bids are used.

2♥/2♠   signoff
3♣   non-forcing 3=2=4=4 distribution, opener may pass with a minimum hand and 3/4 clubs or may correct to 3♦
3♥/3♠   game invitational in bid suit either 4 spades or 4 hearts
4♣/4♦   establishes hearts/spades, respectively, and is Roman Keycard Blackwood with kickback; more keycard and slam bidding later in Chapter 3.
4♥/4♠   signoff

All response to the 2NT* bid must be alerted.

Opening 2NT

The opening bid of 2NT requires a balanced hand (4-3-3-3, 4-4-3-2, or 5-3-3-2), which may have a five-card minor suit. The opening point count requirements for a 2NT opening bid are between 20-21 starting points and having all suits stopped. With 20-21 points and a five-card major, one also tends to open the hand 2NT since if a hand was opened one of a major there is a chance partner may pass and game may be missed. When opening 2NT, the bid is not forcing; your partner may pass with a weak hand. Recall that the number of points for game is 24-26 points; partner will pass with five or less points. With 6+ points, your goals are to bid a game in a major or notrump. Slam requires about thirty-three points.

After the bid of 2NT with a balanced hand and 6-11 points and no four-card major bid, one merely bids 3NT (to play) showing no interest in slam. One investigates slam with 12+ points.

Stayman after 2NT Notrump (basic)

After the bid of 2NT, the Stayman Convention uses the asking bid of 3♣ as an artificial bid to inquire whether or not partner has a four-card major. The convention is so engrained in bridge that it need not be alerted. Opener's responses are:

3♦   no 4 card major
3♥   denotes a 4 card heart suit, but may have 4 spades
3♠   denotes a 4 card spade suit

To initiate the convention requires 6+ starting points and at least one four-card major.

Responder's rebid, with game going values, will be either 3NT or a raise of opener's major to game with a fit. With more than an opening hand, cuebids or jump bids are used to investigate slam.

What happens if partner bids 3♦ (no four-card major)—then the bid of 3♥/3♠ shows a hand that is 5-4 in the majors where the suit bid has five cards. There is not Smolen or Quest Transfers when opening 2NT. If you are 6-4 in the majors, one again uses, as with the one notrump opening, extended transfer bids (more on this soon).

Is there a Garbage Stayman Convention over 2NT? Yes, it works as follows. After the bid of 3♣, if partner responds 3♦, your next bid is 4♣ "pick a major" (careful, some partnerships may use the bid of four diamonds). Remember, you need at least 6+ points to use this option. I prefer the four club bid; it is like "extended Stayman."

With less than 6+ points and the magic 4=4=4=1 distribution, you may still use Drop Dead Stayman and pass any suit bid by the opener after bidding three clubs.

A major disadvantage of Stayman is it does not allow one to easily find a 5-3 major suit fit when the 2NT opener has a five-card major (one may use Modified Puppet Stayman).

Jacoby Transfers four-way

Over the bid of 2NT, transfers to the majors when responder has 5+ cards are called Jacoby Transfers. They are again used with a variety of hands: weak, invitational, and strong. Point counts are not required with Jacoby Major Suit Transfers. Responder will clarify the nature of his hand with subsequent bids. We have added to the Jacoby Major Transfer transfers to the minors. Jacoby Transfers are used when you have a long major or are 5-4 in the majors. With a weak hand, you can transfer to the major and pass. When you are 5-4 in the majors, you transfer to the five-card major and bid the four-card major. The minor suit transfers are used with either a very weak hand with a 6+ cards in minor or very strong minor suited hands (12+ starting points) with slam interest in a minor. All bids are announced as transfers.

After the bid of 2NT, responder makes the following bids, promising at least 5+ cards in the transfer suit (the bids are announced, not alerted).

3♦	transfer to hearts
3♥	transfer to spades
3♠	transfer to clubs
3NT	transfer to diamonds

Opener's responses for **majors suit transfers**

3♥	shows only 2 hearts
4♣/4♦	shows 5 hearts and at least 4 cards in the bid minor with slam interest
4♥	shows 4 hearts and mild slam interest
4♠	Roman Keycard Blackwood with kickback for hearts (Chapter 3)
3♠	shows only 2 spades

4♣/4♦ shows 5 spades and at least 4 cards in the bid minor with slam interest

4♠ s hows 4 spades and mild slam interest

4NT Roman Keycard Blackwood for spades (Chapter 3)

When responder is 5-4 in the majors, the other major is bid showing the distribution.

Opener's responses for **minor suit transfers**

3NT shows good clubs, 3 pieces with 2 of top 3 honors (e.g., AQx, AKx, KQx, etc.—super accept)

4♣ poor clubs or doubleton

Pass shows good diamonds, 3 pieces with 2 of top 3 honors (e.g., AQx, AKx, KQx,
etc. —super accept)

4♣ poor diamond support

4♦ diamonds no honors or doubleton

After a club transfer, responder can next bid, after 3NT, 4♣ to play with 6+ clubs and a very weak hand (less than six points). Any other suit bid (4♦ /4♥/4♠) shows slam interest with perhaps four cards in the bid suit.

After a diamond transfer, you can correct the bid of four clubs to five diamonds with 6+ diamonds and a weak hand (you cannot pass). If you have interest in a diamond slam, bid 5♣ as super Gerber over four clubs. After the bid of 4♦, bid 4♥ as Roman Keycard Blackwood with kickback.

Texas Transfers (4♦* and 4♥*) and Extended Texas Transfers

After opener bids 2NT, suppose you have a six-card major with game going values and no interest in slam. Using the principle of fast arrival, one employs the four-level bids of

4♦* transfer to hearts

4♥* transfer to spades

* Alert

When you are 6-4 in the majors, you again bid 3♣ (Stayman), and then bid:

4♦* transfer to hearts (shows 6-4 in the majors)

4♥* transfer to spades (shows 6-4 in the majors)

*Alert

Modified Puppet Stayman (3♣*)

When opening 2NT, one often has a five-card major. Puppet Stayman was designed to help locate a 4-4 major suit fit, a 5-3/5-4 spade fit, or a 5-3 heart fit. However, it is does not allow responder to show a hand with five spades and four hearts. To correct this problem, there is a convention called the Modified Puppet Stayman Convention (I have also seen it called Muppet Stayman). It allows one to find all 4-4 major fits and 5-3 heart or spade fits. It is identical to Puppet Stayman except that the meaning of 3NT and 3♥ in Puppet Stayman are switched in meaning (hence the modification).

It works as follows: 2NT - 3♣* (Modified Puppet Stayman or Muppet Stayman)

3NT*   shows 5 hearts. Responder can either pass if he has spades, or if responder wants to play it in hearts, bids 4♦* as a transfer to hearts which allows the strong hand to play the contract in 4 hearts

3♠*   shows 5 spades

3♦*   **has 1 or 2 four-card majors or if he has a 3-card spade suit**

3♥*   shows no 4-card major or no 5-card major may have 3 spades. Responder will usually now bid 3NT. But, if responder has 5 spades and 4/3 hearts, he can now bid 3♠, looking for the 5-3 major fit in spades.

When opener bids 3♦*, responder makes the following rebids.

3♥*   Responder bids the major he does not have (like Smolen). This sequence shows 4 spades and denies 4 hearts. Opener either bids spades or 3NT.

3♠*   Responder bids the major he does not have. This sequence shows 4 hearts and denies 4 spades; opener either bids hearts or 3NT.

4♣*   Responder has both majors, it asks partner to pick the major.

4♦*   **Most p**artnerships play the bid of 4♦ to show slam interest, pick a slam.

* Alert

We next consider a few examples. Partner opens 2NT. What do you bid with the following hands?

♠ A1054 ♥ 4567 ♦ 67 ♣ J32

You have a weak hand, bid 3♣*, and if partner bids a major, support the major; if opener bids three diamonds, bid 4♣ to ask partner to pick a major.

♠ AQ54 ♥ 456 ♦ 67 ♣ J1032

You want to find a 5-4 spade fit or a 5-3 heart fit. If partner responds 3NT* showing five hearts, you would next bid 4♦ as a transfer to hearts. If partner bids 3♠, you simply raise the bid to four.

♠ AK542 ♥ Q65 ♦ 67 ♣ 1032

You want to find your 5-3 spade fit or perhaps a 5-3 heart fit. If partner bids 3NT* finding the heart fit is no problem. If partner bid 3♥* (showing no four—or five-card major, but may have a 3-card spade suit), responder next bids 3♠ to show that he is 5-3/4 in spades and hearts. Opener with only three spades would next bid four spades.

If responder is 5-5 in the majors, over 3NT by opener he may bid 4♥ to show his 5-5 shape.

Note: Using Puppet Stayman, the 5-3 spade fit could be found and using Jacoby Transfers one would lose the 5-3 heart fit; Modified Puppet Stayman finds both fits.

What do you do if you are 5-4 in spades and hearts?

For example, you have the hand: ♠ AK542 ♥ K653 ♦ 67 ♣ 103

Using Modified Puppet (Muppet) Stayman, bid 3♣*, if partner bids 3NT, you can pass or bid 4♦ as a transfer to hearts; if opener bids 3♥, then bid 3♠.

If you have five hearts and four spades, you do not need Muppet, transfer to hearts and bid spades.

♠ AKJ2 ♥ KQ53 ♦ K7 ♣ 1032

You have fifteen starting points. You are in the slam zone for a major or notrump. But suppose you hear the response 3♦*. You have two options: four clubs or four diamonds.

If you bid 4♦, it allows opener to pick the slam (perhaps notrump). The bid of 4♣ asks partner to pick a major. With a marginal hand, say only eleven starting points, you would definitely make the bid of four clubs since you need to know how the hands fit.

♠ 1032 ♥ 67 ♦ KQ53 ♣ AK1032

You have nice diamonds and clubs. The bid of 3NT does not describe your hand, partner may pass. Bid 3♠* as a transfer to clubs, if partner bids 3NT, you would jump to 6NT. If partner bids 4♣* (pick a major), you would next bid 4♦ to show your distribution. Partner is now the captain of the hand.

♠ 1032 ♥ AK9876 ♦ 53 ♣ 32

You have a weak hand with a six-card heart suit. Bid 4♦* as Texas transfer to your heart; you have no interest in slam. Fast arrival principle. What if you had one more spade? See the next example.

♠ J1032 ♥ AK9876 ♦ 53 ♣ 7

Now use Modified Puppet Stayman and bid 3♣*; after the bids 3♦/3♥/3♠, use the extended transfer bid of 4♦* to show your 6-4 distribution. What if opener bids 3NT*? You have a great heart fit (eleven hearts). Bid five hearts which invites six; partner's values are outside of hearts.

In summary Modified Puppet (Muppet) is superior to Puppet in three ways.

1. It allows the strong hand to declare all major suit contracts.
2. It avoids the often disastrous use of a transfer bid when responder holds 5 cards in one major and 3 cards in the other major and allows responder to look for a 5/3 fit in either major. Holding 5-3-3-2 (♠-♥-♦-♣) responder bids 3♣ to first look for a 5/3 heart fit. Opener will rebid 3♦ with a 4 card major opener and the auction proceeds as in standard puppet. And opener will rebid 3♠ with a 5 spades. Now for the modifications of Puppet: Opener will bid 3♥ rather than 3NT to deny a 4 or 5 card major. If Responder holds 5 spades and 3 hearts, responder will rebid 3NT to show the 5 card spade suit enabling opener to declare in 4♠ with 3 spades and the right sort of hand. If responder does not hold 5 spades, responder rebids 3♠ relaying opener back to 3NT.
3. When holding 5 hearts and 4 spades, responder can transfer to 3♥ and to show 4 spades will rebid 3NT after opener accepts the transfer. This allows the strong hand to declare in 4♠ with a 4-4 spade fit. If responder does not have 4 spades, then after opener accepts the transfer, responder rebids 3♠ relaying opening to 3NT.
4. Muppet also allows opener to bypass a transfer to 3♥ and rebidding 3♠ when holding 5 spades and 2 hearts. Using both Jacoby and Texas transfers, if responder holds a 6 card heart suit and mild slam interest, responder will transfers to 3♥ at 3-level and, when opener bypasses the transfer to rebid 3♠, responder will have to rebid 4♦ to retransfer opener to 4♥ (showing mild slam interest and inviting opener to make a slam try).

If you understand and use Puppet Stayman after any strong 2NT opening or 2♣-2♦-2NT sequence, it is easy to remember Muppet if you just remember that responder must always bid in such a way that the strong hand will declare the hand in a NT or Major suit contract.

SUMMARY

Muppet Stayman is simple Puppet stayman but with opener's 3NT and 3♥ bids reversed (3NT shows five hearts; 3♥ denies a 4+ majors). This allows Responder, over 3♥, to bid 3♠ to show 5♠/4♥, an otherwise unbiddable shape below 3NT when playing Puppet.

So, suppose you have 5♠/4♥ and partner bids 3♦. You have both majors, but they are imbalanced 5-4 so bid 3♥ to show five spades and fours hearts. Or bid 3♠ to show five hearts and four spades.

Now, suppose that you have 5-5 in the majors. Muppet still works. If partner has a 4-card major, nothing can go wrong. If he has a 5-card major, wow. If you hear 3♥, bid 3♠ to show 5♠ or 3/4♥. If opener declines (3NT), you can bid 4♥ to complete the picture.

If either Muppet or Puppet is too complicated for you, another option is to employ the Flip-Flop Flannery Convention.

<u>Flip-Flop Flannery Convention</u>

The Flip-Flop Flannery Convention was developed by Carolyn King and Dr. David S. Shade and published in the "Bridge World" magazine, February 1997.

The Flip-Flop Flannery Convention allows one to find a major suit fit regardless of the partnership distribution. In addition, it also employs the transfer principle allowing the 2NT bidder to become the declarer as in Muppet Stayman. The bids for the convention follow, after the bid of 2NT,

3♣   asks about length in the majors; the opener rebids:

   3♥/3♠ 5-card major
   3♦   4-card unspecified majors; in his turn responder bids 3♠ with 4 hearts and 3♠ with 4 spades; and opener places the final contract in 3NT, 4♥, or 4♠.

3♦   5-card heart suit, transfer; after the completed transfer by opener, responder bids

   3♠   at most 3 spades 3NT
   3NT   4 spades; thus if a fit is found in spades opener become the declarer and places the contract.

3♥   transfer to spades, 5 spades but no hearts

3♠   transfer to 3NT, no 4-card or 5-card major

3NT 5 spades and 4 hearts

Using Flip-Flop Flannery, you are able to find a major fit without going beyond 3NT and it right-sides the contract.

Soloff Bids

If you do not like Muppet Stayman and want to continue with Puppet Stayman, you may want to play the Soloff Convention. This will allow you to continue with Puppet. The bids follow.

- 3♣ Puppet Stayman
- 3♦ Transfer to Hearts
- 3♥ Transfer to Spades
- 3♠ Relay to 3NT
- 3NT shows 5♠ and 4♥

Bids after 3♠ relay to 3NT

- Pass with any hand that wants to play 3NT
- 4♣ shows 4♣ and 5♦, 4♠ agrees diamonds, 4NT denies an 8 card fit
- 4♦ shows 4♦ and 5♣, 4♥ agrees clubs, 4♠ agrees diamonds, 4NT denies an 8 card fit
- 4♥ is a one suited slam try with long clubs. 4NT now by opener shows honor doubleton. 5 ♣ shows a low doubleton. Any other bid is a cuebid with at least 3 card club support.
- 4 ♠ is a one suited slam try with long diamonds. 4NT now by opener shows honor doubleton. 5 ♦ shows a low doubleton. Any other bid is a cuebid with at least 3 card club support.
- 4NT is a slam try with at least 5-5 minors

3♠ Transfer

An alternative to the Soloff bids to finding a slam in a minor is to employ the following simple transfer structure; similar to minor suit stayman.

Opener Responder Meaning

2 NT   The range of the 2 No Trump opening bid is 20 to 21 high card points.

3♠   Responder wishes to inquire about the holding in the Minor suits.

3NT   Relay bid

If responder is 5-5 in the minors, he bids 4♥ or 4♠ to show shortness in the major.

After these bids, 4NT is used to investigate slam. Because you may have a double fit in the minors some use the bid as DRKCB.

If responder is distributional with one long minor, he bids the minor he does not have 4♦ to show clubs and 4♣ to show diamonds.

After 4♦, 4♥ is 1430 to investigate slam and after 4♣, 4♦ is 1430 minorwood. Again some use the bid as DRKCB.

If the opening bidder has 2344 or 3244 distribution with good minors and weak majors, he bids 4NT which is a non-forcing, slam try.

To employ the 3♠ relay bidding sequence, responder must have 12 dummy points.

Opening 2♣

Playing the 2/1 game force system, the opening bid of 2♣ shows a hand with 22+ starting points or 8 ½-9 playing tricks; it is artificial and forcing. To count playing tricks, you only look at the first three cards in each suit where an ace, king, or queen is a winner and all other cards among the first three are losers. With less than three cards, there are these loser honor combinations: AQ=½, Kx= ½, KQ=1, K=1, Q=1, Qx=1.

Independent of points, also open a hand **2♣,** with a 5+ major and at least 4+ quick tricks (A=1, K=½, KQ=1) and no more than four losers; **the rule of forty-four** and then bid the major not notrump.

Partner may not pass the bid of two clubs, even with zero points. With a balanced hand (4-3-3-3, 4-4-3-2, 5-3-3-2, 5-5-2-2), opener may jump into notrump. The notrump bidding schedule follows.

2NT shows 22-24 starting points
3NT shows 25-27 starting points
4NT shows 28-30 starting points
5NT shows 31-33 starting points

When partner opens two clubs, responder's first responsibility is to communicate something about the value of his hand. This permits the opener to show the nature of his hand by bidding notrump or a suit. When responding to partner, partnerships have several options. Based on a survey conducted by bridge expert and teacher Karen Walker, when asked what general structure respondents used for responses to a strong 2♣ in their favorite partnership, they offered the following answers (with the percentage of "votes" for each):

- 36% 2♦ semi-positive, 2♥ immediate negative
- 25% Control-showing step responses

- 21% 2♦ waiting, cheapest minor second negative
- 10% 2♦ negative, 2♥ balanced positive
- 4% Point-count step responses
- 4% Other artificial systems (e.g. ace showing responses)

From Ms. Walker's survey, we observe that the MOST common approach is to use 2♥ as a bust (no ace or king), and 2♦ as semi-positive (a king or more). Others prefer showing controls or they use two diamonds as a waiting bid. We will discuss the three most popular approaches.

Controls

This approach is popular because it allows responder to show his most important cards (aces and kings) immediately, in one bid. Counting each king as one control and each ace as two, responder makes one of the following step responses:

- 2♦ 0 or 1 control (K=1)
- 2♥ 2 controls (A or KK)
- 2♠ 1 ace and 1 king (3 controls—AK in different suits)
- 2NT 3 kings (3 controls—KKK or AK in same suit)
- 3♣ 4+ controls

If the opponents INTERFERE, then a double (or Re-Double) are the weakest bids you can make (one or fewer controls and less than 5 HCP). Bidding would show 1+ controls and a good 5+ card suit.

After a 2♣ opening and any response, if RHO (right hand opponent) bids, a DOUBLE shows shortness in the RHO suit. If you have a 6+ card suit, then a bid is ambiguous as to the length in RHO suit but is preferred to an X for shortness. However, with a void with 6-4-3 shape, then X.

While the control bids communicate values, it does not allow the responder to make a natural bid to show a suit with, for example, two of the top three honors with 5+ cards. It at time uses up valuable bidding space and may wrong-side the hand. For example, showing two controls, hearts, may be opener's suit and responder plays the hand.

A few players define "controls" by steps to show points; this has little value because it makes no distinction between jacks and aces. The 2♣ bidder seldom needs to know partner's total points; information about aces and kings is more helpful.

Two diamonds waiting

This approach is widely used among longtime players. The bid of 2♦ is automatic and provides an opportunity for the opener to describe his hand by bidding notrump or a suit. It is not alerted but a waiting bid.

With a very weak hand, less than four starting points, responder may pass after a notrump bid. If a suit is named and responder is weak, there is a second negative bid. The second negative bid is either the cheapest minor or the cheapest bid, known as the Herbert Convention. The primary advantage of the two diamond bid is that it does not consume space. The major disadvantage is that specific suit strength is not immediately communicated and it may take time for responder to describe his hand.

Two hearts negative and two diamonds semi-positive

Using this approach, the bid of 2♦* (alerted) is a game force bid promising a king or an ace. The bid of two hearts is non-forcing, **but it does not deny points**. For example, you may have two queens and a jack or three queens. The bids for this approach follow.

2♦*	promises a king or an ace and is game forcing (some also include 2 Queens)
2♥*	denies a king or an ace but does not deny some values
2♠	shows at least a 5-card suit with 2 of the top 3 (7+ points)
2NT	shows at least a 5-card **HEART** suit with 2 of the top 3 hearts (7+ points)
3♣/3♦	shows 2 of the top 3 but with 6+ cards in the minor suit bid (7+ points)

After the bid of two diamonds, with a balanced hand, opener may bid notrump as described above; however, the bid of a suit indicates a non-balanced hand.

After the bid of two hearts, the only bid responder may pass is 2NT. Otherwise, he must provide a second negative bid. This is usually the cheapest minor or using Herbert, the cheapest bid available.

In the above responses, observe that the bid of two spades and the three level minor suit bids wrong-side the contract. To avoid this problem, one may consider the following bids for the convention.

2♦*	promises a king or an ace and is game forcing (some also include 2 Queens)
2♥*	denies a king or an ace but does not deny some values
2♠	shows at least a 5-card **heart** suit with 2 of the top 3 (7+ points)
2NT	shows at least a 5-card **spade** suit with 2 of the top 3 hearts (7+ points)
3♦	shows 2 of the top 3 but with 6+ cards in the **club** suit (7+ points)
3♣	shows 2 of the top 3 but with 6+ cards in the **diamond** suit (7+ points)

This option/modification should be discussed with your partner.

Interference note when playing the 2♥* bust

If your partner bids two clubs and your right hand opponent interferes, then a pass* (alert) shows values (ace or king) and a redouble* (alert) denies an ace or a king. Both bids must be alerted. If the opponents interfere with a suit bid at the two—or three-level (or double), again a double (redouble) shows no values and a pass shows values.

Let's consider a few example hands.

Opener   ♠AQ54 ♥ KQ10 ♦ K52 ♣ AKQ

You have 23 HCP. Open the hand 2NT; you have stoppers in all suits.

Opener   ♠KQ754 ♥KQ10872 ♦ void ♣ AK

This hand contains 17 HCP + 3 length points = 20 starting points. Some may open this 1♥ and then bid spades. What if partner passes? Let's look at playing trick for the hand. You have 13-5 losers = 8 playing tricks. You must open the hand 2♣, forcing partner to bid.

Opener   ♠AJ98 ♥AQJ10872 ♦ K ♣ Q

You have 18 HCP + 3 length points—2 dubious honor singletons = 19 starting points. In addition to looking at playing tricks, the hand has 13-3 =10 playing tricks. Open the hand 2♣ and then show your great heart suit. Opening 1♥, partner may pass.

Opener   ♠AJ98 ♥AQJ10872 ♦ K ♣ Q
Responder   ♠Q1092 ♥456 ♦ QJ78 ♣ 97

The bidding sequence for this hand playing the 2♥ bust option would be:

Opener	Responder
2♣	2♥*
3♥	4♥

With three heart support and a bust hand, partner must support hearts. Provided partner takes a call after opener bids 1♥, one would still reach the game. The bidding may go:

1♥—1NT;
3♠ (jump shift)—4♥.

But, why take a chance; partner with only 5 HCP may pass the bid of 1♥!

Ace—Showing Responses

This is a common convention used in Europe. The responses are:

2♦	negative
2♥/2♠	ace-showing
2NT	8+ HCP, but no aces
3♣/3♦	ace-showing
3NT	two aces

The convention is also employed by many over weak two-level bids.

Kokish Relay

When opening 2♣ with a 25+ point hand, responding 3NT and above takes up a significant amount of bidding space; to eliminate this problem some employ the Kokish Relay.

After the bid of 2♦, the bid of 2♥ becomes a relay bid asking partner to bid 2♠. Now with a balanced big hand, partner next bids 2NT.

The following sequences ate used with unbalanced holdings.

Opener		Responder		Meaning
2 ♣				An opening bid showing strong values.
		2♦		Normally either a *waiting bid* or a *negative bid*.
2♥				This is the *Kokish Relay*, a puppet for responder to bid an automatic 2♠ in order that the opener clarifies his holding.
		2 ♠		The puppet bid.
2 NT				Opener promises 25 plus points and a balanced distribution.
3♣				Opener promises a two-suited holding with Hearts and Clubs.
3♦				Opener promises a two-suited holding with Hearts and Diamonds.
3♥				Opener promises a one-suited holding with Hearts.

This allows the bidding to be at a lower level which allows one to more easily find a fit.

With a balanced hand, one employs the folling Kokish sequences.

Example 1

North	South	Meaning
2 ♣		An opening bid showing strong values.
	2 ♦	Normally either a *waiting bid* or a *negative bid*.
2 NT		This promises a balanced distribution and a point count between 20-21 points. The partnership remains on the two level, which is the key of this concept.

In this bidding sequence we did not employ the Kokish Relay bid since the holding does not require a relay to communicate the information that the holding is balanced with values of 20-21 points.

Example 2

North	South	Meaning
2♣		An opening bid showing strong values.
	2 ♦	Normally either a *waiting bid* or a *negative bid*.
2 ♥		This is the *Kokish Relay*, a puppet for responder to bid an automatic 2 Spades in order that the opener can clarify his holding.
	2♠	The puppet bid.
2 NT		North shows a balanced distribution of 23-24 points, a holding too strong for a normal 2♣ - 2 NT rebid. The partnership remains on the two level, which is the key of this concept.

This sequence uses the Kokish relay to show a balanced holding with 23-24 points the opener opens with a strong, artificial 2♣ and puppets the responder to 2♠ in order to clarify the point range of the balanced holding.

Example 3

North	South	Meaning
2 ♣		An opening bid showing strong values.
	2 ♦	Normally a *waiting bid* or a *negative bid*.
2♥		This is the *Kokish Relay*, a puppet for responder to bid an automatic 2♠ in order that the opener can clarify his holding.
	2 ♠	The puppet bid.

3 NT			North shows a balanced distribution of 25-27 points, a holding too strong for a normal 2♣ - 3NT rebid. This rebid is not part of the original version of the Kokish Relays, but could be used as an extension of this concept by partnership agreement if an opening bid of 3NT is Gambling.

By-Passing the Relay

We said that the sequence **2♣ 2♦, 2♥** is a relay to 2♠, allowing opener to describe his hand. However, once in a while responder may have a sufficiently unusual hand to make it worthwhile to by-pass the relay to show a long suit. One common approach is to use transfers whenever you break the relay. So, after **2♣ 2♦, 2♥**, a bid of 3♣ (breaking the relay) would show Diamonds.

When should you not relay! Here is a set of hands responder may have to break the relay.

KJ97643	Very good.
KJ9764	Still OK.
K97643	Starting to get borderline.
Q97643	Not good enough, this will not usually play for one loser opposite **Kx**
Q987643	Now the extra length makes it OK.
QJ10764	This one's fine.

Rule: Play for one loser opposite Ax or Kx.

Mexican 2♦* Convention

Developed by **Mr. George Rosencrantz,** it is a feature of the **Romex System;** however, it is becoming more common among partnerships playing the 2/1 game force system.

The problem arises with hands containing 18-19 starting points (some partnerships only count HCP) that are balanced or semi-balanced with 4-6 losers and possibly a five-card major suit. Never use the bid with a singleton or a void.

Consider the following hand: ♠AQJ102 ♥KJ7 ♦ KJ5 ♣ A10

You have 19 HCP + 1 length point—1 dubious honor doubleton = 19 starting points. Clearly, you want to open, but how can you communicate strength in one bid? You have only a six loser hand. Playing the Mexican Two Diamond Convention, you would open 2♦.

The responses for the call are:

1. A Negative Response with 0-4 starting points is to pass with Diamond support (6+ diamonds).
2. A 2♥* bid is artificial and a relay bid to 2♠ (opener accepts with five) or bids his own five-card suit (clubs, diamonds, or hearts) or 2NT to show a balanced hand; responder passes all bids with 5-7 points. With 8+ points, partner may bid 3♣ as Stayman (basic) with one or two four-card majors, bid 3NT or with support (three cards) for the suit bid by the opener, he raises partner's bid suit to the three levels, an invitational raise to game.
3. A response of 2♠ (showing 7-9 starting points) and a balanced hand transfers the opener to two notrump.
4. Any Positive Response on the three-level, 3♦/3♥/3♠, promises at least 8+ plus high card points and a broken six-card suit. However 3NT is usually a transfer to clubs and 3♣ Puppet Stayman.
5. A Positive Response also includes the use of Texas Transfers (4♣/4♦), the purpose of which is to have the stronger hand concealed during the play. The transfer bids are used only when the partner realizes he holds enough values for game or slam, not a part score.

Karosel 2♦* Convention

This conventional method was created by **Mr. Charles L. L. Dalmas** of Sarnia, Ontario, Canada, and first published in the ACBL *Bridge Bulletin*, June, 2002, pages 50-52.

Employing the Karosel Two Diamonds conventional method, one again opens with 2♦* (alerted) with 18-19 high card points and is limited to holdings with a distribution of from 7-2-2-2 to more balanced distribution, no singletons and no void. Since an opening of two Diamonds describes the holding precisely to the partner, then the partner becomes the captain and sets the contract via the ensuing auction.

The ten possible responses, as described by the author, are as follows:

Opener	Responder	Meaning
2♦		This opening bid describes a semi-balanced hand with exactly 18-19 high card points.
	Pass	Shows a weak hand with 5 plus Diamonds and no other side values.

		2 ♥		Shows 0-5 points and is a negative response. This response strongly suggests that the opener rebid 2 NT to play unless opener has a long suit (6/7 card length), which is rebid instead.
		2 ♠		This response is Minor Suit Stayman showing at least a 5-4 distribution in both Minor suits and at least 6+ points. This response is game-forcing and could indicate slam interest.
		2 NT		This response promises a two-suiter in both Major suits. The opener bids the better Major by rebidding either 3 ♥ or 3 ♠. The responder then bids either game or shows slam interest.
		3 ♣		This first response is Puppet Stayman. The responder promises at least 3 cards in each Major suit.
Rebids				
3 ♦				The opener promises at least one 4-card Major suit. The continuing auction is the same as with the Puppet Stayman convention. After 3 ♦, the responder bids the Major suit not held or 4 ♦ with both Major suits.
3 ♥				The opener promises a 5-card Heart suit.
3 ♠				The opener promises a 5-card Spade suit.
3 NT				The opener holds neither a 4-card nor a 5-card Major suit.
		3 ♦		This response is a transfer to Hearts showing at least a 5-card plus Heart suit and at least 6 plus points. In the 2 ♦ opener only accepts the transfer by rebidding 3 ♥, then the opener is showing a 3 - or 4-card Heart suit and no slam interest. If the opener super-accepts when holding a 4-card Heart suit, then this strongly indicates a mild slam interest if the responder has additional values. If the responder is interested in a slam try, then after acceptance or even super-acceptance the responder may bid 4♠, which is then Roman Keycard Blackwood 1430.

In Competition:

In competition, if the opponent doubles the Karosel 2♦ opening bid, then the responder can redouble holding 9 plus high card points. If the opener holds a 5-card plus Diamond suit, then the opener may pass the redouble since the result of making 2♦ redoubled would result in a better score. If the Karosel 2♦ opener does not have a 5-card Diamond suit, then the Karosel 2♦ opener should rebid 3NT.

In competition, if the responder of the Karosel 2♦ opening bid has absolutely no values to improve the contract, then the responder may pass the double and/or overcall. In this auction, all other agreements are "system off" and/or not binding. A pass informs the opener of the values held by partner. In this instance, as strongly suggested by the author, the partnership **shifts to Rescue Mode**.

This action requires the opener to pass if the right hand opponent bids. If, however, the right hand opponent passes, then the opener rebids his/her 5-card suit at the cheapest level, but with a 4-3-3-3 distribution the preference is to redouble if the overcall after the Karosel 2♦ opening bid was a double. If the left hand opponent, who has doubled then passes for penalty, then the partner of the Karosel 2♦ bidder bids his/her longest suit. This is the so-called Rescue Mode. In the case that the left hand opponent bids over the redouble, then the partner may pass knowing that the distribution is 4-3-3-3 and the preference is to defend.

Opening 3NT* Gambling

Playing Standard American, many were taught to open a balanced hand with 25-27 starting points 3NT. In the 2/1 force system of bidding, this is accomplished by opening 2♣ and then bidding 3NT. Instead the bid is used for Gambling 3NT.

To use the bid of Gambling 3NT*, you must have a solid running minor suit with 7+ cards with the AKQ and possibly the jack. However, when it comes to strength outside the minor suit, not all agree on the requirements. The bid must be alerted.

In first seat, most play the bid with no values in any outside suit vulnerable or non-vulnerable. However, if vulnerable, some require a stopper in the other minor, but no stoppers in the majors. Why? With no stoppers outside, partner will bid 4♣, asking partner to bid his minor. With all suits stopped, he will leave the bid stand. However, when vulnerable, partner only needs stopper in the majors, knowing partner has a long minor and the other minor stopped he will leave the game bid of 3NT to play if vulnerable with stoppers in the majors.

When responding to the Gambling 3NT bid, Marty Bergen makes the following recommendations for responder bids.

Responses to 3NT (Per Marty Bergen)

4♣ says let's play in a part score 4♣ or 4♦

4♦* is asking opener to bid a singleton; responses are:

4♥	heart singleton
4♠	spade singleton
4NT	minor suit singleton
5♣	no singleton

Example: Responder has   ♠ AKQ7 ♥ 76 ♦ AKQ7 ♣ 432

With a heart singleton, you want to play in six clubs otherwise you would bid five clubs.

4♥ and **4♠** are signoffs in responder's long suit. Opener must pass.

4NT is invitational to slam, asking opener to bid a minor suit slam with an outside trick.
5♣ asks opener to play in a minor suit game

5♦ is a sign-off by responder, responder knows that the opener has long diamonds and wants to play game from his side.
5NT is a grand slam try, to play in 7♣ or 7♦.

Responder has no losers outside the trump suit but is usually void of the trump suit and is afraid of a trump loser.

6♣ is to play slam in 6♣/6♦; opener is to pick the suit.

A bid of **6♦** by responder is to play slam in diamonds; responder knows that it is the long suit.

ACOL* 4NT Opening

An opening bid of 4NT asks for specific aces. The responses are:

5♣	0 ace
5♦/5♥/5♠/6♣	shows the ace in the suit bid
5NT	shows 2 aces

* A bridge bidding system played primarily in Great Britain.

The ACOL 3NT convention is also used in Great Britain. It shows 19-21 HCP and is to play. All suits must be stopped. If you use this convention, the ressponses by partner are:

4♣	Gerber
4♦/4♥/4♠	Transfers to Hearts, Spades, and Clubs
	To bid dimonds, one corrects after 5♣ to bid 5♦
4NT	Quantitative

Opening Two of a major

Because we recommend that the bid of 2♦* has special meaning (e.g., Flannery, Extra Shape Flannery, Mini Roman, or Mexican two diamonds), we exclude the bid here. Why tell the opponents you have a weak hand with diamonds? Two-over-one game force players should use the weak two diamond bid; it has no value.

Weak two bids in the majors are used to interfere with the opponents' bidding structure. The bids are preemptive showing a good six-card suit with between 5-10 starting points. The bids are constructive. Partner with a good hand may put you in game. If vulnerable, we recommend that the major suit have two of the top three honors. When not vulnerable, you may relax this requirement.

For example, with the hand ♠ 103 ♥ AK10987 ♦ J3 ♣ Q32, you would open the hand 2♥ vulnerable or non-vulnerable. However, replacing the king of hearts with a jack, you should not open the hand vulnerable.

Rule of 17

When responding to a major two-level opening bid, one may use the RULE OF 17. The rule goes as follows. If the number of Dummy Points and the number of cards in the major suit bid total seventeen, bid to the four level in the major.

With 12-15 Dummy Points and two-card support raise the two-level bid to three, a weak competitive raise that is non-forcing. It is called by some "raise only non-forcing" (RONF). With 15-16 starting points, responder makes a forcing 2NT bid, which asks the opening bidder to describe his hand and is invitational to game in the major with at least two-card support or perhaps notrump, independent of vulnerability.

Bidding 2NT by some players asks partner to bid a feature, an ace or king in an outside suit, bid the suit. It is used to determine if an entry exists in dummy to allow one to access the long suit. More importantly, one needs to know about strength in the major and strength of the hand. The convention one may use is known as OGUST.

The OGUST Convention

After a weak two bid (usually a six-card suit), the convention allows for a detailed description of the opener's hand. It is invoked by the artificial 2NT bid made by the responder. The reply to a weak two bid shows strength and asks whether the opener is weak (5-7/6-8 starting points) or strong (8-10/9-11 starting points) and how many of the top three honors are held in the major. The replies are most commonly as follows.

3♣ minimum, 1 top suit honor (BAD/WEAK Hand and BAD/WEAK Suit)
3♦ minimum, 2 top suit honors (BAD/WEAK Hand and GOOD/STRONG Suit)
3♥ maximum, 1 top suit honor (GOOD/STRONG Hand and BAD/WEAK Suit)
3♠ maximum, 2 top suit honors (GOOD/STRONG Hand and GOOD/STRONG Suit)
3NT all 3 honors, A-K-Q-x-x-x and little else

A simple way to remember this is to picture Mamma Mia dancing—1-2, 1-2, 1-2-3 . . . These refer to the order of the top honors in the major as shown above. The bids represent HAND and then SUIT—**NOT SUIT and then HAND!**

Note: Some players interchange the bids of three diamonds and three hearts. The 1-1, 2-2, 1-2-3 dance step!

Some players incorrectly use the convention to show first suit and not hand. Discuss this convention with your partner. The word OGUST may have a different meaning to your partner! This is why a description of any convention is better than simply using the words "I play Ogust." The OGUST Convention is used instead of "asking" for a feature (ace or king).

What if responder has his own suit? We have said that a raise in opener's suit is non-forcing. When partner bids his own suit, it is most often played as forcing for one round and asks partner to support the suit bid with three-card support . . . or to pass. If you do not play it as forcing, you must alert the new bid as non-forcing "it appears in red on your convention card."

Modified OGUST Convention

Because bidding is becoming more aggressive, many partnerships will open weak twos with a five-card major one-suiter. If you do, one may use Modified OGUST rebids to describe the hand. Again, the 2NT bid is used to ask about the hand. Using this convention, the bids are:

3♣   5-card suit GOOD/STRONG hand
3♦   5-card suit BAD/WEAK hand
3♥   6-card suit BAD/WEAK hand
3♠   6-card suit GOOD/STRONG hand
3NT   either a 5- or 6-card suit or a semi-solid 5- or 6-card suit plus ace or king in a side suit

Observe that the 3♣ bid is used to show a stronger HAND in order to leave more room for further investigation since all responses describe only the **"HAND"** and say nothing about the quality of the suit.

After the response of the 3♣ bid, if responder wants to find out about the **SUIT,** he bids 3♦*. The opener now clarifies the suit strength with the following bids.

3♥*   BAD/WEAK suit and 1honor
3♠*   GOOD/STRONG suit and 2 honors
3NT*   GOOD/STRONG suit and 3 honors

Following OGUST, one describes the HAND and upon request, then the SUIT.

A common practice is to use five-card OGUST Non-Vulnerable and six-card OGUST Vulnerable!

If you do not make this distinction (five and six cards) in your partnership agreement, there is yet another convention called the TWO-STEP OGUST Convention developed by Daniel Zenko. It is discussed in the April 1997 issue of "The Bridge World."

While experts use OGUST-type responses for two-suited 6-4 hands in the majors, the responses become complicated and will not be discussed.

Opening three—and four-level bids

Opening bids at the three-level are preemptive showing a weak hand (5-10 starting points) and able to take about five tricks in the trump suit bid. To open the bidding, one usually has a seven-card suit and no ace or king in an outside suit or four cards in a major. Vulnerable, you should hold two of the top three honors in the suit bid. **Once you make a three-level bid, you have described your entire hand, do not bid again, unless partner makes a forcing bid.** The only ways partner can force are by bidding a new suit, by cuebidding the opponent's suit, or by asking for aces.

Opening at the four-level is also preemptive showing a weak hand (5-10 starting points) and now able to take six tricks in the trump suit. You need an eight-card suit, no outside ace or king, no four-card major, and three of the top five honors. You only get one bid.

Rule of 2/3

A guide to preemptive opening bids and overcalls is that one cannot afford to be set more than 500 (two or three tricks vulnerable and non-vulnerable when doubled) unless one is saving against a slam contract. One often assumes that a vulnerable partner can make two tricks, and a non-vulnerable partner three tricks. Thus, a player who opens 4♠ should have an eight playing trick hand if vulnerable and a seven playing trick hand if not vulnerable.

To count playing tricks, only the first three tricks in a suit are counted. Winners are the A, K, or Q only in the suit. With less than three cards, AQ=½, Kx= ½, KQ=1, K=1, Q=1, Qx=1 loser.

What does that mean? The Rule of 2/3 states that with a weak hand and a long, strong suit, you should count your playing tricks and add three when non-vulnerable, and add two if vulnerable.

To illustrate, we consider two hands:

A) ♠AKQ10653 ♥ 8 ♦ 854 ♣ 96
B) ♠ void ♥ 63 ♦ AQJ876432 ♣ 87

In Hand A, we have six losers (0 in spades, 1 in hearts, 3 in diamonds, and 2 in clubs). Thirteen cards-six losers=seven **playing tricks**. Non-vulnerable, adding 3 = 7+3=10 so you should open 4♠. If you open at only the three levels, you would be underbidding your cards. You would open 3♠ only if vulnerable (7+2=9).

It is obvious that the opponents are able to more easily bid over three spades than four spades.

In Hand B, we have five losers and therefore eight playing tricks; adding three non-vulnerable takes us to eleven. Therefore, one would open 5♦. Vulnerable, one would open 4♦.

Responder bids to three-level preempts

When partner opens the bidding at the three-level, responder has to place the contract. With a weak hand and no fit, pass. To set the contract, you must think about playing tricks and consider the vulnerability.

Opening at the three-level, partner has said he can make five tricks in the trump suit. Thus, for game in a major you need to add five tricks outside the major to raise to the four-level. When opening a minor, bid 3NT if you have four more tricks. A simple raise in the minor shows a minor trump fit without game interest. If you bid another suit, not bid by partner, it generally shows a preemptive hand in the suit bid at the three-level and is lead directing since it is very likely that the opponents will get the contract.

If you are unsure what to do, use OGUST, **only for major suit reempts.** You must have enough points for game in the major with 19+ starting points or have slam interest. We use the bid of 3NT* and the responses follow the bid of 2NT; however, now the bid must be alerted.

Ogust over three-level preempts (bid 3NT*)

4♣*   minimum, 1 top honor (BAD/WEAK Hand and BAD/STRONG Suit)
4♦*   minimum, 2 top honors (BAD/WEAK Hand and GOOD/STRONG Suit)
4♥*   maximum, 1 top honor (GOOD/STRONG Hand and BAD/WEAK Suit)
4♠*   maximum, 2 top honors (GOOD/STRONG Hand and GOOD/STRONG Suit)
4NT*   all 3 honors, A-K-Q-x-x-x and little else

We consider a few examples.

♠7 ♥ KQ10653 ♦ A54 ♣ Q6

You have five losers, or 13-6 = 7 playing tricks. Non-vulnerable, you expect partner to cover three losers, so open 4♥. You would open it at the three-level vulnerable.

♠974 ♥ 7 ♦ AQJ863 ♣ Q62

You have six losers or 13-6 = 7. Non-vulnerable, open 3♦, **pass if you are vulnerable**. Just because you have a six-card suit does not mean you should open the hand with a preemptive bid.

♠A3 ♥ 10987 ♦ void ♣ KQ108762

You have a five loser hand, strong club suit and four hearts. Pass and wait to see what partner bids. Do not preempt your partner in the first seat.

Preempted Openings

Most of the bridge literature has been written about defending against weak three-level bids. Examples include the optimal double, 3NT for takeout, Fishbein, Lower Minor, Smith, Weiss, FILM, Reese, and Two-Suiter Takeouts, etc. Many of these approaches involve numerous artificial bids that most players FORGET. Our goal is to keep it simple because there is no optimal system. The underlying principle that you must use is to devise a system that enables you to reach your own BEST contract and do not worry too much about penalizing the opponents.

Opening Five-level Bids

To play straight penalty doubles at this level does not make sense. Opener will always have a long and strong single suit and the opponents are trying to steal the contract! DOUBLE should always be for takeout, not penalty, and the bid of 5NT shows the two lowest unbid suits. This can be played in both the second and fourth positions.

Opening Four-level Bids

When the preemptive bid is made at the four-level, one has more options. We consider each in turn. (1) Over 4♣ or 4♦

Again, a double is for takeout suggesting a good hand with no clear-cut bid and all four-level bids are natural. A cuebid usually indicates a two-suiter (both majors) or perhaps a three-suited rock crusher. (2) Over 4♥

Here, 4NT is not natural but a takeout bid for the minors. Double is for PENALTY, but I have tolerance for the other suits, particularly for spades. Partner, please decide. (3) Over 4♠.

Here, 4NT is generally takeout and again double is primarily for penalty. Partner will again pull the double on a very shapely hand. Alternatively, a double may be used for takeout; then, 4NT is used to show the minors. Discuss this with your partner.

For more information, see Brian Senior's (1984) "Defending against Pre-empts," by Apsbridge Services Ltd.

Roth Four Club Convention

Previously, we have suggested how to defend against preempt bids. However, if your partner preempts, there are also ways to investigate the preempt bid further. For two-level preempts, one may bid 2NT to ask your partner for a feature or you may use the Ogust Convention. Or, you can play modified Ogust, Two-step Ogust, Roudinesco rebids, Romex rebids, McCabe Adjunct Convention, etc.

What method can you employ if your partner bids at the three-level and you have a very good hand? A convention that is similar to Ogust 3NT* ask is called the Roth Four Club Convention. It is usually a slam-try allowing one to assess the partnership's prospects for slam without going beyond a safe contract.

After the three-level bid, partner bids 4♣* which is artificial and asks partner to describe his hand further. The responses are similar to Ogust and go like this:

4♦   bad hand, bad suit.
4♥   bad hand, good suit (2 of the top 3 honors in the preempt suit).
4♠   good hand (1 or 2 honors outside the preempt suit), bad suit.
4NT good hand, good suit.

The responses are similar to Ogust but use different steps. What do you think? Other systems like Thomas' Four Diamond system use keycard responses that are more difficult to remember. However, some recommend Asking Bids that are discussed next.

What about the four-level preempt with slam interest? One may simply modify the Roth Four Club approach!

Asking Bids after a Preempt

How many times have your partner opened at the three-level and you find yourself with a very good hand? What do you bid? Often neither Blackwood nor cuebids help. To consider a specific example, suppose you pick up the hand: ♠AQ4 ♥AKQ654 ♦ AT ♣ 84

And, your partner opens three spades. What do you bid? The problem revolves around what your partner has in the club suit.

Or, consider the following three OPENING hands:

(1) ♠KJ109765 ♥32 ♦K76 ♣2,
(2) ♠KJ109763 ♥32 ♦K9 ♣J10, and

(3) ♠KJ109543 ♥32 ♦87 ♣A2.

Opposite hand (1), six spades is a lay down. With hand (2), six cannot be made because of the two club losers. And, with the third hand, seven is a lay down. The same problem occurs when your partner opens four spades. With hand (3), Blackwood (Chapter 3) solves the problem, but what about hands 1 and 2? A solution is to play ASKING BIDS whenever one opens at the three/four-level.

For a three-level bid, any JUMP response in a suit is an asking bid in that suit.

Thus, after 3♠ followed by 5♣ asks, what do you have in clubs?
After 3♦ followed by 4♥ asks, what do you have in hearts?
Following a FOUR-level bid, any five-level bid becomes an asking bid.
After 4♥ the bid of 5♦ asks, what do you have in diamonds?
After 4♠, the bid of 5♣ asks about clubs.

These bids do not interfere with normal bidding procedures because a new suit in response to a preemptive bid is usually forcing so that responder need not jump to game. Thus, the jump bid may be used more profitably. When opening at the four-level, opener should have a powerful suit and responder is not likely to have a better suit. Hence, responder is more likely to make an asking bid.

Responses to Asking Bids

Let's consider an example with the sequence: 3♠ followed by 5♣. What do you have in clubs?
Responses to asking bids ALWAYS start with the next suit.
First Step—two or more quick losers' xx, xxx, xxxx
Second Step—singleton
Nearest notrump regardless of step = king
Fourth Step—ace
Fifth Step—A-K or A-Q
Sixth Step—Void
Example 1:

Opener's Hand: ♠K4 ♥65 ♦AJ109432 ♣43.
Responder's Hand: ♠87 ♥AKQJ109 ♦K4 ♣AKQ.

The bidding goes, 3♦ followed by 4♠. What do you have in spades? The bid of 4NT shows a KING, closest NT, and responder bids 6NT to protect the king. Notice that in this case, the first step is notrump, showing the king. With two or three small spades, opener would have responded 5♣ to the 4♠ asking bid.

Example 2:

Opener's Hand: ♠AKJ98765 ♥32 ♦2 ♣54.
Responder's Hand: ♠QT4 ♥J7♦AKQJ ♣AKJ10.

The bidding goes, 4♠ followed by 5♥. What do you have in hearts? Opener bids 5♠, first step, to show two or more quick losers in hearts. Responder passes.

Some recommend using only five steps for asking bids against preempts. They combine singleton and a king (steps 2&3) into step 2. Then step 3 is an ace, step 4 is A-K or A-Q, and step 5 becomes a void. Always discuss how you play asking bids with your partner.

Warning: THERE IS NO DISASTER WORSE THAN A MISUNDERSTOOD ASKING BID! The asking bids discussed here are based upon: Edwin B. Kantar (1974), "Bridge Conventions," Wilshire Book Company.

Grand Slam Force after a bid suit

A bid of 5NT after a three-level or four-level bid suit is called the Grand Slam Force and is used most often when the bidding has shown a strong hand and an agreed upon **major suit**. The definition of a strong hand is: (1) a preemptive opening bid or overcall when vulnerable, (2) a jump rebid, (3) a rebid in your original suit after your partner has made a jump shift. Then, a bid of 5NT by partner is the Grand Slam Force bid asking about the strength of the **major**. It was originally proposed by Josephine Culbertson in 1936, asking partner if he has two of the top three trump honors in the agreed upon major. If the answer is yes, one bids seven. If a trump suit has not been agreed upon, it is usually the last suit bid major. However, this approach only handles about 40 percent of the hands. Hence, since 1936 there have been several proposed modifications to the bid. What follows is as a result of Edwin B. Kantar. There are other variations for the bid so you should discuss it with your partner! Kantar recommends the following responses.

6♣	1 of the top 3 honors, almost always the ace or king.
6 of the agreed suit	2 of the top 3 honors.
7 of the agreed suit	3 of the top 3 honors.

Some also play the bid even if the bidding does not show a strong **major** suit. For example, a preemptive bid not vulnerable. Then the responses are:

6♣	queen or less.
6♦	ace or king with minimum length.
6♥	ace or king with more than minimum length.
6♠	two of the top three honors.
7♣ (or 7 of the agreed upon suit)	the top three honors.

Many times the responder must first find out about aces before using the Grand Slam Force. Then, the bid of 6♣ becomes the Grand Slam Force bid! An example follows:

Opener	Responder	Opener Bid	Responder Bid
♠KQJ109876	♠A	4♠	4NT
♥9	♥AKQ765	5♥	6♣
♦7	♦AK54	6♠	7NT
♣A98	♣KQ2		

The bid is also often used after 1NT asking the opener to pick a suitable slam contract. Or, it can be taken as quantitative looking for 7NT. Again, these bids should be discussed with your partner. You may also consult: Magnus Lindkvist (2002), "Bridge Classic and Modern Conventions," Arta Grafica S.A., Romania.

Namyats

NAMYATS was created by Sam Stayman who, after creating the Stayman 2♣ response to partner's notrump opener, coined the NAMYATS Convention using his name in reverse order. The NAMYATS Convention, part of the 2/1 game force system, allows one to differentiate between a strong distributional hand, which may provide a slam opportunity with less opponent interference, and a preemptive bid that has no slam opportunity.

The bid requires a 7+ card suit in hearts or spades, and like the strong two club opener, requires 8 ½-9 playing tricks. The major suit has two of the top three honors non-vulnerable and three of the top five honors vulnerable, and both require an outside ace or protected king. Thus, you almost have game in hand; partner has to only cover one loser in a major game contract. The bids use the minor preemptive four-level bids:

4♣*   transfer to hearts
4♦*   transfer to spades

If responder bids the transfer suit, this usually denotes no interest in slam. However, if one bids the next step, it indicates slam interest in the major.

4♣*   4♦ slam interest
4♦*   4♥ slam interest

General

In first and second position, 4♣ and 4♦ openings show "good" four-level preempts in hearts and spades respectively. The requirements for such an opening are:

1. exactly two key cards (five aces and trump king), and
2. no more than one uncontrolled suit, and
3. a losing trick count of at most five, and

4. at most three of the nine side-suit aces, king and queens, with no side suit containing all three of these honours, and

5. a main suit at least as good as
    1. KQT9xxx or KQJxxxx or a side void, when holding a seven card main suit, or
    2. KQxxxxxx when holding at least an eight card main suit, and

6. if holding a void, opener must also hold
    1. an uncontrolled suit and a main suit of at least AKQxxxx or AKxxxxx, or
    2. a suit lacking first—or second-round control but holding third-round control (doubleton or queen) and a weaker main suit.

A controlled suit is one in which the ace or king is held, or one in which at most one card is held.

Responding to Namyats openings

After a Namyats 4♣ opening

Responder may inquire with 4♦ when holding at least 2 key cards and some prospects of slam, or make other descriptive slam tries, or sign off in opener's suit at the four level. After the inquiry, in auctions where specific holdings are shown, "strong" holdings (void and honour combinations) are shown naturally, and uncontrolled suits are shown in the order other-major, clubs, diamonds.

4♦				Inquiry, showing at least two key cards
	4♥			Minimum requirements
	4♠			Better than minimum, unspecified void
		4NT		Inquiry
			5♣/5♦/5♥	Club/diamond/spade void
	4NT			Better than minimum, no void, all suits controlled
	5♣/5♦/5♥			Better than minimum, no void, no control in spade/club/diamond suit
	5♠			AKQxxxxx with two singletons and a KQx suit, or AKQxxxxx with one singleton and two Kx suits, or KQJxxxxx with two singletons and a AKx suit
		5NT		Inquiry

			6♣/6♦/6♥	Club/diamond/spade suit with KQx, Kx or AKx respectively according to the hand type held for the 5S response
	5NT/6♣/6♦			AKQxxxx and a spade/club/diamond suit of KQJx with two singletons, or AKQxxxx and a spade/club/diamond suit of KQx with a singleton and a Kx suit
	6♥			AKxxxxxx, two singletons and a Kx suit
4♥				To play
4♠/4NT/5♣				Spade/diamond/club void, slam interest and at least one key card
5♦				Small doubleton trump, three side aces and possibly nothing else
5♥				Small singleton trump, three side aces and nothing else

After a Namyats 4♦ opening

Responder may inquire with 4H when holding at least 2 key cards and some prospects of slam, or make other descriptive slam tries, or sign off in opener's suit at the four level. After the inquiry, in auctions where specific holdings are shown, "strong" holdings (void and honour combinations) are shown naturally, and uncontrolled suits are shown in the order other-major, clubs, diamonds.

4♥				Inquiry, showing at least two key cards
	4♠			Minimum requirements
	4NT			Better than minimum, unspecified void
		5♣		Inquiry
			5♦/5♥/5♠	Diamond/heart/club void
	5♣			Better than minimum, no void, all suits controlled
	5♦/5♥/5♠			Better than minimum, no void, no control in heart/club/diamond suit

	5NT				AKQxxxxx with two singletons and a KQx suit, or AKQxxxxx with one singleton and two Kx suits, or KQJxxxxx with two singletons and a AKx suit
		6♣			Inquiry
			6♦/6♥/6♠		Diamond/heart/club suit with KQx, Kx or AKx respectively according to the hand type held for the 5NT response
	6♣/6♦/6♥				AKQxxxx and a club/diamond/heart suit of KQJx with two singletons, or AKQxxxx and a club/diamond/heart suit of KQx with a singleton and a Kx suit
	6♠				AKxxxxxx, two singletons and a Kx suit
4♠					To play
4NT/5♣/5♦					Heart/club/diamond void, slam interest and at least one key card
5♥					Small doubleton trump, three side aces and possibly nothing else
5♠					Small singleton trump, three side aces and nothing else

Holding the following hand, what do you open?   ♠AK109653 ♥7 ♦9 ♣KJ73
The hand is too strong to open 4♠. Playing Namyats, one would open the bidding 4♦*.

Mc Cabe Adjunct

When your partner opens a weak two bid and they double, what are your options?

With a weak hand, the contract usually belongs to the opponents; hence your partners bid should help you with the lead since it may be the opponent's contract. A convention developed by Mr. J. I. McCabe of Columbia, South Carolina, United States does just that. His article was published in *The Bridge World*, issue of January 1994.

The Mc Cabe bids are:

A simple raise of partner's weak two bids shows an Ace or a King in the bid suit. With this information the weak two-bidder may lead the suit. A bid in a lower ranking suit is also lead directing. It also shows an Ace or a King. And it suggests to the weak two—bidder to bid again without interference.

Without a fit, partner bids 2NT as a relay to three clubs. Responder then corrects or bids a new suit at the three level. The opening bidder must pass. However, if responer next bids partners weak two bid suit at the three level, after the relay bid of three clubs, he denies a good lead and it again shows an Ace or King in the weak two-bidder's suit and a good hand.

Some partnerships reverse the meaning of Mc Cabe's Adjunct.

Mc Cabe Adjunct (reversed)

In this method, raising partner bid suit **denies** an Ace or a King and merely advances the preempt. A new suit at the two level is to play. A three level bid over a major suit bid shows an Ace or King in the major bid. 2NT is again a relay to three clubs and is as in the Mc Cabe Adjunct. A redouble of the bid suit shows a strong hand, it is designed to punish the opponents.

To be more specific with reverse Mc Cabe, we have the following structure.

2♥ - X then   Redouble shows a strong hand
                2♠   =Spades
                2NT   =Clubs (partner bids clubs)
                3♦   =transfer into suit shows A/K of Hearts
                3♥   =No A/K of Hearts

2♠ - X then   Redouble shows a strong hand
                2NT   =Clubs (partner bids clubs)
                3♥   =transfer into suit show A/K of Spades
                3♠   =No A/K of Spades

Over 2♦ all two level bids are natural and 3♣ shows A/K of diamonds; the bid of 3♦ shows the A/K. The bids over 2♦ are of course modified if you play Flip-Flop over the double of a diamond bid.

Chapter 3

Slam Bidding

To reach a slam, the partnership should have roughly thirty-three Bergen points. In addition to a trump fit and count, slams require controls (aces, kings, voids, and singletons). The more controls between the partners, the easier the slam. To evaluate whether or not the partnership has the required controls, one uses cuebids and Blackwood Conventions. Blackwood Conventions reveal how many aces and kings for example, while cuebidding or control showing bids reveal where they reside.

The Blackwood Convention

The most used and perhaps abused convention in bridge is the original Blackwood Convention developed by Easley Blackwood Sr. because many believe it will handle all situations. It does not. While the convention does not require knowing the trump suit, it does require that one knows whether or not slam is possible. The convention augments this knowledge by helping one find the number of aces and kings.

The convention should not be used when:

    (1) Holding two or more cards in an unbid suit with no ace or king (e.g., xx, Qx, Jx).
    (2) Holding a void.
    (3) One has a slam invitational hand (e.g., 1NT facing 1NT hands).

To use the convention, the captain bids 4NT which is the asking partner for the number of aces held.

The responses are:

5♣	0 ace or all 4 aces
5♦	1 ace
5♥	2 aces
5♠	3 aces

If two aces are missing, the captain signs off in five of a suit. If one ace is missing, one may bid 6NT or six of a suit. When spades is not trump, the bid of 5♠ asks partner to bid 5NT.

What do you do if you have a void? Do not count it as an ace. With an even number of aces (two or four) bid 5NT and with an odd number (one or three) bid the suit at the six-level. It works. If you have no aces and a void (ignore the void), bid 5♣ since the void may be in a suit in which your partner has an ace.

Knowing you have all the aces, 5NT is the king's ask (without a void response); the responses are:

6♣	0 king or all 4 kings
6♦	1 king
6♥	2 kings
6♠	3 kings

Having all the aces and kings, one is in the grand slam zone; recall it requires about thirty-seven Bergen points.

The major problem with the Blackwood Convention is you have no way of knowing about the ace and king of trump and the specific location of aces are unknown. To solve these shortcomings, one uses cuebids and the Roman Keycard Blackwood Convention, which has replaced the Blackwood Convention.

Roman Keycard Blackwood (RKCB) Convention—1430

The most authoritative book (in my opinion) on this convention is by Eddie Kantar (2008), "Roman Keycard Blackwood the Final Word" 5th Edition, Master Point Press, Toronto, Ontario, Canada.

To use the RKCB Convention, one must have agreed upon a trump suit. Knowing the trump suit, there are two Roman Keycard Conventions known as 1430 and 3014. When the strong hand asks, Kantar recommends that one play the 1430 version (marked as 1430 on the convention card); if the weak hand asks, he recommends 3014 (marked as RCK on the convention card). While Kantar has several criteria to determine which hand is considered strong and which is the weak hand, because more often than not the strong hand usually asks, we recommend always using the 1430 Roman Keycard Convention. Let's not get too complicated.

When using the RKCB Convention, there are now five keycards, the four aces, and the king of trump. Another keycard is the queen of trump. If you do not use kickback (to be explained later), the 1430 RKCB ask is again 4NT. The responses are:

5♣	1 or 4 keycards (the 14 step)
5♦	3 or 0 keycards (the 30 step)
5♥	2 (or 5) keycards without the queen of trump in the agreed upon suit
5♠	2 (or 5) keycards with the queen of trump in the agreed upon suit

When one responds five clubs or five diamonds, the queen ask may be needed. After the response five clubs, the bid of 5♦ is the queen ask (when hearts or spades are the agreed upon trump suit). After the bid of five diamonds, the bid of 5♥ is the queen asks.

Queen Asks

In review, after five clubs and five diamonds, the queen asks are:

5♦ and 5♥   queen asks

Responding to the 5♦ ask

    (1) If you **do not** hold the queen, responder **returns to the agreed upon suit at the five—level.**
    (2) **5NT shows the queen, but no outside king!**
    (3) With both (Q of trump and one or two kings), bid at the six-level of the lowest ranking king.

Responding to the 5♥ ask

If you do not hold the queen, pass; with the queen, bid 5NT. With the queen and a king in the lower ranking suit, bid the suit. If it is a higher ranking king, return to the six-level.

King Asks

Knowing you hold all the aces and king-queen of trump (note some players do not require holding the queen), **5NT is the specific king's ask!**

The specific king ask is needed for a grand slam try in the agreed upon suit or notrump.

Responses are:

    (1) Return to the agreed upon trump suit at the six-level denies any kings.
    (2) With two kings, bid the cheapest at the six-level (below agreed upon trump suit); if the second king is of higher rank, bid 6NT.
    (3) With three kings, bid 7NT.

To find a second king below the trump suit, bid the suit. Without the second king, responder bids the trump suit at the six-level. With the king, bid as follows.

    (1) Make a first step response, including 6NT with Kxx(x),
    (2) Make a second step response with Kxx, and
    (3) Raise the ask suit with Kx.

Queen and King Asks Combined

To make the best use of bidding space when one holds the trump queen, one may also show specific kings as well.

Assuming hearts are trump:

4NT (RCKB)	5♣ (1 or 4)		
5♦ (next suit = queen ask)	5♥	=	no queen (next suit up)
	6♥	=	queen but no kings (trumps at lowest level)
	5♠	=	queen and king of spades
	6♣	=	queen and king of clubs
	6♦	=	queen and king of diamonds
	5NT	=	queen and 2 kings

4NT (RCKB)	5♦ (0 or 3)		
5♠ (next suit = queen ask)	5NT	=	no queen (next suit up)
(5♥ would be sign off)	6♥	=	queen but no kings
	6♠	=	queen and king of spades
	6♣	=	queen and king of clubs
	6♦	=	queen and king of diamonds
	6NT	=	queen and 2 kings

Assuming spades are trump:

4NT (RCKB)	5♣ (1 or 4)		
5♦ (next suit = queen ask)	5♥	=	no queen (next suit up)
	5♠	=	queen but no kings (trumps at lowest level)
	6♥	=	queen and king of spades
	6♣	=	queen and king of clubs
	6♦	=	queen and king of diamonds
	5NT	=	queen and 2 kings

4NT (RCKB)	5♦ (0 or 3)		
5♥ (next suit = queen ask)	5♠	=	no queen (next suit up)
(5♠ would be sign off)	6♥	=	queen but no kings
	6♣	=	queen and king of clubs
	6♦	=	queen and king of diamonds
	5NT	=	queen and 2 kings

Playing 1430 RKCB, the standard is to use the specific king ask; however, some still may play the number of kings from "Blackwood" excluding the trump suit—YOU BETTER ASK your partner.

Responding with voids

Using the 1430 convention, and have a void the responses to 4NT are:

5NT = 2 or 4 an even number of keycards with a void (with 0, bid 5♦—ignore the void)

6 of suit below the trump suit = odd number keycards (1 or 3)

6 trump suit = odd number of keycards (1or 3) with a void in higher ranking suit

Specific Suit Asks (SSA)

We have seen that one may ask for keycards, the queen of trump and having both, ask for specific kings. When searching for a grand slam, one may also need to know about an outside suit (not the trump suit). For example, do you have a queen in the suit, a doubleton, or a singleton? To ask and answer this question, one makes a Specific Suit Ask (SSA).

The specific suit asks is usually done when the captain has the queen of trump after the Keycard responses of 5♣ or 5♦.

After 5♣   6♣, 6♦ is SSA.
After 5♦   5♠, 6♦, 6♥ is SSA

The responses are:

  (1) Make a first step response, including 6NT with third-round control Qx(x), Ax, AQx, xx
  (2) Make a second step response with second-round control Kxx(x)
  (3) Make a third step response with Kx
  (4) Raise the ask bid with KQx and JUMP to the trump suit with a singleton

Over Interference DOPI-ROPI or DEPO

When the opponents interfere, most players play DOPI/ROPI. Another option is to use DEPO. While most do not use both, I recommend the use of both which depends on the level of interference.

If the opponents interfere at the five levels with a bid, use DOPI,

Pass   One Keycard
Double   No keycards
1st Step suit above Two keycards
2nd Step up   Three keycards

If the opponents interfere at the five levels with a double, use ROPI,

Pass   One keycard
Double   No keycards
1st Step suit above Two keycards
2nd Step up   Three keycards

If the opponents interfere at the **six-levels**, use DEPO,

Double	Even Number of keycards (0, 2, 4)
Pass	Odd Number of keycards (1, 3)

Kickback or Redwood and Minorwood

When the agreed upon suit is a minor, the use of 4NT as a keycard ask will often get the responses too high. To avoid this problem, one uses Roman Keycard Blackwood with kickback. It works as follows: if clubs is trump, then 4♦ is used to ask. If diamonds is trump, the 4♥ is used to ask. If hearts is trump, either 4♠ (in order to avoid problems with the queen ask) or 4NT is used to ask. When spades is trump, one always uses 4NT to ask.

One responds to the ask using each suit in order. For example, suppose the agreed upon suit is diamonds so 4♥ is the ask, the responses are:

4♠	1 or 4 keycards (the 14 step)	1st step
4NT	3 or 0 keycards (the 30 step)	2nd step
5♣	2 (or 5) keycards w/o queen of trump in agreed suit	3rd step
5♦	2 (or 5) keycards with queen of trump in agreed suit	4th step

What is the queen ask? After 4♠, it is 4NT and after 4NT, it is 5♣! Note that with no queen, you again return to the five-level of the agreed upon trump suit. If you have the queen, bid six. It works! All extensions follow.

Instead of playing Kickback or Redwood, some partnerships play **Minorwood.** The Minorwood Convention uses four of the agreed minor for the RKCB ask. For example, in the auction 1♦ - 2♦, the bid of 4♦ is Minorwood; it is used instead of 4♥, kickback, or redwood. It can also be played in a sequence when kickback may be confusing. For example, if the bid of 4♠ is confusing, one may jump into four of a minor instead of using Kickback RKCB. I have heard this called the "Bothwood" convention.

Minorwood

Over 4♣

4♦	1 or 4 keycards (the 14 step)	1st step
4♥	3 or 0 keycards (the 30 step)	2nd step
4♠	2 (or 5) keycards w/o queen of trump in agreed suit	3rd step
4NT	2 (or 5) keycards with queen of trump in agreed suit	4th step

Over 4♦

4♥	1 or 4 keycards (the 14 step)	1st step

4♠	3 or 0 keycards (the 30 step)	2nd step
4NT	2 (or 5) keycards w/o queen of trump in agreed suit	3rd step
5♣	2 (or 5) keycards with queen of trump in agreed suit	4th step

Slam Bidding with No Agreed Upon Suit

When playing 1430 RKC, how should one proceed if there is not a prior agreement on the trump suit? Some recommend that (1) it should always be the last-bid suit, some suggest that (2) one should not play any form of RKC, but instead just use Blackwood as an ace only ask (no keycards), others recommend (3) that RKC be used only if the last-bid suit is a minor (opener or responder) but not a major and some play (4) that it is the last-bid suit of the responder. What is your agreement?

The approach you use must be discussed with your partner when you make out your convention card. There is no "best" or standard approach. However, let's consider a few examples.

Suppose you open one spade and partner responds two hearts (a 2/1 response), and as opener, you hold the hand: ♠AKQJ763 ♥4 ♦KQ53 ♣7

If you play the last-bid suit, you cannot bid 4NT. You might try three spades and then 4NT, but if partner bids four hearts over three spades, you are back to square one. If your agreement allows you to agree that the last-bid major with a forcing three-level raise or a splinter jump (even a fake splinter jump!) below game and this is not done, the last-bid suit is not the agreed upon suit. In the previous example, a strong case could be made to make spades the agreed upon suit if opener jumps to 4NT over two hearts. The last-bid suit works whenever you have a fit for the last-bid suit. But if you do not, it usually does not work. We consider an example.

Opener	Responder
♠KQJ863	♠A2
♥KT942	♥J7
♦Q8	♦AK5
♣Void	♣AKQJT4

The bidding goes:

Opener	Responder
1♠	2♣
2♥	3♦
3♥	4NT
6♣	7NT
Pass	

Responder leaps to 4NT to ask for keycards. Since the last-bid suit was hearts, opener bids 6♣ which shows an odd number of keycards, the king of hearts and a void in clubs. Thinking that the one keycard is the ace of hearts, responder bids a grand slam, 7NT. Whose fault? The fault was that they lacked a mutual agreement as to what 4NT means when there is no agreed upon suit.

If you play the last-bid suit, you will only survive a 4NT ask when you intend to play in your own suit as long as you hold the king of the last-bid suit. Partner is forced to answer only aces! In the above example, responder did not hold the king. Because there was no agreed upon suit, one would bid 5♣ (zero keycards). Partner would bid 6NT.

The above example suggests that one use Blackwood if there is no agreed upon suit.

To illustrate, suppose the bidding goes one heart-two clubs-two hearts-4NT. Then, since the last-bid minor suit of responder was clubs, 4NT agrees clubs. If responder wanted to agree hearts, and the partnership plays that a raise to three hearts is forcing, it is easy enough to bid three hearts and then 4NT. If a raise to three hearts is not forcing, then a jump to four diamonds agrees hearts and if partner bids four hearts, 4NT can be bid. If the responder wants to agree spades, he bids two spades or three spades, and then bids 4NT.

Thus, if you do not have an agreed upon suit, you can play Blackwood or agree that one may play the last-bid minor suit of opener or responder.

With no agreed upon suit, here are my suggestions.

1. Use Keycard after any four-level bid.
2. All Kickback auctions are RKCB.
3. If two suits are agreed upon, the **FIRST SUIT BID** is trumps for RKCB purposes.
4. When none of the previous applies, use Blackwood as ace only asks.

Overview: Roman Keycard Blackwood 1430*

4NT when hearts or spades are the agreed upon suit (Keycard Ask)

5♣ = 1 or 4 keycards
5♦ = 0 or 3 keycards
5♥ = 2 or 5 keycards without the queen of trump
5♠ = 2 or 5 keycards with the queen of trump or holding a fifth trump

Kickback

Use four diamonds as keycard ask when CLUBS is the agreed upon suit
Use four hearts as keycard ask when DIAMONDS is the agreed upon suit

Voids

5NT = 2 or 4 an even number of keycards with a void (5♦=0, ignore the void)
6 of suit below the trump suit = odd number keycards (1/3)
6 trump suit = odd number of keycards (1/3) with a void in higher ranking suit

DOPI/ROPI Interference at the 5 level **DBL/RE-DBL:** 0 or 3 keycards and **PASS:** 1 or 4 keycards

DEPO Interference at the 6-level **DBL:** Even # keycards (0/2/4) or **PASS:** Odd # (1/3)

QUEEN ASK: After 5♣, 5♦ is Queen Ask **AND** After 5♦, 5♥ is Queen Ask

Responses:

> **Denial:** Return to the five-level of the agreed upon suit
> **6 Level of agreed Suit:** With queen and **no** side-suit king or extra trump
> **6 Level of Lower King Suit:** With queen and 1/2 side-suit kings
> **5NT:** With queen **without** a side-suit king, but trump extra

5NT is a Specific King ASK (NOT NUMBER OF KINGS)

YES: Bid Lowest King Suit BELOW the agreed upon trump suit
NO: Return to the agreed upon trump suit (or king is above agreed trump suit)
To ask for a SECOND king, the asker bids the suit. **Without,** return to the agreed suit.
Holding a SECOND king: Make a first step response, including 6NT with Kxx(x)
                                           Make a second step response with Kxx
                                           Raise the ask suit with Kx

SPECIFIC SUIT ASK (SSA) After 5♣: 5♥, 6♣, 6♦ is SSA. After 5♦: 5♠, 6♦, 6♥ is SSA.
Make a first step response, including 6NT with third-round control Qx(x), Ax, AQx, xx
Make a second step response with second-round control Kxx(x)
Make a third step response with Kx
Raise the ask bid with KQx and JUMP to the trump suit with a singleton

*NO AGREED upon SUIT; some use standard BLACKWOOD CONVENTION for Ace Asking and 5NT for NUMBER of Kings Ask

Let's consider some examples on the use of RKCB.

Slam 1
Opener   ♠A7 ♥AQ65 ♦84 ♣AKQ98
Responder   ♠KQ5 ♥ K843 ♦KQJ6 ♣7

Opener	Responder
1♣	1♥
4♥	4NT
5♦	5♥
6♣	6♥

The opener has 19 HCP + 1 length - 1 dubious doubleton = 19 starting points. Responder has fourteen starting points. Opener bids 1♣, responder bids 1♥. Finding a fit, opener reevaluates his hand. He has 19 starting + 2 doubletons = 21 Dummy Points and bids 4♥; we have game. Finding the heart fit, responder bids 4NT (alternatively, he could use kickback and ask by bidding 4♠). The response of 5♦ shows 0 or 3 keycards. The bid of 5♥ is the queen asks. The bid of 6♣ shows the queen of hearts and the club king. Opener bids the slam 6♥.

In this example, we did not use kickback. We should have because it may be difficult to determine if the bid of 5♥ is sign-off or queen ask. Instead of bidding 4NT, suppose one bids 4♠; we would then have:

Opener	Responder
1♣	1♥
4♥	4♠
5♣	5♦
6♣	6♥

Now, 5♣ shows 0 or 3 keycards and 5♦ becomes the queen ask. Denying the queen, the bid would be 5♥, which is short of game. However, 6♣ shows the queen plus the king of clubs. Responder again bids 6♥.

Slam 2
Opener   ♠AJ7 ♥AQJ753 ♦AQ4 ♣7
Responder   ♠K5 ♥ K1084 ♦8765 ♣AK9

Opener	Responder
1♥	2NT*
4NT	5♥
5NT	6♣
6♦	6♥

Opener has 18 HCP + 2 length points + 1 quality suit = 21 points. Responder has thirteen starting points.

After the bid of 1♥, responder bids 2NT* (Jacoby). Instead of showing his singleton, he bids 4NT. With two keycards, the bid is 5♥. Opener has the queen of trump, bids 5NT, which is the specific king ask. With the king of clubs, responder bids 6♣. The bid of 6♦ is the second king's ask. Without the king, responder again signs off in the heart slam.

Slam 3
Opener   ♠AJ7 ♥AQJ753 ♦AQ98 ♣ void
Responder   ♠K5 ♥ K1084 ♦8765 ♣AK9

You have the same hand, but now you have a void. You cannot bid 4NT with a void. However, you have two options, Cuebidding or using another convention called Exclusion Keycard Blackwood (EKCB). We will consider both; however, because Cubidding a void can be risky, we first consider EKCB.

Exclusion Roman Keycard Blackwood (EKCB) Convention

The convention is only played when a known major suit agreement is a major and you know you are in the region of slam. For example, after a Jacoby 2NT bid, a concealed splinter bid, or perhaps a Swiss bid. The convention may also be played whenever the last-bid suit is a major (with or without an agreement). The convention is initiated by an unusual jump to the five levels above game in your void suit. You are asking for keycards for the agreed upon major or the last-bid major excluding the void suit. Partner does not count the ace in the void suit bid; now there are only four keycards, three aces and a king. **There is no such thing as 1430 or 3014 EKCB**. The responses are steps above the bid suit.

Responses to EKCB

First Step	0 keycards
Second Step	1 keycard
Third Step	2 keycards without the queen
Fourth Step	2 keycards with the queen
Fifth Step	3 keycards (very unusual)

The only exception to a five-level bid is that one may use 4♠ if you agree that hearts is trump at the two-level. However, you cannot do this if you play kickback. Thus, I would only recommend that it be used with bids at the five-level.

As with 1430 RKCB, the bid of 5NT is again the specific king ask. The next step after a 0 or 1, including the void suit (but excluding 5NT), is the queen ask. Finally, the bid of any suit that is not the queen ask is the SSA.

What do you do after an EKCB ask with a void? You must always ignore it.

Returning to our Slam 3 example, opener bids 5♣ (EKCB). Excluding the club suit, responder has one keycard (king of hearts) and bids 5♦. Partner with all the aces and a void in clubs knows it is the king of hearts. Having the queen, what next? He bids 5NT which is again the specific king ask, without the king of diamonds, partner again signs off in six hearts.

Double Agreement Roman Keycard Blackwood (DRKCB)

With a double agreement, there are now six keycards (four aces and two kings), NOT FIVE, so we have what are called Double agreement 1430 Roman Keycard Blackwood (DRKCB). We consider DRKCB responses for some double agreements.

1. Major-Major Agreements

a) Opener	Responder		b) Opener	Responder
1♠	2♥		1♥	2♠
3♣	3♠		3♠	4♥
4♥	4NT		4NT	

Then 4NT is a DRKCB ask.

When responding to DRKCB asks, there are now six keycards. And, **there are no void-showing responses.** The first two responses (5♣ and 5♦) of DRKCB are the same as 1430 RKCB; however, there are now three queens showing responses:

5♥	2 with neither queen
5♠	2 with one queen
5NT	2 with both queens

Note that in the second step (5♠), you do not know which queen. However, if partner makes a first or second step response to a DRKCB ask (5♣ and 5♦), unless the asker has both of the agreed-upon suit queens, the queen situation is unknown. To now ask about queens, the asker uses the next available "free bid" step, excluding the trump suits, but including 4NT for a queen ask. The four-response steps now become:

1st step	2 with no queen
2nd step	2 with lower-ranking queen only
3rd step	2 higher-ranking queen only
4th step	2 both queens

When investigating a small slam in double-agreement sequences, you are looking to have at least five of the six missing keycards plus at least one queen of the agreed upon suits.

We now consider two **major-major** examples.

(A) Opener	Responder	Comments
♠A10732	♠KJ5	
♥A982	♥KQJ63	
♦K2	♦A94	

♣Q7   ♣A5

1♠	2♥	(1) Double Agreement
3♥	3♠ (1)	(2) DRKCB
4♥	4NT (2)	(3) 2 with neither queen
5♥ (3)	6♥ (4)	(4) Q♠ is missing

(B) Opener	Responder	Comments
♠A8732	♠KJ5	
♥AQ95	♥KJ632	
♦A2	♦K94	
♣A5	♣Q7	

1♠	2♥	(1) Double Agreement
3♥	3♠ (1)	(2) DRKCB
4♥	4NT (2)	(3) 1 or 4 keycards
5♣ (3)	5♦ (4)	(4) Queen ask with double agreement
5NT (5)	6♥ (6)	(5) Q♥ (2nd step, lower-ranking queen)
		(6) Q♠ is missing

Note that if the response in example (B) was 5♦ (0 or 3) instead of 5♣, one could not ask for the missing queen! No "free-bid" step is available for a queen asks since one must bypass all five-level bids. The five-level bids are sign-offs and 5NT is the king ask.

Queen asks are more easily used with kickback DRKCB sequences.

Quantitative Bids

When one opens 1NT or 2NT, a jump bid to 4NT is usually quantitative; it is asking partner if he is at the top of his bid. If he is, he should bid 6NT, otherwise, pass. While it is most often played when opening notrump, it may also be used with strong suit bid responses.

Examples of some common Quantitative bidding sequences follow.

1NT - 4NT   Partner passes with a minimum or bids 6NT

1NT - 2♦/2♥   Jacoby Transfer to hearts/spades
2♥/2♠ - 4NT   Quantitative, partner passes or bids on with extras values/length

2♣ - 2♦   Semi-positive
3NT - 4NT   Quantitative, partner passes with a minimum or 6NT with good values

1♣ - 1♠
2♦ - 2♥   Reverse by opener showing 17+ points, fourth suit forcing

3NT - 4NT	Quantitative, partner passes with a minimum or 6NT with good values

1NT - 2♣	Stayman
2♥ - 4NT	Quantitative, partner passes or bids 6NT

1x - 1y	
1NT - 4NT	Quantitative, partner passes or bids 6NT

1M - 2m	
2NT - 4NT	Quantitative, partner passes or bids 6NT

1NT - 2♣	
2♦ - 4NT	Quantitative partner passes or bids 6NT

2NT - 3♣	Stayman
3♠ - 4NT	Quantitative partner passes or bids 6NT

Baron Bids after 4NT

After an invitational quantitative 4NT bid, opener need not bid 6NT since finding 12 tricks may be difficult. It is ofter better to play slam in a suit which allows you to ruff losers. If you have four losers you may not want to play in notrump, but a suit. Since the bid of 4NT invites a slam, any bid by the opener says "I accept" the invitation to slam, and is forcing; one may also stop in 5NT. Instead of bidding 6NT, one usually bids 4-card suits up-the-line which allows the partnership two chances to find a suit fit.

Let's look at an example:

West	East
♠54	♠AK7
♥K67	♥QJ9
♦KQJ2	♦A10985
♣AK54	♣J2

In this example, West has 4 losers and the bidding goes 1NT - 4NT; since East has 15HCP and a 5-card suit, he invites slam. With four losers, East accepts by bidding 5♣, the cheapest 4-card suit. East does not like clubs, but is happy to bid 4♦. West likes his quality diamond suit and his two small spades are only an asset in a suit contract. Hence, he bids 6♦. In six diamonds, west can ruff a spade for the 12th trick; if the contract was in 6NT, only 11 tricks can be made.

Let's consider a second example.

West   East

♠AKJ   ♠Q72
♥AQ67   ♥K9
♦A102   ♦K752
♣KJ106   ♣Q842

In this case, the bidding goes:

2♣	2♦ (ace or king)
2NT	4NT
5♣ (Baron bid)	6♣

Finally suppose we have the following hand.

West   East

♠AJ2   ♠KQ43
♥KQ87   ♥52
♦KQ6   ♦AJ103
♣AK8   ♣J102

Here the bidding goes:

2NT	3♣ (Stayman)
3♥	4NT
6NT	

You have bid your suits so that the bid is quantitative for a slam in notrump.

Grand Slam Force after 1NT—Is the bid of 5NT. It may be used after a notrump opening or after one has agreed upon a suit.

To use the bid after a one notrump opening requires 20+ HCP. If opener is at the top of his bid, 17 HCP, he bids 7NT; otherwise he bids 6NT.

After a suit bid, for example 1♠ - 5NT or 4♥ - 5NT, with two or more controls in the bid suit, partner bids:

- **6 of the agreed trump suit** if holding **one** of the top three trump honors (e.g., the ace)
- **7 of the agreed trump suit** if holding **two** of the top three trump honors (e.g., the king and queen)

Pick a Slam—Without a known fit or when the opponents interfere, a jump to 5NT is used to ask partner to pick slam. For example, he may go: 1♣ - 1♥; 2♦ - 5NT or the bidding may go 2♣ - 3♠; 4♣ - 5NT.

Baby Blackwood in Serious 3NT

The bid of 3NT may be used in a variety of artificial ways in possible slam auctions when playing 2/1. Consider auctions of the following type:

West	East		West	East
1♠	2♥		1♠	2♣
3♥	3NT		2♥	3♠
3NT				

What does the bid of 3NT mean?

Clearly, not to play! The problem is that neither player has limited his hand. At this point, both east and west could have near maximum hands with reasonable controls or could have substantial extra values. In both bidding sequences, we have agreed upon a major, hearts and spades, respectively, at the three levels.

At this point, some play the bid of 3NT as Baby Blackwood. It begins the keycard sequence at a low level and allows one to bail out at the five-level of the major.

This can also be a part of the "Serious" 3NT convention proposed by Eric Rodwell. If one does not bid 3NT, one begins a cuebidding sequence! With less than 15+ HCP or the equivalent, one uses a cuebid to show a minimum hand. It is a courtesy cuebid in case partner has substantial extra values. The cubidder usually has a near minimum. If he has substantial extras, he bids 3NT, saying that he is "serious"—"baby" Blackwood with slam interest. Hence with a minimum, the bidding might be:

West	East		West	East
1♠	2♥		1♠	2♣
3♥	3♠/4♣/4♦		2♥	3♠
			4♣/4♦	

This sometimes is referred to as non-serious notrump or frivolous notrump.

With no interest in slam, one would sign off in four of the major and not bid 3NT or cuebid. If you cuebid, there are some important rules:

(1.) A cuebid in partner's 2/1 suit shows one of the top three honors (A/K/Q). (2.) A cuebid in your own 2/1 suit shows two of the top three honors. (3.) A cuebid in an unbid suit shows any first or second round control (A/K/singleton/ void). Cuebidding is always done up-the-line.

By skipping a step, you deny an appropriate "control" in the step you skipped. 4NT is always RKCB (usually 1430).

Ace-asking bids at the level of 3NT or below and usages on the first round (other than Blackwood and Gerber) require **an immediate Alert**. Unusual ace-asking bids above the level of 3NT starting with opener's second turn to call require **a delayed alert**. Delayed Alerts for the declaring side's auction are made before the opening lead and for the defending side's auction after the opening lead.

Slam bidding is the most rewarding and possibly one of the toughest aspects of the game. You have to make one-trick decisions, and if you're wrong (either way), the penalties are severe. Serious 3NT is a tool that may help you improve your decision-making.

When using this convention or others, it's important to remember the three aspects that make slams:

1. Power. For a slam purely on HCP, you need thirty-three for the six-level, thirty-seven for seven. Playing tricks can make up for some of the power, of course, provided the other criteria are met.
2. Controls. If the opponents can take the first (in seven) or first two (in six) tricks in any suit, you will go down. So you need to assure you have the necessary first and second round controls.
3. Trumps. Obviously, not important for NT slams, but in a suit, the trump suit must be both long enough to generate tricks and solid enough to not lose two.

Examples of using serious 3NT and the cuebidding style in some 2/1 auctions follow.

Cue 1:

♠KJ567	♠AQ2
♥A89	♥7
♦Q2	♦AKJ1098
♣Q56	♣A45
1♠	2♦
2♠	3♠
4♦	4NT
5♥	7NT

Opener's 4♦ denies serious slam interest (else 3NT) and denies first or second round club control (else 4♣) but shows one of the top three honors in diamonds. Responder can count thirteen tricks.

Cue 2:

♠AQJ98	♠K234
♥Ax	♥KQ
♦K987	♦AQJ43
♣Q7	♣J9
1♠	2♦
3♦	3♠
3NT	4♥
4♠	PASS

Opener's 3NT shows serious slam interest. Responder's 4♥ bid shows two keycards. Opener's 4♠ bid is an absolute sign-off. Responder, despite holding extra values, must pass. Note: If you did not use "Baby 3NT," you may have over bid!

Cue 3:

♠AJ1087	♠KQ2
♥KJ9	♥654
♦7	♦AKQJ98
♣Q987	♣A
1♠	2♦
2♠	3♠
4♥	4NT
5♦	6♠

4♥ denies serious slam interest but shows a heart control. A heart control is all responder needs to know about. What would happen if you exchange opener's honors in hearts?

Cue 4:

♠AJT34	♠KQ7
♥Q108	♥543
♦7	♦AKQJ98
♣KJ87	♣A
1♠	2♦

2♠	3♠
4♣	4♦
4♠	PASS

When responder bids 4♦, he is announcing serious slam interest. This is due to the fact that opener has denied serious slam interest by not bidding 3NT. Responder would sign off over 4♣ if he did not have serious slam interest of his own. Opener is now obligated to show a heart control if he has one. When opener bids 4♠, responder knows that the defense can take at least the first two heart tricks.

Cue 5:

♠K98	♠Q7
♥AJ10765	♥K32
♦79	♦AQ10654
♣K7	♣AQ
1♥	2♦
2♥	3♥
3♠	3NT
4♥	Pass

When hearts is agreed at the three-level, opener must bid 3♠ if he has a control in spades. Any other bid would deny spade control (3NT would be Baby Blackwood—Serious 3NT). Responder has extra values and shows this by bidding 3NT. 4♥ shows two keycards, and responder passes.

If there is one lesson to be learned from this discussion, it is that there is significantly more too effective bidding than merely writing down the name of a convention or a system on your convention card. Good partnership agreements are considerably more important than the system you play. If you and your partner decide to play a complex non-standard system, put in the time and do it right. Discuss your auctions and make sure you understand why you make bids and what they mean! When you truly understand your system, you will start to see the benefits in your results.

This section is based upon material in the book by Brian Senior (2001), "Conventions Today," Chess & Bridge LTD and an article by Fred Gitelman, "Improving 2/1 Game Force" published in *Canadian Masterpoints*, a magazine for expert players. This article with extensions (including the Last Train Convention) may be found on the Web: www. imp-bridge.nl/artiles/2over1.htm.

Cuebidding for Slam

Cuebidding sequences are critical to reaching a slam in 2/1 game force auctions. In addition, we have been warned: (1) don't use Blackwood with a worthless doubleton; (2) if you use Keycard Blackwood (without kickback) and want to investigate slam in a minor, the use of 4NT can be disastrous. So, how do you investigate slam? The answer is by using cuebidding. The material in this section follows the basic principles set forth by Ken Rexford (2006) in "Cuebidding at Bridge—A Modern Approach," published by Master Point Press, Toronto.

To stimulate how you might use cuebidding, we look at two examples from the 2005 Bermuda Bowl round-robin event (Rexford, page 180). How would you bid the following hands?

Hand 1

West	East (dealer)
♠ Q10832	♠ K754
♥ K2	♥ A84
♦ AK1085	♦ Q74
♣ 5	♣ A92

Hand 2

West (dealer)	East
♠ AKJ974	♠ Q10
♥ A	♥ Q53
♦ AK1097	♦ Q82
♣ 6	♣ J10432

Before we analyze the two hands, we put forth Ken's simple principles.

TEN BASIC PRINCIPLES OF CUEBIDDING

P1. Cuebids of a side suit belonging to the cuebidder show **two** of the top three honors.

West	East
1♥	2♣ (GF)
2♦	2♥
3♦	

P2. Cuebids of a side suit belonging to partner show **one** of the top three honors.

West	East
1♥	2♣ (GF)
2♦	2♥
3♣	

P3. 2NT as a cuebid denies good trumps (denies two of the top three honors).

West	East
1♥	2♣ (GF)
2♦	2♥
2NT	

P4. Bypassing 2NT as a cuebid promises good trumps.

West	East
1♥	2♣ (GF)
2♦	2♥
3♣	

P5. A cuebid of trumps shows **two of the top three honors**, or the MISSING top honor if partner has already shown the other two top honors.

West	East
1♥	2♣ (GF)
2♦	2♥
3♣	3♥

P6. Cuebids of unbid suits show first or second round control, in the form of honors (ace/king) or shortness (singleton/void).

West	East
1♥	2♣ (GF)
2♦	2♥
3♣	3♠

P7. Bypassing a cuebid denies the ability to make that cuebid.

West	East
1♥	2♣ (GF)
2♦	2♥
3♦	

P8. Bidding 3NT shows serious slam interest.

West	East
1♥	2♦ (GF)
2♥	3♥
3NT	

P9. Bypassing serious 3NT denies slam interest.

West	East
1♥	2♦ (GF)
2♥	3♥
4♣	

P10. The last train cuebid below you're agreed upon suit is an artificial bid, a "Last Train to Clarksville" cuebid, used to show slam interest with insufficient information to commit to slam or to use 1430 RKCB.

Finally, you must be able to **infer the meaning** of the skipped cuebid step. Let's look at two examples:

(1) The bidding goes:

West	East
1♥	2♣ (GF)
2♦	2♥
2NT	

Having established hearts as the trump suit and bypassing the cuebid of 2♠, west denies a spade control and shows poor trumps (P3). Alternative, consider the example:

(2) The bidding goes:

West	East
1♥	2♣ (GF)
2♦	2♥
3♣	

Now, opener holds one of the top three honors in clubs (P2) and again lacks a spade control since the control bid was skipped. Furthermore, since the bid of 2NT was bypassed, opener must have two of the top three honors in hearts!

Continuing, suppose responder now bids 3♦; we now know that responder holds a diamond card (P2). But, do we know more? The purpose of cuebidding is to get to slam and from the bidding we know that opener lacks a spade control, and responder did not sign-off in 4♥, but cuebid 3♦. We now know by logical inference that responder must have a spade control.

If opener now bids 3♠ after 3♦, he bypassed 3♥ so he lacks a third heart control but shows third round control in spades.

CORRECT INFERENCES IN CUEBIDDING ARE CRITICAL TO SUCCESS

With the above basic principles and the ability to infer meaning to gaps in cuebidding, one may begin to develop the "art" of cuebidding in his partnerships. For more complex principles like picture jump cuebids, cuebidding after splinters, complicated auctions (e.g., two-way Checkback Stayman, Wolff Signoff, Flag Bids, the Golady Convention), and how to handle interference, see Rexford (2006). We now return to our two examples.

Hand (1)

West	East (dealer)
♠ Q10832	♠ K754
♥ K2	♥ A84
♦ AK1085	♦ Q74
♣ 5	♣ A92

Before we begin, let's examine the starter points in both hands.

East has 13 HCP with no adjustments.

West has 12 HCP +2 length points (diamonds and spades) - 1 worthless doubleton point (K2) + 1 quality suit point (three of the top 5 honors) = 15 starter points and since the number of as and 10s (2) - 1 (Q's +J's) = 1 there was no adjustment for the hand.

East should open 1♦ with 13 HCP; west bids 1♠. East now bids 2♠ to establish the suit. Having determined a fit in spades, west must reevaluate his hand by adding 2 points for a singleton, 1 point for the doubleton, and 1 more point for the quality side suit, hence west has 15 + 2 +1 = 18 Dummy Points. With the possibility of a slam near the thirty-three point level, west must begin a cuebidding sequence. He should not bid 4NT since he has a doubleton heart suit!

However, you must plan your bids. With eighteen Dummy Points, he wants to show slam interest and so bids 3♣; the bid of 2NT is bypassed since it would convey a weak spade suit. Now, east knows there is game in spades, but is there more since he is not sure that the bid of three clubs is help suit or a cuebid? With a balanced hand, east does not believe his hand is worth a slam try, even with the ace of clubs (he has thirteen Starter Points and thirteen Bergen points since he can add no extra values for short-suits, extra length in trumps, or side suit quality—a four—or five-card suit), so he bids 3♠. Next, west bids "serious 3NT" (not Baby Blackwood). East cuebids 4♣. What does east now know? (1) west is serious about slam and (2) west's 3♣ call was a cuebid. Now, west cuebids 4♦ and east should next cuebid 4♥. Thus, west must think slam and not sign-off. He must bid 5♦ to show a second control in diamonds. East now bids 5♠ to show a spade control and east bids 6♠. In summary, the bidding follows:

Hand (1)

East	West
1♦	1♠
2♣	3♣
3♠	3NT
4♣	4♦
4♥	5♦
5♠	6♠

Did you reach the spade slam? If you did not, do not feel bad, the contract by both teams in the Bermuda Bowl was four spades making six.

Let's look at our second example:

Hand (2)

West (dealer)	East
♠ AKJ974	♠ Q10
♥ A	♥ Q53
♦ AK1097	♦ Q82
♣ 6	♣ J10432

At the Bermuda bowl, the bidding went:

West	East
1♠	1NT (semi-forcing)
3♦	3♠
4♣	4♠
5♥	5♠

What a shame! What would you do?

First, let's evaluate the hands. West has 19 HCP + 3 length points (spades and diamonds) + 2 points for the quality suits—1 point for the ace singleton = 24 Starter Points. And, east has 7 HCP + 1 for club length equal 8; since As +10 minus Qs + Js =2-4 there is no further adjustment.

We would agree with the bidding through the bid of 4♣. Instead of bidding 4♠, west must bid 4♦ to show one of the top three diamonds. With this information, west would launch into RKCB, bidding 4NT. Upon hearing 5♦ (0/3 keycards), opener next bids 5♥ (queen ask). With the queen and no extras, east bids 6♠. In this example, we have combined cuebidding with 1430 RKCB.

Scroll Bids (Modified)

With Bergen Raises

When playing Bergen Raises, some use concealed or ambiguous splinter bids. Recall that when opening a major, a jump into the other major indicates a singleton somewhere and four-card support with 13+HCP. For example, if one opens one heart, then three spades indicates 13+HCP with four hearts and a singleton somewhere; if one opens one spade, then a response of three hearts shows four spades, 13+HCP and a singleton somewhere.

To locate the singleton, the opener uses scroll asking bids. Thus, the bidding goes: 1♥ - 3♠, 3NT or 1♠ - 3♥, 3♠. The responses after the 3NT scroll asks are: 4♣, 4♦, 4♠* which shows singletons in clubs, diamonds, or spades, respectively; and the corresponding responses after bidding 3♠ are: 3NT=♣, 4♣=♦, and 4♦=♥, the suit below the singleton. However, club members have asked me: How do you indicate not a singleton, but a VOID when using the concealed/ambiguous splinter bids?

*Note: For the bidding sequence 1♥ - 3♠, the scroll ask is 3NT; however, with a spade void it is often better to use 4♥ to show the spade void with a minimum hand. This allows the opening bidder to pass the heart game with no slam interest. Furthermore, for consistency for the two options, one may also after the bid of 3♠, use the following option: 3NT=♥, 4♣=clubs and 4♦=diamonds.

To show either a singleton or a void, one continues with a scroll bid. Then up-the-line bids are used to show a singleton or VOID and simultaneously provides one with information about keycards for the agreed upon suit. After hearing the response to the asking scroll bids (3NT or 3♠), one uses the next sequential up-the-line bid to determine the nature of the shortage. The responses are: Step 1 (the next cheapest bid) says it is a singleton, and Steps 2-5, the next four bids, indicate one has a void and simultaneously shows keycards.

To illustrate, suppose we are playing 1430 RKCB. And the bidding goes: 1♥ - 3♠, 3NT and one hears the response 4♣. To ask about the nature of the shortage (singleton or void), one uses the next sequential up-the-line bid to ask, bids 4♦. The responses for showing a singleton and/or associated keycards for the major suit (hearts) with a void are:

4♥	club singleton (next cheapest step)
4♠	club void with 1 or 4 keycards (step 2)
4NT	club void with 0 or 3 keycards (step 3)
5♣	club void with 2 keycards w/o the queen (step 4)
5♦	club void with 2 keycards with the queen (step 5)

If you play 0314 RKC, you merely interchange steps 2 and 3 above.

In a similar situation, after hearing 4♦, one would use the up-the-line bid of 4♥ to ask about the nature of the shortage. Now, 4♠ shows a singleton diamond and the keycard steps 2-5 are: 4NT, 5♣, 5♦, and 5♥. After hearing the response 4♠, the up-the-line asking bid is 4NT. Then, 5♣=singleton in spades and the keycard steps (2-5) are: 5♦, 5♥, 5♠, 5NT.

Opening one spade, to show a singleton somewhere with 13+HCP and four-card support is 3♥. After hearing the bid of 3♠, one indicates a singleton with the bids 3NT=♣, 4♣=♦, and 4♥=♠. To ask about the nature of the shortage, one again uses the up-the-line bids: 4♣, 4♦, and 4♠. Again, the next cheapest up-the-line bid indicates a singleton and steps 2-5 are used to show a void and simultaneously keycards for the major suit spades. To illustrate, following the bid of 4♣, the shortage bid is 4♦. The responses follow.

4♥   diamond singleton (next cheapest step)
4♠   diamond void with 1 or 4 keycards (step 2)
4NT   diamond void with 0 or 3 keycards (step 3)
5♣   diamond void with 2 keycards w/o the queen (step 4)
5♦   diamond void with 2 keycards with the queen (step 5)

The responses to the shortage bids of 4♥ and 4♠ follow similarly.

To illustrate how the bid may be used, we consider an example.

Opener   **Responder**
♠AQJ762   ♠K984
♥3   ♥AQ92
♦9872   ♦void
♣KQ   ♣A7632

Opener   **Responder**
1♠   3♥ (shortness somewhere)
3♠ (shortage asking bid)   4♣ (singleton/void in diamonds)
4♦ (modified scroll ask)   4NT (void in diamonds with 0 or 3 keycards)
6♠ (if you have 3, bid 7)   7♠

Using the sequential scroll bids and up-the-line shortage bids, adapted from bids suggested by the Australian champion George Smolanko for splinter bids, allows one to further investigate the nature of the shortage, a singleton, or a void with information about the keycards in the agreed upon major suit.

Observe that the scroll bids and up-the-line shortage bids may also be used with the Jacoby 2NT response to a major. If you play that, a three-level bid denotes a singleton or a void and a four-level bid shows a strong (not a void) five-card suit; however, now one uses "modified" scroll-like bids to ask about shortage with Keycard responses.

After Jacoby 2NT

When playing Jacoby 2NT after a major suit opening, the three-level bid by responder is alerted and says that one has a singleton or void in the suit bid. **The bid of 2NT in response to partner's opening bid of one of a major shows at least four trump and 13+ points in support of the major suit. And, in response to the bid of 2NT, opener's bid at the three levels shows a singleton or a void.**

What does responder do next?

With a minimum and no interest based on opener's response, responder usually jumps to game in the agreed suit. All other bids show at least some slam interest. Responder's new suit bids are often cuebids looking for slam.

Are there other options?

Yes, one can use modified Scroll bids!

Let's look at two bidding sequences:

(A) 1♠ - 2NT - 3♣/3♦/3♥ which shows a singleton or a void in the suit bid.

(B) 1♥ - 2NT - 3♣/3♦/3♠ which shows a singleton or a void in the suit bid.

To determine whether or not partner has a singleton or a void, one bids as follows.

For sequence (A), one bids: 4♣/4♦/4♥, and for sequence (B), one bids: 4♣/4♦/4♠. A scroll-up bid at the four levels. Do you have a singleton or a void?

Responses become:

Next cheapest bid shows a singleton
(Step 2) shows 1 or 4 keycards with a void
(Step 3) shows 0 or 3 keycards with a void
(Step 4) shows 2 keycards without and a void
(Step 5) shows 2 keycards with the queen and a void

Thus, one is easily able to determine singleton and void with Keycard Blackwood. Let's look at an example:

Opening one ♠ and responding 2NT, suppose partner hears the bid 3♥ that shows a singleton or void in hearts. After hearing the bid of 3♥, one next bids 4♥ to ask whether it is a singleton heart or a void (**note, the bid of 4 is a sign-off**).

The responses follow.

4♠	heart singleton (next cheapest step)
4NT	heart void with 1 or 4 keycards (step 2)
5♣	heart void with 0 or 3 keycards (step 3)
5♦	heart void with 2 keycards without the queen (step 4)
5♥	heart void with 2 keycards with the queen (step 5)

Similarly, opening one ♥, the responses after hearing for example 3♠ (a spade singleton or void), and one would bid 4♠.

The responses follow.

5♣	spade singleton (next cheapest step)
5♦	spade void with 1 or 4 keycards (step 2)
5NT	spade void with 0 or 3 keycards (step 3)
5♥	spade void with 2 keycards without the queen (step 4)
5♠	spade void with 2 keycards with the queen (step 5)

Note that the asking bids and responses provide all the information required to bid slam or to sign off at the five-level, below slam.

After Jacoby 2NT—Examples

Previously, I discussed how one may use Scroll Bids with Bergen Raises (when using concealed or ambiguous splinter bids) and after Jacoby 2NT. We now consider two examples of the method when responder bids Jacoby 2NT after a bid of a major.

We consider the Jacoby example found in the July 2009 issue of "Bridge News" that is available at www.pitt.edu/~timm by clicking on item 4, BRIDGE NEWS under Current Projects. "Bridge News" is published monthly by the author.

Dealer East N-S   vulnerable

	♠ J9	
	♥ A984	
	♦ J109	
	♣ Q1087	

♠ K10642	**N**	♠ AQ875
♥ 10762	**W E**	♥ 3
♦ AQ		♦ K765
♣ A3	**S**	♣ K42

	♠ 3	
	♥ KQJ5	
	♦ 6432	
	♣ J965	

Suggested Bidding:

West	North	East	South
		1♠	Pass
2NT*	Pass	3♥*	Pass
4♥*	Pass	4♠*	Pass
4NT	Pass	5♣	Pass
6♠	Pass	Pass	Pass

*Alerts

West's 2NT is Jacoby 2NT, showing a game-forcing raise with at least four spades.
The bid of 3♥ shows a singleton or void. Hearing shortness, and with four hearts, east bids 4♥ to ask whether or not west has a singleton or a void. The first level bid of 4♠ shows a singleton. Now, west bids 4NT (Keycard Blackwood) to ask about keycards. The response (5♣) shows one or four; with an ace missing, west signs off in 6♠.

We next consider an example with a minor suit void:

Dealer North N-S Vulnerable

	♠	KJ832	
	♥	A92	
	♦	Void	
	♣	AJ1084	

♠	Q9	N	♠	5
♥	10764		♥	J83
♦	A965	W E	♦	KQJ103
♣	97	S	♣	Q653

	♠	A10764	
	♥	KQ5	
	♦	872	
	♣	K2	

For this example, the bidding goes:

North	East	South	West
1♠	Pass	2NT*	Pass
3♦*	Pass	4♦*	Pass
4NT*	Pass	5NT	Pass
6♣	Pass	7♠	All pass

*Alerts

Counting high card values and length, north has thirteen HCP and two length points or fifteen starter points and opens 1♠. South has only twelve starter points, however, hearing a major suit bid, reevaluates to thirteen Dummy Points, counting the doubleton, and uses the Jacoby 2NT bid that opener alerts. Opener now bids 3♦ to show the diamond singleton/void. Hearing the shortness bid and with three diamonds, south has slam interest and bids 4♦ to see if north has a singleton or a void, knowing game is ensured. North's response of 4NT (step 3) shows 0 or 3 keycards. South now asks about kings by bidding 5NT, 6♣ shows the king of clubs. North bids 7♠, a grand slam (with only twenty-five HCP).

Can you reach the slam without the Modified Scroll Bids? Perhaps; the bidding may go:

North	East	South	West
1♠	Pass	2NT*	Pass
3♦*	Pass	4NT	Pass
6♦	Pass	6♠	Pass

        Pass   Pass
*Alerts

The bid of 4NT is Keycard Blackwood and 6♦ shows an odd number of keycards with a void in diamonds. Yes, one can now bid 6♠, but note that getting to the grand slam is difficult.

If you do not play Keycard Blackwood, just Blackwood, Eddie Kantar recommends bidding 5NT with a void and two aces. Again, getting to seven spades is difficult.

If south does not bid 4NT, but instead bids four spades, in neither case would one reach the slam.

The use of "Scroll Bids" should enhance the convention card for those who use Bergen Raises (Reverse Bergen Raises or Combined Bergen Raises) playing 2/1, Standard American, or Precision.

After a Bergen Raise—Example

You hold the following hand ♠ KQ762 ♥ Q742 ♦KQ4 ♣A

You open the bidding 1♠ and playing combined Bergen raises partner bids 3♣ showing 7-10 dummy points. Not knowing the exact values, you bid 3♦ to ask, and partner next bids 3♥ showing four spades and 10-12 dummy points. Are you interested in slam?

In May 2008, Marty Bergen asked 60 experienced bridge players this question and found that five would bid 4♠ at matchpoints, but investigate slam in IMPS or a team game, 26 would sign-off in fours spades, and 29 would investigate slam. What would you do?

You know partner has 10-12 dummy points. What about your hand?

You have 16 HCP plus one point for length, subtracting a point for the dubious ace; you have only 16 starting points. However, with a fit you may add two points for the singleton and one more for the good side suit. You have 19 Bergen points. Adding 19 to 12 yields only 31 total points; short of the required 33 points required for slam.

Hence do not investigate slam!

The complete deal follows

Dealer South N-S Vulnerable

	♠	9543	
	♥	A3	
	♦	A1065	
	♣	K75	

♠	A108	**N**	♠	J
♥	J86		♥	K1095
♦	83	**W** **E**	♦	J972
♣	QJ1032	**S**	♣	9864

	♠	KQ762	
	♥	Q742	
	♦	KQ4	
	♣	A	

If you would have reached slam, using perhaps the following bidding sequence

North	South
	1♠
3♣	3♦
3♥	3♠
4NT	5♠ (two key cards with the Queen)
6♠	

West would lead the ♣Q and 6♠ is down two. Declares loses two spades and one heart.

Think before investigaing slam, an overbid usually leads to a bad result.

Roman Keycard Gerber (RKCG)

When is 4♣ asking for aces (Gerber)? When is 4NT asking for aces (1430 RKCB)? When is 4♣ a cuebid or a splinter? When is 4NT quantitative? What is 4♣ after a transfer? And after Stayman?

These are all questions partnerships must discuss. In general, most partners tend to play Gerber over first and last notrump bids. That means if one opens 1NT or 2NT or if in the bidding sequence one bids 2NT or 3NT, the bid of 4♣ is Gerber.

However, after one agrees on a major, the bid of 4♣ is often played as 1430 Keycard Gerber when not playing Baby Blackwood. Partnerships that do not play kickback also use 1430 Keycard Blackwood to keep the bidding at a low level, in place of 4NT. Still others may not play Gerber over the first and last notrump and instead always use 4♣ as keycard Gerber. The responses to the bid follow 1430 RKCB.

Responses to 4♣ RKCG

4♦	1 or 4 keycards
4♥	0 or 3 keycards
4♠	2 keycards without the queen
4NT	2 keycards with the queen

To show a void with two or four keycards, bid 5NT; with and odd number of keycards, bid the void at the six-level.

King Ask in RKCG

After a response to the number of keycards, the next step in Keycard Gerber is the king ask (Progressive Gerber bid). It requests the number of kings, excluding the trump suit.

The steps are respectively 0, 1, 2, 3 etc.

After a suit response to an opening bid followed by the opener rebidding 1NT or 2NT, a follow-up bid of 4♣ by responder is RKCB with responder's suit agreed.

Responding to 2NT with both Minors

Option 1—After the bid of 3♠

1. Opener can agree to a minor by bidding 4♣/4♦.
2. 4♥/4♠ is RKCB for clubs/ diamonds, respectively.
3. 3NT is to play

Option 2—After the bid of 3♠ (opener must bid 3NT)

1. Responder bids 4♣/4♦ to show diamonds and clubs in order to right-side the contract. Over 4♣, 4♦ (by opener) is Minorwood for diamonds and over 4♦, 4♥ is RKCB for diamonds.
2. Responder bids 4♥/4♥ to show singleton heart/spade.
3. Responder bids 4NT (non-forcing) to show 5-5 or 5-4 in the minors

The advantage of Option 1 over Option 2 is that one may sign-off in 3NT; however, with Option 2 you must plan in 4NT.

Roman Keycard Blackwood over Preempts

When your partner preempts, there are ways to investigate the hand further. For two-level preempts, one may bid 2NT to ask your partner for a feature or you may use the Ogust Convention. Or, you may play Modified Ogust, Two-step Ogust, Roudinesco rebids, Romex rebids, the McCabe Adjunct Convention, etc.

What method do you employ if your partner bids at the three-level and you have a very good hand? A convention that is similar to the 2NT asks is the Ogust 3NT ask. The responses are

4♣*   minimum, 1 top honor (BAD/WEAK Hand and BAD/STRONG Suit)
4♦*   minimum, 2 top honors (BAD/WEAK Hand and GOOD/STRONG Suit)
4♥*   maximum, 1 top honor (GOOD/STRONG Hand and BAD/WEAK Suit)
4♠*   maximum, 2 top honors (GOOD/STRONG Hand and GOOD/STRONG Suit)
4NT*   all 3 honors, A-K-Q-x-x-x and little else

However, a diadvantage of this approach is that 3NT is no longer to play!

Alternatively, you may also employ the Roth Four Club Convention. It is usually a slam-try allowing one to assess the partnership's prospects for slam without going beyond a safe contract.

After the three-level bid, partner bids 4♣ which is artificial and asks partner to describe his hand further. Recall that the responses go like this:

4♦   bad hand, bad suit.
4♥   bad hand, good suit (2 of the top 3 honors in the preempt suit).
4♠   good hand (1 or 2 honors outside the preempt suit), bad suit.
4NT   good hand, good suit.

The responses are similar to Ogust but use different steps.

Need better information regarding the trump suit. Then, another option is to use 4♣ as RKCB [used with weak two bids (2♦/2♥/2♠) and three level (3♦/3♥3♠) bids]. The bid of 4NT should not be used since it may get the auction too high.

The responses are:

4♦   first step 0 keycards in the agreed suit
4♥   second step, 1 keycard without the Queen
4♠   third step, 1 keycard with the Queen
4NT   fourth step, 2 keycards without the Queen
5♣   fifth step, 2 keycards with the Queen

The only step in which the queen is not known is the first-step. The next bid of 4♥ is the Queen ask - 4♠ = no and 4NT = yes. A jump over the four hearts bid (5♣/5♦/5♥/5♠) is the Specific Suit Ask (SSA).

After the premptive bid of 3♣, the bid of 4♣ is natural and advances the preempt; a jump to 4♦ is RKCB for clubs.

Let's look at an example.

Opener	Responder
♠ A 7	♠ K 2
♥ K 10 9 8 7 6 5	♥ A Q 2
♦ 7	♦ A Q 6 5 4 2
♣ 3 4 5	♣ A 7

3♥	4♣ (1430 RKCB for hearts)
4NT (2 w/o)	5♦ (SSA for diamonds)
6♥ (singleton ♦)	7♥

Scroll Bids (Simple)

The Scroll Bids discussed in this chapter allows one to determine whether one has a singleton or a void; and if one has a void, the 1430 responses are incorporated into the responses. Is there another option that is perhaps less complex?

Yes, but you must give up weak jump shifts when opening one heart.

The System works as follows:

Opener Responder Opener Explanation

1♥	2♠		Game Force with a singleton
		2NT	Opener asks responder to bid suit of singleton (4♥=♠)
	3♠		Game Force with a void
		3NT	Opener asks responder to bid void suit (4♥=♠)
1♠	3♥		Game Force with a singleton/void
		3♠	Relay bid
			Responder bids singleton suit
			With a VOID responder bid 3NT; Opener relays again 4♣
			Responder bids 4♦=♦, 4♥=♥, 4♠=♣

This method is simple and works well when opening a major. To investigate slam one may use 4NT or 4♠ if the agreed upon suit is hearts. The method is simple and always allows one to stop short of game, if necessary. It was suggested to me by Ted Deflippo.

Chapter 4
Third and Fourth Seat Openings

Up to this point, we have assumed that one was in the first or second seat to open a hand with no interference. If two players have passed and you are in the third seat, you may have a full opener with 12+ starting points and two quick tricks or you may have less. In the third seat, the requirements to open are less stringent; you need only ten starting points and 1 ½ quick tricks. Some players will even open a good four-card major.

Rule of 22/20 (seats 1-3)

Another option is to employ the rule of 22 (some use the rule in the first three seats). The rule goes like this: count your starting points and the total number of cards in your two longest suits, they must add to 20. Next, add the number of quick tricks, if that total is 22 or more, open the hand. The rule of 20 does not require counting the number of quick tricks.

Rule of 15 (fourth seat)

In the fourth seat, one usually has a full opener 12+ starting points and two quick tricks. The only exception is when you hold 4+ spades and 11+ starting points. Now you add your starting points to the number of spades held, if the total is 15+, open the hand either a minor or with 5+ spades one spade (some may open the hand one spade with only four).

To determine whether your partner has a full opener, some variation of the Drury Convention, developed by Douglas Drury, is used when partner opens one of a major (1♥ or 1♠) in the third seat (some also use it in the fourth seat, discuss this with your partner).

Reverse Drury Convention

The Reverse Drury Convention employs an artificial bid of 2♣* used by a passed hand after partner opens 1♥ or 1♠ in third seat (some also use Drury it in the fourth seat; I do not recommend this practice. It is best if opener has at least 11+ starting points—nearly a full opener). The artificial bid of two clubs shows 3+ card trump support and 10-11 Dummy Points and a fit.

In the original Drury Convention, opener rebids 2♦, to show a light opening. With **Reverse Drury** (more common today), a rebid of two of opener's original major suit shows a light opening (that is, no game interest) and responder is expected to pass. Any other rebid by opener confirms a full opening hand (or better) and shows game interest. With a good hand, say 15+ starting points, opener may simply jump to game (four of the major suit). Other bids tend to be natural and descriptive.

Two-Way Drury

The Two-Way Drury Convention (the basic convention) employs two artificial bids: 2♣* or 2♦*, again used by a passed hand after partner opens 1♥ or 1♠ in third seat (again some may use the convention in fourth seat; I do not recommend this practice, it is best if opener has at least 11+ starting points—nearly a full opener). The artificial bid of two clubs shows three-card trump support and 10-11 Dummy Points; the artificial bid of two diamonds shows 4+ card supports for the major and 10-11 Dummy Points. The complete convention follows playing Bergen Raises.

With no interference, the bids over 1M bid are:

A simple raise of partner's major suit bid usually shows three-card support and 6-9 starting points (Drury and constructive raises are off).

2♣*	limit raise, 3 card support and 10-11 starting points
2♦*	limit raise, 4 card support and 10-11 starting points
2NT	10-11 points and 5-5 in minors (opener's rebids are "pass or correct")
3♣	preemptive in clubs
3♦	preemptive in diamonds
1♥-3♠*	4 card limit raise with concealed/ambiguous singleton/void
1♠-3♥*	4 card limit raise with concealed/ambiguous singleton/void
1♥-2♠*	preemptive in spades (6+)
1♠-2♥*	preemptive in hearts (6+)

* Alert Bids—3-level bids are part of Bergen Raises (regular or reverse)—**If you use the Two-Way "Reverse" Drury Convention, the bids of two clubs and two diamonds are interchanged.**

Opener's CONTINUATIONS AFTER DRURY BIDS:

1♥/1♠ - 2♣/2♦ (2♥/2♠ is sub-minimal hand) all other bids are natural and promise a full opener (12-17 starting points).

Two of other major after 2♣* allows one to investigate whether one has a 4-4 fit in other major.

Non-jump suit bid (other than two-level bid of other major) below 3M = help suit game try:

Three-level bid of major is invitational.

Double jump bid (e.g., 4♣/4♦, etc.) = splinter.

2NT = DRURY SLAM TRY (18-19 starting points without a splinter)

- 3♣, 3♦, 3♠ = singleton.
- 3♠ = more-than-minimum strength with a ruffing value (a good 11+ points).
- 3NT = balanced maximum (11+ high-card points).
- 4♣, 4♦, 4♥ = 5-card suit with at least two of the top four honors (QJxxx or better).
- 4♠ = minimum values, no singleton.

3NT = 15-17 starting points with balanced hand and denies other four major
4 of bid major is to play with no slam interest
4NT is RCKCB with slam interest

In competition:

Over DBL or 1♠ - Drury is off
over 1NT - Drury is off
over 2♣ - 2♦ is omnibus limit raise
after 1♠-2♥, DBL = limit raise (Drury double)
After 1♥-2♠, DBL = limit raise (Drury double)

Two/three-level bids are usually defined by partnership agreement.

The two-way Drury Convention allows a pair to avoid guessing on game contracts when partner has already passed. By playing Drury, you get the benefit of staying at the two-level with all balanced or semi-balanced 10-12 points hands that has trump support.

Example (1)

First Seat   ♠KJ2 ♥J1094 ♦ KJ76 ♣ 98

Third Seat   ♠1096 ♥KQ852 ♦ 72 ♣A53

The person in first seat has nine starting points and would pass. Partner in the third seat has ten starting points and 1½ quick trick and opens 1♥. Not playing Reverse Drury, partner has four-card support for hearts and ten Dummy Points and bids 3♦ (Bergen on with a passed hand showing 10-12 points with four-card support). Partner must bid 3♥.

Alternatively, playing Two-Way Drury, one would bid 2♦ to show 10-12 points with four-card support. Partner bids 2♥ (not a full opener) and the correct contract are reached.

You are playing Reverse Drury and hold the following hands and partner has opened 1♥. What do you bid?

Example (2) ♠KJ42 ♥A65 ♦ K976 ♣ 98   Bid 2♣* 11 starting points with three hearts

Example (3) ♠Q942 ♥A6 ♦ J76 ♣ KJ108   Bid 1♠ 10 starting points

Example (4) ♠A2 ♥A7 ♦ K10543 ♣ 653   Bid 1NT only two-card support 10 points

Example (5) ♠42 ♥QJ76 ♦ 1076 ♣ AKJ10   Bid 2♦* 11 starting points with four hearts

Fit Showing Jump Bids (Majors)

Fit showing jumps are bids made by a passed hand (because some always play Bergen Off with a passed hand) that has both constructive and preemptive properties when partner opens a major suit. Fit Showing Jumps (FSJ) require 8-11 starting points, length in partner's suit (4+ cards), a minor side suit with 4+ cards with working honors, and a singleton or void (no flatter than 5-4-2-2). The bid is a jump to the three level in the long minor. The bid allows partner to bid at the three-level of the major or go on to bid game with a double fit in the minor. The major advantage of FSJ over Drury is that the bids show strength and are not artificial. Thus, it is less likely that the opponents would double a fit bid. This is a disadvantage of Drury.

A disadvantage of FSJ bid is that there are many hands where partner is forced to pass since the criteria for the bid are rather stringent. In the Drury Example (1) above, playing fit bids, partner would pass or perhaps bid 1NT.

Two-level Major Suit bids in the third and fourth seats

In the first two seats, preemptive major suit bids at the two-level show 5-10 starting points and a six-card suit. In the third /fourth seat this is not the case. A two-level bid is stronger since your partner has passed. You should have 12+ starting point (an opening hand) and a six-card major suit. When responding to your partner's preempt, remember you are a passed hand so game is unlikely.

Three—and four-level preempts in the third seat

In the first two seats, we suggested that the rule of 2 or 3 be used. However, in the third seat, one may use the simple 2-3-4 rule.

1. Overbid by two tricks at unfavorable vulnerability (vulnerable vs. not vulnerable)
2. Overbid by three tricks at equal vulnerability
3. Overbid by four tricks at favorable vulnerability (not vulnerable vs. vulnerable)

Returning to the hand used above with the rule of 2 or 3:

♠AKQ10653 ♥ 8 ♦ 854 ♣ 96

We would bid as follows. Open 2♠ at unfavorable; open 3♠ at equal; open 4♠ at favorable vulnerability.

Recall using the rule of 2 or 3, we have six losers (0 in spades, 1 in hearts, 3 in diamonds, and 2 in clubs). 13 cards-6 losers=7 playing tricks. Non-vulnerable, adding 3 = 7+3=10 so you should open 4♠. You would open 3♠ only if vulnerable (7+2=9). The rules provide very similar results.

Chapter 5
Bidding with Interference

We have assumed up to this point in our 2/1 Game Force bidding that the opponents have not interfered. If there is direct interference with, for example, a suit bid or a double, **the 2/1 game force is off**.

2/1 Bids with Interference

1) You open one heart and your LHO doubles, partner bids two diamonds. Is it forcing to game? No—it is not even forcing for one round.

2) You open one heart and your LHO bids one spade. You again bid two diamonds. Is the bid forcing to game? NO—However, since the overcall was at the one level, it is foricng for ONE ROUND! Opener must bid again.

3) You open one heart and your LHO bids two spades. Partner next bids three clubs, is it forcing to game or for one round? When responder bids a new suit at the three level, it is not only forcing for one round, it is forcing to game!

4) You open one heart and your LHO bid three diamonds. Partner bids three spades. Is the bid forcing? Over the preemptive bid, the bid is only forcing for one round, but not nessasarily to game. Alternatively, you can double and bid a new suit. This sequence is forcing to game. Note, some 2/1 partnerships play that all three level bids are forcing to game over a preempt.

Many partnerships also play that Bergen Raises are off. I do not support this approach; you may, so please decide what is best for your partnership.

If one makes a game force bid, and the opponents choose to bid, the game force remains on.

When a partnership is committed to game and the opponents choose to interfere, opener may double the contract of the opponents instead of proceeding to game, if he believes the double would result in a better score. Doubles (penalty, responsive, cooperative, etc.) will be discussed in more detail in Chapter 8. For now, if the bidder is on the opener's right (he is sitting behind the bidder), a double is usually for penalty. When the bidder is on the opener's left, it is called a cooperative double and partner may leave it or choose to bid. Finally, opener may make a cuebid (western of the opponent's suit usually at the three-level) used to investigate whether or not partner has a stopper for notrump. Cuebids of suits not bid are used for slam investigation as discussed in Chapter 3 or they may show exceptional hands with voids and significant strength, Chapter 8.

Cuebids by opener (Western Cue)

The term "Eastern Cuebid" refers to a style of low level cubidding of the opponent's suit showing stoppers in the bid suit. It has been replaced by the more popular "Western Cuebid" that asks for a full stopper in the opponent's suit. One is a telling bid while the other is an asking bid. The repeat "Western" cuebid (sometimes called a Directional Asking Bid) is usually asking for more information at low levels below 3NT and the cuebidder is asking for a partial stopper (Qx or Jxx). The Western, Eastern, and repeat Western cuebids (DAB) are used to help the partnership reach a notrump contract. An example follows.

West	North	East	South
	1♠	pass	2♦
2♥	3♥#	pass	3NT

the 3♥ cuebid is asking south for more information. South has a heart stopper and bids 3NT. Cuebids are not alerted or announced.

When the opponents interfere, they may or may not take up bidding space. When the overcall allows you to bid at the one-level, your response is natural, limited, and non-forcing. If the opponents bid a suit, you may have room to bid your own suit or notrump. For example, if you open one club and the opponents overcall one diamond, the bid of a major show 5+ starting points. However, the bid of 1NT shows a stopper in the overcalled suit. If you are allowed to make a bid at the one-level, it is the same as if the overcall did not occur. This is also the case when the opponents make a takeout double.

Responder Bids after a takeout double

When the opponents make a takeout double over partner's one-level bid suit, it usually shows support for the other suits (at least three cards) with an opening hand of 12+ starting points. The takeout double asks the doubler's partner to bid a suit and implies shortness in the suit doubled (Chapter 6).

Many play that all systems are on over a takeout double (some have devised special systems over a double such as those who play BROMAD and Modified Jacoby 2NT over a double). Most players ignore the double and make their normal responses, assuming the double did not occur. The following guidelines apply.

1. A new suit is forcing at the one-level.
2. A bid suit at the two-level is weak (a weak jump shift) and is non-forcing.
3. 1NT is semi-forcing, shows a stopper in the overcaller's suit with lack of fit.
4. All Bergen Raises are on when opening one of a major.

One may also redouble the double. It shows 10+ points with or without a fit (some play that it always implies no fit).

Responder Bids Over a one—or two-level suit bid

When the opponents interfere over a major suit bid, the Combined Bergen Bids follow over a double, suit bid (at the one or two-level), or for a passed hand. The following schedule summarizes the bids when partner opens one of a major.

Combined Bergen Raises with Interference
Max Hardy Swiss Bids and Concealed/Ambiguous Splinters

Dummy Pts	No Interference	Double	Suit bid	Passed Hand
		2 Trumps		
5-9 Pts	*1NT then 2 Major	pass	pass	pass
		3 Trumps		
5-9 Pts	*1NT then 2 Major	pass	pass	pass
8-10(bad) Pts	@2 Major (Constructive)	2 Major	2 Major	
10-12 Pts	@3♦**	@2♣	Cuebid	Drury (2♣*)
13+	2 over 1 Bids	Redouble	Cuebid	N/A
16+ Pts Balanced	@4♣ (Swiss)	@4♣	@4♣	N/A
		4 Trumps		
0-6 Pts	@3 Major (Weak)	@3 Major	@3 Major	@3 Major
7-12 Pts	@3♣**	@3 Clubs	2 Major	2 Major
	Bid 3 Diamonds to Ask 3♥=7-9, 3♠=10-12			
13+ Singleton	@3 Other Major	@3 Other Major	@3 Other Major	N/A
(Concealed Splinter) then Step Bids# (see footnote#)				
13+ No Singleton	2 over 1 Bid	2 over 1 Bid	2 over 1 Bid	N/A
15/16+ Pts	@Jacoby 2NT	@Jacoby 2NT	@Jacoby 2NT	N/A

	5 Trumps			
0-11 Pts	Bid Game	Bid Game	Bid Game	Bid Game
12-15 Pts	@4♦ (Swiss)	@4♦	@4♦	N/A

Note: With five HCP and three-card trump support, pass, unless holding either a singleton or at least one trump honor with all other HCP in one side suit. *Semi-Forcing **=Forcing, @=Alert

after 3♠ bid 3NT to find singleton/void, then 4♣/4♦/4♥/4♠ denote Singleton/void. After 3♥, bid 3♠, again, steps denote the singleton. For example, 3NT denotes club singleton/void, etc. If you want to know if it is a singleton/void, bid next suit up which are Scroll Bids?

The above table also applies to Bergen Raises, one only need change the bid of 3♣** to show 7-9 points with four-card support and 3♦** to show four-card support with 10-12 points, 1NT* followed by three of the major to show 10-12 points with three-card support and Jacoby 2NT requires only 13+ starting points and four-card support.

If the overcall is at the two-level, we also use the Bergen bids; however, if the bid is, for example, 2♣, the bid of 3♣* may show three—or four-card support because of its cuebid nature.

Truscott Jordan 2NT

In the Combined Bergen Convention, we have chosen not to include the Truscott Jordan 2NT bid. If used, it is not the same as the Jacoby 2NT bid. The bid is typically used to show a limit raise with three—or four-card support for the bid of a major over a double (it must be alerted). We recommend the Redouble that shows 10+ points with or without a fit. After a redouble, one next supports the major (shows 13+ with three—or four-card support for the major). If you redouble and bid your own suit, you are denying a fit. Discuss these options with your partner.

We recommend the Jordan 2NT over a minor suit opening if you do not play Flip-Flop. It shows 5+ card support and a limit raise. Recall that playing Flip-Flop, 2NT is weak and a three-level bid of the minor shows a limit raise.

Responder Bids when opponent (advancer) interfers after 2NT

To illustrate suppose the bidding goes: 1♥-P-2NT-3♦

4♥	-is signoff, no shortness
Pass	-forcing pass, shows shortness in opponent's bid suit
New Suit	-shows shortness in bid suit
3NT	-medium or maximum hand, no shortness

After a forcing pass bid by opener, rebids by responder are:

Double—Penalty

3M	-new Major, Ace in suit and 0-1 losers in opponent's bid suit
3NT	-King in Opponent's bid suit
4m	-Ace in suit bid and 0-1 losers in opponent's bid suit

Opener's Rebids after a redouble

Partner's redouble after a double shows 10+ starting points. If the opponents make a runout bid to compete and the opener cannot double the bid for penalty, it is always best to pass and allow responder to bid. Partner will show his suit or support for the opening bid suit. In most situations as opener **you should pass a redouble.** This allows your partner to show his hand; do not be quick to bid.

However, if opener has a long suit or a strong two-suited hand that is not suited to a penalty double, opener must bid. For example, a reverse would show a strong hand.

When the opponents bid over a redouble, a rebid of the suit shows a long suit with a weak hand, a double usually shows 4+ cards in the opponent's bid suit. A bid (or jump bid) of a new suit shows 5-5 distribution and a weak hand. A pass is forcing. If responder passes first and then bids, it shows a stronger hand, usually 5-5 in the two suits and 15+ starting points.

Negative Doubles by Responder

The **negative double** is like a takeout double. It is made by the responder after his right-hand opponent overcalled at the first round of bidding. A negative double guarantees that responder has at least **ONE** of the unbid suits (there is one exception, if partner bids a minor and the opponents overcall the other minor a double always implies both majors; however, some may do it with only one). In addition, if partner bids a major, the negative double usually shows support for the other major.

The starting point requirements for a negative double provided the overcall bid is no higher than 3♠, the most popular option (this is marked on the back of the convention card, some may play that they are in effect with higher level bids, e.g., 4♥), is:

You need 6 starting points   **to double at the 1-level**

You need 8 starting points   **to double at the 2-level**

You need 10 starting points   **to double at the 3-level**

You need 12+ starting points   **to double at the 4+ level**

Negative doubles never apply after a NT bid or a two-level cuebid such as Michaels (discussed soon).

After one Minor—(one or two of Major), a negative double promises only the single unbid major. It says nothing about the unbid minor.

After one Major—(one or two of Other Major), a negative double promises only **one minor,** not both. It does not deny both.

After one Minor—(two of Other Minor), a negative double promises **both** four-card majors.

After responder's negative double, opener must make a rebid that describes both his strength and his support for the suit partner may have shown with the double.

Opener Rebids—one/two-level overcalls with negative doubles

When responder makes a negative double, the only way to create a forcing auction on the next round is to cuebid the opponent's suit. If partner opens a minor and you double for a major and next bid, it usually shows a weak hand. Rebidding a major after bidding it the first time shows more values. Neither of these bids is forcing. The only way to make a forcing bid is to cuebid the opponent's suit on your next turn to bid. It is often used to reach a notrump contract and called a Western Cuebid. If partner does not bid notrump, returning to opener's first bid suit shows a strong hand. An overview of bids by Opener follows.

A cuebid is forcing to game.
All jumps below game are invitational.
1NT for one-level overcalls and 2NT for two-level overcalls usually promise a stopper in overcaller's suit.
Opener may be forced to rebid a five-card suit or introduce a three-card suit.
A double jump to 3NT shows length and strength in the suit opened and a bid hand. It does not require a balanced hand.
Double and triple jump to game in a major show great shape and is weaker than a cuebid followed by a jump to game.
A reverse bid by opener is forcing to game.

We consider two examples of cuebidding.

A cuebid is the only forcing bid a negative doubler may make. This cuebid often shows a good hand with no other clear course of action.

1♣ - 1♥ - Dbl - pass

2♣ - pass - 2♥

The two heart bidder may hold ♠AQ94 ♥763 ♦AK75 ♣J5. Responder is hoping the opening bidder has a heart stopper and can bid 3NT. For example, opener may have the following hand: ♠K5 ♥KJ6 ♦63 ♣AQ10987.

Jumps by a negative doubler are non-forcing, but highly invitational. For example:

1♦ - 1♠ - Dbl - pass

2♦ - pass - 3♥ which shows less than ten starting points, and 6+ hearts - an invitational bid. The 3♥ bid may be based upon: ♠7 ♥KQJ965 ♦Q87 ♣987. With ten starting points and 5+ hearts, for example, with a hand as: ♠7 ♥KQ965 ♦A87 ♣954 or ♠A6 ♥AQJ107 ♦876 ♣954, responder would not double but bid 2♥. The negative double at the two-level shows a hand with only four hearts and unlimited point count or five or more hearts and not enough points to bid at the two-level.

Opener Rebids—three-level overcalls with negative doubles

A cuebid is forcing to game.

3NT guarantees a stopper in clubs.

Opener may be forced to rebid a five-card suit and rarely introduce a three-card suit.

After (one Level and 3♦ or one Level and 3♥ or one Level and 3♠), the negative double is called a trump double by Marty Bergen. It asks partner to bid 3NT with a stopper in the opponent's overcall suit (with a stopper do not use a negative double, bid 3NT directly).

Opener in general has three types of hands when responding to a negative double.

Minimum (12-15 starting points)	with support for suit—partner's implied suit with the double, you should bid it.
Invitational (16-17 starting points)	Jump one level to show support
Game values (18+ starting points)	Jump to game or Cuebid the opponent's suit, this allows partner to show his suit

Instead of a negative double, one may bid a new suit at the two-level with 10+ starting points. These are called a "standard" free bid. However, some play **Negative Free Bids.** Negative free bids usually require only 6-10 starting points and show a long suit. Negative free bids must be alerted, if played. If you play negative free bids, it also affects the negative double, since now, playing negative free bids, you have to double and bid with 10+ values.

Responder Bids used with minor suit openings (without flip-flop)

While we have stressed major suit openings, there are also several bids that may be used when the opponents interfere over a minor suit opening. Let's suppose you open 1♦ and the opponents bid a major. A summary of responses follow.

1♦ - 1M

Double	Negative double shows other major
1NT	8-10 starting points, 3 diamonds and a stopper in the major
2♦	Less than 10 starting points, 4 diamonds (inverted minors is off)
2♣/2♥	Natural with 10+ starting points
2M	Cuebid, 12+ starting points and asking for a major stopper
2NT*	11 - 12 starting points with a major stopper and 5+ diamonds
3♣	Splinter (singleton/void) in support of diamonds
3♦	Weak raise 6-10 starting points
3M	Splinter in major with 5+ card support in diamonds

*Truscott Jordan

Balancing Double by Opener

Often, your partner bids and your right hand opponent (RHO) interfere and you have their bid suit. You make what is called a trap pass. When the opponents pass, your partner often makes a **balancing double** when holding only two cards in the overcall suit he is asking you to bid. Do you bid or pass the double? To decide, one uses the rule of nine. It works as follows:

Rule of 9

Add the level of the contract (usually one or two) to the number of trumps you hold in the overcaller's suit, plus the number of honors including the ten. If the total is nine or more, pass, leaving the double in, otherwise bid to take out the double.

This action may cause the overcall bidder to bid a new suit. If you had enough to leave the double in the first time, you should also double the second suit. Partner may pass for penalty holding a strong hand with a good holding in the second suit bid, rebid his original suit, or perhaps bid notrump. A direct cuebid of overcaller's second suit shows a strong hand and a desire to play in the overcaller first suit.

Responder calls after a 1NT overcall

When the opponents interfere by bidding 1NT, they usually have the suit bid stopped, a balanced hand showing a notrump opener with 15-17/18 starting points. If this is not the case, the bid must be alerted. Some partnerships play that the bid of 1NT for takeout with shortness in the bid suit to interfere with the opponents' agreements.

When the opponents bid 1NT, responder's options are limited. The bid has taken away the negative double. Responder may pass, raise his partner's suit, or **double for penalty**. Observe that if partner has 12+ points and the overcaller has fifteen, the remaining points shared between the remaining hands are only thirteen.

With 5-9 points and at least three-card support, raise your partner's major suit. A jump raise in partner's major shows 10-12 points with support with three or four-card support. Unless you have 10 + points and a good 5+ card suit, do not bid it.

With 10+ starting points or a very good suit of your own (8+ cards), consider doubling for penalty.

Unusual 2NT Overcall

The Unusual 2NT overcall is used after one has made a majors suit bid. A 2NT overcall shows at least five cards in each of the lowest unbid suits; partner is expected to bid the one he likes best. Some examples:

1♣ - 2NT	2NT shows the lowest two unbid suits, diamonds and hearts.
1♦ - 2NT	2NT shows clubs and hearts.
1♥ - 2NT	2NT shows clubs and diamonds.
1♠ - 2NT	2NT shows clubs and diamonds.

In each of these cases, the partner of the 2NT bidder normally corrects to the suit for which he has the most tolerance. With equal length in both suits, especially with two doubletons, he bids the cheapest suit. If he has a weak hand with at least four-card support, he can consider making a preemptive jump bid to the four-level in one of the known suits.

When the opponents interfere using the 2NT overcall bid, you may use the convention known as **Unusual over unusual 2NT** which is a series of cuebids to show support for your partner's bid suit.

Because we know the two suits when the opponents use employing the unusual 2NT bid, we can use this information to your advantage. One uses the suits of the opponents (the cheapest suit and their second suit, as cuebids) and the two natural available bids to describe the hand of the responder:

Cheapest Cuebid: A limit raise or better in the bid suit.

Second Cuebid: Game forcing hand in the fourth unbid suit.

Raise in the fourth suit: Natural and non-forcing.

Raise in the bid suit: Competitive raise (weak).

An example follows.

1♥ - 2NT (clubs & diamonds) -(?)

3♣	the Cheapest Cuebid, is a Limit raise or better in hearts.
3♦	the Second Cuebid, is a game forcing bid in spades.
3♥	is a competitive raise and weak.
3♠	is natural and non-forcing

NOTE: Some play the second cuebid as invitational only, not forcing; it depends on your partnership agreement. Check with your partner!

What about bids above the three-level? Discuss these with your partner.

3NT is usually natural with stoppers in the two suits.
4♣/4♦ is splinter raise in hearts (for our example).
4♠ is natural.

When should the double be used? It usually shows 10 + starting points (with or without a fit) and is primarily used as if the bid of two notrump was a double (for our example, 1♥-Dbl).

Thus, a double after the bid of 2NT is like a redouble. Because the opponent's bid of two notrump is forcing, the opener can now double the opponent's bid with good trumps, make a descriptive bid with an offensive hand, or make a forcing pass.

Some partnerships also play unusual 2NT in the balancing seat: 1♥ - pass - pass - 2NT, showing the minors.

Michaels Cuebid

This is a direct cuebid of the opponent's opened suit (one club by RHO, two clubs by you) to show 5+card length in two other suits. One of your suits is always a major, but the exact two you promise depend upon the opening bid.

- Over a **minor-suit opening**, a Michaels Cuebid (1♣-2♣ or 1♦-2♦) shows **both majors**.
- Over a **major-suit opening**, a Michaels Cuebid (1♥-2♥ or 1♠-2♠) shows **the OTHER major and an unspecified minor**.

When using Michaels and the two suits of the opponents are known, the bids by responder are identical to those used in Unusual over Unusual 2NT. To illustrate, after the bids of 1♣-2♣ (the majors, hearts and spades), we have that

2♦	is natural and non-forcing.
2♥	the Cheapest Cuebid, is a limit raise or better in clubs.
2♠	the Second Cuebid, is a game forcing bid in diamonds.
2NT	is natural and invitational.
3♣	is a competitive club raise and weak.
3♦	is natural and forcing.
3♥/3♠	is splinter raises in clubs.
3NT	is natural with stoppers in the two suits.
4♥/4♠	is splinter raise in clubs.
5♣	is natural.

A double shows 10+ starting points with or without a fit.

What about when the second suit of the Michaels bid is ambiguous? (See footnote (*) below.) Then only **one** suit is known; for example, with the bids 1♥-2♥, and 1♠-2♠. Now, we can no longer do everything since we have only one known cuebid. For example, for the bid 1♠-2♠ (shows hearts and a minor), we have the following bids.

2NT	is natural and invitational.
3♣	is a non-forcing club raise.
3♦	is a not forcing diamond raise.
3♥	the only cuebid, shows a limit raise in spades.
3♠	is competitive and weak.
4♥	is splinter raise for spades.

If the opener doubles the opponent's three-level bid after Michaels or Unusual 2NT, it is generally for penalty, not takeout.

(*) Some play that the opponents' cuebids show the upper two unbid suits; then one heart followed by two hearts would show spades and diamonds; and one spade followed by two spades would show hearts and diamonds! It is called Modified Michaels and all suits are known. Hence, the responses may be patterned after the one club-two club bid discussed above.

Some partnerships also play Michaels if the bidding goes, for example, 1♣ - pass - pass - 2♣; or if the bidding goes 1♣ - pass - 1NT - 2♣, a balancing seat Michaels.

Michaels bids need to be alerted. YOU MUST AND SHOULD ASK WHAT THE CUEBID MEANS. For additional details, consult Marty Bergen's (1986) "Better Bidding with Bergen, Volume Two, Competitive Bidding Fit Bids, and More," by Devyn Press.

After Weak Jump Overcalls

After a preemptive jump overcall, for example 3♦, after partner has bid a major you have several options: pass, support, bid your own suit, etc. If you have support for partner's major and 10-12 starting points, show support immediately. With a stronger hand, make a cuebid or bid your own suit freely and the support partner's major. The advantage of bidding your own suit is that if the opponents compete in the auction, opener (your partner) will be a better position to decide whether or not to double the opponents for penalty or bid on.

Fishbein Convention

The **Fishbein Convention** is a bidding convention developed by Harry Fishbein. It is in the direct seat when the opponents preempt at the two or three levels. Instead of doubling for takeout (negative), one bids the next higher suit (excluding 2NT) for takeout. Then double is for penalty. The bid of 3NT is usually to play.

Some examples

When the opponents interfere, there are number of strategies one may consider. We review several applying the principles reviewed in this chapter.

(1) The bidding goes:

South	West	North	East
1♠	Pass	2♦	2♥
(?)			

South has the following hand: ♠ KQJ76 ♥ J54 ♦ AQ5 ♣ 107.

South has fourteen starting points and his partner responded with a 2/1 game force bid. However, the opponents interfered with the bid of two hearts. South has no more to say and must pass. The auction will not end since his partner (north) has given a 2/1 response and will bid. The pass by the opener is called a forced pass; south has bid his hand and is not required to bid again. What would a double show? The overcaller (east) is on the opening bidder right. It would be for penalty.

(2) The bidding goes:

South	West	North	East
1♠	double	2♦	2♥
(?)			

South has the same hand, but west has made a takeout double. Partner has taken a free bid at the two-level showing 10+ starting points. South knows that his partner has diamonds and with three, he competes by bidding 3♦. This allows partner to return to spades at the three-level for a partial score. Partner did not use Bergen; game in a major is unlikely.

(3) The bidding goes:

South	West	North	East
1♠	2NT	3♣	3♦
(?)			

The bid of 3♣ by partner is a limit raise for spades (the bid of 3♦ would be a game force bid in hearts) showing 10-12 starting points. Partner may invite or bid game. A cuebid of three diamonds would show interest in slam.

(4) The bidding goes:

South	West	North	East
1♥	pass	2♣	2♠
(?)			

   (a) North has the following hand: ♠ 765 ♥ A2 ♦ AQ5 ♣ AJ1076.
     Without a spade stopper, south cannot bid notrump. Instead, south bids 3♠ asking for a spade stopper. Without a stopper, north bids 3♥.
   (b) North has the following hand: ♠ AKQ ♥ 82 ♦ K65 ♣ KQJ43.
     With a spade stopper, north bids 2NT (with eighteen starting points). Depending on opener's response, may show his extra values later in the bidding sequence.
   (c) North has the following hand: ♠ 87 ♥ K54 ♦ KQ5 ♣ AK1043.
     With three-card support for hearts, show your support, bid 3♥.

(5) The bidding goes:

South	West	North	East
1♠	3♦	(?)	

North has the following hand: ♠ 874 ♥ K5 ♦ KQ5 ♣ AK1043.

Do not show your five-card suit, show your support immediately.

(6) The bidding goes:

South	West	North	East
1♠	2♣	(?)	

(6) North has the following hand: ♠ 874 ♥ K5 ♦ KQ5 ♣ AK1043.

A bid of 3♠ shows a weak hand, cuebid 3♣ to show support even with three in this case.

Partner should bid game.

(7) An example of the Fishbein Conventions (from the World Championships in Sao Paolo, Brazil).

	♠ A3 ♥ AQJ3 ♦ K2 ♣ 106543	
♠ Q42 ♥ K1097652 ♦ 6 ♣ 87	N W E S	♠ J10765 ♥ 4 ♦ J975 ♣ KJ2
	♠ K98 ♥ 8 ♦ AQ10843 ♣ AQ9	

In this example, the bidding goes

South	West	North	East
1♦	3♥	(?)	

You have a heart stack against the opponents; you cannot make a negative double since you do not have spades. Playing the Fishbein Convention, one would double for penalty. Not playing the convention, you must pass and hope partner reopens with a double. Do not bid 4♦.

Responding to 3NT after a three-level preempt

While a bid of 3NT over a three-level bid is to play, when you have a big hand you need a method to investigate slam since you know partner has stoppers and at least a strong notrump hand with 15+ starting points. How do you investigate slam when you have a strong hand or a very distributional hand? With a balanced hand, 4NT would be quantitative. And transfers would be on where 4♦/4♥ are transfers to a major are non-forcing slam try in the major suits, hearts and spades, respectively. While a direct bid of a major is to play. Now, 4♦ may be used as an artificial enquiry with the following responses.

4 of a suit	minimum hand to play
4NT	15-18 balanced hand
5 of a suit	good hand with slam interest
5NT	19-21 balanced hand
6 of suit	great hand 6+ cards
6NT	22+ balanced hands

Chapter 6
Takeout Doubles

Standard Takeout Doubles

As seen in Chapter 5, a takeout double is a competitive bid used to show an opening hand with at least 12+ starting points when used in the direct seat. The purpose of the bid is to get into the auction. The ideal hand for the doubler is 4-4-4-1 or 5-4-4-0 where the singleton or void is in the opponent's bid suit. It tends to deny a five-card major. The doubler usually has two kinds of hands, weak or strong. With a weak hand, the doubler will usually pass any bid made by his partner; with a stronger hand 16/17+ starting points, he will double and bid his own suit. With 19+ starting points, the doubler will generally double and cuebid. When the opponents bid after partner responds to a double, the second double is usually for penalty.

The doubler will normally have no more than three cards in the opponent's opening suit (do not double with a stack in the opponent's suit, make a trap pass, if partner balances with a double, use the rule of nine to see whether you pull the double or leave it in for penalty). When the doubler doubles a major suit opening, he will usually have four cards in the other major or a strong hand where he will bid his own suit or cuebid.

The takeout double is not restricted to the direct seat. It occurs when partner has not yet bid, passes do not count but redoubles are considered bids, and the double is of a suit bid (not notrump) at the 1, 2, or 3 bidding levels. Thus, one may also use a takeout double in the fourth seat when the bidding has gone 1x - pass - pass - double. The double is for takeout since partner has not yet bid; it is virtually never used for penalty in this situation.

Let's look at some simple auctions:

South	West	North	East
	1♦	1♥	3♦
Pass	pass	double	

Because partner south has not bid, the double is for takeout.

South	West	North	East
1♥	pass	1NT	double

In this example, the double by east is equivalent to a direct takeout double of the heart opening bid. If opener had bid a minor, the double is more than likely asking for a major suit.

Additionally, the double by east is equivalent to a direct takeout double of the heart opening bid.

Getting more complicated, E-W vulnerable and N-S non-vulnerable

West	North	East	South
	1♦	1♠	pass
Pass	double	pass	pass
2♥	double		

What is the second double by north? South's pass of the first double is a "penalty pass," equivalent to bidding spades since the first double of the spade bid should have showed hearts (at least three and maybe four) with a shortage in spades. Even though partner has passed in the auction, it is not for takeout but for penalty. When three different suits have been bid, the second double is usually for penalty.

Suppose north does not double but passes the bid of two hearts; if south holds the hand: ♠ KQ75 ♥ AJ102 ♦ 7 ♣ 9865, using the rule of nine, he must double for penalty at the two-level.

Takeout Double or Overcall

When an opponent opened the bidding, you can make a simple overcall with 8+ to 16 starting points and a five-card suit major, never a minor (for example, if the opponents open one club and your distribution is 3=3=5=2, double). If your overcalls have to bid at the two-levels, you'd better have 13+ points. Jump overcalls are preemptive. If you have a balanced hand, you can make a notrump overcall with 15-18 points (careful, some use it as a takeout bid). If you have strong hand with shortness in opponents' suit, you should make a takeout double. Overcalls are explained in Chapter 7.

Responding to a Takeout Double

When partner makes a takeout double and the opponents do not bid, you must respond; the double is forcing. Your options are:

Suit bid	6-9 starting points and 3+ card suit (usually 4+)
Jump Longest Suit	10+ starting points 4+ cards, forcing one round
Double Jump	13+ starting points 5+ cards, forcing to game, may bid game
1NT	8-10 starting points balanced with a stopper, no 4-card major
2NT	11-12 starting points balanced with a stopper, no 4-card major
3NT	13-15 starting points balanced with a stopper, no 4-card major
Cuebid	12+ points, over natural bids, artificial and forcing

Pass   Converts the double into a penalty, Rule of 9.

Cuebids in response to takeout doubles

A cuebid is the only forcing bid an advancer may make to a takeout double. All other bids, including jumps, are non-forcing.

With a good four-card suit or 5+ card suit and an opening hand, it may be easy to get to game after a double; however, suppose you have good values and two suits, what do you do? For example, with equal length and perhaps even equal strength in two suits when the bidding proceeds:

1♣ - Dbl - pass and the advancer holds one of the following hands.

1) ♠K986 ♥K986 ♦A8 ♣K64

2) ♠A975 ♥A975 ♦A98 ♣J3

3) ♠KQ9 ♥KJ10 ♦AQ43 ♣765.

With two four-card majors (hands 1 and 2), you must cuebid 2♣. It asks partner to bid his best major.

With hand 3, if the takeout doubler bids spades, advancer may repeat the cue (3♣) that suggests less than four-card support for the doubler's major suit but with game going values. The doubler would often bid 3NT with stoppers in the opponent's suit.

Responding to a Takeout Double with Interference

A freely-bid suit shows 6+ points and at least a four-card suit. If the takeout double is redoubled, all bids are natural but jump suit bids are now preemptive, not strong, showing at least five cards and 0-9 points.

How high to play takeout doubles is a matter of partnership agreement. Many partnerships play takeout doubles through the 3♠. A double above the bid of three spades is then taken as penalty. However, some may play it to the level of 5♦. You should discuss the level with your partner.

In the preceding three examples there was no interference; suppose the bidding now goes:

1♣ - Dbl - 1NT - (?). Now what do you bid?

You again invoke the Michaels cuebid of 2♣ in the balancing seat for the first two hands; however, with hand (3), a double is used to show the two lower ranking suits (hearts and diamonds). Note you must be at least 4-4 to use the cuebid or the double.

If the opponents open a diamond and the bidding goes 1♦ - Dbl - 1NT - (?), again 2♦ shows the majors and a double shows clubs and hearts.

The bids may also be used with a major suit opening where now a cuebid of the major shows the other major and a minor and again a double is used to show the lower ranking suits. Be careful here since if partner does not have the major, you are at the three levels in a minor. You should have 10-12 points to cuebid the major.

Rebids by Doubler

When making a takeout double, remember, partner may have nothing. You have forced partner to bid. Partner may have no more than nine starting points. After a minimal response, you will need at least 16+ points for game in partner's bid suit. You can invite with 16-18 starting points. With 19-20 or 21+ jump, bid at the three - or four-level, respectively. If partner bids at the two-level, make a single raise with 16-19 starting points and a double jump to game in a major with 20+ points.

Summary:

With a Minimum Hand (12-15 points)

- Responder made the cheapest possible response—pass
- Responder jump, pass, raise to invite or bid game, you must decide

With a Medium Hand (16-18 points)

- Responder made the cheapest possible response—raise one level to invite, game is still possible.
- Responder has jumped, raise to game

With a Maximum Hand (19-21 points)

- Responder has made a cheapest possible response—jump raise
- Responder has jumped, raise to game

Takeout double over weak two bids

Playing Fishbein, recall that a double is for penalty, one has to bid the next level suit for takeout. If you do not play Fishbein, a double is for takeout. While in most cases you would bid your best suit, suppose you have zero points; partner doubles the bid of 2♠ and you have a weak hand with four hearts:

♠ 872 ♥ 7654 ♦ 983 ♣ 876

What do you do? You cannot bid 3♥; you have less than six points. You bid 2NT* as a relay bid which is part of the Lebensohl or Transfer Lebensohl systems played over interference to 1NT (Chapter 9). It asks partner to bid 3♣* so you may sign off at the three-level in a suit with no interest in game. If the doubler does not accept the relay and bids any other suit, it shows a 20+ HCP hand. If you do not bid 2NT, but bid a suit at the three-level you are showing about 6 HCP.

2NT followed by 3NT denies four of the other majors and shows a stopper in the weak suit bid. A direct cuebid of the weak suit shows a very strong hand; it is game forcing.

Fishbein is played the in direct seat over a weak two or three-level bid and does not use 2NT. 2NT over a weak two bid always shows a strong 1 NT opener (14/15-17 points).

Doubling 1NT (penalty or takeout)

The double of a 1NT opening may be for takeout or penalty. Whether the double is for penalty or takeout usually depends on the convention you play as defense over notrump. Several approaches will be discussed in Chapter 9. However, before we get there, let me explain what you need to double a 1NT bid for penalty with a balanced hand.

If the opponents are playing 15-17, you need 18+ to double for penalty.

If the opponents are playing 12-14 or 10-12, you need 15+ to double for penalty.

I am of the opinion that in the direct seat, one should always double the contract of 1NT for penalty when you can or if not pass, but in the balancing seat and the bidding has gone 1NT—pass—pass then it should be for takeout. In either case, the double must be alerted.

The experts do not agree on whether a double should be for penalty or takeout; however, all have opinions. You may read about it at: www.clairebridge.com/defensevsnt.htm.

Some partnerships use the simple rule that all doubles when partner has not bid are for takeout. Your agreements must be discussed.

Examples

(1) The opponents open 1♦ with either of the following hands you must make a takeout double with shortness in diamonds.

♠ AK65 ♥ KQ65 ♦ 98 ♣ K42   ♠ Q972 ♥ AK65 ♦ 7 ♣ KJ43

You will pass any bid partner makes, even if it is clubs, you do not have sufficient values (16/17+) to double and bid.

However, with the following hand you would again double:

♠ AKJ1094 ♥ KQ ♦ 7 ♣ AK87

and bid spades. If the opponents opened 1NT, you would double for penalty.

(2) The bidding goes 1♣—double—pass—(What do you bid?)

a) ♠ 652 ♥ K5 ♦ KQ82 ♣ A976   you can bid 1♦ or because you have a stopper, try bidding 1NT. You do not want to play in a minor.

b) ♠ 652 ♥ 75 ♦ KQ982 ♣ 762   you have a weak hand, bid 1♦.

c) ♠ 542 ♥ K5 ♦ KQ1082 ♣ AK7   you have a strong hand, bid 2NT. You do not want to play in a diamond game

d) ♠ 92 ♥ 10987 ♦ K865 ♣ 632   bid 2NT as a relay to three clubs

e) ♠ AKJ1094 ♥ KQ ♦ 7 ♣ 8765   bid 4♠, jump to game to show values

(3) The bidding goes:

South	West	North	East
1♦	double	pass	1♠
Pass	(?)		

And you have a four-card spade suit, do you raise or pass? With 16+, raise, otherwise pass; remember you forced your partner to bid.

(3) Suppose the bidding goes:

West	North	East	South
		1♦	double
pass	1♠	2♦	(?)

You again hold four spades, but you have less than 16+ points. Do you pass or bid on? Do not let the opponents steal the bid; you are only at the two-level with the master suit. You must bid 2♠, even vunerable versus non-vulnerable. Never let the opponents play at the two-level holding the master suit or if they do not have a fit.

(4) The bidding goes:

South	West	North	East
	1♦	pass	1♠
2♥	pass	pass	(?)

And you again hold spades ♠ AK543 ♥ 7 ♦ 985 ♣ AQ76. What do you do? You have two choices—support diamonds or double for takeout, hoping partner will bid spades with only two.

(5) The bidding goes:

South	West	North	East
			1♥
pass	pass	Double	(?)

And you hold ♠ 9876 ♥ 7 ♦QJ832 ♣ K87. What do you do? The opponents have passed, so your partner must have a very good hand; even though you have four spades, bid your best suit, bid 2♦. If partner does not bid spades, bid them at the next turn.

Chapter 7

Overcalls

Overcalls are complicated and countless books have been written about them. However, there are basically only four common types of overcalls: simple overcalls, notrump overcalls, jump overcalls, and two-suited overcalls (in Chapter 5, we discussed two-suited overcalls: Unusual 2NT and Michaels Cuebids, but not the responses to the bids).

The 1NT overcall

The ACBL regulations state that a direct overcall of 1NT shows 15-18 starting points and a stopper in the opponent's bid suit. This is considered "standard" and need not be alerted. For now, let's assume you are playing the standard approach. Then the bids for a notrump overcall are as follows.

15-18	Overcalls 1NT
19-20	Double and then bid Notrump
21-23	Double and then jump in Notrump
24-26	Double and rebid 3NT (or double and cuebid)

If you play the "standard overcall" strong 1NT bid, one next has to ask whether or not you play systems on or off. This must be marked on your convention card.

Systems On or Off

ON

Most partnerships play that all systems are on which means you do not differentiate between a 1NT openings from the overcall of 1NT. Thus, Stayman, Jacoby Transfer, etc. are all in effect.

OFF

Alternatively, you may play that systems are off. If you do, one does not use Stayman or any of the transfer bids. Why take this approach? Are not the two situations the same? No.

Consider this: If your LHO opens 1♠ and your partner overcalls 1NT, you can only play one of the remaining three suits at the two-level, and that's hearts. What if you want to play two diamonds or two clubs? You can't if you play systems on.

If your LHO has about twelve starting points and your partner has sixteen, then there are only about twelve points left for your RHO and you. Sometimes you don't get your fair share, right?

Take a look at your partner's hand and yours.

Opener   ♠ KJ9 ♥ AJ107 ♦QJ8 ♣ K87
Responder   ♠ 876 ♥ 7 ♦109762 ♣ 5643

Where do you think it plays best? Not 1NT. Your hand has no value for partner, but if you play it in two diamonds, your hand can take several tricks. If the A-Q of spades and the ♣A are on your left, you will make two diamonds.

If you don't play natural bids at the two-level, you will either have to pass and apologize for such a poor hand or play at the three-level. Good luck.

Suppose you have a good hand? When you hold points there are several ways to show them.

You can cuebid the opponent's suit and partner should respond as though it were Stayman. You can discover a 4-4 fit by using a cuebid, the convention is called Cuebid Stayman.

You can bid 2NT with an invitational hand that is balanced, and of course you can always bid 3NT.

You can also jump to the three levels with an unbalanced hand and a good suit. Let your partner decide what to do.

Summary

When you have some points, you don't have a problem playing Systems On. It's when you don't have them, which is more likely, that you need a way to find the best contract using Systems Off. Rather than playing in a hopeless notrump contract, you might consider not playing Systems On, your partner overcalls 1NT and bids naturally. If you only have 4-8 points and a balanced hand, you should pass.

You have to discuss with your partner whether Systems are ON or OFF after a 1NT overcall.

Over 1NT, some play that a bid of 2NT shows a 1NT hand (14/15-17), it is not unusual for the minors. Be careful; it must be discussed with your partners.

1NT overcalls in the balancing seat (Range/Inquiry Stayman)

When playing 2/1, the bid of 1NT in the balancing seat usually shows 10/11-14 HCP. However, if partner doubles and then bids 1NT, he should have 15-17 HCP when playing a strong notrump 2/1 system. With 18-19 HCP, a balancing 2NT bid is used. To show 20-21 HCP, one doubles and bids 2NT. This usually works well when the opponents open with a minor; however, when opening with a major there is less room to bid since partner must now bid at the two level.

To solve this problem, over a major suit opening bid the balancing notrump bidder usually has more values, 14/15-16 HCP. To avoid getting too high, one uses the Range/Inquiy Stayman convention. Now a bid of 2♣ is not only Stayman, but also and asking bid. With 10/11-14 HCP, you make the normal response of 2♦ with no 4-card major or two of the major if you have one. If however you are in the 14/15-16 HCP range you bid 2NT, delaying your normal Stayman response. Partner next continues with the re-Stayman bid of 3♣ if he wants to know if you have a four card major.

Suit Overcalls

A simple overcall at the one-level shows 8-15/16 starting points. A one-level overcall usually shows a 5+ card suit and one of the top two honors (ace or king). Why do you need one of the top two honors? The bid always suggests an opening lead if you do not win the contract. If you do not satisfy this criterion, it is best to pass and wait for partner to bid. **Do not overcall with a jack high six-card suit.** With 16-17+ starting points, one doubles and bids. If you have a medium sized hand, you may again double and pass partner's bid suit.

Many duplicate bridge players are afraid to overcall with a 4-card major. This may be because they are afraid they will be penalized, or they are a afraid partner will raise with only three card support, or if after passing they may be afraid partner will return to the major suit bid. All these fears are unfounded.

The advantages of the major overcall are that it is lead directing, allows one to compete aggressively for a part score, allows one to get a bid in early even if one has a five card minor, and often disturbs the bidding of the opponents.

When overcalling with a four card major one may use the following guidelines.

1. The four card major overcall should only be made at the one level.
2. The overcall major should have 3 of the top 5 honors with an ace or king.
3. Overcall with a good hand (10+ HCP) and a poor suit, only two of the top three honors in the major.

4.   Overcall at the two level with 12+ HCP.

Examples of major suit holdings at the one level:

AJ107   KQJ6   AKJ8

Holding only AJ93, one needs 12+ HCP.

Overcalls at the two-level require both a great hand and a good suit and should have 12+ starting points.

Responding to a Suit Overcalls (Major or Minor)

With 3+ card support, provided the opponents pass, you should:

Raise one level	with 7-9 starting points
Jump-raise	with 10-11 starting points
Bid game	with 12+ starting points

With no major suit fit, bid notrump provided you have a stopper in the opponent's bid suit.

1NT	with 8-10 starting points
2NT	with 11-12 starting points
3NT	with 13+ starting points

If you do not have a stopper, or three-card support for partner's overcall suit, bid your own five-card suit if you have 9+ starting points. How do you play a new suit? You may play it Forcing for one round, Non-forcing constructive, or Non-forcing (see the back of your convention card). What is the meaning of a cuebid of the opponent's suit?

In general, a cuebid of the opponent's suit is always forcing. All good hands start with a cuebid! However, the responses to a major overcall and a minor overcall are different.

Let's look at the major overcall, the bidding goes:

1♣ - 1♠ - pass - (?)

1NT	8-10 starting points, with club stopper and non-forcing
2♣	asking bid, how good is your overcall (shows fit with 6-10 HCP)
2♦/2♥/2♠	non-forcing
2NT	11-12 starting points, with club stopper and non-forcing
3♣	**Fit Bid forcing with 4-card support**
3♦/3♥	Very good suit, non-forcing constructive
3♠	Preemptive non-forcing

3NT   13+ starting points, to play with stopper

If partner overcalls diamonds, you can follow the same general rules as above. However, if you have stoppers in the opponent's suit and 10+ starting points, you should consider not raising partner's suit but instead bid notrump. Notrump will often be the easiest game to make, especially if you have at least a partial fit with partner's suit (a doubleton honor, for example).

Responding to a Weak Jump Overcall

Partner's jump overcall is preemptive, so you need a fit and quick trick (aces and kings) to consider a game. If you're weak or if you lack support for partner's suit, you should generally pass. If you do have a fit (three-card support) and a few tricks, you can make a simple raise below game. A raise is not invitational; it is only furthering the preemptive bid. Partner will always pass a simple raise.

Overcall or Double Revisited

When you overcall, partner does not know whether you have eight or sixteen starting points while a double usually shows at least twelve starting points. What is the "best" strategy?

Advantages of Overcalling

1) It is usually lead directing.

You should have an ace or a king in the bid suit! Do not overcall with junk. However, if you have two bids and an opening hand, it is usually better to double provided you have support for the other three suits.

For example, with the hand: ♠975 ♥975 ♦ AK1096 ♣ 75, you would overcall 1♦ after the opponents bid 1♣.

But, with the hand: ♠K75 ♥A75 ♦ AK1096 ♣ 75, it would be better to double. Telling partner you have at least an opening hand and support for the other three suits is much better than telling him to lead a diamond.

Suppose partner has the hand: ♠642 ♥KQ9864 ♦ 4 ♣ A84 and you overcall a diamond. The bidding went: 1♣ - 1♦ - 3♣ - (?), partner would probably pass fearing a misfit and only moderate values. However, if you instead double so the auction was: 1♣ - X - 3♣ - (?), partner would confidently bid 4♥.

What do you do in the fourth seat? The bidding goes 1♥ - P - 1♠ - (?). And you hold the following hand: ♠8732 ♥K ♦ KQJ9 ♣ K764. Your partner has passed and you are not going to outbid the opponents. Clearly, a lead directing bid of 2♦ is better than a takeout double. In addition, your bid will certainly not be doubled for penalty.

2) An overcall does not give the opponents (or your partner) information about your distribution.

This may be important for declarers when deciding to finesse a queen in a suit that you have doubled for takeout. This is the price you pay for describing your hand accurately with a double. You have to weigh what information you need to give partner versus the opponents.

3) You can sometimes bid a second suit, clarifying your distribution.

Suppose you hold the following hand: ♠AK875 ♥7 ♦ AJ10652 ♣ A and the RHO opens 1♣. What do you bid?

You have to overcall a diamond and then bid spades (reverse by overcaller). You have two very good suits, always bid the longer. However, if instead you had the hand: ♠AK875 ♥7 ♦ 987652 ♣ A, bid 1♠, you do not have the strength to reverse.

Disadvantages of Overcalling

1) The bidding may die before you can show support for the other suits.

This may happen if you have a strong hand on which you have decided to overcall instead of double. Sometimes it is better to describe your two-suited hand which may only happen if the bidding continues.

2) A fit in another suit may be missed. It happens.

3) Defensive values are undervalued or overvalued.

Partner does not know whether you have eight or sixteen starting points, this is a significant drawback when you have support for all unbid suits. Even though you are very distributional, it is sometimes better to double and take a change since partner knows you have at least an opening bid.

4) You may get doubled and go down when you have a fit elsewhere.

Advantages of Doubling

1) Shows high card strength.

A double shows at least twelve starting points and hence defensive values; partner better able to place the contract with this information.

---

2) Allows partner to double the opponents.

Even though you have twelve starting points, you should not always double. For example, suppose you have the following hand: ♠ Q42 ♥KQ109 ♦ KQJ75 ♣ 5. With this hand you should bid 1♦ over 1♣. Even with twelve starting points, you do not have defensive values to double.

3) Allows partner to bid a suit confidently, knowing you will have at least three-card support.

4) A new suit bid by you later shows a hand too strong for a simple overcall.

For example, the opponents open 1♠ and you have five hearts and 17+ points. Do not overcall, double and bid hearts. If your partner now bids 4♥ and the opponents go to four spades, you can then double for penalty.

5) Avoids being doubled when you have a better fit.

If you overcall and are doubled, usually you just have to sit and take your medicine. It is often too dangerous to scramble around trying to find the right spot. Starting off with a double, you have a better chance of finding a fit.

Disadvantages of Doubling

1) Partner may miss the best lead.

This is especially true against a notrump contract. However, unless you have a very top-heavy suit, doubling may in fact be your best chance of getting the defense off to the right start.

2) You might misjudge your fit.

It is easy to make the wrong decision as to how high to bid, or what defensive values you have, as you may have a nine-or ten-card fit which you think is only an eight-or nine-card fit. This issue is often overlooked. For example, over a heart opening, you have a choice of bidding 2♦ or to double with the following hand: ♠Q86 ♥98 ♦ AKJ107 ♣ J64. Again, any bid may work; however, if you overcall and partner is all diamonds, he will know either to preempt or keep quiet hoping the opponents misgauge their fit. Let's look at an example.

	♠ J752	
	♥ J75	
	♦ Q1984	
	♣ 9	
♠ K1043	**N**	♠ A9
♥ Q6	**W** **E**	♥ AK1043
♦ 632	**S**	♦ Void
♣ AK73		♣ Q10852
	♠ Q86	
	♥ 98	
	♦ AKJ107	
	♣ J64	

With east-west vulnerable, if south doubles east's 1♥ opening, the bidding might go:

West	North	East	South
		1♥	Dbl
Rdbl	1♠	2♣	Pass
3♣	Pass	5♦*	Pass
5NT	Pass	7♣	All Pass

* Exclusion Keycard Blackwood, asking partner not to count keycard in the diamonds.

However, if instead you bid 2♦, things may go:

West	North	East	South
		1♥	2♦
Dbl	6♦	Dbl	

Down four for =800 for east-west, instead of +2140.

The material in this section is based upon information in the book by Neil Kimelman (2008) "Improve your Bidding Judgment" by Master Point Press. A must-read for any serious bridge players since bidding is where you often win or lose at the game. There are many more topics in the book to help bridge players know when to be passive or aggressive. Neil Kimelman is a Canadian expert bridge player.

Cuebidding Principles

Cuebids have become an integral part of contract bridge and you do not have to be an expert or an advanced player to use them. They allow one to reach the appropriate level for a part-score, game, or slam. They are used to show support for partner's overcall, responses to takeout doubles, looking for notrump contracts, getting to slams, as conventions and more. There are more than fifty conventional cuebids listed in the Official Encyclopedia of Bridge. We review a few common uses that may help to improve your partnership agreements. A comprehensive overview of cuebidding is provided by Dee Berry (author of "Two over One in a Nutshell") in her recent book "Cuebids in a Nutshell" (2008) published by PDI Bridge Supplies.

How good is your overcall?

In most bidding systems, overcalls in an unbid suit are natural and usually include a five-card or longer suit with 8-16 HCP for an overcall at the one-level and 10-17 HCP for an overcall at the two-levels. Given these wide ranges, how good is the overcall? To find out, one may make an asking cuebid! For example, suppose the bidding goes 1♣ - 1♠ - pass - **2♣.**

The bid of two clubs to the overcaller is the only forcing bid partner may make and is asking partner how good is your overcall. It usually promises 6-10 Dummy support points with a fit (3+ cards). A jump cuebid is most often played as a limit raise with four-card support; however, some play the jump fit cuebid as a Mixed Raise with four trumps and less than a limit raise (8-11) and some defensive values.

A rebid of the suit (by the overcaller) at the lowest level conveys a "minimum overcall." Any other bid (a new suit, notrump, or a jump) shows a sound overcall with an opening hand (12-15/16 HCP). With more points, the overcaller would double and bid! If the opener doubles the advancer's cuebid (showing a good suit), a pass by the overcaller shows the lightest overcall, a rebid of the suit shows a respectable overcall, and a new suit or jump shows approximately an opening bid or better.

In the prior example, the 2♣ bidder's hand may look like ♠QJ5 ♥K9 ♦KQJ876 ♣975. If the overcaller has the hand ♠AK876 ♥Q4 ♦A43 ♣J82, a bid of 2♥ shows an opening bid or better and is forcing for one round. Alternatively, one may have the hand: ♠AK1098 ♥Q4 ♦543 ♣AJ8 and bid 2NT which promises at least one stopper in the opponent's suit and preferable two. Some may even bid 3NT; alternatively, with the hand ♠AK1086 ♥AQJ64 ♦54 ♣8, one may bid 3♥, a game forcing bid, showing five hearts. A bid of 2♠ would show a minimum overcall, for example: ♠AK1087 ♥54 ♦10965 ♣AJ. And, if the opener were to double the bid of two clubs, the overcaller would pass.

Cuebids by responder (after Opponent's Overcall)

A cuebid by responder shows a limit raise or better in opener's suit, with at least three-card support for opener's major suit or at least four-card (and preferable five-card) support for opener's minor suit.

1♥ - 1♠ - 2♠ promises a limit raise or better in hearts. Responder may hold:

(1) ♠842 ♥K763 ♦AK65 ♣54

(2) ♠94 ♥Q875 ♦Q864 ♣AKQ6

(3) ♠A54 ♥987 ♦AQ109 ♣Q87

A cuebid is a one round force. With the second hand, some responders would prefer to bid 2♣ since that bid is forcing (any new suit by an unpassed responder is forcing) and hearts could be supported later. And, with the third hand, some would perhaps bid 2♦ for the same reason.

If the cuebid forces your partner to the four-level, it shows an opening bid or better.

1♥ - 1♠ - 3♠ shows a game forcing heart raise with at least three-card supports. Hands could be:

(A) ♠92 ♥QJ76 ♦9874 ♣AKQ

(B) ♠K5 ♥A632 ♦A543 ♣K75

(C) ♠876 ♥AK7 ♦A8432 ♣K6

In 2/1, a jump to three or four hearts is preemptive showing at least four trumps and weak, less than nine starting points.

What if the bidding went 1♥ - 1♠ - pass - 4♥? A double jump cuebid is a splinter in support of spades and game forcing.

Sandwich 1NT/2NT and Skew Cuebids (Hess Bids)

Sandwich 1NT/2NT

The bid of 1NT is usually made in the fourth seat after your partner has passed and the opponents have bid two suits at the one-level. It must be alerted and shows five-five or better in the unbid suits and less than a full opener. You are usually willing to play at the two-level (eight losers non-vulnerable, seven losers vulnerable).

With the same distribution (five-five or better) and 16+ starting points, you bid a Sandwich 2NT (also called a Roman Jump Overcall). Now, you are willing to play at the three-level.

Example 1: 1♦/pass/1♥/1NT with ♠KJ987 ♥7 ♦109 ♣QJ543, bid 1NT.

Suppose instead of the hand in the Example 1, you have the hand:

Example 2: ♠KQ987 ♥K7 ♦A ♣AKJ87. Now, one would bid 2NT.

When one is four-four in the two unbid suits or five-four in the unbid suits, the Sandwich NT bids are replaced by a Takeout Double or Skew Cuebids, respectively.

Skew Cuebids (also called Hess Cuebids)

When the opponents have bid two different suits, then a cuebid of the higher ranking suit shows five cards in the higher unbid suit and four cards in the lower unbid suit. A cuebid of the lower bid suit shows five cards in the lower bid suit and four cards in the higher unbid suit. Use this bid instead of the Sandwich 2NT bid to show shape and extra values, 16+ starting points.

Takeout Double

The takeout double has more HCP and less shape. For example, the distribution may be: ♠KQ76 ♥98 ♦456 ♣AKJ2, more than an opening hand when partner is forced to bid at the three-level. But, if partner is forced to bid at only the two-level, the doubler need only 12+ starting points, an opening hand.

Overcall

The previous bids are used to represent shape and values. In general, the shapelier the hand, the lighter the values may be. An overcall of an unbid suit at the two-level will show length in the suit with little value. As in the case of the sandwich NT bid, if the bid is made at the two-level, one must again have about eight losers non-vulnerable and seven losers vulnerable. A three-level bid requires extra values.

Some Examples

1♦/pass/1♥/1NT	shows clubs and spades with 5-5 shape, but not strength.
1♦/pass/1♥/double	shows clubs and spades with 4-4 shape and opening values.
Pass/1♣/pass/1♠/1NT	shows diamonds and hearts with 5-5 shape, but not strength.
1♠/pass/2♣/2NT	shows diamonds and hearts with 5-5 shape and 16+hcps.
1♠/pass/2♣/2♠	shows hearts and diamonds with 5-4 shape and 16+HCP.
1♠/pass/2♣/3♣	shows diamonds and hearts with 5-4 shape and 16+HCP.

Final Note: In the sequence 1♣, pass, 1♠, pass / pass/1NT, the 1NT bid is not Sandwich; it shows some values and you do not want the opponents to play at the one-level.

Leaping Michaels

Leaping Michaels utilizes the 4♣ and 4♦ bids. Similar to the Michaels cuebid, in case this minor suit overcall is in the opposing suit, both major suits are implied. In case the overcall is not a cuebid, the suit bid plus a major suit is indicated. So, on preempts of the opponents (indicated between brackets), the following applies when playing Leaping Michaels:

(2/3♥) - 4♣: Clubs and spades
(2/3♥) - 4♦: Diamonds and spades
(2/3♠) - 4♣: Clubs and hearts
(2/3♠) - 4♦: Diamonds and hearts
(3♣)   - 4♣: Majors
(3♣)   - 4♦: Diamonds and an undisclosed major
(3♦)   - 4♣: Clubs and an undisclosed major
(3♦)   - 4♦: Majors

All bids show 5-5 shape.
After 3♦ or 4♣, the bid of 4♦ asks for a major. The bids 4♥ and 4♠ are to play. Following 3♣ or 4♦, the bid of 4♥ is played as pass-or-correct.

Some partnerships prefer to interchange the meanings of the 4♣ and 4♦ bids following a 3♣ preempt so that 4♣ denotes diamonds and an undisclosed major. This has the advantage that the 4♦ becomes available to ask for the major suit. The 4♥/4♠ responses may then be played as natural (to play). Discuss this with your partner!

Leaping Michaels can be utilized after natural two-level preempts and also after conventional preempts such as the **Muiderberg Convention,** also called the Dutch Two opening. It is a preemptive opening based on a two-suiter with precisely a five-card major and a minor suit (four-cards or longer). In Muiderberg, the 2♥ opening denotes five hearts and an unknown minor suit, while 2♠ denotes five spades and an unknown minor suit.

It can also be played against a weak 2♦ bid; here, Leaping Michaels may be utilized to good effect:

(2♦) - 4♣: Clubs and an undisclosed major (4♦ asks for the major)
(2♦) - 4♦: Diamonds and an undisclosed major (4♥ is pass-or-correct).

If you currently play 2/1 using Michaels Cuebids, you may want to consider adding the Leaping Michaels Convention.

An alternative to using Leaping Michaels (strong hand) with Michaels (weak hand) is to employ the Liberalized Leaping Michaels Convention. Using this convention, one again uses the Leaping Michaels bids as defined above, but it is now used to show a weak two-suiter with 9-10 HCP. Using the Liberalized Convention, a cuebid of the 2/3 level bid is used to show a strong two-suiter. The bids are flip-flopped. Mike Cappelletti suggested the Liberalized Leaping Michaels Convention in the July 1988 issue of "The Bridge World." The advantage of the convention is that it allows for more bidding room when one has a strong hand and takes less bidding space with a weak hand. Hence, the opponents have less room to investigate slam.

Responding to Michael Cuebids or Unusual 2NT

In Chapter 5, we introduced Michaels Cuebid and Unusual 2NT as overcalls and showed how the opponents (opener and responder) may use cuebids when it is used. The two bids are used with either very strong 5-5 hands or with weak hands in a competitive auction. With between with 12-16 starting points, one may use either an overcall or a double.

Now, we need to discuss advancer responses to the bids. Recall that Michaels shows both majors or a major and a minor. Unusual 2NT shows the two lowest unbid suits, either both minors or a major and a minor.

Let's first look at Michaels:

1) Without a good fit for either of the known suits, give simple preference for the one you like best (or dislike least);
2) With a good fit for a known suit, make a single raise or double jump in a known suit with 12+ starting points;
3) With an even better hand (17+ starting points), cuebid the opponent's suit as a game force bid. The suit will be revealed later;
4) With a strong balanced hand (16+ starting points), and stoppers in opener's suit and the "other" suit, one may bid 3NT
5) After 1♠ - 2♠ or 1♥ - 2♥ overcaller's second suit is not known. A reply of 2NT is forcing and asks which minor is held;
6) A bid in a suit not promised by the overcaller is natural and non-forcing, based on a very long suit. Overcaller will not bid again unless he is extra strong.

When the opponents interfere above the level of 2NT, a bid of 4♣ is a request to play in the minor at the four levels and the bid of 4NT is forcing to game in the minor.

Without interference, a bid of 3NT is to play and the bid of 4NT is Blackwood, no agreed upon suit. A direct cuebid of the opponent's suit shows a strong hand and is game forcing. If your partner bids a suit not bid by the opponents or shown by the cuebid, it is natural and wants to play in the suit bid.

If after a Michaels Cuebid or Unusual 2NT and partner responds with a weak bid and partner bids again, 17+ starting points, like a double and bidding a suit.

The responses to the 2NT overcall are similar.

Reverse Good Bad 2NT

Let's suppose you have the following HAND: ♠ K8754 ♥ 6 ♦ KQ862 ♣ Q2 and the bidding goes:

West	North	East	South
	1♣	pass	1♠
2♥	pass	pass	?

What do you bid?

For this situation, Marty Bergen ("Better Bidding with Bergen," page 112) recommends what he calls the "good-bad" 2NT bid. Originally, following Lebensohl, you would bid 2NT with the hand, followed by 3♦ over partner's relay bid (alert) of 3♣*, while with a stronger hand (10+ starting points), you would bid 3♦ immediately which is forcing for one round. However, based upon two articles in the 1999 "Bridge World," Reverse Lebensohl is now more popular, then a bid of a new suit at the three-level is weaker than bidding 2NT first.

Similarly, the modern tendency for those who play good-bad 2NT is to reverse the bids. Then, the immediate three-level bid (to take up valuable bidding space) shows a weak hand (and is non-forcing) and 2NT, followed by a bid shows a forcing hand. This is called reverse good-bad 2NT. Clearly, the reason for the modern change is that with a weaker hand, you want to get your bid in before the opponents compete further since you are too weak to show your suit at the four-level. When you hold the stronger hand, the opponents are not likely to compete further (and if they do, they may be sorry), so you will be able to finish describing your hand. Because these are new concepts, we consider the (reverse) good-bad - 2NT by opener first. After:

West	North	East	South
			1♦
Pass	1♥	2♠	?

And as opener (south), you have the following hands, from Bergen:

	♠	♥	♦	♣
a)	97	J8	KQJ873	AJ8
b)	97	J8	AKQJ87	A92
c)	97	KJ74	AK952	J10
d)	97	KJ7	AK952	K108
e)	97	AJ92	AKJ92	K8

f)	♠ 97	♥ 8	♦ AK952	♣ AQ843
g)	♠ 97	♥ A	♦ AK952	♣ KJ843
h)	♠ K7	♥ 6	♦ AKJ92	♣ AQJ42
i)	♠ 7	♥A7	♦ AKJ92	♣ AQ842

On hand (a) you would bid 3♦ while with (b) you would bid 2NT; followed by 3♦. With hands (c) or (d), you would bid 3♥ (support doubles do not apply at this level, only usually through 2♥, Chapter 8); hence, a double to show three-card support is not an option. With (e), bid 2NT followed by 3♥.

The only real problem occurs when you as opener have a minor two-suiter. With an average or skimpy 5-5, you would bid 3♣, as in hands (f) or (g). With a very strong minor two-suiter you would start with 2NT and then, over 3♣, bid 3NT with a spade stopper—hand (h)—or cuebid 3♠ without a stopper—hand (i). Both 3♠ and 3NT guarantee five clubs and a very good hand.

Over 2NT by opener, the 3♣ bid by responder is forcing since opener hasn't shown which type of hand he has, so responder must relay to 3♣ over 2NT to find out. With extra values, responder can bid more after opener finishes describing his hand, but with a minimum hand and a long, independent suit of his own, he should rebid his suit (non-forcing) instead of bidding 3♣. For example, suppose as responder you hold:

♠ 875   ♥ QJ10974   ♦ 86   ♣ K10

Bid 3♥, which might enable opener to raise to game with a good hand but skimpy heart support. Add a king to responder's hand and he would be too strong for a non-forcing 3♥ bid, so he must bid 3♣, followed by 3♥ (forcing), if opener's rebid is 3♦.

Following the philosophy of the Wolff sign-off bid, suppose responder bids 3♦, instead of 3♣ after the opener bids 2NT. This would suggest that responder is near minimum with a decent five-card heart suit or a very weak six-card suit. He is not strong enough to bid 3♣ and the 3♥ (forcing), hence he bids the "reverse" check-back bid of 3♦. Now, if the opener has the hand:

♠ A8   ♥ 7   ♦ AQ107654   ♣ KJ8

He would pass. And bid 3♥ with the hand

♠ A8   ♥ 7   ♦ AK754   ♣ Q9

Or bid 4♥ with

♠ A8   ♥K75   ♦ AK10754   ♣ A9

Let us think about how we handle responder's problems with the "reverse" 2NT bid. Suppose the auction goes:

West	North	East	South
	1♦	pass	1♥
2♠	pass	pass	?

And you hold the hand: ♠ J8   ♥ AJ876   ♦ Q75   ♣ K87.

Double on this hand! A double in front of the bidder is for takeout. You don't know whether partner bids 3♥ with three-card support, bids 3♣ (over which you bid 3♦), bids 3♦, or pass (with four spades).

However, with the hand: ♠ J8   ♥ AJ87   ♦ Q75   ♣ K875.

Do not bid 3♥; instead bid 3♦. Because support doubles are not applicable at this level, you have to gamble that partner has five diamonds.

We consider four more examples:

j)   ♠ J8   ♥ AJ84   ♦ 7   ♣ K87542
k)   ♠ J8   ♥ AQJ875 ♦ 7   ♣ J875
l)   ♠ J8   ♥ AQJ875 ♦ 7   ♣ K875
m)   ♠ 8   ♥ AJ876   ♦ Q75 ♣ K875

With hand (j), bid 2NT, intending to pass partner's bid of 3♣. With (k), bid 3♥, expecting partner to pass. With hand (l), bid 2NT, followed by 3♥ to show the kind of hand where you would have bid 3♥, invitational, if LHO had passed. Finally, with hand (m), bid 3♦. Although a double would be for takeout, partner would pass with four spades. You don't like to defend doubled contracts at the two-level when the opponents have eight trumps.

Well, what do you think? Some people even play reverse good-bad 4NT! Partner opens one heart and the RHO bids four spades.

Which do you think would be more useful, playing 4NT as Blackwood or showing extra values? If you choose the latter, 4NT transfers to 5♣, and if responders bids 5♥, it is invitational to slam. While a bid of 5♥ opener should have extra values. A bid of 5♣ is natural and invitational to slam in hearts. With a weak hand, he would bid 4NT and pass 5♣! Similarly, if opener bids 4♠, a double is for takeout/penalty and 4NT is a relay to 5♣.

Reference: Marshall Miles (2002), "Competitive Bidding in the 21st Century," Master Point Press.

Scrambling 2NT

Another use of the 2NT bid is in the auction 1M - pass - 2M - 2NT. The bid of 2NT is for takeout and only played over major suit bids. You usually have no more than two cards in the major bid and it asks partner to bid his four-card suits up-the-line. It allows you to perhaps find a partial contract in a minor or the other major. It may also force the opponents to an un-makeable three-level contract. Playing duplicate bridge, you never allow the opponents to play in a one-level contract, and you normally do not want them to play in a two-level partial. If the two-level bid is announced as constructive, you have to be more careful when vulnerable.

An Overcall System

Following is an overcall system of bids developed by John E. Fout with permission from John Twineham. It is non-standard so be carefull.

When the opponents open the bidding, they have already garnered an advantage. Standard defensive bidding methods generally allow you to compete, but this requires holding a good hand. We never have good hands[1]; we want to compete anyway. The only problem presented to us is that our partner can never take a joke if we're bidding on a distributional hand. The Structure, thus, has been created so that partner will not hang you.

The questions arise: why do we want to compete on these "bad" hands, and isn't that dangerous? We believe that competing at the one and the two level is superior to balancing at the three level which can be very dangerous as both opponents have already communicated their values. One note about our style before we go on: all of our bids are made according to relative vulnerability as it relates to sanity. We aren't insane; we just like to compete. This is what advancer (partner of overcaller) must keep in mind because 90% of the time it will be advancer's job to make the decision about how high to compete on the combined offensive values of the partnership. Advancer should definitely remember that many calls are limited in values, and more importantly do not promise defensive values!

In order to understand this competitive style properly, we encounter several theoretical considerations. The Law of Total Tricks best explains why and how to compete. On most hands we possess at least an eight card fit which usually will allow us to compete successfully at the two level; sometimes we will have two eight card fits which will allow us to compete at the three level. If we have a nine card fit, the three level should be safe, etc. The opponents of course attempt to do the same depending on how big their trump fits are, but there exists a limited number of tricks available because of a limited number of trumps and a limited number of values or working high cards. In essence, on every hand everyone aims to compete to the par spot.

But not everyone truly comprehends the idea of the par spot. People think of it as being a plus position. This is not always the case. Frequently, the par spot translates to out competing the opponents, and actually going minus; for example, we go to three spades over the opponents' three hearts, down one. The opponents can make three hearts. We win. Many times we only have a minus score available, and strive to reduce that minus. It certainly can be difficult to decide how much to bid at certain vulnerabilities in conjunction to reaching the par spot. But having this understanding of the par spot and competing on a greater number of hands, however, over time will lead to better hand evaluation, better judgment and better results.

How are we going to compete more effectively? Using these tools:

Simple Overcalls, No Trump for Takeout, Power Doubles, Roman Jump Overcalls, the two suited cue bid, Intermediate Jump Overcalls, NAMYATS, and a few other gadget bids. Using this structure, it will become apparent that we have found the easiest way to enter effectively into the auction.

The Simple Overcall at the One Level

The simple overcall (SO) occurs most frequently and the inferences drawn from a SO or a pass are many. Because the overcaller has several available bids, making a SO denies possession of the other possible hands, and remember that partner will always take inference. Let's see what this means.

We make a SO for several reasons. We have a suit that we want led; we have too many values to pass, e.g. a good 10-14 hcp; we want to find out which of our suits to lead; we want to preempt at a low level; we have a hand that seems conducive to competition. So what are we overcalling on? Many times one level overcalls only have four card suits, and tend to show length in opener's suit. It denies holding a side five card suit or probably even a four card suit unless you're 4-4, 5-4 or 6-4, and no other available systemic bid describes your hand. As these overcalls are so aggressive, we cautiously raise partner. We thus employ support doubles and redoubles[2] after an overcall and interference. Occasionally, we must conceal three card support on hands people might commonly raise with in standard. Be more conservative especially when holding three small, Jxx or Qxx of LHO's suit which is known as the "Death Holding" or a 4333 hand with a bad six or seven count.

What about suit quality? There exist no specific requirements here except that you hold four cards in that suit. For example, if holding S KQx H T9xx D xx C AKxx, and RHO opens 1 club, we would not pass but rather overcall 1 heart. The average suit quality with which someone would overcall on approximates to KJ9x. Again, these bids are all relative to vulnerability or the ability to get to another spot if necessary.

Responding to a SO—Uncontested Auction

The aggressive nature of our overcalls requires a delicate response structure to handle various possibilities:

1) A 1 over 1 response is not constructive merely suggesting an alternative spot. This strongly suggests 2 or fewer cards in overcaller's suit (check LHO's pulse to find out how few partner has!).

2) 1 No Trump is not natural! It is Lebensohl with three distinct purposes:
   a) Run out to another five card or longer suit[3].
   b) Invitational in a new suit that could not have been bid previously as invitational, or invitational in no trump.
   c) A flower bid in opener's suit (see 3 below); shown by rebidding partner's suit.

3) Non-jumps at the 2 level are flower bids; fit showing with 3+ card trump support, 4+ cards in the bid suit, limit raise values, but non-forcing.

4) Cue-bid of opener's suit is a strong no-fit game try; advancer looks for game either in no trump or in his own suit.

5) Single jumps in suits, even jump cue-bids, are mini-splinters; generally 4+ trumps and around limit raise values (more if subsequent action is taken).

6) 2 No Trump is jacoby style; an opening hand with 4+ trumps; not forcing to game if overcaller responds with a minimum.

Responding to a SO—Contested Auction

The responses are similar but modified. A 1 over 1 tends to be more constructive. A new suit at the two level is a flower bid in that suit or length with that suit and enough values to force a level higher. Cue-bids are a limit raise or better for partner's suit while single jumps are still mini-splinters. Remember that support doubles and redoubles apply and come up quite frequently.

The inferences from partner passing in an auction like this: 1♣ - P - 1♠, are very revealing. It's known that partner could not even compete at the one level. Partner almost surely denies possession of all the hands mentioned in the second paragraph on the SO, and denies also the three-suited takeouts, two-suited hands, etc., as will be described ahead. The hands most likely to be passed are 4x3 hands with length in opener's suit or any hand with opener's suit, very weak hands, and hands with a bad suit and only average values, i.e. Jxxx or worse and 6-9 HCP, depending on the hand.

One Notrump for Takeout (NTO)

All other bid have been centered around the one No Trump Overcall (NTO). The NTO comes up frequently and creates havoc in the opponent's auction while letting us know in what suits we should be competing. The NTO can be described as a light three suited takeout, showing three cards in all the unbid suits, and generally 6-15 HCP at equal vulnerability. The minimum shape here is 4-4-3-2 up to as shapely as 7-3-3-0. People always ask, would you really overcall a NTO with six spades and a stiff club, 6-3-3-1 shape over a one club opening? We say YES, and tell them about the number of times we have buried the opponents' heart fits. Furthermore, you must bid a NTO on these hands; otherwise, partner gets confused about your shape and will be unable to accurately place or accurately defend the hand.

Responses to a NTO—Uncontested Auction

1) Any response in a new suit at the two level is to play. If the NTO bidder raises, expect a shapely max with four card support (in some cases it could be blocking with 5+ card support).

2) Cue-bidding opener's suit first asks partner for a four card major, but if advancer later bids a new suit, then this reveals an invitational sequence for a major but not necessarily invitational for a minor. A follow-up cue-bid by advancer demonstrates a strong interest in game—probably in the suit you've bid—opposite any hand with reasonable cover cards[4].

3) Jumping in a suit at the three level is preemptive even if opposite a maximum, unless bid red versus white. This shows any six card suit or a good five card suit with a little shape.

4) Bidding 2 No Trump over 1 NT tends to show minors, but could be a hand with a minor and a major. This depends on the auction.

All other game or four of a minor bids are to play. Here's an interesting example; at imps both vulnerable, you hold: ♠ Jx ♥ AKTxxx ♦ J9xx ♣ x. Over a one diamond opening by LHO, partner bids a NTO while RHO follows with 2 clubs. You gamble out a 4 heart bid. It goes down one—barely—when partner holds a mere six count, but the opponents are gin for 5 clubs, win 10 imps. Here's another interesting hand from a matchpoint session: ♠ QJxx ♥ Qxxx ♦-♣ QJxxx. Your RHO opens 1 diamond; you bid a NTO. Your LHO doubles, and partner leaps to 5 clubs! What does partner have? You pass, happy for now until your LHO chimes in with 5 hearts while partner and RHO pass it around to you. What does partner have? Well, work it out; with any six card suit partner should bid 3 clubs; with a little shape and a good six card suit that would constitute a 4 club bid. So, partner must have 7 clubs and it seems likely partner has one or fewer hearts. Since partner couldn't hammer five hearts, you're going to have to follow the LTT and bid six clubs with a 12 card fit. Score it up. Partner held: ♠ Kxx ♥-♦ Jxx ♣ AKTxxxx; the kind of hand you would expect. It's unlikely standard bidders could possibly draw these inferences from such a short auction, and find a way to preempt the opponents out of their cheap six diamond save.

Responding to a NTO—Contested Auction

1) The opponents double. We play a runout system that helps us find our eight card fits. Over the double, a direct suit bid by advancer promises a five card suit; a redouble shows exactly four cards in the highest unbid suit. A pass denies either of the above, but advancer could still have a lower four card suit. After advancer's pass, a redouble by overcaller shows possession of a five card or longer suit. Advancer then responds in the lowest suit that would be reasonable to play in opposite a five card suit. If overcaller doesn't redouble, bidding a suit starts a runout looking for 4-4 fits[5].

2) The opponents bid a new suit or raise opener's suit. A double is responsive style showing at least one of the unbid suits—usually the other major—but not promising both. 2 No Trump in these sequences is minors, or the unbid suits with a weaker

hand. It's hard to imagine a hand where bidding 2 NT as natural would be right. Bidding a new suit is non-forcing and usually lead directing. While cue-bidding, then, bidding a new suit shows a good hand.

There will be times when a certain hand will force you to bid a NTO with extra values and the wrong shape to make a Power Double (PD). The PD tends to show a doubleton or greater length in opener's suit because responder will more often convert a PD for penalties. So for example, if holding ♠ AJT9 ♥ AQTx ♦-♣ KQxxx, and your RHO opened 1 Diamond, bid a NTO. Even though you hold considerable extra values, a double on your second turn would communicate these greater values.

The Power Double—Option One

This bid is the easiest to understand and the simplest to use. Essentially, it shows a good 15/16+ HCP that tends to be balanced like a strong no trump overcall, but doesn't guarantee a stopper. Certain hands have been eliminated from the PD as alluded to above, and come up as either an Intermediate Jump Overcall or some of the strong two suited bids.

Responding to the PD is very similar to a standard takeout double except that opener always has a good hand which makes bidding easier for responder. Free bids tend to limit hands in that they contain less than invitational values; any jump would show invitational values as in standard although we invite more frequently with distributional hands. A cue-bid is forcing. Both responder and the PDer follow up with natural bids allowing room to find the best spot. We play South African Transfers: a transfer to four of a major by bidding the corresponding minor, ♣ => ♥ & ♦ => ♠, and this allows the PDer to super accept by bidding the step in between. The ranges for responding in no trump are slightly adjusted as compared to standard: 1 NT = a good 4 to a bad 7, 2 NT = a good 7 to a bad 9, 3 NT = 10-14, etc. This works out well because many times we right side the no trump, forcing the strong hand to be on lead, resulting in an overtrick. Notice that we also avoid the danger of overcalling a no trump and getting doubled off for penalties.

A definite advantage to the PD comes from the ability to penalize the opponents at a low level, especially if we're white and they're RED. For example, if holding ♠ Kxx ♥ Axx ♦ QJ9x ♣ xxx and partner made a PD over LHO's 1 diamond opening, we would float the double. We'll make 3 NT, but LHO won't enjoy playing this one out of his hand. Floating the double is probably right on two types of hands. The type of hand given in the example that's all primed, balanced with a couple trump tricks or a hand with just LHO's suit and no side suit precluding your side from having a big fit. These aggressive passes have been successful; a further benefit develops from passing these doubles. If opener runs from the double, it's a reasonable possibility that their bid was psychic and partner would now play any of your bids in that suit as natural. It becomes very difficult for the opponents to dink around as we can draw so many more inferences from an auction than in standard.

The Power Double—Option Two

Another alternative system for the PD is to treat is as if your partner opened a strong one notrump with 15-17 HCP. Now you play the PD exactly as you did with your strong notrump system with all transfers on. However, is best now not to play 4-way transfers? But, Texas tranfer bids and Lebensohl (or Transfer Lebensohl) is on.

The Two Level Overcalls

The TLO is kind of a tweener bid. Sometimes it fits right into our system while other times it resembles more closely a standard TLO. If an Intermediate overcall is available, then a TLO is either a more or less standard overcall—with only a five card suit—or it is a preemptive bid[6]. If there's no Intermediate available, then it's more difficult to tell exactly what the overcaller has—especially when the hand appears to be inappropriate for a PD or other action—which could be anywhere from a preempt to an ok intermediate.

The best way to respond to this bid is to treat the TLO as a standard overcall, but try not to hang partner. Maybe have a little extra for a natural 2 NT, and try not to raise on a bad hand with honor doubleton for support. Two level bids in a new suit aren't forcing, which is different from standard, but partner will strive to raise you with a good hand and support. In competition, we play that a double or a redouble by advancer shows a good raise to three of partner's suit while the direct raise is merely blocking, not guaranteeing values. A cue-bid in these sequences just promises a good hand either in support of partner or in another suit.

The Roman Jump Overcall

The two cheapest jump overcalls over a one level bid by opener show the suit bid and the higher touching suit with generally 6-15 HCP. There will always be at least nine cards in the two suits. If there are only 9 cards, the lower ranking will always have five cards and the higher ranking will have four. The bids are as follows with minimum holdings and tendencies:

> 2♦/1♣: 5 diamonds & often 4 hearts
> 2♥/1♣: 5 hearts & often 4 spades
> 2♥/1♦: 5 hearts & often 4 spades
> 2♠/1♦: 5 clubs & 4 spades; 5-5 if vul
> 2♠/1♥: 5 clubs & 4 spades; 5-5 if vul
> 3♣/1♥: 5 clubs & 4 diamonds; often 5-5
> 3♣/1♠: 5 clubs & 4 diamoonds; often 5-5
> 3♦/1♠: 5 diamonds & 4 hearts; often 5-5

The point ranges and limitations are very sensitive to relative vulnerability. Non-vulnerable vs. vulnerable opponents, 2♥/1♣ with ♠ Jxxxxx ♥ Txxxxx ♦ x ♣ - , would be acceptable. Vulnerable vs. non-vulnerable opponents, 2♥/1♣ with ♠ KJxx ♥ AJxxx ♦ Qx ♣ KQ, would be reasonable, as opposed to a double, especially opposite a passed partner. One hand that you will never have is 4-5-3-1 shape with shortness in opener's suit because that is a NTO.

Responding to a RJOC—Uncontested Auction

1) Cue-bid shows the best possible hand; either interested in one of overcaller's suits or the fourth suit. Responding in the cheapest possible fashion shows the worst hand by overcaller. Certain responses are logical. For example, if the auction proceeded 1♦ - 2♥ - P - 3♦; P - ?, then a 3♥ response shows any minimum, 3♠ shows a 5-5 relative minimum, 3 NT shows relative extras with a diamond stopper (probably 4-5-3-1 shape), 4♣/♦ both show relative maximums with shortness in that suit, and 4♥ shows 6 hearts and 4 spades with a little extra.

2) 2NT response promises at least invitational values, and leaves more room to investigate. It also tends to show interest in the higher ranking suit. Again, follow the maxim that the cheaper the response, the worse the hand overcaller has. Jumps are still like in the cue-bid above, showing shortness and extras7.

3) Any raise of either the higher ranking or the lower ranking suit is blocking whether a single or double raise. A double jump of the higher ranking suit is mildly invitational red v. white.

4) Bidding the fourth suit as a non-jump is non-forward going but a single jump in the fourth suit would be a splinter while a game bid in the fourth suit would be to play. This can be a little confusing, but doesn't come up very often.

Responding to a RJOC—Contested Auction

1) If the opponents double, redouble is equivalent to a cue-bid above. Pass is to play. Any other bid is essentially as above.

2) If the opponents raise or bid the 4th suit, a double replaces the cue bid. A double at a very high level just shows values. Any raises of the higher ranking suit aren't necessarily invitational, but remember advancer is under pressure. We would probably re-raise to game with a maximum.

We have auctions where responder quickly leaps to game following a RJOC. What frequently happens on these hands is that no one knows who can make what, nor do the opponents have the courage to double us, fearing that it will be a lucky make. Many times we go down two, maybe even vulnerable. Even so, most times the opponents have a game in a side suit, and can't find it because responder is forced to pass on certain hands over a RJOC while opener can't take action at the four or five level. We thus have an effective tool for finding good sacrifices; sometimes even good sacrifices versus their partscores. Try to utilize this preemption whenever possible.

The Two Suited Cue Bid (QB)

This bid shows the two suits left out by the RJOC, or the suits above and below the cue bid suit. The only difference between the QB and the RJOC is that the upper range to the QB remains unlimited. Here's a list of the suits shown:

2♣/1♣: 5 diamonds & 4 spades
2♦/1♦: 5 hearts & 4 hearts
2♥/1♥: 5 diamonds & 4 spades
2♠/1♠: 5 clubs & 4 hearts; often 5-5

The responses for these are exactly the same as for the RJOC, but overcaller, here, has to remember his hand is unlimited unlike the RJOC. If advancer makes any forward going motion, make sure you keep bidding with a rock crusher.

The 2 No Trump Overcall

The 2NT bid shows a strong two suited hand. One suit is always known, which is the non-touching suit, over 1 club it's hearts and over 1 diamond it's spades and vice versa. What do we mean by strong, a hand that has fewer than 4 1/2 AKQ losers, according to the Losing Trick Count—LTC. Here's an example 2NT bid over a 1 heart opening: ♠ A ♥ x ♦ AK9x ♣ KQT9xxx. This is a pretty good three loser hand; the hand has a loser in every suit outside of spades. Slams would be a pretty good bargain opposite an ace and queen fourth or fifth in either minor. As it turned out, we were in slam opposite the ace of hearts, JTxx of diamonds and a stiff club, which worked when the diamond hook was on through the opening bidder. Although the 2NT can be off-shape as in the example, the normal would be 5-5 or a good 6-4, like ♠ x ♥ QJTxx ♦ AKQxxx ♣ x. The advantage we have comes from quickly describing our hand, allowing advancer to make a good decision even with a modicum of values. It's never this easy in standard.

Responding to 2NT—Uncontested Auction

1) Bid of known suit is to play with a very weak hand.
2) Bidding the cheapest non-cuebid suit also shows a weak hand looking to play in the back suit.
3) Bypassing the cheaper non-cuebid suit implies an ok hand for the higher suit and a tolerance to play in the anchor suit, but essentially it's still weak.
4) Cue-bid asks for further description; tends to be a good invitation or better. Doesn't promise more than 1 trick, since 2NT has 4 1/2 losers or fewer.
5) Jump in known suit either to play in game or invitational if not already game.
6) Jump in unknown suit or opener's suit is a splinter for overcaller's known suit.

Responding to 2NT—Contested Auction

1) If the opponents bid a suit:
   a) Bid of anchor suit is to play—weak.
   b) Double is the same as cue bid if anchor suit could be bid at 3 level. Value showing if anchor suit cannot be bid at 3 level, and tends to deny fit for anchor suit.
2) If the opponents double:
   a) Bidding anchor suit is to play; redouble is the same as cue bid above.
   b) Pass forces a redouble or bid of second suit if lower than anchor.

These auctions come up quite infrequently, but are awesome when they do. Just be familiar with the general process involved and go from there. When these auctions come up, remember to look at the potential cover cards in your hand because many of these positional games and slams roll home as the points have already been located.

The Intermediate Jump Overcall

Bids at the 3 level when higher than the two cheapest jump shifts show a single suited hand with the values to bid to the 3 level in competition. The hands generally range from 12 HCP and a 7 card suit to a bad 17 HCP with a six card suit9. Suit quality is generally about a 1 loser maximum. The available bids are: 3♦-3♥-3♠/1♣, 3♣-3♥-3♠/1♦, 3♦-3♠/3♥ and 3♥/1♠. Treat with respect to vulnerability. In a major, one top trick and a fit by responder is usually sufficient to bid game vulnerable vs. nonvulnerable, but nonvulnerable vs. vulnerable even 1 & 1/2 tricks with a fit would probably be insufficient (overcaller has a NAMYATS bid available showing 8 to 8 1/2 tricks). All game bids are to play, and 4 level bids below game are usually slam tries for overcaller's suit.

Miscellany

Namyats

Bids at the 4 level are NAMYATS style showing 8 to 8-1/2 playing tricks. Bid 4 of the corresponding minor to show the strong hand while bidding 4 of the major shows the more preemptive hand: 4♣ => 4♥ and 4♦ = > 4♠. Over 1♥ and 1♠, 4♣ and 4♦ are normal 4 minor preempts.

Responding to NAMYATS

1) Accepting the transfer denies interest in slam.
2) Bidding the step in between, shows slam interest
3) Bidding a new suit asks for a control in bid suit; 4NT=RKC

2 Spade Jump Over 1 Club

This is the only existing jump preempt available below the 4 level; treat this as you would in standard. A 1 spade overcall of 1 club thus tends to deny the preemptive style hand.

3 Level Jump Cue Bid

One of the easiest bids in the system asks advancer for a stopper in the bid suit and tends to show a long minor with a couple outside cards.

Alerts in the Overcall Structure

Clearly, many calls in the structure are alertable as they differ greatly from standard practices, such as a NTO. An alert "problem" materializes from our natural overcalls. Even though they are natural, they still diverge from standard whether or not you happen to hold an unusual hand systemic for us). We believe it's only fair to alert these calls; generally, we are only alerting the opponents to the negative inferences from the call. This unfortunately elicits confusion. The best way to avoid this is to try and pre-alert the opponents to our unusual methods. When the opponents ask for explanation, give them just a general understanding of the bid while letting them know there's more information available if they are interested.

Putting it All Together

The hardest thing to remember at first is to bid with a "bad" hand. You must be relentless. Partner expects this from you, and will definitely blame you for not bidding or misbidding a hand10. Other keys, responder normally maintains control of the auction which means getting in and out after having bid the limit of the partnership's offensive values without leaving any burn marks around partner's neck! Something to be aware of is balancing—especially over a 1 of minor opening—because partner would have already pre-balanced by overcalling. Pay attention to vulnerability. Down two undoubled is a great score non-vulnerable at matchpoints, but vulnerable it's definitely bad news.

We aim at certain strategic targets when playing against standard bidders using five card majors. If the opponents open 1 of a minor in standard, we want to use whatever means we can to preempt the auction, making it difficult for them to locate their fits. For example, utilizing the preemptiveness of the Intermediate Jump Overcalls, the RJOC are also very preemptive as is bidding a NTO and having advancer preempt at the 3 level. Whenever you eat up a level of bidding, the opponents will be forced to guess at a final contract. It's been our experience that they guess wrong.

The basis for our system is that we trade off ease in handling a few relatively infrequent strong hands to increase our use of lighter and more frequent hands. We, furthermore, try to increase our percentage of success with these more common hands. We use specific description to reduce the strength necessary to compete successfully in an auction. The tradeoff is that less strength is required when less time is needed in the auction to find your proper position. You may be weaker, but if your exposure to danger is shorter, you do not need as much raw power to be relatively secure.

Glossary for the Overcall System

Advancer: the fourth person at the table who happens to be the partner of an overcaller. Balancing: any time someone is in the passout seat and has to decide to take action.

Cover Cards: a corollary of the Losing Trick Count that says to evaluate the number of losers you can reasonably cover in partner's hand with your cards in conjunction with the LTC (not always easy to do).

Flower Bids: bids that show a suit in addition to a fit for partner in other words fit showing.

Intermediate Jump Overcall: single suited hand with the values to bid to the 3level in competition characterized by a good suit with generally about a six loser hand.

Jacoby Raise: a conventional raise showing a forcing hand with 4 or more card trump support for partner asking for greater description.

Law of Total Tricks: a bidding theory that attempts to explain how many tricks are available to be taken on any given hand depending on the number of available trumps. For general purposes, assume that you can compete to an equal level to the number of trumps held between two hands.

Lebensohl: a conventional understanding that characterizes the use of a no trump bid as a puppet rather than natural in order to delineate certain hand strengths.

Losing Trick Count: a hand evaluation theory or formula that states when a trump fit has been located to add the number of losers of your hand and your partners hand together and subtract that number from 24 to find the number of tricks available ([your losers + partner's losers] - 24 = number of tricks).

Mini-Splinter: a bid showing shortness in a suit with support for partner that gives your hand limit raise values.

NAMYATS: a conventional bid showing a major suit preempt with about 8 to 8.5 tricks made by bidding four of corresponding minor while a direct bid shows less than that.

No Trump for Takeout: a conventional call that shows a three suited takeout at the one level rather than making a takeout double.

Par Spot: a theoretical spot to be reached on a given hand assuming that both sides take proper action and that the par spot thereby will be reached.

Power Double: a defensive double that shows 15+ HCP and tends to be balanced like a strong no trump overcall and tends to show two or more cards of the bid suit.

Psychic bid: any bid made that is deceptive in nature and does not describe the hand actually held. Roman Jump Overcall: a jump overcall that shows the suit bid and the higher touching suit. Simple Overcall: a natural overcall made at the cheapest possible level without jumping. South African Transfer: a jump transfer that allows partner to super accept or not super accept.

Support Doubles and Redoubles: a conventional bid that allows one to make a raise showing an exact number of cards, usually three while a direct raise shows four or more.

Footnotes for the Overcall Syatem

1. When your RHO opens, the frequency of high card points you will hold is as follows: 0-5 HCP => 18.18%, 6-8 HCP => 27.65%, 9-11 HCP => 28.55%, 12-14 HCP => 19.02 %, 15+ HCP => 6.60%, 38+ HCP => 00.00%. Notice, the great majority are the weaker hands.

2. Support doubles and redoubles are conventional calls allowing one to show exactly three card trump support with unlimited strength. A direct raise shows four or more trumps. The exchange of information about the number of trumps we hold eases three level decisions.

3. Direct action has proven to be tactically superior to passing and pulling a double. Even if you run from one 5-1 to another 5-1, unless the direct seat can hammer it without knowing about the strength of their partner's hand, then the person in the passout seat many times is stuck and cannot take a call.

4. Cover cards is a theory expounded by George Rosenkranz, and is a corollary to the Law of Total Tricks. Cover cards cover losers in partners hand, allowing for hands to fit better. For example, if you have AKQ opposite partner's void, you don't have any cover cards, but if you have only an A opposite partner's stiff you have a cover card. We usually assume any fitters in partner's suits are cover cards, and potentially A's and K's in side suits where its known partner probably does not have shortness.

5. This is one area where many people believe the Overcall Structure gets nailed when trying to runout. Sometimes we do get nailed. But the number of times we've gotten nailed here versus the number of times you get nailed balancing at the three level is still fewer. Many times when the opponents think they have nailed us, it's because they're cold for game or slam their way.

6. Remember that there are no preempts below the four level; it's just possible that partner has a preempt. Of course, the opponents will let you know by having a strong auction.

7. Decisions about whether to show extras depend upon vulnerability and what partner would expect at a given vulnerability

8. Count a loser for every AKQ missing in a suit. Distributionally count none for a void, one for a singleton, and two for any Qx doubleton or worse. Some suits have

only half losers whenever a finessing position can be assumed, e.g. AQJ, AKJ, AJT, KJT, etc. The number of losers calculated assumes that we will have an eight card or better trump fit.

9. We have no requirements set in stone. The basic idea is to make a descriptive bid showing a single suited hand that doesn't require very much to make game.

10. Under certain circumstances, it's acceptable to make a simple overcall instead of bidding a NTO or a two suited bid. This only happens when you're red v. white with a suit that's more important to overcall for a lead director, and you don't want to risk going for 500.

The Overcall Structure—Summary

(THIS APPLIES IN THE DIRECT SEAT ONLY)

RHO opens - > You bid:	1♣	1♦	1♥	1♠
2NT	Strong 2-suiter (8.5+ playing tricks) Non-touching suit + another			
Double	15/16+ HCP Any shape			
1♦	Simple Overcall 6-14 HCP 5+ diamonds			
1♥	Simple Overcall 6-14 HCP 5+ hearts			
1♠	Simple Overcall 6-14 HCP 5+ spades			
1NT	1NT Takeout 10-14 HCP (12-14 vul. & passed hand) 3+ card support for all unbid major suits (1N over 1M promises 4 in other major)			
2♣	Two-suited cue bid (touching suits) 5+ diamonds 4+ spades 10+ HCP	Two level overcall 5+ clubs 11-14 HCP		
2♦	Two-suited jump overcall 5+ diamonds 4+ hearts 10-14 HCP	Two-suited cue bid (touching suits) 5+ clubs 4+ hearts 10+ HCP	Two level overcall 5+ diamonds 11-14 HCP	

2♥	Two-suited jump overcall 5+ hearts 4+ spades 10-14 HCP		Two-suited cue bid (touching suits) 5+ diamonds 4+ spades 10+ HCP	Two level overcall 5+ hearts 11-14 HCP
2♠	Weak jump overcall < 6 HCP 6+ spades	Two-suited jump overcall 4+ spades 5+ clubs 10-14 HCP		Two-suited cue bid (touching suits) 5+ hearts 5+ clubs 10+ HCP
3♣	Asks for stopper for 3NT	Weak jump overcall <6 HCP 6+ clubs	Two-suited jump overcall 5+ clubs 5+ diamonds 10-14 HCP	
3♦	Weak jump overcall <6 HCP 7+ diamonds	Asks for stopper for 3NT	Weak jump overcall <6 HCP 7+ diamonds	Two-suited jump overcall 5+ diamonds 5+ hearts 10-14 HCP
3♥	Weak jump overcall <6 HCP 7+ hearts		Asks for stopper for 3NT	Weak jump overcall <6 HCP 7+ hearts
3♠	Weak jump overcall <6 HCP 7+ spades			Asks for stopper for 3NT
3NT	To play			

Priority: 1. Strong 2-suiter; 2. Power Double ; 3. Roman Jump Overcall; 4. Cue Bid; 5. Simple Overcall; 6. Two Level Overcall; 7. Weak Jump Overcall; 8. 1NT for Takeout

Ghestem—Two Suited Overcalls

Roman Jump Overcalls and Cue Bids are used to show 5-4 and 5-5 hands. Recall that we learned that Michaels Cue bids and the Unusual 2NT bids (UNT) were used to show 5-5 hands.

Another scheme called The Ghestem System is used to show 5-5 suits.

The Ghestem bids are defined:

Direct cue bid = highest + lowest suits
2NT   = 2 lowest suits
3♣   = 2 highest suits

So we have: -

Opening bid: Overcall: Meaning

1♣	2♣	♠'s and ♦'s (highest + lowest)
1♣	2NT	♦'s and ♥'s (two lowest)
1♣	3♣	♠'s and ♥'s (two highest)
1♦	2♦	♠'s and ♣'s (highest + lowest)
1♦	2NT	♣'s and ♥'s (two lowest)
1♦	3♣	♠'s and ♥'s (two highest)
1♥	2♥	♠'s and ♣'s (highest + lowest)
1♥	2NT	♣'s and ♦'s (two lowest)
1♥	3♣	♠'s and ♦'s (two highest)
1♠	2♠	♥'s and ♣'s (highest + lowest)
1♠	2NT	♣'s and ♦'s (two lowest)
1♠	3♣	♦ 's and ♥'s (two highest)

Now this really is not too difficult to remember. 2NT is the same as the unusual NT, so always the two lowest. That leaves the cue bid and 3♣. 3♣ is always the higher bid and it means the two highest suits. That just leaves the cue bid for what's left (the highest and lowest).

There are just six of these two-suited combinations. So playing Ghestem we have: -

Hand 1	Hand 2	Hand 3	Hand 4	Hand 5	Hand 6
♠ 6	♠ 6	♠ KQ942	♠ 6	♠ KQ942	♠ KQ942
♥ 95	♥ KQ942	♥ 6	♥ K8742	♥ 6	♥ K8742
♦ KQ942	♦ 95	♦ 95	♦ KQ942	♦ K8742	♦ 6
♣ K8742	♣ K8742	♣ K8742	♣ 95	♣ 95	♣ 95

Hand 1: Over an opening bid of 1♥/♠, bid 2NT. This shows the two lowest

Hand 2: Over an opening bid of 1♦, bid 2NT. This shows the two lowest
        Over an opening bid of 1♠, bid 2♠. This shows the highest and lowest

Hand 3: Over an opening bid of 1♦, bid 2♦. This shows the highest and lowest
        Over an opening bid of 1♥, bid 2♥. This shows the highest and lowest

Hand 4: Over an opening bid of 1♣, bid 2NT. This shows the two lowest
        Over an opening bid of 1♠, bid 3♣. This shows the two highest

Hand 5: Over an opening bid of 1♣, bid 2♣. This shows the highest and lowest
        Over an opening bid of 1♥, bid 3♣. This shows the two highest

Hand 6: Over an opening bid of 1♣/♦, bid 3♣. This shows the two highest

Hand 7 Now Ghestem is basically pre-emptive. But most people play that it may also be very strong. So with this hand we bid the 2NT over a

1♦ opening and we bid 2♣ over a 1♠ opening.
But after partner's response we then make a forcing bid or bid game.

♠ 6
♥ KQ942
♦ A
♣ AKQ642

Hand 8   But hand 8 is different; it is neither weak nor very strong. So with intermediate
hands like this we simply overcall.

♠ 6
♥ KQ942
♦ A5
♣ AQ642

There are a couple of drawbacks with using Ghestem: -

1-   You loose 3♣ as a weak jump overcall or whatever it normally means in your
system.
2-   Sometimes you have to bid higher than you would have using UNT/Michaels. For
example with Hand 6 we bid 3♣ but playing Michaels it would be a cuebid of two of
the minor and so we are a level lower using Michaels.

Chapter 8
Conventional Doubles

Support Double and Redouble

Support doubles, invented by Eric Rodwell in 1974, are used when the opponents overcall after they have bid a suit. For examples: the bidding goes 1♦ - Pass - 1♥ - 2♣ (overcall)—double*. The double is not for penalty, it shows three-card supports (support double) for hearts. A bid of 2♥ shows four-card supports. The convention is usually played through 2♥ or 2♠. If instead of bidding two clubs, one doubles then the double is replaced by a redouble to show three-card supports for hearts. Support doubles and redoubles must be alerted.

Support doubles are unusually only played for the majors; however, some play them for all suits.

If the auction goes 1♣ - pass - 1♦ - 1♥ - and opener has a four-card spade suit, he should not use the support double with three hearts, but instead show the spade suit. If now the RHO bids 1NT instead of a suit, the double would be for penalty. Some examples follow.

1♦ - Pass - 1♥ - 1♠ (overcall) - double*
The double shows three-card supports for hearts

1♣ - 1♦ - 1♥ - 2♦ (overcall) - 2♥
Shows four-card supports for hearts.

1♥ - pass - 1♠ - 2♠ - 3♥
Shows 6+ hearts and denies spade support (less than three).

Some partnerships playing 2/1 do not like support doubles since it precludes making a penalty double of the overcall. Because penalty is not as likely at the two-level, this is not a problem for most players.

For more information on support doubles, read the article by Eric Rodwell on the web site: www.bridgetopics.com.

Responsive Doubles—Opponents Bid And Raise (OBAR)

A double used for takeout after partner has made a takeout double or a simple suit (not NT) overcall, and RHO has raised the suit bid by opener.

Example   1♦ - double - 2♦ - double (responsive)

Example   1♦ - double - 3♦ - double (responsive)

In this auction, you should be 4-4 in the majors and you are asking partner to pick a major. To use the responsive double, you should have 6-9 starting points at the two-level and 10+ at the three-level.

If the bidding were to go:
Example 1♣ - double - 1♥ - double

The second double is not responsive but shows hearts (4+ cards).

Responsive doubles are usually played through the same level as negative doubles, most partnerships use 3♠.

What if the bidding goes?

Example   1♦ - 1NT - 2♦ - double

You need an agreement for this double; it is either penalty or transfer. Playing systems on over the notrump bid, it would be a transfer to hearts. If systems are off, it is probably for penalty. Few play the double for takeout (unlikely).

Maximal Support Double

A double of a three-level bid that asks partner to bid game.

Example: 1♠ - 2♥ - 2♠ - 3♥ - double (maximal double). The double asks partner to bid 3♠ with a minimum and 4♠ with a maximum. If you merely compete by bidding 3♠, partner may take the bid as only competitive.

Snapdragon and Rosencrantz Doubles

If partner has overcalled a minor and all suits have been bid, the snapdragon double shows three-card support for the minor and a five-card major.

Example: 1♣ - 1♦ - 1♥ - double

This is a snapdragon double that shows three-card support for diamonds and a five-card spade suit.

Alternatively, suppose partner overcalled a major:

Example: 1♣ - 1♠ - 2♣ - double

This is a Rosencrantz double which is a spade raise promising an ace, king, or queen. The bid of two spades would deny a top honor. In the above, the bidding could also go:

Example: 1♣ - 1♠ - double - redouble

This is also Rosencrantz, showing three-card supports with an honor (A, K, or Q).

Because the goal is to get to major suit contract, I recommend that Snapdragon Doubles be played over a minor overcall and that Rosencrantz Doubles/Redoubles be played over major suit overcalls.

Lead Directing Doubles

A lead directing double is used when the opponents make an artificial bid. For example, if the opponents Stayman after the bid of 1NT, a double of Stayman asks partner to lead a club. To make the double, you must hold either Ax or Kx. They may also be used over transfers, any artificial bid, and Splinter bids.

Fisher Double

Invented by Dr. John W. Fisher, the Fisher double is used when opening 1NT or 2NT. The double of the final notrump contract at any level asks for a lead in a minor suit, CLUBS if the 2♣ Stayman Convention was NOT used and diamonds if Stayman was used but it was not doubled. A final note: some partnerships use the convention asking for a diamond lead, no matter if clubs were bid or not. Discuss this bid with your partner!

Lightner Slam Double

This convention was designed by Theodore Lightner and asks the partner of the opening leader to make a lead directing double of a slam contract.

If doubler has bid a suit, (1) partner MUST NOT lead the suit, (2) DO NOT LEAD a TRUMP, (3) assume that the double is based on a void or an unexpected AK (or AQ) in a suit bid by the opponents. (Very often dummies first bid suit.)

If doubler has NOT bid a suit, (1) partner MUST NOT lead the unbid suit, (2) DO NOT LEAD a TRUMP, (3) assume that the double is based on a void or an unexpected AK (or AQ) in a suit bid by the opponents or perhaps declarers side suit (second bid suit).

If both the doubler and the doubler's partner have bid a suit, (1) partner MUST NOT lead the suit bid by the doubler, (2) DO NOT LEAD a TRUMP, (3) partner is forbidden to lead his own suit, (4) lead the unbid suit.

Doubles of notrump slams usually ask partner to lead dummy's first bid suit or an unusual lead.

CONVENTION CARD: Special Doubles

On the back of the ACBL convention card, there is the section called **SPECIAL DOUBLES.**

Special Doubles
After Overcall: Penalty ☐ _____
Negative thru _____
Responsive ☐ thru _____   Maximal ☐
Support: Dbl ☐ thru _____   Redbl ☐
Card-Showing ☐   Min. Offshape T/O ☐

We have discussed all Special Doubles on the Convention Card except for the card-showing doubles and offshape doubles, which we now define.

Card-showing Doubles

If your low-level competitive doubles show values without being strictly penalty or negative in nature, check this box. For example, if partner opens 1♣, RHO bids 1♥, and you double simply to show a good hand regardless of the pattern, this would be a card-showing double.

Minimum Offshape Takeout Doubles

A takeout double of an opening bid usually shows a hand with at least opening values and shortness in the opener's suit. It also suggests support for the unbid suits. However, some players will make a takeout double on any hand with minimal opening values (twelve to fourteen HCP) even if the pattern isn't classic! For example, after RHO bid of 1♥ opening, and if you would double with the hand:

♠ A5 ♥ K873 ♦ KJ52 ♣ Q98.

CHECK THE BOX.
While the Box is not YET in Red on the Convention Card, it should be—just like Walsh bidders should alert their bid (not required by ACBL) in the sequence 1♣ Pass 1♦!

SOS Redouble

Many times the opponents will double a part score suit contract at the two or three-level for penalty. When partner redoubles the penalty double, it is called an SOS Redouble. It asks partner for his best rescue bid.

Chapter 9
How to Interfere with Their Bidding

The Rule of 8

When defending against notrump, interference is typically based upon a weak one—or two-suited hand using some convention like Brozel, Cappelletti, DONT, etc. The question is how weak is weak? Mel Colchamiro proposed the rule of eight, published in "The Bridge Bulletin," October 2000.

The rule follows:

Holding a minimum of six starting points; deduct from the total number of cards in your two longest suits the total number of losing tricks. If the difference is TWO or greater, you should interfere.

If it is less than TWO, do not interfere.

Examples:

     1)   ♠ A Q 9 4 3 ♥ K 6 2 ♦ 7 4 ♣ K 8 6

You have a total of eight cards in your two longest suits. Subtracting seven losers (one in spades plus two each in the other suits) is equal to one. You must NOT interfere even with thirteen starting points.

     2)   ♠ K 7 6 5 2 ♥ K 9 5 3 2 ♦ 8 3 ♣ 6

You have a total of ten cards in the long suits. Subtracting seven losers (two each in spades, hearts, diamonds, and one in clubs) is equal to three. You should interfere despite the weakness of your hand, only eight starting points.

The Rule of 2

Mel has another rule that is used in the balancing seat called the Rule of 2.

It is used in the sequence 1NT-Pass-Pass - ?

Should you bid or pass? You should bid only if you have two or more shortness points, regardless of vulnerability, otherwise pass. Let's consider some hands.

♠Q84 ♥ A63 ♦9 ♣ J8642 (yes-bid two clubs)

♠A84 ♥ K963 ♦K92 ♣ K86 (No—better to defend—no shortness points)

♠10643 ♥ Q1095 ♦10 ♣ Q965 (yes—bid two clubs)

Interference over Notrump Conventions

In the October 2007 issue of the ACBL "Bridge Bulletin," several experts recommended and discussed systems they play over the bid of a strong 1NT (14/15-17 HCP). Even if you have read the article (also available at www.clairebridge.com/defensevsnt.htm), you still may not have a clear picture regarding which system is "best."

A well-known British tournament director David Stevenson has posted 55 notrump defenses at: http://blakjak.org.def_1nt01.htm.

What system should you play over a weak 1NT (12-14 or 10-12, say), should your approach change playing Match Points vs. IMPS, and should the system change depending upon whether you are in the direct or balancing (pass-out) seat? There is no clear or best system for all situations: weak vs. strong notrump, Match Points vs. IMPS, direct vs. balancing seat. We consider each in turn, and then recommend an approach. When considering a system to play over the bid of 1NT (weak or strong), the first question you should ask yourself is whether or not a double should be value-showing and penalty-oriented.

Clearly, over a weak NT bid, a double has to show values (15+) and be for penalty. Over weak notrumps, if you do not double, but defeat the 1NT contract by one or two tricks, you will get an inferior score at Match Points or IMPS. Furthermore, over a weak notrump bid, it is critical to show both majors even if you are 4-4 and have only 10-11 HCP. You may easily compete at the two levels. Thus, over weak notrumps (Match Points or IMPS) you need a system where a double is for penalty and that is able to show the majors (80 percent of all game bids are played in a major). Finally, over the weak NT bid, it does not matter whether or not the declarer is in the direct or pass-out seat. Hence, it is best to bid your suit, as soon as possible, especially if it is spades! A system designed with these requirements is Mohan. Like most systems designed to interfere over weak notrumps, it is based upon transfers (e.g., Weber). This allows the overcaller a second opportunity to bid, especially with a moderate to good holding.

The John Mohan system follows:

Mohan

Double   Penalty

2♣*   Shows both majors (4-4 or 5-5)

2♦*	Transfer to hearts
2♥*	Transfer to spades
2♠*	Spades and a minor
2NT*	Hearts and a minor

All three-level bids are natural, usually a six-card suit and preemptive.

What if the bid is a strong NT (14/15-17 HCP)? Again, most would agree that a double is value showing and penalty oriented. NOT ALL AGREE ON THIS. Cappelletti is unwavering in his view: "It must be penalty-oriented. On a particular hand it might not work, but in the long run it's best. Remember that you're 'over' the 1NT opener and that you get to make the opening lead." If you agree, do not adopt any system (IN THE DIRECT SEAT) where a double is not for penalty. Hence you would not use, for example, DONT, Meckwell, or Brozel. Even though Larry Cohen likes DONT because it allows you to show all one—and two-suit hands without having to bid at the three-level, the double is NOT for penalty. Furthermore, the system must be able to show the majors at the two-level either directly or indirectly and one usually wants the strong hand on LEAD. If you agree with the above comments and want a system that may be played over either weak or strong notrumps (Match Points or IMPS) it is, in my opinion, the best system is Modified Cappelletti.

Modified CAPPELLETTI

Double: Any double over weak notrump is for penalty. However, over strong notrump bids it may be used for takeout/penalty.

2♣: Shows a single-suited holding in diamonds OR a two-suited holding in an unspecified major suit and an unspecified minor suit. After a pass by the partner of the notrump bidder, the advancer can bid 2♦, which is forcing for one round. Then the overcaller will either pass or raise with a single-suiter in diamonds if holding stronger values OR bid the major suit if the holding is a two-suiter.

If the overcaller shows the two-suited holding after the 2♦ bid, then the advancer can bid 2NT to return to the actual minor suit (clubs or diamonds) or pass if the major suit is preferred.

2♦: Shows both major suits (as in Cappelletti).

2♥: Shows a single-suited holding in hearts. Partner should pass after a notrump opening by an opponent.

2♠: Shows a single-suited holding in spades. Partner should pass after a notrump opening by an opponent.

2NT: Shows both minor Suits (5+ in each).

WHAT SYSTEM SHOULD YOU ADOPT IN THE PASS-OUT SEAT? Clearly, in the pass-out seat, a double for penalty is not as valuable since the doubler is not on lead against 1NT. In the pass-out seat you should use Modified DONT also called Meckwell.

Modified DONT (Meckwell)

Double: Shows a one-suited hand (6+ cards) or both majors.

2♣: Shows clubs and a major suit (5-4 or 4-5 or longer).

2♦: Shows diamonds and a major suit (5-4 or 4-5 or longer).

2♥: Shows hearts (5+)

2♠: Shows spades (5+)

2NT: Shows both minor suits (5+in each).

In my opinion, Modified Cappelletti and Modified DON'T (Meckwell) are my selections for interference over notrump. There have been many methods proposed. I like these methods because they both show the majors immediately and may be used with two-suited or single suited hands.

In both of the above conventions, 2NT was used to show the minors. This is sometimes modified to show an equivalent notrump hand. Discuss this option with your partner.

Multi Landy Over 1NT

While the number of conventions used to interfere over notrump is many, I came across a new system developed by Martin Johnson on the Web site: www.freewebs.com/bobbybridge/conventions/conventions.htm.

The convention is very similar to the ones I have recommended; it is called Multi Landy which is a relatively new defense to the opponent's 1NT opening. While it is similar to the conventions I have recommended, the clear advantage is that it may be played in both the direct and balancing seats. One convention for both the direct and balancing seat is attractive. The system Martin Johnson suggested follows; also included are his comment and analysis regarding systems one should use over notrump openings.

	1NT(opponent)	?

	2 ♣ - Landy (at least 5-4 or 4-5 in majors). Advancer bids 2♦ to ask opener to show longer major (over weak notrump, may be 4-4).
	2♦ - Multi (one-suiter in a major). Advancer bids 2♠ with good spades, else 2♥.
	2♥/2♠ - 5 card suit with a minor suit (usually 5-5). Advancer bids 2NT to ask for minor suit.
	2NT - minors
	3m - 6+ suit, sounds vulnerable, may be pure preempt not vulnerable
	Double - 4-card major and 5-card minor, typically opening hand or better. Advancer may pass with a decent hand, otherwise bids 2♣ to ask opener to show his minor (passing with clubs, else 2♦) or 2♦ to ask for the major (will usually be 4-4 at least in majors), or 2M to play (own decent six-card suit).
	Double - Versus a weak notrump, double is played as for penalty.

Analysis by Martin Johnsons: "Multi Landy seems clearly superior to Cappelletti (Hamilton). The 2 ♣ bid to show majors allows room to sort out the overcaller's major, which the Capp 2♦ bid does not. The Multi 2 overcall allows advancer to determine overcallers suit if responder bids a major, whereas the Capp 2♣ one suited bid does not. Furthermore, the Capp 2♣ can be doubled as a Stayman response and the Multi 2♦ cannot. The Multi double showing a major with a longer minor is another hand type that Capp does not handle at all. The only other notrump defense that handles that combination is Astro (2♣ =♥ and lower, perhaps 4-5, 2♦=♠and other, often 4-5), but Astro will get you to the three-level in most cases where you belong in the minor, whereas Multi Landy does not.

"Another popular defense is DONT (Double=one-suiter, 2x=that suit and a higher suit). DONT handles Astro style hands okay, but the double to show a one-suiter has no preemption value, and overcaller's suit can easily be lost. The 2♥ overcall to show the majors also leaves insufficient room to determine overcaller's long major. More significantly, DONT has no penalty double of 1NT, which is a must versus a weak notrump."

Extending the Multi Landy defense: In the standard American auction: 1♦-pass-1NT-(?), the responding hand almost invariably has length in clubs. It is therefore a reasonable idea for the sandwich bidder to use Multi Landy in this sequence. An overcall of 2♣ can be used for major takeout, at least 5-4, a 2♦ cuebid as a weak one-suiter in a major, and a 2M overcall as either a sound overcall (opening strength or better) or as that suit with secondary clubs. Double can be a normal takeout of diamonds or something else if you wish. I don't have much experience to assess the merits of this treatment, but the loss of a natural club overcall is certainly not a problem.

My only issue with the Multi Landy is that a double over strong NT (14/15-17) is not for penalty. However, I believe that it is superior to DONT.

Marvin French System

Mr David Stevenson on his notrump site has a very nice overview of the Marvin French (bridge expert from San Diego California) system. It is rather unique in that the system may be used to show a three-two-or one-suited hands. The bids are:

Direct Seat or Balance SEAT over Strong NO TRUMPS

Double:	**♣♦♥ or ♦♥ or ♥ (weak or strong)**
2♣	**♦♥♠ or ♥♠ or strong ♠**
2♦	**♥♠♣ or ♠♣ or strong ♣**
2♥	**♠♣♦ or ♣♦ or strong ♦**
2♠	**♠**
2NT	**one or two minors (weak ♣ or weak ♦)**
3♣	**♣♥ (non-forcing)**
3♦	**♦♠ (non-forcing)**

In the four three-possible-suit cases, advancer, with no special strength, chooses among the three suits, preferring a major to a minor; intervenor will usually pass or correct but may raise or jump with a very stong hand. With game interest advancer can bid two notrump to inquire.

Over intervenor's two notrump, advancer will usually bid three clubs, past-or-correct. If intervanor then bids a forcing three of a major, he cancels the orighinal message and announces a two-suiter too strong for an initial jump to three of a minor.

If intervenor's call is doubled or redoubled, a pass or a bid is to play; a redouble asks intervenor to clarify. If responder bids a suit, advancer's double is negative unless it is a bid in intervenor's anchor suit, a bid is to play, and a pass is nocommital.

In the direct seat, if you want to double one notrump, you may use two spades with the meaning shown for the double and add weak spades to the list for the bid of two clubs.

When the Opponents Interfere Over 1NT Opening

Lebensohl is a common convention used over weak two bids, reverses, and interference over notrump. However, an even better convention is the Rubinsohl Convention, which uses transfer bids over disruptive interference bids. The basic convention uses the combination of transfers and Lebensohl in a competitive auction aimed at allowing a player to show his distribution with both weak and strong hands. It is similar to the "stolen bid" convention played by many of club players. The method was introduced by Bruce Neill of Australia in an article in "The Bridge World" in 1983. The concept was based upon the article published in the same magazine by Jeff Rubens, who used the term Rubensohl. However, the method had been previously used in the United States by Ira Rubin, and therefore named Rubinsohl and not Rubensohl. Both names (Rubinsohl and Rubensohl) appear in the Bridge Literature.

Lebensohl

Lebensohl is used after one opens notrump when the opponents interfere to show game forcing hands immediately. However, the downside of Lebensohl is that you must go through relay bids to find out partner's real suit and if RHO competes you might never know that you have a good fit. In today's game, the opponents always seem to use their "toy" to disturb your notrump and the RHO is getting into the action more and more to re-preempt the auction. Ira Rubin and Jeff Rubens thought it was better for partner to announce his suit directly and to show strength later.

The structure of Lebensohl is, briefly:

Double is for penalty.
Two-level bid is to play.
Three-level bid is forcing to game.
Two notrump is artificial, forcing opener to bid three clubs.
An immediate cuebid by responder is Stayman (except after two clubs, double is Stayman).
A direct jump to 3NT denies a stopper.
Two notrump followed by a cuebid of the enemy suit after opener's forced club relay bid is Stayman.
Two notrump followed by three notrump, after a relay to three clubs, shows a stopper and asks opener to play in three notrump.

For example, consider the hand where opener has (♣, ♥, ♦, ♠) xxx AQxx AKxx Kx and the bidding goes: 1NT-2♠-2NT-4♠ and your partner has the hand: x Kxxxxx xx QTxx. You are forced to pass and miss the huge heart fit. Or, you hold xxx Ax Axxx AKxx and the bidding goes 1NT-2♠-2NT-3♠ and partner holds x xxx QJTxxx Qxx and you guess that he was competing in hearts so you pass. You missed the five diamond contract. In the first hand, it would be better to transfer to hearts, and in the second, one would want to transfer to diamonds.

To avoid these disasters, one may play Rubinsohl or Rumpelsohl that is part of the Kaplan Sheinwold bidding system.

I do not recommend either; instead, my system of choice is Transfer Lebensohl.

The Major disadvantage of Lebensohl is that it results in the play of a hand from the WRONG side; since it is a relay based system instead of a transfer based system. This is not the case for Basic Rubinsohl and Transfer Lebensohl.

Transfer Lebensohl

A close cousin to Basic Rubinsohl, and often confused with it, is Transfer Lebensohl. The conventional bids follow. The primary difference in the two systems is in the meaning of the bid of three spades. First off, all two-level bids are to play, identical to Lebensohl. However, it may also be played over weak two bids and more as seen below.

Transfer Lebensohl over notrump and weak two bids.

After   (1) 1NT (2X)?
            (2) (2X) Dbl (P)?

(a) X = Diamonds/Hearts/Spades.

    Double = Penalty/negative (ov 2♠ or higher)
    2Y to play where Y is not equal to X.
    2NT: Puppet to 3♣
        -> Pass /Lower Suit: To play.
        3X cuebid Stayman with stopper GF
        Over X=H, 3♠=both minors
    3NT with stopper.
    3♣: Transfer to diamonds, INV or better. *
    3♦: Transfer to hearts, INV or better. *
    3♥: Transfer to spades, INV or better. *
        * If transfer to opponents—> Stayman w/o stopper
    3♠: Transfer to clubs no stopper
    3NT: To play, but no stopper
    4m: Leaping Michaels. 5-5 up.
        (X=M: 4♣=C+oM. 4♦=D+oM.
        X=D: 4♣=C+One major. 4♦=H+S.)
    4M: Unbid: NAT. with stopper.
        Jump Cue: Minors. Strong.
    4NT: Minors. (Weak if X=M.)

(b) X = Clubs.

    Double = Cuebid Stayman w/o stopper
    2Y where Y is not equal to X: To play.
    2NT transfer to diamonds no stopper (weak).
        -> 3♦=Accept. 3♣=Decline.
    3♣: Stayman with a stopper GF
    3♦: Transfer to hearts, INV or better.
    3♥: Transfer to spades, INV or better.
    3♠: Transfer to diamonds no stopper (INV)

3NT: To play but no stopper

4m: Leaping Michaels.

4M: NAT. with stopper.

It may also be played in the sequence 1X - Dbl - 2X?

The best system to play after an overcall of partner's 1NT bid has a long history in "The Bridge World." For an informative discussion, one may consult the May/June 1989 Issue of "Bridge Today" and the article by Alvin Roth (one of America's foremost bidding theorist) "Doctor Roth's What Do You Bid and Why?" pages 39-41. He recommends that one NOT play Lebensohl but use a transfer based system like either Transfer Lebensohl or Basic Rubinsohl. The Basic Rubinsohl bids follow.

Over a natural 2♠ overcall

2NT=transfer to clubs

3 ♣= transfer to diamonds

3 ♦= transfer to hearts

3 ♥ (transfer into their suit) is Stayman without a stopper

3 ♠ is a transfer to 3NT with a stopper

3NT= natural with a stopper in the bid suit.

Over a natural 2♥ overcall

2 ♠ is natural and non-forcing

2NT= transfer to clubs

3 ♣= transfer to diamonds

3 ♦ (transfer into their suit) is Stayman without a stopper

3 ♥ shows spades with a heart stopper

3 ♠ shows spades without a stopper in hearts

3NT= natural with a stopper in the bid suit.

If the opponents overcall a natural minor, the treatment is as follows. Two-level bids are natural and non-forcing. With the overcall 2♦, 2NT shows clubs as usual, but 3♣ is Stayman for both majors and asks if partner has a diamond stopper. If no major or stopper, one accepts the transfer. Jumps in the majors are natural and forcing. The bids of 3♦/3♥ are transfers. But, 3♠ is partnership defined most, use it to show a club bust (Minor Suit Stayman). A bid of 3NT shows a stopper in diamonds.

With a 2♣ (natural or not) overcall, a double is Stayman without a club stopper and two-level bids are natural and competitive. 2NT is usually defined as Stayman with a club stopper. A jump to a three-level bid is a transfer and forcing.

What if their bid shows two suits, then transferring into their lower ranking suit shows the next higher suit which is not the opponents? So if their bid shows hearts and a minor, transferring into hearts must show spades.

With so many "toys" being used over 1NT, Rubinsohl and Transfer Lebensohl have a distinct advantage over Lebensohl since you know your suit early and it ignores the RHO getting into the act. In both systems, a double is not for penalty but for takeout.

Simple Lebensohl

When playing in club games, I have noticed that most club players do not play Lebensohl, Transfer Lebensohl, Rubinsohl, or Rumpelsohl; they are too complicated. What I find is that many play the very limited "Stolen Bid" convention.

The purpose of the stolen bid double is to allow Stayman and Jacoby transfer sequences to proceed as if no overcall had been made. Thus, in the sequence

Partner	Opponents	You
1NT	2♣	Dbl

playing "stolen bids", a double is Stayman. In this following sequence,

Partner	Opponents	You
1NT	2♦	2♥

is a transfer to spades or if the bidding sequence is:

Partner	Opponents	You
1NT	2♥	Dbl

Then double also requests a transfer to spades.

There are two very serious problems with "stolen bids" after 1NT openings.

(1) They do not allow use of a penalty double which is a powerful deterrent to opponents contemplating an overcall after a strong 1NT opening.
(2) It is not always possible to make a stolen bid, especially when the overcall is artificial, as in for example with the Landy and Cappelletti defenses to no trump openers. In Cappelletti, 2♦ shows the majors, so you can hardly want your partner to transfer into hearts with a stack of hearts behind him/her. The same is the case with Landy where now 2♣ shows majors. Now Stayman doesn't make a lot of sense.

Playing any more sophisticated system like Lebensohl or Transfer Lebensohl, a double of an artificial two—suited hand is for penalty. However, if the bid of 2♣ shows an unknown single suited hand, it remains Stayman. Other bidding sequences are more complicated and most club players will not invest the time to learn either more fully.

If you are not going to learn a more complicated alternative, and would still like to penalize them for interfering, what can you do? Give up "Stolen Bids" and play Simple Lebensohl over a strong 14-17 notrump opening. The Simple Lebensohl system of bids takes bids used in both Lebensohl and Transfer Lebensohl with simplification.

Simple Lebensohl Bids

Over a Double

Pass = no interest in competing

Redouble = relay to 2♣ (unless advancer bids) then responder passes or corrects to 2♦

2♣ Stayman

2♦/2♥ Jacoby transfer to hearts and spades, respectively

2♠ Transfer to clubs with a correction to diamonds

2NT Natural 8-9 HCP

3NT To play

4♣ 5-5 in the majors

4♦/4♥ Texas Transfers

Another option is to play 4-way transfers, but most club members do not use this option so I do not recommend it in "Simple Lebensohl".

Overcall 2♣ (Natural/Undefined/Two Suited)

Double Penalty

If 2♣ is natural, then 3♣ is Stayman

If 2♣ is undefined, then bid your 5-card suit at the two level (transfers are off)

If 2♣ is a known two suiter, then a cue-bid of the lower ranking know suit is Stayman and a cue bid of the higher ranking suit is game force

2NT is a relay bid to 3♣ (Lebensohl)

3NT to play with stoppers if suits are know

4♣ 5-5 in the majors

4♦/4♥ Texas Transfers

Natural Suit Overcalls (2♦/2♥/2♠)

All Doubles are for penalty

All cheapest two level bids are to play

Three level bids are transfers and a transfer into their suit is Stayman without a stopper.

2NT is a relay bid to 3♣ (Lebensohl) over a suit bid

3NT to play with a stopper

4♣ 5-5 in the majors

4♦/4♥ Texas Transfers

After 2NT Overcall (Strong/Minors)

Double is Stayman (if Strong) and 3♣ is Stayman (if Minors) and 3NT to play with stoppers in Minors

3♦ is transfer to hearts with a correction if needed to spades

3♠ is natural

3NT to play with stoppers

4♣ show 5-5 in the majors

4♦/4♥ Texas Transfers

Defense against Transfer Bids

In duplicate bridge, transfer bids (e.g., Jacoby, Texas, and NAMYATS, etc.) are almost standard. How do you defend against these systems?

The following defenses against transfer bids will allow you to show two-suited hands with one call. They may be employed not only against transfers but against any bid that shows specific suits (e.g., 2NT to show the minors). A major disadvantage of transfer bids is that they give the opponent two opportunities for action: immediate or delayed. This aid to defensive bidding accuracy should be utilized.

When Your Side Has Been Silent

When the transfer bid occurs before your side has bid or doubled (e.g., vs. Jacoby or Texas response to a 1NT opening, or vs. an opening preemptive transfer bid), use the following defense:

-   A notrump bid asks for a preference between the lower two suits, excluding the one indicated by the transfer bid.
-   A double of the transfer bid shows the higher two suits.
-   A "cuebid" (in the suit indicated by the transfer bid) is top-and-bottom, asking for a preference between the top and bottom suits.
    For instance, after a 2♦ Jacoby response to a 1NT opening

South	West	North	East
1NT	Pass	2♦	2NT—both minors
			Dbl—spades/diamonds
			2♥ - spades/clubs
			2♠/3♣/3♦ - one-suited hand

The double may be made with less strength than any of the other two-suited calls. One of the suits indicated by the double is the suit bid by the opponent, so partner can pass with an unsuitable hand. This sequence has an easy mnemonic: Dbl for Diamonds and the other major, Cuebid for Clubs and the other major. Bids over a 2♥ transfer to spades have the same mnemonic.

When given a choice of suits in which you have equal length, prefer a major to a minor, hearts to spades, and clubs to diamonds. Partner can keep this in mind when deciding whether to overcall or pass with a marginal hand.

The immediate overcall with a one-suited hand should be quite sound. With a doubtful hand, simply pass and reopen the bidding if the transfer suit gets passed:

South	West	North	East
1NT	Pass	2♦	Pass
2♥	Pass	Pass	2♠/3♣/3♦

These reopening bids can be made with moderate hands, since partner is marked with some high cards when the opponents stop at the two-levels.

The soundness of immediate natural overcalls applies at higher levels, too:

South	West	North	East
1NT	Pass	4♦	4♠/5♣/5♦—sound bids
			4NT—for the minors

Remember that a direct bid of 4NT is for the minors and a balancing 4NT bid is natural. That is the general rule and for the sake of consistency it must be followed even at this level.

With a doubtful hand, perhaps taking a deliberate save with many playing tricks but little defense, east can pass on this round and bid next time. This policy may help partner when he has to make a double/bid/pass decision.

You may sometimes have a three-suited hand with shortness in the suit indicated by the transfer bid. In that case, pass the transfer, then double for takeout on the next round. You can do this with a huge hand, since the transfer bid is forcing; there is no need to jump into the bidding immediately:

South	West	North	East
1NT	Pass	2♥	Pass
2♠	Pass	Pass	Dbl—takeout double strong 1NT

If 1NT was weak, this double is optional, just showing a strong balanced hand.

When the transfer is an opening bid that shows a preemptive bid in the next higher suit, the same principles apply. An immediate notrump overcall still shows the lower two "unbid" suits. A reopening notrump bid is therefore natural:

South	West	North	East
3♦	Pass	3♥	Pass
Pass	Dbl normal takeout double		
	3♠ competitive reopening bid		
	3NT natural		

South's 3♦ bid shows a preemptive type hand. The double is not a reopening action, since an immediate double would show a two-suited hand with spades and diamonds. It is true that passing 3♦ with a nine-trick notrump hand gives north a chance to make a preemptive raise in hearts, but that must be chanced. There are two advantages to this approach: (1) a two-suited hand in the minors can be easily shown by an immediate 3NT bid, and (2) the general principles of countering transfer bids remain the same, with no exceptions. We consider an example.

South	West	North	East
3♣	Pass	3♦	3♥/3♠/Dbl

Believe it or not, east is actually making a reopening call. North has indicated that he would have passed a normal 3♦ opening bid, so east pretends that is just what has happened. He is no worse off than he would be with a normal preemptive 3♦ opening. This is especially true if he is short in diamonds. The hand short in the opposing suit must be quick to act, since partner probably cannot.

Against Strong NAMYATS

The NAMYATS Convention uses a 4♣* opening to show hearts and a 4♦* opening to show spades. Even in the "strong" version a 4♥ or 4♠, the bids are usually weak in high cards (only 7-7 ½ quick tricks), while a 4♣* or 4♦* opening shows a good hand (8-8 ½+ quick tricks) that would welcome a slam contract. The fact there is an intervening suit between the transfer bid and the indicated suit affects the usual defense against transfer bids:

- Passing and then doubling opener's major on the next round retains the same meaning: a strong three-suited hand short in opener's suit.
- Immediate overcalls in the ranking suit (i.e., the suit lying between opener the opening bid and opener's major) may be weaker than overcalls in the remaining two suits. If you don't bid now, you have to bid higher next time.
- Immediate overcalls in the remaining two suits are very sound, because you can pass and bid on the next round with a sacrifice type hand, at the same level that an immediate bid would require.
- Jump overcalls are extra strong.
- The immediate double, "cuebid" of opener's suit, and notrump bids all retain the same meaning: major/diamonds, major/clubs, and both minors, respectively:

South	West
4♣*	Dbl—Diamonds and hearts
	4♦ - diamonds, may be a stretch
	5♣ - Clubs and spades
	4♠/5♣ - good hand
	4NT - minors
	5♦/5♠ - extra strong

With a sacrifice bid of 4♠ or 5♣, west could pass and bid on the next round. The immediate overcall shows a good hand both offensively and defensively. The difference may be important if partner has to decide what to do when the opponents go to 5♥.

There are two ways to show spades and a minor: double/cuebid, or bid 4♠ and then bid the minor (if you get the chance). Choose the natural bid when spades are strong and longer than the minor, the conventional call otherwise. You are not going to run if 4♠ gets doubled, so the spades had better be pretty good. When you show the suits conventionally, partner will not take a false preference in order to play the major suit.

There at least two ways of showing both minors: bid 4NT immediately or on the second round. Common sense says that an immediate 4NT bid is stronger than a delayed one. The immediate bid promises a good hand, both offensively and defensively, while a delayed bid implies poor defense.

When the opening is 4♣*, you can also show diamonds and clubs by bidding them instead of overcalling 4NT, which provides a third way of showing both minors. Show the minors this way when the clubs are not longer than the diamonds. Partner will then prefer diamonds with equal length. After a 4NT bid, he prefers clubs with equal length.

There are also three ways to get to 5♦ after a 4♣* opening: bid 5♦ immediately; bid 4♦, then 5♦, or pass and then bid 5♦. The jump is stronger; the delayed bid (passing first) is weaker. Bidding diamonds twice (a seemingly illogical action) allows room for partner to bid 4♠, so it could be based on a good hand with some spade support.

When the opening is 4♦* it is the immediate major suit bid that may be a stretch:

South	West
4♦*	Dbl - Diamonds and hearts
	4♥ - may be a stretch
	4♠ - clubs and hearts
	4NT - minors
	5♣/5♦ - sound bids
	5♥ - extra strong

West has three ways to get to 5♥: bid 5♥ immediately, obviously the strongest action; bid 5♥ on the next round (weakest); or bid 4♥, then 5♥, which is somewhere in-between.

There are two ways to show hearts and a minor: double/cuebid or bid both suits. With hearts longer than the minor, one bids 4♥ and then the minor. When the two suits are of equal length or the minor longer, double or cuebid.

There is no way left to double opener's eventual game bid for business, unless you are able to overcall in the ranking suit and then double on the next round. That is not a big deal, because doubling a strong NAMYATS game bid is seldom profitable and often disastrous.

Against Weak NAMYATS

When the opening bid of 4♣ or 4♦ shows a weak major suit preempt, we must have a way of doubling the major for business. The delayed double therefore becomes a little more optional than takeout, not necessarily a three-suited hand. Otherwise, the defense is the same as against the strong version of NAMYATS.

NAMYATS NOTE: When playing strong NAMYATS, most people will open 4♥/4♠ directly with weak preemptive hands and long major suits. Warning, if **NAYMYATS is not played by the partnership, the "preemptive bid" may be strong!** Even if you play strong NAMYATS, you should discuss it with your partner. For example, some partnerships play the refusal of the transfer (4♦ over 4♣ and 4♥ over 4♦) to allow opener to play game (usually no tenace) while others use the intermediate bid to request partner to bid an ace if he has one or to sign off without an ace. For a review of bidding sequences, visit: members.shaw/convention/ Namyats.htm.

Action vs. NAMYATS by Fourth Seat

When the opening has been passed by second seat, third seat will either bid four of partner's major or bid the next higher suit (as a query bid or as a "retransfer" to let opener play the hand).

—When third seat signs off in opener's suit, a double is for takeout and a 4NT bid shows both minors:

South	West	North	East
4♣*	Pass	4♥	Dbl—takeout
			4NT—minors

Against the weak version of NAMYATS, the double of 4♠ is more optional than takeout, just as it would be over a normal preemptive 4♥ or 4♠ opening.

—When third seat bids the ranking suit so that opener can play the hand that is treated like a transfer bid:

South	West	North	East
4♣*	Pass	4♦	Dbl—spades and diamonds
			4♥ - spades and clubs
			4NT - minors

South	West	North	East
4♣*	Pass	4♥	Dbl—hearts and diamonds
			4♠ - hearts and clubs
			4NT - minors

Other defensive actions are similar in meaning to those used in the second seat.

Defense over Forcing Notrump

Using the 2/1 convention, after a major opening the opponents bid 1NT and announce the bid as forcing. How do you compete?

Suppose the bidding goes 1♥/1♠—Pass—1NT—? And you want to compete. While some may play all bids as natural, sometimes you need a way to show hands that are widely varying in strength, without misleading partner, or a two-suiter. A clever way is to switch some bids around that allow one to compete in the fourth position. Using the Useful Space Principle (USP), one may employ the Vasilevsky Convention.

In the above forcing 1NT sequence, you bid as:

Dbl	Transfer to clubs
2♣	Transfer to diamonds
2♦	Transfer to the unbid major
2 of the bid major	Good, distributional takeout "double"
2 of unbid major	Weaker takeout double, guaranteeing four of the major bid
2NT	Distributional takeout for the minors
3♣/3♦	Natural, but shows 6-4, the four being the unbid major

Let's see how it works. The bidding goes 1♥—Pass—1NT—?

And you hold:

a)   ♠Q10654 ♥A5 ♦9 ♣KJ1076

Double to show clubs. If opener passes and partner bids 2♣, you next bid 2♠, showing a two-suited 5-5 hand. If you were 6-4 in clubs and spades, you would bid 3♣.

However, suppose you are 4-4 in clubs and spades. You have the hand:

b)   ♠AJ54 ♥7 ♦AK93 ♣A874

You now bid 2♥, showing a strong takeout double.

With either of the following hands:

c)   ♠AJ54 ♥72 ♦Q87 ♣KJ74

d)   ♠9542 ♥7 ♦KJ854 ♣Q107

You would bid 2♠, a weak takeout double.

When you are a passed hand, Vasilevsky no longer applies. Since intervener's hand is limited, he doesn't need two bids.

The only disadvantage of the convention is that one may not penalize a 1NT bid; however, this does not occur that often. The advantage is that, using transfers, the calls are logical, hence easy to remember and show exactly the distribution and strength needed to compete.

The Useful Space Principle (USP)

The Vasilevsky Convention is based upon the Useful Space Principle developed by Jeff Rubens. The principle has formed the basis for the creation and development of many modern day conventions; for example, Roman Keycard Blackwood with Kickback.

The definition of USP follows:

"When allocating bidding space under partnership agreements, assign it where most useful without deference to natural or traditional bridge meanings of calls."

Let's apply the principle in some situations.

Suppose the bidding goes: 1♣—Dbl—1♥—?

What do you bid if you are weak and have four spades? Bid 2♥. With 10+ points and five spades, bid 2♠.

Recall that Leaping Michaels is a reasonable way to show a two-suited hand over weak level bids. Using the USP, suppose the bidding goes:

2♠ - Pass - 3♠ - (?)

How do you now compete? Consider the following bids.

4♣   shows clubs and hearts
4♦   shows diamonds and hearts
4♠   shows game in a long minor and asks partner to bid 5♣ which may be corrected, if
       necessary, to 5♦
4♥   natural
4NT   shows both minors

The previous are just two examples of exchanging the normal meaning of bids; you can invent many more if you are so inclined. For additional suggestions, consult "Competitive Bidding in the 21st Century" by Marshall Miles (2000) published by Master Point Press.

Chapter 10
Review of Common "Bridge Rules/Laws"

Rule of 2

You should interfere over the bid of 1NT in the balancing seat if you have two shortness points. Otherwise, do not interfere.

Rule of 7

When playing NT contracts and having only one stopper in the suit led headed by the ace, one may use the Rule of 7 to decide how many times to hold up. Rule: subtract the total number of cards you and dummy hold in the suit from seven. This is the number of times you should hold up when the suit is led by the opponents. The rule is also used with suit contracts.

Rule of 8

Provided you have at least six starting points, you should interfere over 1NT in the direct seat if the number of cards in your two longest suits minus the number of losers in your hand is two or more. Otherwise, do not interfere.

Rule of 9

A reopening double by opener is for takeout. Responder is expected to bid his best suit or pass for penalty with the correct hand. What is the correct hand? The Rule of 9 may help one decide whether to pass for penalty or bid. To use the rule, add the level of the contract, the number of the trump, and the number of trump honors held including the ten. If this sum is nine or more, pass the takeout double for penalty. If the number is eight or less, bid something, do not let the double stand.

Rule of 11

The Rule of 11 is used for placing the outstanding higher cards when partner makes a fourth best lead. One subtracts the spot of the card led from eleven to determine the number of higher cards in the remaining three hands. Since the high cards in the dummy and your hand can be seen, the remaining cards are with declarer. This information is quite useful in deciding which card to play on the trick and how to play the suit if you take the trick. If the answer does not make sense, the card led may not be fourth best.

Rule of 10/12

When playing third and fifth best leads the concepts remain the same. Using fifteen as the base, subtract from fifteen the card led **(third or fifth best).** If partner's lead is third best, subtract spot card from twelve (15-3). If partner's lead is fifth best, subtract spot card from ten (15-5). If you are not sure, try both; one of the answers is likely to make more sense than the other, giving you an idea of partner's holdings.

Rule of 15

A rule used for opening the bidding in fourth seat. You should open the bidding if the number of high card points and the number of spades equals fifteen. This assumes that spades are likely to be evenly divided between the two partnerships and that a fit in spades may exist.

Rule of 17

When your partner preempts with a weak major suit two bid, you have to decide whether to compete at the three-level or bid game. To help, one may use the Rule of 17. Add your high card points to the number of trump held. If this total is seventeen or more, bid game; if the total is more than ten but less than seventeen compete to the three-level. If you are still unsure, use OGUST and bid 2NT; if the response is 3♥ (good hand, bad suit) or 3♠ (good hand, good suit), bid game, compete to only the four-level, otherwise, raise the bid to the three-level.

Rule of 20/22

To determine whether or not to open a hand in the first or second seat, one often uses the rule of 20/22. If the number of high card points and the number of cards in your two longest suits add to twenty and you have two quick tricks, open the hand. In the third or fourth seats, one only needs 1 and one-half quick tricks (the rule of 21 ½).

Rule of 24 (Losing Trick Count)

Losing trick count is a method of evaluating the hand to determine the proper bidding level. The method is most effective with unbalanced hands with an eight-card or better trump fit when the two hands have different distributional patterns. The Rule of 24 goes as follows.

STEP 1: Count your losers and assume seven losers in your partner's hand. Rule: 24-7—(Your losers) = Number of Tricks. Reduce the number of tricks by six to determine the level of the bid.

STEP 2: Partner will correct the bid with fewer than seven losers.

Note: Only the first three cards in each suit are considered when counting losers in each suit. With three cards, only the A, K, and Q are not losers. With less than two cards, then AQ=½, Kx=½, KQ=1, K=1, Q=1, Qx=2 represent losers.

Rule of 26

When opening one of a major, some partnerships play direct splinters or concealed/ambiguous splinters. In either case, a splinter bid usually shows four card support for the major suit bid and 13+ HCP.

When should the opening bidder consider slam?

One may apply the Rule of 26.

Opener merely adds his HCP in his suits outside the known splinter suit and if the total is 26+, you should consider slam in the major suit bid.

This rule works because once the partnership can ignore an entire suit, you can expect to make a small slam with only 26+ game points; you do not need 33+ points which is required when you have to take into account all the suits.

Rule of 44

When you open 2♣, should you bid 2NT or two of a major?

If you intend to bid 2NT, you should have 22-24 HCP and notrump distribution. This is not the case when you bid a major 2♥ or 2♠. What are critical are losers and quick tricks, not points! What is needed?

To open 2♣ and then bid a major requires at least five cards in the major, NO MORE THAN FOUR LOSERS and a minimum of FOUR QUICK TRICKS (A=1, K=½, KQ =1); **the rule of 44.**

Given these two requirements, open TWO CLUBS, independent of points.

Let's look at an example: You hold the hand ♠ AKQJ2 ♥ AKQ10 ♦76 ♣ 7. You have only 19 HCP + one length point or twenty starting points. But you have three losers in the minors (less than four losers) and four quick tricks (two aces and two KQ combinations); **using the rule of 44, open the hand 2♣.**

Marty Bergen in the September 2009 issues of the "Bridge Bulletin" (page 50) also reviews this rule, but he did not name it the Rule of 44.

Rule of 64

When opening a hand that is 6-4 in the majors, show the four-card suit only if the number of HCP in the four-card suit is greater than or equal to the number of HCP in the six-card suit. If this is not the case, rebid the six-card suit and do not show the four-card suit.

Rule of 2/3

This was reviewed in Chapter 2, recall that a guide to preemptive opening bids and overcalls is that one cannot afford to set more than five hundred unless one is saving against a slam contract. One often assumes that a vulnerable partner can make two tricks, and a non-vulnerable partner three tricks. Thus, a player who opens 4♠ should have an eight playing trick hand if vulnerable, and a seven playing trick hand if not vulnerable.

Tricks = 13—losers +3 if non-vulnerable, and Playing tricks = 13—losers + 2 if vulnerable. If the number of trick is 10, open the bidding at the 4 level, if the number is 9; open the bidding at the three level. The quantity 13—LTC is called the number of plaing tricks.

The Law of Total Tricks

In his book, Larry Cohen (1972) "To Bid or Not to Bid," Cohen states the Law of Total Tricks as: the **Total Number of Tricks** available on any deal is approximately equal to the total **Number of Trumps.** The total number of trumps means the combined total of cards in both sides' best trump fit. For example, if north-south's best (longest) fit is a 5-4 spade fit, and east-west's best (longest) fit is a 4-4 diamond fit, then the Total Number of Trumps would be 9+8, or 17. Now for the Rule: Never outbid the opponents at the three-level with sixteen trumps. But, always outbid the opponents at the three levels with eighteen trumps. With seventeen trumps, it is usually right to outbid them on the three levels, if not vulnerable.

Note: With 10 trump in a major suit partnership fit, it is usually correct to bid to the 4-level (Due to Marty Bergen, not the Law).

Lets look at the Law in more detail, for example with only sixteen trumps and both sides vulnerable Cohen shows that it is better to let the opponents play in three hearts and for you not to bid three spades when both sides have only 16 trumps. He calls this "chart logic". To see this more clearly lets look at the chart, assuming nobody doubles.

Both Sides Vulnerable with 16 Trumps

Contract played in three spades		Contract played in three hearts	
Our Tricks won	Our Score	Their Tricks won	Our Score
10	+170	6	**+300**

9	+140	7	**+200**
8	- 100	8	**+100**
7	- 200	9	**- 140**

From the chart, we see no matter how the trumps break, when both are vulnerable, that it is better to allow the opponents play the contract in three hearts.

Rule: When both are vulnerable do not compete to the three level with only 16 trumps.

Or, given that both sides have eight trumps between them, both can be expected to make eight tricks, making either two hearts or two spades. This being the case, you must bid to the three level in hearts; however, do not compete to the three level in spades when both sides are vulnerable—this is the "LAW"!

In Larry's new book "Following the Law" the sequel To Bid or Not to Bid, he has a simple formula that may be used when both sides are **vulnerable.**

Formula: $\sum$ Trumps - 11 = $\sum$ Bids

Where the symbol $\sum$ denotes "SUM OF"; thus, applying the formula 16-11 = 5. The bid of 3♥ + 2♠ = 5 so do not bid to the level of three spades.

Important Note: The formula should only be used when both sides are vulnerable.

What happens when both sides are non-vulnerable? Again, we may make a chart, again assuming no doubles:

Both Sides Non-vulnerable with 16 Trumps

Contract played in three spades		Contract played in three hearts	
Our Tricks won	Our Score	Their Tricks won	Our Score
10	**+170**	6	+150
9	**+140**	7	+100
8	- 50	8	**+50**
7	**- 100**	9	- 140

From the chart we see that by competing to the three level, when both sides are non-vulnerable, succeeds in three out of four cases. Thus, while the formula fails we may always use chart logic and bid to the three level when non-vulnerable and having only16 trumps.

What if the spade bidder is vulnerable and the heart bidder is non-vulnerable. Then we have the following chart, again assuming no doubles.

Spade (V) and Hearts (NV) with 16 Trumps

Contract played in three spades		Contract played in three hearts	
Our Tricks won	Our Score	Their Tricks won	Our Score
10	**+170**	6	+150
9	**+140**	7	+100
8	- 50	8	**+50**
7	- 200	9	**- 140**

And finally, suppose the heart bidder is vulnerable and the spade bidder is not. Then we have the following chart with no doubles.

Spade (NV) and Hearts (V) with 16 Trumps

Contract played in three spades		Contract played in three hearts	
Our Tricks won	Our Score	Their Tricks won	Our Score
10	+170	6	**+300**
9	+140	7	**+200**
8	- 50	8	**+100**
7	**- 100**	9	- 140

From the charts we have the following rule.

Rule: Never compete to the three level when both sides are vulnerable or with unfavorable vulnerability with only 16 trumps. However, with favorable vulnerability or both non-vulnerable, compete to the three level playing three spades over three hearts.

The above rules are based upon our chart analysis and bidding the majors. What if one side is bidding a major and the opponents are bidding a minor? Again, when both sides are vulnerable, we may use the simple formula. Looking at an example, suppose the opponents open the bidding 2♦ and your partner bids 2♥ followed by a bid of 3♦ by the opponents. Should you bid 3♥ with three hearts?

Applying the formula there are probably 9 (diamonds) + 8 (hearts) = 17 trumps and 17-11 = 6. Thus, bid 3♥ over 3♦.

However, suppose the bidding went:

RHO	YOU	LHO	PARTNER
2♦ (weak)	pass	3♦	Dbl
Pass	??		

Now what do you bid? At equal vulnerability bid your three card major. However, it they are vulnerable and you are not, pass.

The next logical question you must ask yourself is what happens when both sides have 17 trumps in the majors? This is more complicated. However, let's begin with a logic chart assuming no doubles.

Both Sides Vulnerable with 17 Trumps

Contract played in four spades		Contract played in four hearts	
Our Tricks won	Our Score	Their Tricks won	Our Score
10	**+620**	7	+300
9	- 100	8	**+200**
8	- 200	9	**+100**
7	**300**	10	- 620

Both Sides Non-vulnerable with 17 Trumps

Contract played in four spades		Contract played in four hearts	
Our Tricks won	Our Score	Their Tricks won	Our Score
10	**+420**	7	+150
9	- 50	8	**+100**
8	- 100	9	**+50**
7	**- 150**	10	- 420

The charts suggest that if the opponents can win only 8 or 9 tricks in four hearts that we should not bid four spades winning the same number of tricks.

Based upon 10000 deals, the likelihood of winning 10 tricks occurs about 10% of the time while winning 8 or 9 tricks occurs almost 33% of the time. Hence, it is best to complete to the four level and bid four spades over four hearts with only 17 trumps. However, if you were to apply the formula, 17-11=6 it would suggest that one not compete to the four level. You will be down at least one trick.

Rule: With 17 trumps (vulnerable or non-vulnerable), one may sometimes complete to the four level when bidding spades over hearts.

Rule: With 17 trumps, never bid to the four level of a minor over a three level major suit bid with equal or unfavorable vulnerability.

When bidding four spades over four hearts and both sides vulnerable, the formula suggested that one **not** compete at the four level. However, by taking into account hand shape (distribution), double fits, and poor honor combinations, one may adjust the "Formula" for the law to better decide whether to bid or pass. Let's see how it works.

1) For hands with poor honor combinations subtract one trick; however, with few honor combinations add one trick.
2) For a double fit in two suits, add one trick; but, for a negative fit subtract one.
3) For balanced (flat) hands, subtract one trick; however, for non-balanced hands add one trick.
4) For poor trump quality, subtract one trick (no A/K/Q); however, with a high honor or good intermediaries add one trick.

Taking these factors into account the formula becomes:

Adjusted Formula: $\sum$Trumps - 11 + positive factors—negative factors = $\sum$ Bids

Adding the adjustments to the formula allows one to apply it in more situations since if the factors allow one to reach the 19 "trumps" level observe that 19-11 = 8, allows each to bid to the four level (e.g. 4♥ over 4♣/4♦, or 4♠ over 4♥, but not 5♥ over 4♠).

We now look at an example. You hold the following hand knowing the opponents hold nine hearts and both are vulnerable.

♠J8765 ♥QJ2 ♦J762 ♣Q

Applying the formula with no adjustment 18-11 = 7 you expect to be down only one so you might bid four spades if you were to make no adjustments. However, with spades as trumps subtract one (-1) for no high honor, for poor honor combinations outside of trump subtract one (-1), for the unbalanced hand add +1.

Using the formula with adjustments we have that 18-11-2 +1 = 6. You should not bid to the four level even with 10 trumps!

Do not apply the law without taking into account adjustments.

We look at a second example from Larry Cohen's new book. Your partner opens 2♥ and you hold the following hands:

1) ♠K104 ♥K876 ♦QJ3 ♣QJ4

2) ♠K43 ♥KJ76 ♦QJ43 ♣54

In both situations you have 10 trumps with say 18 total trumps, 18 - 11=7 so do you bid 4♥ over 3♠?

Let's look at each of the hands. With hand (1) you have the King of trump (+1), but many Q's and J's in the other suits (-1), and a flat hand (-1) thus 18 - 11 - 2 +1 = 6, do not compete to the four level!

With hand (2) you also have the King of trump (+1), a flat hand (-1), but fewer minor honors in the other suits; thus, 18-11-1+1=7, compete to the four level.

To read more on making adjustments to the LAW of Total Tricks, read Larry Cohen's (1995) book "Following the Law the Total Tricks Sequel."

Mike Lawrence and Anders Wirgren's (2004) "I Fought the Law of Total Trick," published by Mikeworks, show that hands that agree with the LAW diminish as the number of trumps increase. With sixteen trumps, it is right only 44.1 percent of the time, but with seventeen or eighteen trumps, the Law is right only 36.0 percent of the time. They claim that it isn't the number of trumps that is important, but distribution which the **Law** ignores. It is the partnership short-suit total (SST) that determines how well the trumps will work.

The Lawrence and Wirgren's LAW is: Estimate the short-suit total (SST) between the hands and subtract it from thirteen. With 19-21 HCP between two hands (about half the high card points); your winner's equal thirteen minus your SST. Say your side has a SST of four (a doubleton in each hand), 13-4=9, you can expect to take nine tricks. BID TO THE THREE-LEVEL. With 22-24 HCP, you have one extra trick; with 25-27 HCP, you have two extra tricks, etc.

8 Ever 9 Never

When finessing for the queen, with nine cards and no information, the odds for a drop are 52:48 vs. 50:50 for finesse! This is a nominal difference. In general, if the finesse is into the safe hand, even with nine cards, one would finesse, with no information from the bidding, it is better to play for the drop of the queen.

Let me explain in more detail. With AJxxx (dummy) and Kxxx (hand), plan (1) is to cash the king, and if the queen does not drop, take the finesse and plan (2) is to cash the ace and king to drop the queen. Plan (1) wins if trumps are 3-1 with three on our left (24.87%), when they are 2-2 with the queen on the left (20.35%), and when they are 1-3 with the bare queen onside (6.22%), for a total of 51.22 percent. For plan (2), when the suit is 2-2 (40.70%) or 3-1 either way round with a bare queen (12.44%), for a total of 53.14 percent. I averaged these two approaches to obtain 52.18 percent or about 52 percent! It works! You say, if the queen does not drop with plan (1), each opponent follows low; do not finesse, but play for the drop. Now, the probability of queen to three on the left is 47.85 percent and queen doubleton on the right is 52.15 percent. Here the difference is 52.15-47.85=4.30%. This has a greater difference than playing for the drop, 53.14-51.22=1.92%. Thus, if no queen falls on first card, still play for the drop.

10 Ever 11 Never

A similar rule applies when finessing for the king; with eleven cards, it is again better to play for the drop; however, with ten cards, finesse. Again, the probability is small, about 52 percent vs. 50 percent. I will not bore you with the details. However, let's look at an example.

If the king is missing and you have 11 cards, only two cards are outstanding in the suit. If they split evenly (1-1) which occures 52% of the time, the king will drop. A 2-0 split occurs only about 48% of the time. Thus play for the drop!

While simple rules may be used for the king and the queen, what happens missing the Jack? Suppose you have Q72 and AK106 in a suit. Do you finesse or play for the drop? You have seven hearts and the opponents have six. If they split 3-3, the jack will drop. This referred to as the Finesse Drop Test "FDT". Simply count the out standing cards!

Losing Trick Count (LTC)

The Losing Trick Count (LTC) method of hand evaluation is used when you and your partner have established an adequate fit (at least 5-3) in a trump suit contract. While the original method was introduced in 1934 by Dudley Courtney in his book "The System of Expert Play," the modern method is due to Ron Klinger with suggestions by Jeff Rubens.

The method works with both balanced and distributional hands (since it does not count twice for duplicated honors in short-suits) and hence is preferred to the "Law of Total Tricks" which does not take into account short-suits! Using the LTC, you are able to evaluate you and your partner's potential losers to give you third round control of all suits and thus the number of tricks you can expect to make in your trump contract.

To use the LTC method, one considers only the top three cards in each suit. The top three cards in each suit ace, king, or queen are counted as winners and all others are considered losers. Thus, LTC counts A-x-x, K-x-x, and Q-x-x as two losers. To compensate for this disparity, Jeff Rubens suggests that if you have an equal number of queens and aces, it does not matter; however, if you have more queens than aces, ADD ½ losers for each queen, and if you have more aces than queens, SUBTRACT ½ losers for each ace. This is called the adjusted LTC Method.

Two examples follow.

Hand (a): ♠ KQ543 ♥ AKQ ♦ J72 ♣ 94 and Hand (b): ♠ 74 ♥ void ♦ 875432 ♣ 96432.

Hand (a) contains six losers (one in spades, none in hearts, three in diamonds, and two in clubs); however, there are two more queens than aces, so one adds 1/2 to the total for 6½ losers and thirteen HCP. Hand (b) has no HCP and eight losers.

Using the adjusted LTC method, one is able to calculate the number of expected tricks your partnership should take (with a trump fit) by subtracting the number of losers you and your partner hold from twenty-four. Why twenty-four? It is the total number of losers the partnership can hold, twelve by each partner.

Using the adjusted method, the partnership should be able to take twelve tricks if there are twelve losers between the two hands (24-12=12), eleven tricks with thirteen losers (24-13=11), ten with fourteen and so on.

To use the LTC method, you must be able to estimate the number of losing tricks you and your partner have. Fortunately, there is a high correlation between the expected number of losing tricks and one's HCP count. It goes as follows.

Opener: 12-14 HCP; seven losers; 15-17 HCP; six losers; 18-20; five losers.
Responses: 6-9 HCP; nine losers; 10-12 HCP; eight losers; 12-14 HCP; seven losers.

Using these guidelines, suppose you open the bidding with eighteen HCP (five losers) and your partner makes a limit raise (eight losers). You have thirteen losers between the two hands. LTC predicts that you can expect to take eleven tricks (24-13). You have game but not slam.

There will not be a dramatic difference between standard point-count hand evaluation and LTC; however, it may offer an additional edge since losers in at least one hand is known.

Let's consider a few examples where partner opens 1♥ and you hold:

Hand (1): ♠ 84 ♥ A764 ♦ K6543 ♣ 92

LTC says you have two losers in each suit and adjusting for the ace-queen factor, subtracting ½ from the total, you have 7½ losers. Adding your total to your partner's, the partnership has 14.5 losers or (24-14.5=9.5) 9.5 tricks, almost "10." Thus, even though you have only 7HCP, a limit raise is appropriate. (Note: With four trumps, the number of effective points is ten). Playing Bergen Raises, one would bid 3♣, 7-9 HCP. All methods seem to lead to the same result. However, consider the following balanced hand.

Hand (2): ♠ J65 ♥ A764 ♦ 754 ♣ KQ8

This hand has nine losers and since the number of queens is the same as the number of aces, no adjustment is necessary. Adding your losers to partner's (9+7=16), and using the LTC formula (24-16=8), you can expect only eight tricks. Hence, with 10 HCP you only bid two hearts. With standard point count methods you may give a limit raise or using Bergen you may bid 3♦. Both may result in game contracts for down one since neither take into account the balanced 3-4-3-3 distribution!

Hand (3): ♠ 6 ♥ A7643 ♦ K8642 ♣ 92

The adjusted LTC method indicates that this hand has seven losers, less ½ because you have one ace and no queens. Hence, you expect to take 10.5 tricks even if partner has a minimum opener. Bid four hearts, no interest in slam. Playing Bergen with Swiss bids, you would also bid four hearts. Using Dummy Points, some may bid Jacoby 2NT! This would be incorrect since you need solid high card points for the bid.

Hand (4): ♠ 6 ♥ K643 ♦ Q932 ♣ Q954

You have seven losers and adding ½ because you have two queens and aces; adding your losers to the opener's seven, you expect to make 9½ tricks, almost ten or you can give a limit raise, even though you have only 7 HCP. Using Bergen Raise, do not bid 3♥, you might also miss game.

Hand (5): ♠ 6 ♥ K643 ♦ AK98654 ♣ 9

This hand has one spade loser, two heart losers, one diamond loser, and one club loser, minus one-half loser (one ace and no queens); a 4½ loser hand. Now, partner has a seven or fewer loser hand. Thus, 24-11.5=12.5 expected tricks. You may have a grand slam! Hence, with your fit in hearts, you must use some form of Blackwood to investigate the possibility of slam.

Bridge is a complicated game. The adjusted LTC method allows one to investigate the potential of your combined hands and should not be ignored by duplicate players. It can be used with 2/1, Standard American, Precision, and other methods as a tool for hand evaluation. You should combine it with your method of choice to play better bridge. Reference: Ron Klinger (1998), "Modern Losing Trick Count Flipper." Also see Klinger's Lecture on LTC at http://members.shaw.ca/conventions/ltc.pdf.

For an overview and discussion of many of the above rules and more, consult Mel Colchamiro's book (2007), "How You Can Play like an Expert" by Magnus Press.

Rule of 210

How many times have your heard bridge players say that the 5-level belongs to the opponents?

THIS IS NOT THE CASE IN COMPETITIVE AUCTIONS!

If you are in a competetive auction and the opponents have bid to the 5-level, do you compete, double or pass. You may use the rule of 210.

With two (2) cards in the opponents bid suit you should DOUBLE for penalty.

With ONE (1) card in their suit pass, and with ZERO (0) cards in there suit, compete to the five level.

For example you are bidding diamonds and they are bidding clubs. Use the rule to determine whether or not you should bid five diamonds over five clubs, double, or pass.

This is also the case for hearts over diamonds or spades over hearts. Remember the rule of 210; simple!

The rule comes from **Negative Slam Doubles** which are used to decide whether to sacrifice or not.

Over a slam bid, the second hand doubles to show no defensive tricks but passes with one or more tricks.

If the second hand doubles, then the fourth hand passes with two or more defensive tricks but sacrifices with zero or one.

If the second hand passes, fourth hand also passes with one or more tricks but doubles with no tricks. Now the second hand sacrifices if he has only one trick but passses with two or more.

Chapter 11

Defensive Carding

Standard Carding

On the convention card under defensive carding, one observes two boxes next to Standard: vs. Suits vs. NT. If these are marked, then standard carding means that on partner's lead, one is playing attitude and on the opponent's lead, one is playing count. Attitude is shown by playing a high card to encourage the suit lead and a low card discourages. The cutoff is the six, which means neither.

Count is given by playing high low for an even number of cards and low high for an odd number of cards. Count does not apply for the trump suit. If you do not play trump suit preference, then a high-low discard shows extra trumps (usually three). When the attitude singnal is not needed (partner has led the ace and the king is in dummy) then one shows suit preference. High cards calls for the higher of the remaining suits that are not trump and a low card implies the lower of the two suits that are not trump.

When a low card is lead, it means BOS (Bottom from Something), an Honor. When partner has bid a suit, then one usually leads the highest card in partner's bid suit.

When leading a card most play fourth best for suits and NT. However, using the Rule of 11, this lead helps the opponents. Instead, one may use 3rd/5th best for suits (the rule of 10/12 defined above) and fourth best versus only NT.

Against NT, if partner leads an ace, it requests partner to unblock, to play his highest honor. If the king is lead, partner is to play his second highest honor. If, however, the queen is lead, partner is requested to play the jack.

When partner leads small or fourth best and you take the trick as appropriate, then the standard return of the suit is the lowest card from three remaining cards or the highest from two remaining.

To show shortness in a suit, one plays high-low. If you do get a ruff, the card returned should indicate whether you want the higher suit returned and a low card asks for the lower of the remaining suits.

If you play standard signals and cannot follow suit, then a high card in a suit is encouraging and a low card is discouraging.

Other Carding Agreements

While the standard carding system is played by many duplicate bridge players, some do not like the system since one tends to waste "high" cards. A popular option is upside down count and attitude which is the opposite of standard.

Upside down Count and Attitude

Playing this system, a low card is encouraging on a lead and a high card is discouraging. Now, a doubleton is denoted by low-high instead of high-low. However on leads, one still uses the high-low single to show a doubleton. If you do not, it must be alerted.

Count is also opposite of standard, high-low is odd and low-high is even. When you cannot follow suit, a low card in a suit is encouraging and a high card is discouraging. Most partnerships playing 2/1 use this approach since high values are not wasted.

Odd-Even Discards

Used when you cannot follow suit the first time, an odd card in a suit is encouraging and an even card is discouraging. A high even card says you like the higher of the suits not led, excluding the trump suit, and a low even card says you like the lower of the two suits not lead, again excluding the trump suit. It is played against both suit contracts and notrump. When played in notrump contracts, a low even card says you want the lower of the two suits, excluding the suit lead.

Lavinthal Discards

Similar to odd even, except a low card (less than six) says you would like the lower of the suits that is not trump and a high card says you want the higher of the two suits that are not trump.

Suit Preference Discard

When you cannot follow suit the first time, a discard of any suit shows your suit preference.

Revolving Suit Discards

When unable to follow suit for the first time, you discard a card from a suit you do not want. A high card asks for the higher-ranking suit, and a low card asks for the lower-ranking suit.

What carding system should you adopt? Let's look at an example where both are vulnerable and north deals.

	♠ AKJ10	
	♥ 32	
	♦ 2	
	♣ AKJ1032	

♠ 9532	**N**	♠ 64
♥ Q1094	**W E**	♥ A765
♦ K1095		♦ AJ65
♣ 6	**S**	♣ 987

	♠ Q87	
	♥ KJ8	
	♦ Q876	
	♣ Q54	

The bidding goes:

North	East	South	West
1♣	Pass	1NT	Pass
2♠	Pass	2NT	Pass
3NT	Pass	Pass	Pass

Opening lead is the 4♥.

Playing upside down signals, east wins with the ace. Now, to defeat the contract, the defense needs red suit tricks, so instead of making the routine return of a heart, east returns a low diamond. West now encourages with the five. East continues with the jack of diamonds and the defenders take the first five diamond tricks to defeat the contract. On a heart return, declarer makes eleven tricks.

If instead of playing upside-down signals, suppose you are playing standard signals and make the same switch. Now you must play the ten or the nine of diamonds, declarer covers the jack with the queen and the defenders get only three diamond tricks and a heart. The contract makes.

Of course, there is no "best" carding system. But why use a high card to encourage partner?

On average, the better carding system is upside down count and attitude against both suit and notrump contracts. Against notrump contracts, one usually leads fourth best; however, for suit contracts, it is usually better to use third and fifth leads (see Chapter 12).

Trump suit Preference

The most "basic" trump echo signal is when declarer begins to draw trump. A high-low signal shows an odd number of trumps and a low-high shows an even number (upside-down count).

Instead of showing count, it is often better to tell partner where your strength is outside the trump suit (Trump Suit Preference). Now, going up-the-line shows strength in lower-ranking suit strength and high-low shows strength in a higher-ranking suit.

On the deal below, most wests would lead the ♥9 against the N-S 4♠ contract. East inserted the ten and allowed south to win the trick with the queen. South was reluctant to begin on diamonds before pulling trump. Playing Trump Suit Preference east played the 9-3 in spades to show hearts. When east wins the A♦, he knows to continue hearts, holding the contract to ten tricks.

			♠	A76		
			♥	K63		
			♦	QJ98		
			♣	Q75		
♠	42		**N**		♠	93
♥	9754				♥	AJ10
♦	A7		**W E**		♦	6542
♣	K10982		**S**		♣	J643
			♠	KQJ1085		
			♥	Q82		
			♦	K103		
			♣	A		

On the following layout, east again plays the ♥10; however, he would play the 3-9 of trumps (low-high) showing suit preference for clubs. West must shift to clubs when he wins the ♦A.

	♠ A76		
	♥ K62		
	♦ QJ98		
	♣ Q76		
♠ 42	**N**	♠ 93	
♥ 9754		♥ AJ10	
♦ A7	**W** **E**	♦ 6542	
♣ K10982	**S**	♣ J643	
	♠ KQJ1085		
	♥ Q83		
	♦ K103		
	♣ A		

While Trump suit Preference is a commonly used carding convention when playing in a suit contract, the Smith Echo convention is used when one is playing against a notrump contract.

Smith Echo

Devised and published in 1963 in the "British Bridge World" magazine by I.G. Smith of Great Britain, the Smith Echo is an attitude signal most often used against notrump contracts to show partner either the desire to continue leading the opening suit or to switch to another suit. Unlike the usual suit signals, the Smith Echo is not made on the opening lead but when declarer is next on lead.

When declarer begins to run his own or dummy's long suit, a high-low signal in this suit by the defenders (opening leader and partner) has the following meaning:

If made by partner of the opening leader, it shows good support for the opening lead and asks partner to continue the suit led when regaining the lead. If made by the opening leader, it says that the suit led was weak and that partner should switch to another suit when gaining the lead.

When playing defense, we are all taught to return partner's suit! However, consider the following situation.

	♠	832	
	♥	94	
	♦	AQ3	
	♣	A10863	

♠	AQ104	N	♠	J965
♥	Q1053	W E	♥	J86
♦	76		♦	J1092
♣	942	S	♣	K7

	♠	K7	
	♥	AK74	
	♦	K854	
	♣	QJ3	

Against 3NT, west leads fourth best 3♥ which was covered by east's jack; declarer wins the king and returns the ♣Q and west sees that that declarer has four club tricks, possibly three diamonds and two hearts. The only hope in setting the contract is in spades. Playing Smith Echo, west follows with the 9♣ telling partner NOT TO RETURN HEARTS. Winning with the ♣K, east does not return a heart, his partner's lead. He can see that the only possible return is a spade: for down one!

Some partnerships play **Reverse Smith Echo** when playing for example upside down conut an attitude. Now low-high is encourging! Be careful, look at the opponents carding scheme.

Foster Echo

This carding procedure was devised by Robert Frederick Foster of New York. He also invented the "rule of eleven."

There are several versions of this convention used primarily against notrump. One is used when the opening lead is an honor and the third hand wants to show four cards in the suit headed by an honor.

With four cards, the Foster Echo always begins by following with the third highest card. If the suit lacks an honor, on the second round partner follows with the fourth highest card, but if headed by an honor, one follows with the second highest. For example, suppose you (third hand) hold:

Hand (1) 8 7 5 2 Hand (2) Q 7 5 2

---

and, partner leads the king, with hand (1) you play the five followed by the two (high-low: have no honor); with hand (2) the five is followed by the seven (low-high: have an honor). This version of Foster Echo allows the opening leader to locate the missing honors in the suit and to help choose the right continuation. If you were playing the upside down carding system, one would discard the eight with hand (1) to discourage and the two with hand (2) to encourage.

Another version (less frequently used) combines an unblocking play with giving count. If the third hand cannot top either the card led or the card played by dummy, he follows with his second highest card; with a four-card holding, on the second round plays the third highest card, next the highest, reserving the lowest for the last round. However, with a three-card holding, on the first round partner also plays the second-highest card in the suit and on the second round the highest card. This may cause some ambiguity if the suit is headed by two honors. Holding, for example, Q-10-x or J-10x, partner would play the ten on the first round; hence, the leader doesn't know if the higher honor is the queen or the jack.

Chapter 12

Bridge Leads

Many books have been written on Bridge Leads, but my favorite is by Sally Brock (2007), "Leading Questions in Bridge" by Master Point Press. While leads are difficult since a contract may be made or fail because of the lead, the most important thing to remember is to listen to the bidding since it may help the most in what one should or should not lead. Then you must decide whether to be Active or Passive.

In general, an active lead is when you lead honors; however, it may give up a winner. Alternatively, you may be passive, which avoids giving the declarer a trick he does not deserve.

Dick Olson at www.slospin.net has provided a comprehensive summary regarding leads, following the principles put forth by Sally Brock. His recommendations follow, Points 1-6.

Standard Leads

(1) Leading a Trump

If you can attack a contract, it is usually best to do so. However, there are times when a trump lead is called for.

Example 1: You have: ♠64 ♥AJ93 ♦AQ105 ♣KJ6

The bidding goes: [1♠ Dbl 2♠ Pass]: [4♠ Pass Pass Pass]

Since leading a side suit is unattractive, lead a trump here.

Example 2: The bidding goes: [1♠ Pass 1NT Pass 2♠]

An optimal time to lead trumps is when dummy denies support for a major suit opener. In Example 2, responder obviously has 0, 1, or 2 card support for spades. This is a good time to lead a trump.

(2) Leads in Suits that include the Ace

Never under lead an ace against a suit contract at trick one.

If you do not have the king, lead the ace only when you are defending against a slam (except 6NT) or declarer preempted, or

Your ace is singleton, or
Your ace is the only unbid suit against five clubs or five diamonds, or
Your side promised length and strength in the suit, or
You have a seven—or eight-card suit.

Lead the ace from AK (unless you play Rusinow Leads); after trick one, lead the king from AK.

(3) Short-Suit Leads

Singletons are invariably good choices.

Doubletons are overrated, especially with one honor.

The best time to lead a short-suit is with trump control, e.g., A63.

Avoid a short-suit lead when you do not need a ruff; e.g., with trump holdings such as QJ9 and KQ10 or when you have trump length. With four trumps it is usually correct to lead a long suit to make declarer ruff (this is called a forcing game).

(a) Basic Leads

In selecting your lead, you must consider your hand as well as inferences from the bidding.

Desirable Leads

Partner's suit, especially if he promised five or six cards. The proper card to lead is the same one you would have led in any other suit. Therefore, lead low from Q63 or K852 (this is called BOS "bottom of something"; however, some lead the top of a suit if partner has bid the suit. It is best to discuss your approach with partner). Top of a three-card (or longer) sequence (top of nothing).

Sequences

It is better to lead top of a sequence than fourth-best (or third and fifth against a suit contract)

A sequence must contain an honor (10 or higher)

Against a suit contract, a sequence can be as short as two cards. Lead the king from KQ53 and the queen from QJ64. However, against a notrump contract, lead low from both holdings.

Partner has Not Bid and There is no Sequence

Prefer to lead a suit the opponents have not shown. In general, try to lead from length against any contract. A lead from Q1074 is more attractive than from Q107. It is acceptable to lead away from a king against a suit contract.

Leading Dummy's Suit

Leading through strength is overrated. Lead dummy's suit only when partner is likely to have length and strength behind him.

(b) Standard Leads Against Suits (3ʳᵈ and 5ᵗʰ)—Preferred

Sequences:

A K x, **10** 9 x, **K** Q x, K **J** 10 x, Q J x, K **10** 9 x, J 10 9, Q **10** 9 x, K Q 10 9

Length Leads with an Honor (X = honor)—lowest-card lead usually indicates an honor:

X x **x**, X x **x** x (start of high-low), X x x x **x** (start of low-high), X x x x **x** x (start of high-low)

Length leads Without an Honor:

x x, x **x** x (MUD to indicate no honor), x **x** x x (start of high-low), x x **x** x x (start of low-high), x x **x** x x x (start of high-low)
Primary signals:
Count is usually first option
Attitude is given if count doesn't make sense
Suit preference is given if neither count nor attitude makes sense (some always give attitude first).

(c.) Standard Leads Against Suits (4ᵗʰ Best)—Not preferred

Sequences:
A **K** x, **10** 9 x, **K** Q x, K **J** 10 x, Q J x, K **10** 9 x, **J** 10 9, Q **10** 9 x, **K** Q 10 9
Length Leads With an Honor (X = honor)—Lowest-card lead usually indicates an honor:
X x **x**, X x x **x**, X x x x **x** x, X x x **x** x x
Length leads Without an Honor: x x, x **x** x (MUD to indicate no honor), x **x** x x (MUD), x x **x** x x (MUD), x x **x** x x x (MUD)

Primary signals:
Attitude is first option
Count is given if attitude doesn't make sense
Suit preference is given if neither attitude nor count makes sense

(4) Standard Leads against Notrump

Length Leads—> 4th best x x, x **x** x (MUD), x **x** x x (MUD if no honor), x **x** x x x (MUD if no honor), **10** 9 x,

K Q x, K **J** 10 x, Q J x, K **10** 9 x, J 10 9, Q **T** 9 x, K Q 10 9
A **K** x x (x)—only against notrump; K asks for attitude

A K J x (x)—only against notrump; A asks to unblock honor; if no honor, then give count

Primary signals: attitude then count

(5) Journalist Leads—"Ten Promises and Jack Denies" (Non-Standard)

Usually against notrump, though some play it against suit contracts. Purpose is to promise or deny one of the top three honors. Whenever the opening lead is a 10, the leader promises the A, K, or Q and an interior sequence. Whenever a jack is led, the leader denies having the A, K, or Q and shows a sequence headed by the jack. Note a lead of the queen always promises the jack or a singleton, never lead from Qx.

Used when you have:
A high honor with an interior sequence—lead the 10 which indicates having the A, K, or Q. An "interior sequence" is defined as QJ10x, J109x, or 109xx (98xx is not considered a sequence here).

An interior sequence with nothing above it—10 which denies having the A, K, or Q

Typical hands where a 10 is lead ("Ten Promises")

AJ109(x), AJ10x(x), KJ109(x), K1098(x), Q109x(x)—lead the 10

but for the sequence QJ109(x) or QJ10x(x)—lead the Q

Typical hands where the J is lead ("Jack Denies")

J109x(x), J10x(x)—lead the J

Other leads that deny holding an A, K, or Q

1098(x) or 109x(x)—lead the 9 (can't lead the 10) which promises either the 10 at the head of a sequence with no high honor or a doubleton 9x.

(6) Rusinow Leads (Non-Standard) normally used against suit contracts and only on the opening lead. Primary purpose of these leads is to remove the ambiguity when using the king lead from AK.

The most difficult play in bridge is the lead. To become proficient, you must listen to the auction. Rules are only helpful when you have limited information. Let's look at an example found in Bridge with the Abbot (David Bird), in the September 2009 issue of the "Bridge Bulletin," page 59.

	♠ 753	
	♥ 742	
	♦ AQ764	
	♣ 83	
♠ QJ1062	**N**	♠ 94
♥ 5	**W E**	♥ 983
♦ K95		♦ J103
♣ 9742	**S**	♣ KQ1065
	♠ AK8	
	♥ AKQJ106	
	♦ 82	
	♣ AJ	

The bidding:

West	North	East	South
			2♣
Pass	2♦	Pass	2♥
Pass	♥	Pass	3♠
Pass	4♦	Pass	6♥
All Pass			

As west, what do you lead? The natural lead is the ♠Q (top of a sequence), but if you listen to the bidding, what have you learned? Clearly, south has a control in spades and north has a control in diamonds. And, a trump lead gains nothing; in general, it is not a good idea to lead a singleton trump. The lead that has a chance of setting the contract is a club lead; lead the club 9. Leading away from the king of diamonds when the opponents are strong in the suit is never a good idea.

For more advice on bridge leads, one should also consult the book by Mike Lawrence (1996), "Opening Leads," Los Alamitos, CA: C&T Bridge Supplies.

Bridge leads Dos and Don'ts

The most difficult task in bridge is the opening lead. It often results in a top or a bottom. You cannot be correct 100% of the time, but there are some does and don'ts. I will go out on a "limb" with the following general guidelines.

Don'ts

1) Don't lead away from a King, if you have another option.
2) Don't lead trump.
3) Don't lead an Ace in suit contracts.
4) Don't lead a singleton when you have a better alternative.
5) Don't lead your partner's suit if he has not shown a good suit or you have trump control.
6) Don't lead the unbid suit when the opponents have jumped to game in notrump.
7) Don't lead fourth best in notrump when your hand is weak or your suit has bad intermediates.
8) Don't lead doubletons.
9) Don't lead from broken honor sequences.

The above are general guidelines, of course there are exceptions. Never say never in the game of bridge.

Dos

1) Lead fourth best in notrump contracts with good intermediaries when you have bid your suit and the opponents have bid notrump.
2) Lead partner's suit, even if you have a good 5-card suit as an alternative, unless you also have an outside entry.
3) When the opponents are in a major suit contract, lead the other major unless you have an alternative lead in a minor suit.
4) Lead the unbid suit in notrump or a suit contract if the opponents reached the contract slowly.
5) When you have a choice between two suits, lead the one with the strongest secondary cards.
6) When partner has bid two suits, lead his second suit. Or, lead a singleton if you know partner has values.
7) When the opponents have bid their suit aggressively, it is time to be passive.
8) Lead an ace against preempts if you have one.
9) When you have a weak defensive hand lead an unsupported honor in partner's suit.

10) Lead a trump when you have five trumps or when partner's double shows good trumps.

The does and don'ts assume that the auction was uninformative. For example, the bidding may go 1x—1NT.

(1) Suppose the bidding goes: (South) 1♠ - Pass - 4♠ - All pass and as west you hold the following hand:

♠ 7 ♥ K873 ♦ KJ53 ♣ K985

You have no information. What do you lead?

Clearly a trump lead is passive and gains nothing for the defense. Do not use the adage "When in doubt lead trump"!

Leading away from your kings in general will give up a trick; do no close your eyes and hope for the best! Observe that by leading a club or a heart will establish at most a single trick. However, if partner were to hold the queen of diamonds then leading a diamond may set up two tricks.

Hence, you must lead the ♦J or the 3.

(2) The bidding goes (South) 3♠ - Pass - 4♠ - double—All pass and as west you are on lead with the following hand. What do you lead?

♠ AQ7 ♥ J5 ♦ 10987 ♣ K653 what do you lead?

The immediate raise to four spades suggests that dummy has a solid suit and your partner has doubled. You have no information, lead the trump ace and after seeing dummy you can decide on your switch to reach partner. Do not guess.

As the opponents' bidding becomes stronger, your opening lead should become easier.

The guidelines may help with no information, but there is no substitute for Listening to the Auction!

Leads against 3NT

The bidding has gone 1NT—3NT and you hold the following cards:

(1)   ♠ Q105 ♥ KQ853 ♦ K83 ♣ 82
(2)   ♠ 953 ♥ Q53 ♦ 762 ♣ J842
(3)   ♠ QJ976 ♥ K5 ♦ J7632 ♣ 7

(4)   ♠ AQ97 ♥ AQ54 ♦ 10987 ♣ 7
(5)   ♠ 73 ♥ A54 ♦ Q1087 ♣ Q753
(6)   ♠ 532 ♥ AQ754 ♦ QJ103 ♣ Q
(7)   ♠ 973 ♥ K4 ♦ 876543 ♣ K7
(8)   ♠ 972 ♥ AJ1094 ♦ 76 ♣ 543
(9)   ♠ Q97 ♥ AJ7 ♦ KJ2 ♣ 8763
(10)   ♠ AQ97 ♥ AQ54 ♦ 10987 ♣ 7
(11)   ♠ K9852 ♥ 7 ♦ QJ1064 ♣ 73
(12)   ♠ A7 ♥ A53 ♦ A76 ♣ 65432

With each of the above hands, you have no information about, what do you lead?

(1)   Clearly your best suit is hearts. Lead 4th best, the ♥5.

(2)   You have a weak hand and should try to fine partner's best suit. Leading an unbid major is usually better than leading an unbid minor. You have values in hearts, lead the ♥3.

(3)   You have five spades to the Queen and five diamonds to the Jack. It is usually better to lead a strong four cad suit instead of a weak five card suit. Lead the ♥Q.

(4)   You do not want to lead from your AQ tenaces, hence, lead the ♦10. Playing coded 9's and 10's it conveys zero or two of the top three honors.

(5)   You have two nice 5-card suits; lead the fourth best from the stronger suit, the ♦7.

(6)   You have two strong suits, one 5-card and one 4-card. Lead from the stronger 5-card suit. Lead the ♥5, fourth best.

(7)   You have two weak suits, spades and diamonds. You will not develop a trick in diamonds. Lead the ♠9.

(8)   Lead the ♥10 to show zero or two of the top honors in hearts.

(9)   You have a great hand, lead top of nothing or the ♣8. Partner when he gets in will switch to another suit.

(10)   Protect your tenaces and lead the ♦10.

(11)   You have two suits of equal length, lead from the stronger suit. Lead the ♦Q.

(12)   You have three entries to your club suit, lead the ♣6.

How did you do?

In our examples we had no information from the bid; however with more information, the easier the lead. Let's consider an example. Suppose you hold the following hand:

♠ J987 ♥ 853 ♦ J83 ♣ A75

And the bidding goes:

West (you)	North	East	South
Pass	1♦	Pass	1♠
Pass	3♦	Pass	3NT
Pass			

Do you have any clues? First, you know that North has a strong diamond suit and that the defense has spades.

Partner did not overcall one heart over the bid of one diamond so that suggests that you should not lead a heart, he does not have first or second round control. However, he might have a club holding and since the opponents stopped at the three level, may have some values in clubs.

You best lead is a low club—not the ace!

The bidding goes:

	North	South
	1♠	1NT
	3♥	3NT

You as west hold the following cards:

♠ A7 ♥ 1098 ♦ J754 ♣ J654

What do you lead?

South has not bid either of the minor suits and did not support the majors bid by his partner. The lead of the 4 of either minor form the Jack is in general not a good lead in notrump, the opponents have the minors. Lead the ♥10.

Always listen to the bidding!

Rusinow Leads

Devised by **Mr. Sydney Rusinow**, and applied at the bridge table with his friends and partners, **Mr. Philip Abramsohn** and **Mr. Simon Rossant**, in the 1930s. Although the leads were original and unique, the ACBL, for undisclosed reasons, declared them illegal and barred the use of this principle at ACBL sanctioned tournaments until 1964, whereupon the ban was lifted. The principle behind the concept of the Rusinow Leads apparently did not sit well with the bridge community in the United States, but they were adopted by many European bridge players. They were employed also by Mr. Walter Avarelli and Mr. Giorgio Belladonna and incorporated into the **Roman System**, which they devised, and became also known as **Roman Leads**. Since the Rusinow Leads have become common practice with many bridge players, they have been incorporated in several bidding systems.

The principle behind Rusinow Leads is simply the leading of the second-ranking of touching honors. Rusinow Leads are used only on the first trick against a suit contract in a suit, which the partner has not bid during the auction, if at all. It is uncommon to employ the Rusinow Leads also against a No Trump contract since the purpose of the lead against a No Trump contract is entirely different in nature, but it is not illegal.

Since the 1930s represented the era of the transition from Whist to Contract Duplicate, many innovations had to be considered and many traditional playing strategies had to be re-arranged and redefined. It was quite normal practice for the defenders to lead the King against a contract, when holding the Ace and King of the same suit. It was also quite standard for the defender to lead the King against a contract, when holding the King and Queen of the same suit. This standard practice sometimes led to unusual situations where the partner of the defender was uncertain as to the better play, since the partner was uncertain as to whether his partner had the Ace or the Queen after leading the King.

	Dummy	
	♠ 654	
Defender		**Defender**
♠ K		♠ J103

The ambiguity of the lead becomes apparent. If West has the King/Queen, East will wish to play the Jack of Spades and encourage West at the same time. However, if West has the Ace/King, then East will wish to play the 3, so that West will choose to change to another suit. If south, the declarer holds the Queen-9-8-x, a continuation will give south at least one winner in this suit.

In the early days of bridge, defenders were looking for new ways to impart information, and to try new strategies. The attempt at leading the Ace from an Ace/King, promising the King, proved unsatisfactory, since leading a single Ace against a suit contract seemed prudent and in hindsight the only lead that would defeat the suit contract. It was concluded that one problematic situation was exchanged for a second problematic situation, and it was not quite clear, which principle should be more favored, or if a new principle should be created for the defense.

Mr. Sydney Rusinow came up with a solution, which was first endorsed by Mr. Ely Culbertson. However, the solution did not gain very much favor and popularity by the bridge community. The solution was to lead the second highest from touching honors, such as leading the King from Ace/King and Queen from King/Queen and Jack from Queen/Jack. Although this solution of leading in this manner was eventually barred from ACBL tournaments, the Europeans seemed captivated by the concept. They were eventually adopted by the World Bridge Federation and especially by the advocates of the Roman Club bidding system, the players of which were looking for innovative ideas.

The main principles of the Rusinow Leads are as follows:

1. **Ace: this lead denies the King, except when holding the Ace-King as a doubleton.**

2. **King: this lead is from Ace-King. The third hand should signal with the Queen or a doubleton.**
3. **Queen: this lead is from King-Queen. The third hand should normally signal with the Ace or Jack, but not with a doubleton if the dummy contains three or four small cards of the same suit. This may be to avoid a <u>Bath Coup</u>, whereby the declarer could possible be holding the Ace-Jack-x, and thereby cash two tricks.**
4. **Jack: this lead is from Queen-Jack.**
    4.1. **Ten: this lead is from Jack-Ten.**
    4.2. **Nine: this lead is from Ten-Nine.**

These leads complement the MUD lead convention, in which the original lead is from three small cards. The first is the Middle card, followed by the higher card, followed by the lower card, when holding only three cards in that suit, or Middle, Up, Down.

5. **In the case that more than two touching honors are held, and a lead has to be made, the card representing the second-highest honor is led. For example, from King-Queen-Jack, the Queen is led. The second card from this sequence, which is then led, is the Jack. The third hand knows that his partner holds the King of that suit.**

Rusinow Leads gave the partner information about the holding, but the Rusinow Leads are used only on the first trick against a suit contract. This fact is very important to remember concerning the communication with the partner. After the first trick, it is important to remember that the highest card should be led from touching honors. This is true whether the lead if from either of the hands of the defenders.

An important side note: the Rusinow Leads were originally devised for use against a suit contract. The experiment was made to use this lead also against a No Trump contract, and the experiment failed miserably, since the purpose of a lead against a No Trump contract is different than against a suit contract. The information needed by the partner is whether the partner has led from his longest suit, and not where his honors are located.

Whether or not Rusinow Leads should be part of the partnership agreement must be considered by the individual partnership. The advantages are obvious and they are presently accepted as a form of defense by the ACBL and most other bridge governing bodies around the world. They must be noted on the Convention Card and must be made known to the opponents.

If you wish to include this feature, or any other feature, of the game of bridge in your partnership agreement, then please make certain that the concept is understood by both partners. Be aware whether or not the feature is alertable or not and whether an announcement should or must be made. Check with the governing body and/or the bridge district and/or the bridge unit prior to the game to establish the guidelines applied. Please include the particular feature on your convention card in order that your opponents are also aware of this feature during the bidding process, since this information must be made known to them according to the Laws of Duplicate Contract Bridge. We do not always include the procedure regarding Alerts and/or Announcements, since these regulations are changed and revised during time by the governing body. It is our intention only to present the information as concisely and as accurately as possible.

This discussion is from Simon's Web page at: members.shaw.ca/conventions/alpha.htm

Chapter 13
Completing the Convention Card

The 2/1 Convention Card

The growth in Bridge Systems since the 1950s has revolutionized the game today, there are numerous systems used by the experts. For example, on Graeme Williams' Web site: www.gwilliamd.org.uk/systems/hdex.html, he discusses the following systems: ACOL, Blue Team Club, Culbertson, Eastern Scientific, EHAA, Goren, Kaplan-Scheinwold, Precision, Roth-Stone, Schenken, Standard American, and 2/1 Game Force.

As a new bridge player, which one should you learn? According to Bert Hall & Lynn

Rose-Hall (1996), "How the Experts Win at Bridge," Jordan Press, the optimum system used by many top players in the world today is 2/1. However, the 2/1 approach includes many conventions. Which ones should you learn?

In this book, I have tried to cover the most played 2/1 conventions. As a guide to the utility of conventions, one must decide upon the effectiveness of the convention, how often it occurs, if it greatly improves your bidding, how it may affect a natural bid, and whether or not your partner understands and remembers it. What one is seeking is a number of conventions that meet these tests, blend together, and effectively handle a range of hands that come up most often. The critical variable in the development of the system is whether or not the conventions BLEND together. Don't play a convention because it is a "present day" gimmick. In this book, we have put together such a set that does just that—blends. Playing 2/1 Game Force, one may include in the Convention Card, the following items.

Notrump
Strong 1NT (14/15-17)
Jacoby transfers
Gambling 3NT
Extended Texas Transfers
Stayman with super accepts
Smolen
4-Way Transfers
Inter over NT (Tran Lebensohl)

Major Suit
5-Card Major
1NT Semi-Forcing
Combined Bergen
-Fit Bids
-Constructive Raise
-Concealed Splinters
-Jacoby 2NT (Scroll)
2-Way Reverse Drury
Lisa Convention

Minor Suit
Convenient Minor
Inverted (13+)
Crisscross (10-12)
Flip-Flop
2NT Invitational
Walsh Club
Bypass 4 diamonds

Slam Bidding
1430 RKCB (kickback)
Gerber+ Super Gerber

Special Doubles
Negative
Responsive

Opening Two Bids
2♣ - Strong
2♦ - XShape Flannery

EKCB
Grand Slam Force
Minorwood
Cuebidding
Pick a Slam

Support D/Re-Dbl
Fisher Double
Cooperative
Maximal
Fishbein

2♥/♠ Weak (5-10)
Ogust + Modified
2NT (20-21)
Muppet Stayman (3♣)

Other Conventions
Two-Way (NMF)
Fourth Suit Forcing to Game
Weak Jump Shifts
Michaels
Leaping Michaels
Sandwich 1NT/2NT
Unusual 2NT
Unusual vs. Unusual
Unusual vs. Michaels
Skew (Hess) Cuebids
Western Cue
3344
Game Try Relay
Wolff Sign-Off with Checkback
Reverse Good Bad 2NT
Serious 3NT
Scrambling 2NT

Defensive Carding
Leads Suit 3rd & 5th
NT 4th Best
Coded 9s & 10s
Signals USDCA
-Attitude
Trump Suit Preference
Smith Echo

Defense Conventions
Inter Over NT
-Modified Cappelletti
-Modified DONT
Transfer Lebensohl

The Bridge World Standard

Bridge World Standard (BWS) is a system based on the majority preferences of approximately 125 leading experts and thousands of Bridge World readers. Its methods were determined by polls: a clear expert preference determined the treatment; close questions were decided by the readers' vote. Because it is a consensus system, BWS is rarely used by regular partnerships. It is, however, very valuable in forming casual partnerships—if both partners know the system, they need discuss only those areas in which individual preferences do not conform to the BWS treatment. BWS is also used as a foundation for voting in the Master Solvers' Club in The Bridge World.

Opening Bids and Responses

Minimum balanced hand: good 12.

1 NT: good 15 to bad 18. Jacoby transfers (splinter rebids; game raise is slam try; two diamonds plus two spades forcing only one round); two spades shows minors; three hearts invitational, major two-suiter; Texas transfers; Stayman (two-spade rebid invitational; two-heart rebid weak; minor rebid forcing); Smolen; three of a minor invitational; Gerber.

2 NT: good 20 to bad 22 (small doubleton acceptable). Jacoby transfers; three spades shows minors; Texas transfers; Gerber; High Gerber.

Two clubs artificial, strong: Natural responses (positive response requires good suit); two diamonds neutral; second negative=cheaper minor to three diamonds.

Preempts: Weak two-bids (two notrump, which asks for feature if maximum, and new-suit responses forcing). "Weak gambling" three-bids. New-suit response to game-level opening asking-bid (step responses).

3 NT: gambling (little outside strength); four-diamond response artificial.

Five-card majors in first and second position: one-notrump response forcing; two-over-one promises rebid; limit jump raises (four trumps; cheapest rebid asks shortness); two notrump strong raise (asks shortness); three notrump natural, 16-17; passed-hand responses: one notrump 6-12, two clubs strong raise, three clubs natural.

Responses to minor-suit openings: Single raise strong, 10 pts. up, denies major; jump raise weak; 1 NT 8-10 after one club, 6-10 after one diamond; two notrump natural, game force; up the line may be ignored with moderate hand; two-club response to one diamond promises a rebid.

Partnership Bidding

Splinter raises: Double-jump shift after suit opening; single jump in fourth suit if one level above a reverse; single jump in third suit if four level, or reverse; double jump in fourth suit; four of opener's minor after new-suit rebid; jump-shift by two-diamond responder to two clubs; new-suit jump after single major raise; double new-suit jump after 1 NT response.

Slam methods: Roman key-card Blackwood with trump-queen ask; DOPI; five notrump (2 keys) or higher response with void; 5 NT rebid invites seven, asks king cue-bidding. Cheapest-weakest responses to grand-slam force. Gerber after one-notrump or two-notrump opening, or rebid. Picture jumps in forcing situations.

Other methods: Fourth-suit bidding: nonforcing by passed hand unless reverse; one spade may be weak; promises another bid at two level; game force if reverse or at three level. Third-suit bidding: game force if reverse or at three level, otherwise does not promise rebid. Opener's suit-over-suit reverse promises rebid; responder's cheaper of 2 NT and fourth suit neutral. All non-jump-shift secondary jumps by one-over-one responder invitational. Opener's jump rebid to four of original minor is strong raise. Unbid minor forcing and artificial after one-notrump rebid, requests support. Three clubs artificial, may be prelude to signoff, after two-notrump jump by opener. Reraise to three of major preemptive.

Competitive Bidding

Negative doubles: After suit opening, through three spades (including opener's suit); after one-notrump opening, at the three level; unlimited; suggests length in unbid major; of one heart shows four spades; of one spade after minor opening shows four or more hearts. Repeat same-suit double by negative doubler for takeout.

Weak jump responses after overcall of minor opening.

Over overcall: jump raise preemptive, cue-bid is at least limit raise; jump cue-bid is splinter.

Over two-suited overcalls: cheapest cue = raise; next cue = unbid suit; unbid suit nonforcing.

Over minor Michaels: unbid suit nonforcing; major suit shows stopper.

Over major Michaels: cue-bid in enemy major is limit raise or better; new suit forcing.

Support doubles and redoubles when raise to two is available, except one club—(pass)—one diamond—(one spade)—double shows hearts.

Over a double of partner's suit bid: new suit forcing at the one level only; jump shift nonforcing; two notrump limit raise or better; double jump in new suit splinter

Lebensohl after two-level overcalls of one notrump (fast denies stop).

Jump cue-bid by opener is splinter raise.

Pass and pull strong in forcing situation.

Defensive Bidding

Michaels cue-bids (in minor: majors; in major: other major plus unspecified minor) in direct and reopening position over suit one-bids and over one-notrump response; weak or quite strong.

Direct jump cue-bid natural over minor, asks stopper over major.

Takeout doubles of preemptive openings through four hearts; otherwise for penalty.

Maximal overcall double of raised suit.

Reopenings: 1 NT, 10-14; 2 NT, 18-19.

In fourth seat over a response: one notrump and cue-bids natural.

After 1 NT overcall: two clubs Stayman; jumps invitational.

Double of free new-suit bid by responder shows fourth suit plus tolerance.

Cappelletti over one notrump (all situations).

Direct two notrump unusual for lower unbid suits; weak or quite strong.

Takeout doubles: may be light with shape; new-suit rebid very strong.

Preemptive jump overcalls and jump raises of overcalls.

Responsive and extended responsive doubles after takeout doubles, at the two level after an overcall, after a preempt.

Mixed-raise advances of overcalls.

Cue-bid by advancer forcing until a suit is bid twice, or game.

Lebensohl after double of weak two-bid, either position by unpassed hand, and following one-notrump overcall.

Opening Leads

Against suit contracts: third from even; low from odd. All other leads old-fashioned.

The Acol Bidding System

As explaned on bridgeguys.com, the Acol Bidding System is not a Standard Bidding System as the Five Card American Standard Bidding System. This means that the Acol Bidding System is rather interpretable and allows stronger latitude in flexibility according to the partnership agreement. We would like to present a General Structure of the Acol Bidding System in order that the bridge player, who would like to learn, has a general concept of the meanings behind the bids.

The General Structure of the Acol Bidding System is outlined below:

Opener:		With 5+ card suits, open the higher ranking longer suit
		With only 4 card suits, such as a 4-3-3-3 distribution, open the 4 card suit. If you wish to guarantee a 5-card 1 Spade opener, the opener will then open 1 Club with 4 Spades, and this is the only situation when you will only have 4 Spades.
		with a 3-4-4-2 touching distribution, open the higher suit. The exception is when your holding is Hearts and Spades as in the distribution of 4-4-2-3, and the general rule is to open 1 Heart.
		with a 4-4-1-4 distribution, open the suit immediately below the singleton. The exception is the 4-4-4-1 distribution, and then the opening should be 1 Heart.
Responder:		A non-reverse change of suit rebid by opener is non-forcing, if the responder bids at the One Level, but is forcing if the responder has made a 2-over-1 response.
		Any change of suit rebid by the responder is forcing except over opener's 1 No Trump rebid.
Opener's Rebid:		A non-reverse change of suit rebid by opener is non-forcing, if the responder bids at the One Level, but is forcing if the responder has made a 2-over-1 response.
		A reverse by opener is forcing for one round with 16+ points and at least 5-4 distribution and the first suit will be longer.

The following principles are major in the general principles of the Acol System. Much of this has to be learned by heart, but once it is memorized, then the auction proceeds with both partners acting as one. Even with the 5-Card American Standard we had to memorize certain guidelines and principles to show length and strength.

Fourth-Suit Forcing is generally forcing, except in the following bidding auction:

Opener		Responder
1 ♣		1 ♦
1 ♥		1 ♠

1.	In this instance, a 1 No Trump rebid shows 15+ HCPs and is generally forcing.
2.	However, rebids by the responder at the Two-Level are non-forcing over 2♣ / 2♦ / 2♥ by the opener.
3.	Three-Level rebids are generally forcing.

Any possibly ambiguous bid by the opener or responder shows values or length in that suit. This is called **fragmenting**, rather than **splintering**, which means that the bid is indicating a stopper, rather than asking for a stopper.

Note: **To fragment means to show a Stopper. To Splinter is asking for a Stopper**, and this is very important to remember.

Over 3 of a Major, when there is a known fit in the Major, 3 No Trump is a natural bid, if Three of a Major is Non-Forcing. But it is a **Trump Cue** if Three of a Major is forcing.

Over 3 of a Minor, Three No Trump is always at least a suggestion to play.

A simple raise of responder's 2-over-1 is Invitational, that is Non-Forcing. A Jump raise to 4 of a Minor is Generally Forcing and suggests slam interest. Hands worth "3-5" Minor raise must find another bid.

The auction 1 Spade - 2 Hearts promises 5 cards in Hearts, but 2 of a Minor promises only a 4-card suit.

A new suit at the Four Level, after partner has shown strength, is a cuebid showing a hand too strong to raise partner's last bid suit directly.

The following bidding auctions should clarify this principle:

Opener		Responder		Meaning
1 ♣		1 ♠		
3 ♥		4 ♦		Shows a strong Heart raise.
1 ♥		1 ♠		
3 ♥		4 ♣/4 ♦		The rebid by responder is a cuebid, and Hearts is the agreed upon suit.
1 ♥		2 ♣		

2 ♦			Forcing bid for one round.
1 ♥		1 ♠	
3 ♥			This bid is invitational.
1 ♥		2 ♣	
3 ♥			This bid is game forcing.
1 ♠		2 ♥	
3 ♥			This bid is invitational.
1 ♣		1 ♥	
2 ♦		2 ♥/3 ♣	Either of these rebids by responder is not encouraging, Non-Forcing.
1 ♣		1 ♥	
2 ♦		2 ♠	Indicates a 4-card Spade suit and is game forcing.
1 ♣		1 ♥	
2 ♦		2 NT	This bid is invitational.
1 ♣		1 ♥	
2 ♦		3 ♦	This bid is forcing for one round.
1 ♣		1 ♥	
2 ♦		3 ♥	This bid is game forcing, because opener has reversed.

In the bidding sequence:

Opener		Responder		Meaning
1 ♥		1 ♠		
2 ♦		3 ♣		

3 ♦	3 ♥	The last bid by the responder is an attempt at slam.
3 NT		This is a **Trump Cue**.

In the bidding sequence:

Opener	Responder	Meaning
1 ♥	3 ♥	
3 NT		This bid gives the responder a choice of the better contract.

These examples show the general principles of the auction using the Acol System. Many of them must simply be memorized. It is not surprising that many bridge players incorporate some/many of the guidelines used in the Acol System. We must remember that many intelligent minds went into devising new methods of bidding and thereby creating new Bidding Systems. Many of these methods and treatments and conventions have become intermixed with other Bidding Systems, and bridge players around the world use them without always realizing that they are an integral part of different Bidding Systems.

Chapter 14

Play of the Hand

There are many great books on Play of the Hand. A new book I would strongly recommend is by Guy Levé (2007), "Encyclopedia of Card Play Techniques at Bridge" Master Point Press. When playing a hand, have a plan and be aware of the bidding, as Levé recommends, STOP—LOOK at DUMMY—LISTEN. Many times, the play to the first trick will make or defeat the contract.

There are numerous techniques and strategies to the play of the hand, such as safety plays, elimination (end) plays, finesses, squeezes, avoidance plays, and more. Two basic principles are to use of the Rule of 12 to guide one on making finesses and the dummy reversal play.

Play of the Hand—Always have a Plan!

You (sitting south) and your partner reach the final contract of 3NT. As south, you bid 1NT and partner bids 3NT. Opening lead is the queen of clubs. Can you make the contract?

North
♠ AJ2
♥ 954
♦ KJ72
♣ K76
South
♠ K96
♥ A873
♦ A54
♣ A94

Many players may go down with this hand because they do not plan their play. The auction was simple and did not reveal anything. All the opponents know is that dummy is not going to have a four-card major and ruffing values.

With the lead of the queen of clubs, your first problem is: Are you going to win the first trick, or are you going to duck the club?

Clearly, you do not want a heart shift that could be more dangerous than the club threat, so you must win the first trick. Now, you have to consider which hand do you win the trick?

Obviously, you want to be in your hand and lead toward dummy. You have five fast tricks outside the diamond suit. How are you going to tackle diamonds? YOU DO NOT KNOW YET! It depends on how many tricks you need in the suit! You must win the trick in your hand and lead a spade to the jack. Next, how will you continue if that loses? Do you play the same way if the finesse wins? NO.

If the finesse loses, you need four diamond tricks, and the only way to get them is to take the finesse and hope the suit splits evenly. But if the spade finesse wins, you only need three tricks from diamonds and can afford a safety play. You would cash the king of diamonds and lead a diamond to the ace. If the queen does not appear, play the jack. That lands the contract any time the queen drops, the break 3-3, or west holds the queen. Great odds! The complete deal follows.

	♠ AJ2	
	♥ 954	
	♦ KJ72	
	♣ K76	
♠ Q53	N	♠ 10874
♥ K6	W E	♥ QJ102
♦ 10983	S	♦ Q6
♣ QJ102		♣ 853
	♠ K96	
	♥ A873	
	♦ A54	
	♣ A94	

Some Card Playing Rules

Rule of 7

When playing NT contracts and having only one stopper in the suit led headed by the ace, one may use the Rule of 7 to decide how many times to hold up. **Rule**: subtract the total number of cards you and dummy hold in the suit from seven. This is the number of times you should hold up when the suit is led by the opponents. The rule is also used with trump contracts.

Let's look at an example.

The bidding goes:

	South	West	North	East
	Pass	Pass	1♣	Pass

1♠	Pass	2NT	Pass
3♠	Pass	4♠	Pass
Pass	Pass	Pass	

Opening Lead: ♥J; the deal follows.

	♠ AK	
	♥ Q972	
	♦ AQJ	
	♣ K742	
♠ Q	N	♠ 8543
♥ J10854	W E	♥ K3
♦ K863	S	♦ 10752
♣ QJ5		♣ A109
	♠ J109762	
	♥ A6	
	♦ 94	
	♣ 863	

West led the Jack of hearts, covered by the queen and the king and taken by the ace. Declarer successfully finessed the jack of diamonds, cashed the ace and king of trumps but then had no fast return to his hand to draw the last rump and repeated the diamond finesse for a club discard. A low heart from the table was taken by West's eight, and the switched to the queen of clubs quickly netted the defenders three tricks in the suit for down one.

South's error was made at TRICK ONE! The rule of seven says that one should duck the heart lead. Now there is no way West can gain the lead. Declarer wins the heart continuation, finesses the jack of diamonds and cashes the table's top trumps, fetching the queen. A heart ruff is the entry to hand to draw the last trump and repeating the diamond finesse. Contract bid and made since the defenders are now limited to two clubs trick to go with the heart trick.

Rule of 9 (Ruff high or low)

Add the number of cards held in a suit between you and dummy to the number of rounds played. If that number is ten or more, a ruff is likely. For example, suppose you hold the AK in a suit and the number of cards in the suit is seven; then a ruff is likely after it is played a third time since 7+3=10; hence, ruff high!

Rule of 12

Consider the following three hands:

1. NORTH Q 10 3 2 SOUTH A J 6 4	2. NORTH J 7 SOUTH A Q 10 5 4 3	3. NORTH Q 9 2 SOUTH A J 10 4 3

One hand has a tenace missing the king. The opposite hand holds one or more cards equal in rank to the lower card(s) in the tenace. In #1, the A-J is the tenace and the Q-10 opposite is equal in rank to the jack, the lower card of the tenace. Given you intend to finesse for the king, how should you handle these combinations, assuming you have plenty of entries to the north hand?

The question is whether you should lead low from north to finesse or whether you can afford to lead a high card from dummy and let it run. The **Rule of 12** provides the answer! It goes as: With 8, 9, or 10 cards in the two hands, if the number of cards in the two hands plus the cards in the sequence totals twelve or more, you can afford to lead a high card opposite the tenace. If the total is less than twelve, lead low to the tenace. WOW!

In hand #1, you have eight cards and three cards (Q, J, and 10) in the sequence, 8 + 3 = 11. Hence, it is **not** safe to lead the Q or the 10 from north. The correct play is to lead low from north to the jack in your hand. If the jack wins, return to north and then lead the queen or the 10 to repeat the finesse. The layout could be:

$$Q\ 10\ 3\ 2$$
$$9\ 8\ 7\ 5 \qquad\qquad\qquad\qquad\qquad\qquad K$$
$$A\ J\ 6\ 4$$

If you lead the queen or 10 on the first round, you lose a trick. Start with a low card from north and you have all the tricks. If entries to the north hand are a problem, take the risk and lead an honor from north.

The answer for #2 is the same: 8 cards + 3 in sequence = 11. Therefore, it is not safe to lead the jack on the first round. Again, king singleton would cost you a trick. As long as entries to north are comfortable, start by leading the 7 to your 10. If that wins, return to dummy and lead the jack for the second finesse.

In hand #3, you have 8 card + 4 in the sequence = 12. It is therefore safe to lead the queen or the 9 for the first-round finesse. Even with a singleton king onside, it does not harm you. Let's consider a few more examples: hands 4, 5, and 6.

4. NORTH	5. NORTH	6. NORTH
A Q 7 6	J 10 2	Q 2
SOUTH	SOUTH	SOUTH
J 5 4 3 2	A Q 7 6 5 4	A J 7 6 5 4 3

In hand #4, 9 cards + 2 in the sequence (Q and J) = 11. The Rule of 12 tells us that you should lead low on the first round, NOT the jack. Play low to the queen. If that wins, cash the ace. To lead the jack first would cost a trick if the king is singleton in this position:

$$A Q 7 6 3 2$$
$$K \qquad\qquad\qquad 10\ 9\ 8$$
$$J 5 4 3 2$$

In #5, 9 cards + 3 in the sequence = 12. Therefore, it is safe to lead the jack or the 10 first.

In # 6, 9 cards + 2 in the sequence = 11. It is not safe to lead queen first. If east has king singleton, playing the queen will cost you a trick while leading the 2 from north avoids losing a trick.

7. NORTH	#7: 10 + 2 = 12. It is safe to lead the jack. In fact, it makes
J 8 7 6 4	no difference whether you start with the jack or lead low
SOUTH	to the queen first.
A Q 5 3 2	

8. NORTH	Again, you should lead the jack first. If east started with
J 8 7 6 4	K-10-9, low to the queen leaves you with a loser, but jack
SOUTH	first can avoid losing a trick.
A Q 5 3 2	

The Rule of 12 also applies when missing the king and queen as here.

9. NORTH	10. NORTH	11. NORTH
10 9 5 2	10 7	9 4 2
SOUTH	SOUTH	SOUTH
A J 6 4	A J 9 5 4 3	A J 10 6 5 3

In hands #9 and #10, 8 cards + 3 in the sequence = 11. Therefore, do not lead a high card on the first round. Start with a low card from north. To lead high from north costs a trick if east has a singleton honor. You can lead high from north for the second round finesse.

In #11, 9 card + 3 in the sequence = 12. It is safe to start with the 9 from north.

For more bridge tips regarding card play, consult Ron Klinger (1998) "Better Bridge with a Better Memory," Cassell Press and the book by William S. Root (1990) "How to Play a Bridge Hand," Crown Trade Publishers, New York may also be consulted.

Dummy Reversal Play

You (sitting south) and your partner reach the final contract of 7♠ and the diamond king is led. Can you make the contract?

	North	
	♠ J98	
	♥ Q43	
	♦ AJ76	
	♣ Q85	
West	N	**East**
♠ 762		♠ 43
♥ 9875	W E	♥ KJ102
♦ KQ1085		♦ 432
♣ 3	S	♣ 9764
	South	
	♠ AKQ105	
	♥ A6	
	♦ 9	
	♣ AKJ102	

Many players may go down with this hand because they assume the contract is impossible. What is the winning line of play? Counting your winners you see from the south hand twelve winners. The problem is in hearts. Do you take the finesse which will win only 50 percent of the time or is there another approach? Walk around the table and sit in north's chair! From this point of view, you have a better idea of how to make the hand!

Although your trump holding is not great (J98), it is good enough to draw the outstanding trump, provided they break 3-2 (approx 2/3=67 percent, see Table in Chapter 16). Your three diamond losers can be ruffed in "dummy." And best of all, your three heart losses can eventually be thrown on "dummy's" club suit.

Win the opening lead of the diamond ace, and ruff a diamond with the spade ace. Lead the spade five to north's eight, and ruff another diamond with the king. Lead the spade ten to north's jack, and ruff the last diamond with south's last spade the queen. Now return to the north hand with the club queen and lead the spade nine. This draws the opponent's last trump, as south you have no spades left, so you discard the heart six. South's hand is now high and the grand slam is home!

The above technique is known as a "dummy reversal." What you have done in effect is made the "short" hand (north) into the master hand. The dummy reversal technique is the major exception to the general policy of avoiding ruffs in the "long" hand (other exceptions are e.g., the trump coup and cross ruffing a hand).

For an explanation of why the technique works, let's consider solely the trump holding for a moment.

North: ♠ J 9 8 and South ♠ A K Q 10 5

You have five trump tricks. The normal way to get an extra trick is to ruff once in the short hand (north) and then draw trumps with the south hand (5+1=6). The *unusual* way to get an extra trump trick is to ruff three times in the south hand and the draw trumps with the north hand (3+3=6).

On the actual hand, declarer has twelve tricks and needs to find a thirteenth. The normal procedure of ruffing a loser in dummy is impossible. But the *unusual* technique of reversing the dummy is the winning approach (the dummy reversal). How do you as declarer know when to use the technique?

First, the trump holding in the short hand must be strong enough to draw the opponents' trumps. In our example, the J98 of spades are all high enough and can take care of the likely 3-2 spade break.

Secondly, the short side suit must be in the hand with the long trumps. In our example hand, the singleton diamond and the spade trump length.

Finally, a dummy reversal will not work unless there are sufficient entries to dummy. In our example, three entries are needed to ruff dummy's three diamonds and one extra entry is needed to draw the last trump. Before embarking on a dummy reversal, declarer must count his entries. The diamond ace and the two trump entries are used to ruff the three diamonds, and the ♣Q is the extra entry to last the last trump. In the play, declarer doesn't trump the diamonds with the A K Q of spades just to be flamboyant. He has to ruff high because the ten and the five spot are his entries to dummy! Let's look at another example. You have reached the contract of 4♥ and the opponent's lead the ♠K. Can you make the contract?

	North	
♠	1065	
♥	Q109	
♦	Q32	
♣	A742	

West		East	
♠ KQ98		♠ A76	
♥ 54		♥ 876	
♦ J1074		♦ 98	
♣ 963		♣ KQ1085	

	South	
♠	J32	
♥	AKJ32	
♦	AK65	
♣	J	

The opponents cash the first three spade tricks and shift to a club, which is won by your ace. There are now three different ways to try to make the contract.

1. Declarer can draw all the trumps and hope that the opponents' diamonds are divided three-three. However, with six cards out, they may not break 3-3 (Chapter 16), and this method of play will work only about one-third of the time.

2. Declared can considerably improve his chances by drawing only two round of trumps before playing three rounds of diamonds. He is still all right if the diamonds are 3-3, and he gives himself the extra chance that the opponent who is short in diamond does not have more than two trumps. This approach will work a little more than half the time.

3. There is also the option of reversing the dummy. After winning the club ace, ruff a club with a high trump. Lead a small trump to dummy, and ruff another club high. Lead the other small trump to dummy, and ruff dummy's last club with south's last trump. Now, enter dummy with the diamond queen and play dummy's last trump, discarding a diamond from the south hand. The ace and king of diamonds win the last two tricks, and the contract is made. This method will work when trump break 3-2, about two-thirds of the time.

Of the three options, the dummy reversal approach is clearly the superior line of play!

Source of Lesson: "Winning Declarer Play" (1969) by Dorothy Hayden Truscott.

Let's look at a final example (a little more advanced) that includes bidding and play (Based upon a hand from "The Bridge World," May 2009, p. 14). You are sitting north with neither side vulnerable with the following hand:

	♠ A53	
	♥ AK10	
	♦ A9865	
	♣ K10	

♠ 10874	N	♠ 9
♥ 32	W E	♥ J984
♦ KJ1032		♦ Q8
♣ 97	S	♣ 865432

	♠ KQJ62	
	♥ Q765	
	♦ 4	
	♣ AQJ	

The bidding goes:

South	West	North	East
		1♦	Pass
1♠	Pass	2NT	Pass
3♥	Pass	4♠	Pass
4NT	Pass	5♦	Pass
5NT	Pass	6♣	Pass
6♥	Pass	7♠	

Bidding

Let's first look at the bidding. 4NT was 1430 RKCB and 5-diamonds shows 0/3 keycards (Clearly, 3 with the bid of 2NT). 5NT was the specific kings ask, and 6 clubs showed the king. 6 hearts was the second kings ask and with the king, north bids 7♠. Note: Some players do not use the specific kings ask, but the number of kings. In this auction they would respond 5♥ (two); however, not knowing that one has the K♥ versus the K♦, the grand slam contract may not be bid (you should discuss whether you use specific king or number of kings option with your partner!).

Play

You have to start with the king-queen of spades. If trumps break four-one, you should play the spade ace, club queen, spade jack (pitching a diamond), heart, ace, and club ace-jack, leaving:

```
North
♠      ----
♥      K10
♦      A97
♣      ----


South
♠      6
♥      Q75
♦      4
♣      ----
```

Now, you must guess what to do. Leading to the heart king gains if the jack drops doubleton and there is no red-suit-squeeze, but ruffing a diamond gains when an opponent started with jack-fourth (or-fifth) of hearts and at least five diamonds. Perhaps the count, discards on the trumps, or some other aspect of the defense carding will help.

If spades break three-two, things are clear. After playing the KQ of spades, one plays the heart ace-king; if the heart jack does not fall (and there is no ruff), diamond ace, three clubs to discard the 10 of hearts, a heart ruff with the ace of trumps, diamond ruff, spade jack.

Best play (Dummy Reversal)—Two trumps, diamond ace, diamond ruff, heart ace, diamond ruff, heart king, diamond ruff, club king, draw the last trump, plus 1510, if not, minus fifty!

Cuebidding for Slam an Example

North-South is Vulnerable. How do you bid this hand?

North	South
♠ 43	♠ AKQJ1075
♥ KJ87	♥ AQ10543
♦ 976	♦ Void
♣ J432	♣ 5

The bidding goes:

West	North	East	South
1♦	Pass	5♦	?

What do you bid and why?

Clearly, the east-west pair is trying to steal the bid. Some may be tempted to bid 6♠ (this was the bid of the pair in the team match at the recent ACBL Summer North American

Championships in Las Vegas, see the October 21, 2008 issue of the Daily Sun). If you bid 6♠, the bidding would go:

West	North	East	South
1♦	Pass	5♦	6♠
Pass	Pass	Dbl*	Pass
Pass	Pass		

* **Lightner Double**

You hold the following hand: ♠986 ♥ 6432 ♦AJ82 ♣AQ. What do you lead? You are looking at the AQ of clubs; clearly, the double is calling for a heart lead, an unusual lead.

The entire deal follows:

	♠ 43	
	♥ KJ87	
	♦ 976	
	♣ J432	
♠ 986	N	♠ 2
♥ 6432	W E	♥ Void
♦ AJ2		♦ Q10543
♣ AQ	S	♣ KQ9876
	♠ KQJ1075	
	♥ AQ1095	
	♦ Void	
	♣ 5	

As the cards lie, the ace of clubs could also defeat the slam (partner would toss the king, asking for a heart return; the higher of the other two suits).

What went wrong?

South should not bid six spades; you can use a six-diamond cuebid. Your partner would bid five hearts and you would find your unbeatable heart slam (some may play that a double of the bid of five-diamonds is for takeout, not penalty and also reach the slam contract).

Bidding Problems

(1) You hold the following HAND: ♠ AQxx ♥ Axxx ♦ Jx ♣ xxx

And the BIDDING goes:

P   1♣   1♦   P
??

What call would you now make?

(2) You hold the following HAND: ♠ Ax ♥ xx ♦ AQJxx ♣ AKJ9

And the BIDDING goes:

1♦   P   1♠   P
3♣   P   3♦   P
??

What call would you now make?

(3) You hold the following HAND: ♠ Ax ♥ AQxx ♦ Qxx ♣ AKxx

And the BIDDING goes:

1♣   3♦   3♠   P
??

What call would you now make?

(1) While you should have three diamonds to cuebid clubs, the best bid is a cuebid of 2♣. It tells your partner you have 10/11 HCP, support for the unbid suits and some support for diamonds. If partner bids two of a major, you would be happy to raise to three!

(2) Clearly, the "Western" Cuebid of 3♥ is in order. With a heart stopper, partner will bid notrump. If he bids 3♠, then you would bid four, since his bid probably shows at least two honors. And, without two honors, he can bid 5♦.

(3) While some may disagree, the best bid is 4♦. While 3NT will probably make, your hand is too strong to sign off in game! If your partner has six good spades and short diamonds, you have a good play for slam. If you bid 4♥, partner may think you hold hearts and clubs and might pass.

Chapter 15
Other Bridge Conventions

Weak Notrump an Overview

Playing 2/1, most partnerships use the strong notrump opening in all seats with balanced hands and 14/15-17 HCP. However, many use different ranges depending upon the seat and/or vulnerability. For example, some play 14-17 in the first two seats and 15-17 in the third and fourth seats, independent of vulnerability (**fried chicken NT**). **Regular chicken** notrump means you open a 12-14 1NT in the first two seats and only at favorable or equal vulnerability. And, **super chicken** NT means you need the vulnerability even more in your favor. You open a weak 12-14 NT if not vulnerable, otherwise, 15-17 vulnerable. For **chicken** notrump, you open 1NT in all seats with 12-14 points; this is the approach used in the Kaplan-Sheinwold bidding system. Should you adopt some form of "chicken" notrump?

Yes, there are certain advantages. It has the (1) preemptive effect, (2) balanced hands occur frequently, (3) rebidding becomes easier, (4) it is easier to punish your opponents, and (5) it provides an improved bidding structure when partner bids one of a minor. In North America, the ACBL does not allow any ranges lower than 10-12 HCP in its tournaments, often called **"Kamikaze"** NT which is part of some systems, for example EHAA (**E**very **H**and **A**n **A**dventure). When playing the Precision System, 1NT often shows a balanced hand with 13-15 HCP or 14-16 HCP. We support the **super chicken** variety since, as suggested by Edgar Kaplan, it supports high, preemptive bidding for weaker hands and allows for no risk when vulnerable.

The primary difference between a weak and a strong notrump is THREE points (a king). Thus, to reach game using a weak NT (12-14), you need 12 HCP and 11 HCP becomes invitational; exactly three more points than the required amount using the strong notrump bid. But, what if you have a strong 15-17 opener? Playing 12-14 NT, you cannot open 1NT. You must open a convenient minor and then bid 1NT to show a balanced hand with 15-17 HCP. If you are unbalanced or have a five-card major, you should bid a major and bypass the 1NT rebid. Simple!

Weak Hands (12-14)

With a weak 1NT opening (12-14), one should have a balanced hand and one of the following distributions: 4-3-3-3, 5-3-3-2, or 4-4-3-2 with length in a minor or a weak non-biddable major. Let's consider a few examples:

(1) ♠ KQ87	(2) ♠ KJ7	(3) ♠ 75
♥ 10853	♥ 93	♥ AJ2
♦ AK3	♦ Q1063	♦ A93
♣ Q3	♣ AQ84	♣ K10875

(4) ♠ KJ7	(5) ♠ AQ72	(6) ♠ 632
♥ J8753	♥ 104	♥ AQ105
♦ AQ6	♦ J84	♦ AQ109
♣ Q5	♣ KQJ5	♣ J6

In hands 1-4, one would open with a weak 1NT. In hands (1) and (2), the scattered honors in three suits and the general weakness of the hand do not allow for a comfortable two-level bid. In hand (3), the club length is useful for a possible NT contract. In hand (4), the heart suit is too weak to rebid. One would not open hands (5) and (6) one notrump. In (5), one would open one club and if responder bids one diamond or one heart, opener can bid one spade. In (6), one would open one diamond, since one can raise hearts or rebid diamonds.

Responder with a balanced hand must take into account that game is possible only if he has a minimum of 12 HCP (an opening hand) and opener has a maximum hand. Hence, with a balanced hand, no five-card suit and fewer than 12 HCP, responder must pass. Responder does not use transfer bids. Two hearts and two spades are to play. Three-level bids are invitational. We review some bids after a weak NT opener.

2♣/2♦ non-forcing/forcing Stayman. Opener bids 2♦/2NT with no four-card major, two of a major with four, where 2♥ may imply both.

After 1NT-2♣-2♦

Pass	Garbage Stayman
2♥, 2♠	to play (2♣)/invitational (2♦)
2NT	invitational
3m	5+ card suit, game forcing, slam oriented. By a passed hand it is invitational with a four-card major and 5+ cards in the minor.
3M	Smolen
4♣	Gerber
4♦, 4♥	Delayed Texas transfer, 6+ 4 in the majors, no slam interest/very strong hand with a void
4NT, 5NT	Quantitative
5M	GSF

After 1NT-2♣-2M:

2NT	invitational
3m	5+ card suit, game forcing, slam oriented. By a passed hand it is invitational with a four-card major and 5+ cards in the minor.
3M	Invitational

Sets M as trump suit, and responder may be planning to RKCB in M in his next bid (kickback/1430).

4m	void, fit in M, slam interest.
4NT, 5NT	Quantitative
5M	GSF
5m, 6X	Signoff

After 1NT opening,

2♥, 2♠	to play
2NT	invitational
3♣, 3♦, 3♥, 3♠	natural and invitational

Interference with weak NT is common.
After double, 1NT-double, the following scheme is used.

Redouble	shows clubs.
2-level bids	Transfers and Signoff.
Pass	Opener is asked to show a five-card minor or to redouble with none. After opener redoubles, responder starts bidding suits up-the-line.
2NT	Two-suited monster
3X	Weak hand 7+ card suit
3NT	Solid 7+ card minor, nothing else outside, opener is expected to bid four clubs without reasonable stoppers.

After the auction: 1NT-p-p-X-p-p:

| Redouble | Five-card minor, opener relays to two clubs |
| 2♣, 2♦, 2♠ | Lower of two four-card suits |

With the auction 1NT-2X, a natural or artificial bid, you can play Lebensohl, Rubinsohl, Rumpelsohl (a combination of Lebensohl and Rubinsohl), or Transfer Lebensohl.

After the auction 1NT-p-2♣-2X

Opener rarely bids. A double would be for penalties. 2M shows a good fitting maximum [4-4-2-3] hand when X=♦, otherwise it shows a maximum hand with a two small cards in X.

After the auction 1NT-p-2♣-X

In general, the opener will indicate whether he should be playing in 2♣-doubled. Therefore, pass shows a good four-card suit allowing opener to redouble for business, redouble shows a five-card suit.

After the auction 1NT-p-2♦-X and 1NT-p-2♥-X

Responses are unchanged except that opener must pass with two cards in partner's suit. Redouble is natural showing a fair 4⁺card suit and willing to play the redoubled contract.

After the auction 1NT-p-p-2X

Opener's double is for takeout, showing exactly xx in opponent's suit. Responder's double is penalty-oriented: opener must take out with xx in the opponent's suit or other poor defensive hand.

As responder, it denies a 5+card major, he may compete on the 2-level showing his cheapest four-card suit or with 2NT showing both minors (or if X=♠, any takeout).

The primary advantage of playing a weak NT is its preemptive value. Let's consider an example taken from the National Championships.

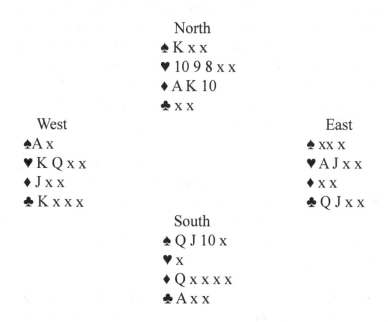

```
                        North
                        ♠ K x x
                        ♥ 10 9 8 x x
                        ♦ A K 10
                        ♣ x x
       West                                East
       ♠A x                                ♠ xx x
       ♥ K Q x x                           ♥ A J x x
       ♦ J x x                             ♦ x x
       ♣ K x x x                           ♣ Q J x x
                        South
                        ♠ Q J 10 x
                        ♥ x
                        ♦ Q x x x x
                        ♣ A x x
```

Playing a weak NT, west opens 1NT. Neither north nor south can afford to overcall at the two-level; so, the contract is played at 1NT. If, however, you opened the west hand one club, north might double and the spade game by north-south would be reached. While the east-west pair cannot make 1NT, the contract should be down two for a north-south score of 200. This is clearly better than the game score of 620. However, north led the ♥10 with no information to guide the lead and the contract was made! South shifted to a diamond upon taking the A♣, but the opponents can only take six tricks before east-west took seven. The opponents were punished because they do not know which suit to attack; they must guess. West is dealer with east-west non-vulnerable and north-south vulnerable.

With a strong hand, playing any form of chicken NT, you cannot open 1NT; instead, you must open one of a minor and then bid 1NT.

Much of the material in this section on weak NT is based upon the book by Andy Stark (2006), "The Weak Notrump, How to Play it, How to Play Against it." Master Point Press. Using a Google search with the string defined by Katzman@math.umn.edu, one may obtain a Kaplan-Sheinwold PDF by Katzman who reviews his system of bids to 1NT using the range 12-14.

Two—Way Stayman

When playing weak Notrumps 11-14 (13-15) HCP, one uses two-way Stayman. In response to a 1NT opening, responses have these meanings:

2♣—Any sort of invitational hand, denies game-going strength opener shows any major, but with both majors he bids 2NT with a minimum and 3♣ with a maximum. This will avoid getting the bidding too high when opener has both majors and a minimum, with responder having neither major. This response can also be made with a weak three-suited hand short in diamonds, planning to pass any two-level bid by opener. If opener ungraciously shows both majors, responder's 3♥/3♠ bid closes the auction, even if opener has shown a maximum hand. Otherwise, any rebid by responder is invitational. That could be awkward when responder has an invitational hand with five hearts and opener bids 2♠. He will normally bid 3♥, which opener will have to pass with a minimum, even with a doubleton heart. To avoid this situation, responder should bid 2NT over 2♠ when holding five hearts and a balanced hand.

2♦—Forcing to game bid. Opener shows a major, bidding 2♠ with both (planning to bid 3♥ later if spades are not raised). When opener responds in two of a major, responder should not jump to 3NT when holding three-card support. Instead, she should bid a forcing 2NT, giving opener a chance to rebid a five-card suit. She should also rebid 2NT when holding four hearts after opener has responded 2♠, in case opener has four hearts, too. A rebid of three in a minor implies some slam interest.

2♥/2♠—Natural signoff bids (not Alertable). While the response denies much interest in game, opener can raise one level (only) to show an extremely good supporting hand.

2NT—Invitational to 3NT (Note: some play this as a puppet to 3♣ with/without a correction to 3♦).

3♣/3♦/3♥/3♠—A six-card suit with two of the top three honors and 9-11 HCP.

Texas Transfers are applicable, but in competition only through 3+ (when both transfers would be jump bids).

Weak Notrump Runouts

Many more players are opening 1NT weak. Any range below the standard 14/15-17 may be considered a weak notrump bid.

When the opponents make a penalty double of your weak 1NT opening bid, your side can be at serious risk of being set and going for a very large penalty (especially if you are playing a weak notrump opening bid). This is particularly true if the opponents can run off a long suit against you in notrump. Consequently, it is imperative in these situations that your side has a mechanism for finding its best fit at the two levels. DONT Notrump Runouts are one such mechanism for escaping the penalty double and finding your fit.

Modified DONT (Meckwell) Notrump Runouts

DONT Runouts bids are similar to the notrump overcall convention; hence, they share the same name. Playing this convention, after the auction has begun 1NT-Double (for penalty), a Redouble shows a single-suited hand and forces partner to bid 2♣ so that you can pass or correct to your suit. All bids at the two levels show a two-suited hand with the bid suit and a higher-ranking suit: 2♣ shows clubs and a major suit, 2♦ shows diamonds and a major, 2♥ shows both majors, and 2NT shows the minors. All three-level bids show a long suit and are to play and Texas transfers are on. If you have a good hand and want to play 1NT doubled, you should pass. For the purposes of runout bids, a hand is two-suited if it is 4-4 or better, and it is single-suited if it contains a six-card or longer suit or a five-card suit without another four-card suit. If 4-3-3-3, it is usually best to pretend the hand is two-suited.

If you don't like the modified DONT runout procedure, you can play standard DONT Runouts or you may use the following.

Exit Transfer Notrump Runouts

If the opponents have doubled your partner's 1NT opening bid, Exit Transfer Notrump Runouts provide you with a way to try to escape the penalty with as little damage as possible. Exit Transfers additionally have the benefit of allowing the Notrump opener to declare most two-level contracts, "right-siding" them.

Playing Exit Transfers after the auction has gone1NT-Double, Redouble is a transfer to 2♣ and shows 5+ clubs, 2♣ is a transfer to diamonds and shows 5+ diamonds, 2♦ is a transfer to hearts and shows 5+ hearts, and 2♥ is a transfer to spades and shows 5+ spades. If you have a two-suited hand, you should pass; your pass forces partner to redouble, then with a hand well suited to play 1NT redoubled you can pass, or else you can describe your two-suited hand by bidding 2♣ to show clubs and a higher-ranking suit, 2♦ to show diamonds and a major, and 2♥ to show both majors.

For the purposes of runout bids, a hand is two-suited if it is 4-4 or better, and it is single-suited if it contains a six-card or longer suit or a five-card suit without another four-card suit. If 4-3-3-3, it is usually best to pretend the hand is two-suited.

Helvic Notrump Runouts

Helvic Notrump Runouts are a convention that is popular in England. Part of the reason for its popularity is that the Standard English/ACOL system contains a weak notrump opening bid, which is significantly more susceptible to penalty doubles.

If the opponents have doubled your partner's 1NT opening bid, Helvic Notrump Runouts provide you with a way to try to escape the penalty with as little damage as possible. Playing Helvic, you can either show a single-suited hand by redoubling or show a two-suited hand by bidding at the two-level. A 2♣ bid shows clubs and diamonds, a 2♦ bid shows diamonds and hearts, a 2♥ bid shows hearts and spades, and a 2♠ bid shows spades and clubs. If you redouble, partner will bid 2♣ as a pass-or-correct bid. And finally, if you wish to play in 1NT despite the double, or if you have a two-suited hand with non-touching suits, you should pass. Your pass forces partner to redouble so that you can play 1NT redoubled or so that you can bid 2♣ to show clubs and hearts or 2♦ to show diamonds and spades. For the purposes of runout bids, a hand is two-suited if it is 4-4 or better, and it is single-suited if it contains a six-card or longer suit or a five-card suit without another four-card suit. If 4-3-3-3, it is usually best to pretend the hand is two-suited.

An Extended Stayman Convention

Everyone plays the Stayman Convention; recall that the bidding goes:

1NT-2♣-2♦ = No four-card major, 2♥ = Four hearts, and 2♠ = Four spades.

It is normal to bid 2♥ with both majors. After using Stayman, a 3♣ rebid by responder cancels the initial message and says you want to play in clubs. This is not the case if you play Extended Stayman, as described here where now 3♣ initiates Extended Stayman (the French use it for Spring Stayman).

Because there are many versions of Extended Stayman, a simple variation follows:

After the sequence 1NT-2♣-2♠-3♣* = do you have another 4 card suit?

Opener's bids are 3♦=4 diamonds; 3♠=5 spades; 3NT=4 clubs, 3♥ shows 4-3-3-3 shape.

After the sequence 1NT-2♣-2♥-3♣*= do you have a 4 card suit?

Opener's bids are 3♦=4 diamonds; 3♠ shows 3-4-3-3 shape; 3NT=4 clubs, 3♥=5 hearts.

After the sequence 1NT-2♣-2♦-3♣* = do you have a 4 card suit?

Opener's bid of 3♦=some five-card minor; and 3♥ by responder asks which five-card minor; opener responses are then: 3♠=clubs and 3NT=diamonds.

A bid of 3♥ (after 1NT-2♣-2♦-3♣*) by opener shows a 2-3-4-4 pattern (Major Fragments and both minors).

A bid of 3♠ (after 1NT-2♣-2♦-3♣*) by opener shows a 3-2-4-4 pattern.

A bid of 3NT (after 1NT-2♣-2♦-3♣*) shows one four-card minor with 3-3-3-4/3-3-4-3 pattern over which one can ask by bidding 4♣ (where 4♦=diamond, 4♥=clubs). One now usually plays in a minor suit game or in a minor suit slam.

* Some bridge players use the bid of 3♦ after the bid of 2♦ to initiate an older version of Extended Stayman used to ask opener to bid his better three-card major. Today, one would use the Mini-Maxi convention and not bid 2♣; instead after 1NT, one bids 3♥ to show 5-5 in majors and weak and the bid of 3♠ to show 5-5 in majors and strong. In addition, some use the bid of 3♣ for SARS (Shape Asking Relays after Stayman); SARS is similar to the version of Extended Stayman provided above as discussed in Chapter 1. However, if you want to use SARS and Extended Stayman, then 3♣ would be used for SARS and 3♦ would be Extended Stayman.

If you do not use 3♦ as Extended Stayman, it may be used for Stayman in Doubt (SID).

Stayman in Doubt (SID)

Stayman is designed to locate a 4-4 fit in the majors. However, some argue that one should not use Stayman if your distribution is 4-3-3-3 or 3-4-3-3. In general, this is bad advice. It is usually better to play in a 4-4 major suit fit rather than in notrump. However, there may be one exception. This is when the opener and partner have identical shape (4-3-3-3 facing 4-3-3-3 or 3-4-3-3 facing 3-4-3-3). Then it may be better to play in notrump rather than a 4-4 major suit fit! To determine whether or not you and partner have the same shape, responder bids 3♦ after the 2-level major suit bid by opener known as the Stayman in Doubt (SID) convention. It says "partner, I am totally flat with four of your major, if you are also totally flat consider bidding 3NT." This allows the partnership to play in 3NT when there is total duplication in shape, even with a fit in the majors! Responder should only use this convention with 12-15 HCP. Then, the value of the combined hand is 27+ HCPS and the notrump will usually yield a higher score than the major suit contract.

Vacant (Worthless) Doubleton Convention

What do you do when your partner opens 1NT (14/15-17 HCP) and you have 10-14 HCP, but a worthless doubleton?

Let's consider a few examples:

Hand 1:

Opener's Hand   ♠A6 ♥AK52 ♦763 ♣KQ92
Responder's Hand   ♠42 ♥Q63 ♦AK42 ♣J654

Hand 2:

Opener's Hand   ♠AQJ4 ♥J7 ♦ AQ6 ♣K963
Responder's Hand   ♠K52 ♥42 ♦K754 ♣A754

With both hands, partner opens 1NT and the next person passes; what do you now bid? The obvious bids for both responder hands are 3NT, but are you not nervous about your worthless doubletons? With the first hand, you may play better in five of a minor or even four hearts with a spade lead. Similarly, with the second hand, making 3NT with a heart lead has zero play. Making ten tricks in spades if spades are no worse than 4-2, as long as clubs divide 3-2 or diamonds 3-3 is a better contract! How do you reach the most makeable contract?

To avoid playing notrump with worthless doubletons (Jx at best), Dave Cliff, who also invented splinter bids, suggested the Vacant Doubleton (VD) Convention. The convention is used when responder has no four-card major and a worthless doubleton. While the notrump bidder may also have a worthless doubleton, the VD convention is used to find responders worthless doubleton, allowing the notrump bidder to conceal his.

For responder to use the convention, we said he must have an invitational notrump hand, no four cards in the major and a worthless doubleton. In addition, there are two more requirements.

1. Responder must have three to an honor in at least one major.
2. Responder does not hold a six-card minor.

How do we proceed?

(1) Recall that in SAYC, a bid of 2♠ is used as a relay to 3♣ to show a weak hand to sign off in 3♣ or 3♦. Opener is required to complete the transfer by bidding 3♣ and responder will pass or correct to 3♦. These are both used to show "bust" hands with 6-8 HCP and a six-card minor.

(2) Playing 2/1 and Minor Suit Stayman, the bid of 2♠ is asking partner to show a four-card minor. It is used to show the following types of hands: 1) a weak minor two-suiter, 2) a weak hand with diamonds, and 3) a strong minor two-suiter. Playing Minor Suit Stayman, Opener shows a four-card minor by bidding 3♣/3♦. Without a four-card minor, opener bids 2NT. Responder passes holding a weak minor two-suiter if opener shows a four-card minor. If opener has denied holding a four-card minor by bidding 2NT, responder's rebid of 3♣ shows a weak two-suiter and asks opener to pass with three-card support, or to correct to 3♦. Opener will always have three cards in one of the minors since with three cards; opener would be 5-4 in the majors and would have opened 1♥/1♠.

To show a diamond bust, responder will either pass a 3♦ rebid by opener or correct opener's 2NT or 3♣ responses to 3♦. Minor suit Stayman followed by a 3♦ rebid is always a drop-dead bid. Any rebid by responder, other than 3♣/3♦, shows a strong minor 2-suiter. Responder's normal rebids are:

3♥/3♠ shows a singleton or void in the suit bid
3NT shows 2-2-5-4 (5-5 in the minors) and mild slam interest
4NT shows 2-2-5-4 (5-4 in the minors) and strong slam interest

A raise of opener's 3♣/3♦ rebid to 4♣/4♦ is usually Roman Keycard Minorwood, however, some play Kickback (the suit above the agreed upon trump suit). If opener shows a four-card minor, all sequences are natural and forcing to game.

(3) In Standard American, one does not employ transfers. The bid of 2♠ is to play.

(4) In modified SAYC, a bid of 2♠ is used as a relay to 3♣ to show a weak hand (6-8 HCP) with a six-card club suit. Opener is required to bid 3♣. A bid of 3♣ is a transfer to 3♦, 6-8 HCP and six diamonds. And, a bid of 2NT is 8-9 HCP and invitational.

Note that none of the aforementioned methods protect one against a worthless doubleton. How might we proceed?

In this book, we recommend four-way transfers, to invoke the Vacant Doubleton Convention; you may not use four-way transfers.

For the Vacant Doubleton Convention, the bid of 2NT is an ASKING bid. What kind of hand do you have?

3♣	minor two-suiter and forcing
3♦	vacant doubleton in clubs or diamonds
3♥	vacant doubleton in hearts
3♠	vacant doubleton in spades

After the 3♦ response showing a VD in either minor, opener now bids 3♥ to ask which minor. Responder's bid of 3♠ shows clubs and 3NT shows diamonds.

When using this convention, the bid of 2NT by responder suggests 8-9 HCP, invitational, but partner may still have a worthless doubleton; however, opener may invoke a Checkback bid as described more fully below.

For Hand 1, responder would bid 2♠. When partner bids 2NT (the asking bid), responder bids 3♠ to show his vacant/worthless doubleton in spades. The rest is up to partner. Over 3♠, he would likely bid 4♥ and play in a 4-3 fit. Note that this contract has a good chance of making if hearts are 3-3. With a spade lead, the 3NT contract has almost a zero probability of making.

For Hand 2, one would again bid 2♠, and after a 2NT bid by opener, one would bid 3♥ to show the vacant/worthless doubleton. Now, partner would bid 4♠. This will make if spades split 4-2, provided clubs split 3-2, or diamonds split 3-3; again, much better than 3NT.

But opener has four clubs, instead of bidding 2NT, suppose he bids 3♣ showing 4+ clubs. Now, responder bids 3♦ and opener must bid 3♠ because of the heart doubleton. With three spades, responder bids 4♠. All is well!

Let's look at one more example.

Hand 3:

Opener's Hand	♠A1075 ♥K52 ♦AK54 ♣Q9
Responder's Hand	♠KJ2 ♥AJ6 ♦Q8762 ♣63

Playing the convention, the bidding would go:

1NT	2♠
2NT	3♦ (doubleton is a minor)
3♥ (which minor)	3♠ (clubs)
4♠	Pass

Now, four spades again has a reasonable chance of making. With a club lead, 3NT has little chance of making.

Whenever responder bids 2NT non-forcing, or Stayman, or transfers to hearts, opener may CHECKBACK for a vacant doubleton. Here is how it works:

Opener	**Responder**
1NT	2NT
3♣ (Checkback)	

Opener	Responder
1NT	2♣ (Stayman)
2x	2NT
3♣ (Checkback)	

Opener	Responder
1NT	2♦ (Transfer)
2♥	2NT
3♣ (Checkback)	

In all cases, opener with enough points to bid game has the option of bidding 3♣ to ask responder if he has a vacant/worthless doubleton. Over the bid of 3♣, responder responses are:

3♦ vacant doubleton in clubs or diamonds
3♥ vacant doubleton in hearts
3♠ vacant doubleton in spades
3NT no vacant doubleton

After 3♦, one may again ask which minor by bidding 3♥ as above. Again, a bid of 3♠ shows clubs and 3NT shows diamonds.

NOTE: It is not useful to show a vacant/worthless doubleton in a suit bid by the opener (e.g., after Stayman, if opener bid spades, responder should not bother to show a worthless doubleton in spades).

We now look at some more examples of the Checkback variation of vacant doubletons.

Hand 4:

Opener's Hand	♠Q42 ♥KJ1054 ♦K32 ♣AK
Responder's Hand	♠63 ♥A76 ♦QJ106 ♣J654

The bids follow.

Opener	Responder
1NT	2NT
3♣ (Checkback)	3♠ (spade doubleton)
4♥	Pass

Opener has five hearts and three spades, to avoid a rebid problem, he opens 1NT. He checks back over 2NT by bidding 3♣ and finds out that partner has a worthless doubleton spade and bids 4♥. (Yes, he could have bid 3♥ over 2NT as a natural bid, but this informs the opponents about his five-card suit, something he would prefer to hide if the final contract is 3NT).

Hand 5:

Opener's Hand ♠AK64 ♥AK ♦QJ102 ♣963
Responder's Hand ♠J82 ♥QJ754 ♦A43 ♣83

The bids follow.

Opener	Responder
1NT	2♦
2♥	2NT
3♣ (Checkback)	3♦ (worthless doubleton in clubs or diamonds)
3♥	3♠ (worthless club doubleton)
4♥	Pass

Hand 6:

Opener's Hand	♠AQ6 ♥AQ2 ♦32 ♣KQ973
Responder's Hand	♠KJ43 ♥10874 ♦65 ♣A52

The bids follow.

Opener	Responder
1NT	2♣ (Stayman)
2♦	2NT
3♣ (Checkback)	3♦ (worthless doubleton in clubs or diamonds)
3♥	3NT (worthless doubleton in diamonds)
4♦ (choose better major*)	4♠

* Called choice-of-game cuebid!

Final note: suppose responder has a VD (worthless doubleton) with a four-card or five-card major. You may want to add the VD option to your agreement as follows.

Opener	Responder
1NT	2♦
2♥	3♣ (Checkback*)

Opener	Responder
1NT	2♣ (Stayman)
2x	3♣ (Checkback*)

Here, the bid of 3♣ is used to show a "game force + VD".

WHAT DO YOU LOSE BY PLAYING THE VACANT (WORTHLESS) DOUBLETON CONVENTION?

The major risk is that it provides information to the opponents. If you had bid 1NT-3NT, the opponents may not have found the lead in your partner's VD (worthless) suit.

To add the VD convention to your partnership agreement and opening 1NT (14/15-17HCP), the bid of 2NT is invitational to 3NT having 8-9 HCP, and bid of 3♣ is then used as a transfer to a six-card diamond suit. The bid of 2♠ is either VD or a transfer to clubs.

This convention is an extension of the "Vacant Doubleton" Convention contained in the 2003 book "Bridge Conventions in Depth" by Matthew and Pamela Granovetter and published by Master Point Press.

Notrump Overcalls

When the opponents open the bidding at the one-level and you overcall with the bid of one notrump, one usually has a strong 15-18 HCP hand and a stopper in the bid suit. As discussed herein, one can play systems on/off over the notrump overcall. That is, if off, then one plays all responses as natural with cuebid Stayman, or with systems on, one uses transfers and Stayman.

However, when the opponents open the bidding, it is less likely that you have a "strong" notrump overcall (it occurs in less than 10 percent of all hands and even less frequently with a stopper). What do you bid after the opponents open the bidding with one of a major and you hold the following hand?

♠ 7 3 ♥ 6 5 ♦ A Q J 9 6 3 ♣ J 8 4

You only have 8 HCP so you should not bid at the two-level and you cannot double since you cannot pass any suit bid by partner. A solution is to play the Gardner Notrump Overcall Convention devised by the World Champion Nico Gardener, London, England. In France, it is called the "Comic Notrump Overcall." Or, one may play The Baron Notrump Overcall Convention developed by Leo Baron from Salisbury, Southern Zimbabwe or the Lindkvist One Notrump Overcall Convention developed by the Swedish champion Magnus Lindkvist (also called the Raptor [Polish] Notrump Convention), among others.

Is there a simpler approach? YES! Use the bid of 1NT as a takeout bid.

If one has a stopper in the opponent's bid suit and 15+ HCP and a balanced hand, one merely doubles. However, with no more than two cards in the opponent's bid suit and 8-14 HCP, one bids 1NT for takeout.

After a double, one responds as if your partner opened a strong notrump (systems on/off per partnership agreement). If the opponents interfere, you again use your agreed upon convention over notrump interference (e.g., Stolen Bids, Lebensohl, Transfer Lebensohl, etc.). Over the 1NT takeout bid, bid your longest suit.

Note: The "ACBL standard" 1NT overcall requires 15-17/18 HCP, a balanced hand, and a stopper in the opponent's bid suit. ANY VARIATION FROM THIS STANDARD must be alerted. If the opponents ask, the bid must be fully explained. For example, standard overcall range of 15-17/18, but our bid does not require a stopper; or our notrump bid is for takeout 8-14 HCP and partner usually has two or fewer cards in the bid suit, etc.

Can a similar practice be used with a 2/3 level pre-emptive opening? Yes, now 2/3NT is for takeout! This practice is sometimes referred to as the Notrump for Takeout Convention.

Reverse Flannery by Responder

How many times as responder with five spades and four hearts with 5-8 HCP has your partner opened one of a minor and you bid one spade and opener rebid his minor and you missed a fit in hearts? To illustrate, suppose you have the following hands:

Opener   ♣ 842 ♦ AQ972 ♥ AKJ ♠ 42
Responder   ♣ J 9 ♦ 84 ♥ Q532 ♠ K9754

And the bidding goes 1♦ - Pass - 1♠ - Pass; 2♦ - Pass - Pass - Pass, so you missed your heart fit.

Or even worse, suppose you have the following hand:

Opener   ♣ J5 ♦ AK853 ♥ AJ94 ♠ J9
Responder   ♣ 7 ♦ J4 ♥ 109742 ♠ KQ853

And again the bidding goes 1♦ - Pass - 1♠ - Pass; 2♦ - Pass - Pass - Pass, so again you missed your heart fit.

This bidding problem is handled by using the Reverse Flannery Convention (RFC). How does it work?

After a minor suit opening, the convention works:

(1) An immediate jump shift to two hearts after partner's minor opening is defined as showing a hand with five spades and four or five hearts, minimum responding values (about 5-8 HCP).

(2) A one-spade response followed by a jump shift to three hearts on the second round is invitational, showing 5-5 distribution or better, originated by Edwin Kantar.

(3) A bid of 2 spades shows 5-4 distribution with 9-11 HCP.

(4) A one-spade response followed by a two-heart rebid is forcing for one round showing a minimum of 9 HCP and no upper limit. A three-heart rebid on the third round is forcing to game.

While the RFC does not allow one to use the weak jump shift in hearts (two hearts), this is not a major problem, since two hearts is of dubious preemptive value if jump shifts are weak, and the strong jump shift of two hearts can be handled by a one-heart response and aggressive rebidding.

Continuation of the auction after RFR is simple. Opener in most cases places the contract by passing, bidding two spades, or bidding three of his original minor. He may invite naturally by bidding two notrump or three of either minor.

Responder's obligations are, usually in order of priority:

(a) Rebid three hearts with five hearts or

(b) Rebid three notrump with stop in the unbid minor or

(c) Raise opener's minor with three or

(d) Raise opposite minor with four-card support for opener's minor (usually a void of opposite minor) or

(e) Bid three spades failing (a) through (d) above.

The RFC can be combined with inverted minors (criss-cross) using the following bids.

1♣	2♣	Game forcing club raise
	2♦	Limit raise for clubs
	2♥	5 spades, 4-5 hearts, 5-8 pts
	2♠	5 spades, 4-5 hearts, 9-11 pts
	2NT	invitational to game, 10-12 pts
	3♣	Limit raise in clubs
1♦	2♦	Game forcing raise for diamonds
	2♥	5 spades, 4-5 hearts, 5-8/9 pts
	2♠	5 spades, 4-5 hearts 9-11 pts
	2NT	Invitational to game 10-12 pts
	3♣	Limit raise in diamonds
	3♦	Weak preemptive raise for diamonds

The TRASH Convention

Most partnerships have their favorite conventions they play over a NT opening. There are a host of conventions: Cappelletti, Modified Cappelletti (also called Hamilton/Modified Hamilton), Astro, Pinpoint Astro, Brozel, Landy, Transfers (Weber), Ripstra, Hello, DONT, etc. and the list goes on. For those who play a convention in the direct seat, they often have a different convention in the indirect seat. In addition, many have yet another convention over a weak NT bid (10-12/12-14) and over the precision strong club bid (e.g., **Co**lor **RA**nk and **SH**ape [CRASH] and Mathe). A convention that may be unknown to many partnerships is the TRASH Convention. It can be played in the direct seat, the indirect seat, over strong bids and over weak bids. It is truly a panacea.

This convention was designed by the American champion and bridge author Harold Feldheim. The TRASH (**TR**ansfer **A**nd **SH**ape) Convention is a defensive convention that can be planned against all strong opening bids (1♣, 1NT, 2♣, 2NT, etc.) and is therefore better than CRASH/Mathe that is usually only played against the one club opening. The convention is similar to the transfer system (sometimes called Weber) played over the strong notrump opening; however, it is better since it allows the defenders to enter the auction with either one—or two-suited hands. The TRASH Convention may also be used over weak 1NT (e.g., 10-12, 12-14, etc.) openings. Now, one has to learn only a single convention for all seats and several bidding systems.

Based on the transfer principle, the TRASH artificial overcall shows either a one-suiter in the next ranking suit (first step) or a two-suiter, second and third step above the bid suit. Only the spade overcall is an exception (since the next higher step is notrump) showing a rounded (hearts and clubs) or a pointed (diamonds and spades) two-suiter. The following table shows the meanings of all TRASH overcalls.

Opening Bid		Overcall	Meaning of Overcall
1♣, 2♣		Double	Diamond one-suiter
	or		
1NT		2♣	Hearts-spades two-suiter
2NT		3♣	
1♣		1♦	Heart one-suiter
	or		
1NT, 2♣		2♦	Spades-clubs two-suiter
2NT		3♦	
1♣		1♥	Spade one-suiter
	or		
1NT, 2♣		2♥	Clubs-diamonds two-suiter
2NT		3♥	

1♣		1NT	Club one-suiter
or			
1NT, 2♣		2NT	Diamonds-hearts two-suiter
2NT		3NT	
1♣		1♠	Two-suiter (unknown)
or			
1NT, 2♣		2♠	Pointed (hearts and clubs)
2NT		3♠	or rounded (spades and diamonds) suits

Over 1NT/2NT **double** is always for penalty.

To use the convention to show two-suited bids over the strong 1♣ opening bid (following Mathe), one may agree to use the 1NT overcall bid to show the minors instead of a club one-suiter and the spade bid for an unknown two-suiter. Now, 1♣-2♣ is natural. With this modification, one should have a hand equal to a strong notrump opener (15-17 HCP).

Responder Bids

Facing a TRASH overcall, partner must transfer to the next ranking suit. The only exception is he has good support for the next ranking suit as well as for one of the other suit, he then bids as follows.

> With a weak hand = jump in the next higher ranking suit
> With a good hand= bid notrump

The intervener now has enough information to choose the best contract for the defending partnership. With a strong hand and holding a one-suiter, he may rebid the original suit or he may rebid the lowest suit of the two-suiter.

TRASH has a strong nuisance effect on the opponents, posing new kinds of problems. It is also useful in finding a good sacrifice or perhaps an ideal contract.

The Mathe Convention

This is a simple convention played over a strong Precision Club Opening developed by Lewis L. Mathe. It goes:

All single suit bids: diamonds, hearts, and spades are natural showing 5+ cards.
1NT shows both minors (5+/5+)
Double shows both majors (4/4 or 5/5 by agreement)

The "Undercall" ♣ Convention—Extended

How many times have the opponents opened a club and you have overcalled a major and then they negative double to show the other major? Or, you make an overcall and win the contract and the weak hand is on lead? Is there a convention you can use that can prevent the often used negative double or ensure the strong hand leads? The answer is YES, but before discussing the convention, let's look at an example.

In the second seat, after the bid of one club, you pick up at favorable vulnerability the following hand:

♠AQJ873 ♥432 ♦ J87 ♣A What do you bid?

With an opening hand and six spades, most would overcall a spade to show a good suit and lead directing! However, if you win the contract, the weak hand is on lead. In many situations it is better to get the strong hand on lead. Thus, you want your partner to play the contract. To accomplish this goal, you may use the "Undercall" Club Convention based upon transfers.

The convention applies ONLY over the opening bid of 1♣. In the second (overcall) seat, your overcall bids are: Opener 1♣

Your bids are:

1♦ = transfer to hearts (5+ hearts and first or second round control)

1♥ = transfer to spades (5+ spades and first or second round control)

1♠ = transfer to diamonds (should have 10-14 HCP with an ace or king) **NOTE: May be played to transfer to Notrump, usually with a club stopper since playing in a minor may not be attractive.**

1NT = shortness in clubs and 8-14 HCP (Optional*—for takeout)

X= 15+ HCP with stopper in clubs (Optional*)

2♣=both majors and weak 8-11HCP
2♦ = Flannery or Extra-Shape Flannery (Optional—depends on partnership agreement).
2♥ = transfer to spades (5/6+ spades and strong 16-21 HCP)
2♠ = 5-5 in the majors and strong (16-21 HCP)
2NT = 5+hearts and 5+diamonds (Optional).

* Some partnerships reverse the meaning of these bids—then 1NT is 15/16-17/18 usually with a stopper and double is for takeout.

That is it! What do you gain by using the transfer bids?

1) You get partner to declare the hand in your long suit, putting the strong hand opening bidder on lead.
2) With diamonds, you preempt their one-level overcall by bidding 1♠.
3) You escape a penalty double if partner happens to hold length in the suit you bid and shortness in the suit you have shown.
4) You get to make two bids (usually) for the price of one, since most of the time partner will bid your suit or something else and you get to make another bid (standard transfer advantage).
5) By transferring into your major suit, it may take away their negative double.

Now, let's look at the complete deal and employ our new "Undercall" club convention.

	♠ AQJ873	
	♥ 432	
	♦ J87	
	♣ A	
♠ 2	N	♠ 64
♥ AQ75	W E	♥ J108
♦ KQ10		♦ 654
♣ K10973	S	♣ Q8642
	♠ K1095	
	♥ K96	
	♦ A632	
	♣ J5	

Not playing the Undercall Club Convention, north would overcall a spade and N-S would reach a part score or game in spades and make eight or nine tricks with east leading the jack of hearts.

Playing the Undercall Club Convention, the bidding would proceed as follows.

West	North	East	South
1♣	1♥*	Pass	1♠
Pass	3♥**	Pass	4♠
All Pass			

*Alert
**Help suit game try—alert

With south playing the contract, west leads the king of diamonds. South wins the ace, cashes the ace of clubs, leads a trump to hand and ruffs a club, draws a second trump, and leads a diamond toward dummy, ending in hand. A heart is discarded on the thirteenth diamond. If west started with two diamonds, he is end-played. If west started with four diamonds, he gets out with a diamond and declarer wins the jack, leads a third trump to hand and plays a diamond, throwing a heart. Now, west is end-played. Four spades bid and made—but only from the south side.

It is true that even if south plays the hand, a club or spade lead with defeat 4♠, but only if west defends perfectly. After winning the first round of diamonds, he must shift to a heart, leading away from AQxx. It is not that easy!

What do you lose by playing the Undercall Club Convention?

You lose the ability to hear partner bid 1♥ or 1♠ as he could after a 1♦ overcall. Also, if you bid 1♠ with diamonds, committing your side to the two levels, you will need a better diamond suit than for a 1♦ overcall.

As in Precision, can you refuse the transfer? Yes, if they pass, bid 1NT without a fit (a void or only one card in the transfer suit, with two/three cards—accept the transfer). Or, you can bid your own 5+ suit. And, if they interfere, you can pass without support or perhaps bid your own suit. Finally, you can bid 2♣ to ask overcaller to bid his second suit.

Let's look at few more examples: The opponents open 1♣ and you hold the following hands:

(1) ♠ 975 ♥ A75 ♦ AK1096 ♣ 75

(2) ♠ K75 ♥ A75 ♦ AK1096 ♣ 75

(3) ♠ A75 ♥ A75 ♦ AK1096 ♣ 75

For hand (1), you would bid 1♠ as a transfer to diamonds (lead directing); however, with hand (2), you would bid 1NT as takeout (tells partner you have an opening hand and can support all suits), and with hand (3), you would double. You would reverse your bids in hands (2) and (3) if you play 1NT as a strong hand and double for takeout!

Finally, with the following hand: ♠ AKQJ7 ♥ 7 ♦ 987652 ♣A, you would bid 1♥ and (if necessary) perhaps bid diamonds later (e.g., if partner bid 2♣).

This is the basic Undercall Club "Transfer" Convention; it is best played only over a ONE CLUB OPENING BID (Provided the club bid is not the strong Precision Club).

However, you may also play transfers over other one-level opening as follows.

WHAT HAPPENS IF THEY OPEN 1♦? Can we extend the transfer bids? Yes!

One can again use transfer bids:

Opener	You
1♦	1♥ = transfer to spades (5+ spades and first or second round control)
	1♠ = transfer to clubs (should have 10—14 HCP with an ace or king)

NOTE: May be played to transfer to Notrump, usually with a diamond stopper.

1NT = shortness in diamonds and 8-14 HCP (Optional*—for takeout)
X= 15+ HCP with shortness in diamonds (Optional*)

2♦=both majors (Optional)
2♥ = transfer to spades (5/6+ spades and strong 16-21 HCP)
2♠ = 5-5 in the majors and strong (16-21 HCP)
2NT = 5+hearts and 5+diamonds (Optional).

* Some partnerships reverse the meaning of these bids—then 1NT is 15-17 and double is for takeout.

WHAT HAPPENS IF THEY OPEN 1♥?

Opener	You
1♥	1♠ = transfer to clubs (should have 10-14 HCP with an ace or king)

NOTE: May be played to transfer to Notrump, usually with a heart stopper.

1NT = shortness in hearts and 8-14 HCP (Optional*—for takeout)
X= 15+ HCP with stopper in hearts (Optional*)

2♥=spades and a minor (Optional)
2NT = 5+clubs and 5+diamonds (Optional)
3♥ = transfer to spades (5/6+ and strong 16-21 HCP)

* Some partnerships reverse the meaning of these bids—then 1NT is 15-17 and double is for takeout.

AND FINALLY, if they open 1♠

Opener	You
1♠	1NT = shortness in hearts and 8-14 HCP (Optional*—for takeout)
	X= 15+ HCP with shortness in diamonds (Optional*)
	2♠=hearts and a minor (Optional)
	2NT = 5+clubs and 5+diamonds (Optional).

* Some partnerships reverse the meaning of these bids—then 1NT is 15-17 and double is for takeout.

The convention proposed here is an extension of the Undercall Club Convention discussed in "Bridge Conventions in Depth" (2003) by Matthew & Pamela Granovetter by Master Point Press.

Note: All of the material in this book is included on the ACBL General Convention Chart. This means they may be played at Clubs, Sectional, Regional, and National ACBL events. This is not the case for the Undercall Club; it is a Mid-Chart Convention meaning it may only be played in events that have no upper master point limit.

Reuben Advances

Bidding a new suit over partner's overcall bid is played as (a) forcing, (b) non-forcing constructive, or (c) non-forcing. Each option works well with some hands and poorly with others. Is there a better option even if it can not be used will all hands? Yes, they are called Reuben advances. Unlike the Undercall club convention, which is a Mid Chart Convention, Reuben advances are allowed in the ACBL General Convention Chart, used in most local bridge clubs.

As motivation for Reuben Advances, recall that over the opening bid of a strong notrump most partnerships play transfer bids. This is done to allow the strong hand to play the contract in order to protect his tenaces on the opening lead. When you make the transfer bid, as responder you may (1) make the bid and pass (2) transfer and raise (3) transfer and bid notrump, and (4) transfer to one suit and bid another. In most cases, you want to bid and make another bid.

Can one employ the notrump strategy when making an overcall bid? Yes! Let's look at an example. Suppose the opener bids 1♣ and partner overcalls 1♠ and your RHO passes.

With the following hand you would like to (1) transfer to 2♥ and pass.

♠7 ♥AQ1098 ♦Q76 ♣ 5432

However, with a better hand you want to (2) transfer and raise to 3♥.

♠76 ♥AQJ98 ♦K76 ♣ 54

or, with a more balanced hand (3) transfer to hearts and bid 2NT

♠76 ♥AQ1098 ♦K76 ♣ QJ2

(3) transfer to hearts and bid 2NT. Finally, with a two-suited hand,

♠7 ♥KQ1098 ♦AJ976 ♣ J2

you might (4) raise and bid a second suit.

If the overcaller holds the following hand:

♠AQJ1098 ♥7 ♦Q76 ♣ 543

He may refuse the transfer and instead bid 2♠. Or, with a strong two-suit hand when the transfer is to diamonds, bid 4♠ if the overcaller had the following hand

♠AQJ1098 ♥7 ♦K765 ♣ 43

This is exactly how Reuben advances work.

Playing Reuben advances, the transfer begins with a cuebid of the opener's suit. In our example 1♣ - 1♠ - pass, 2♣ is a transfer to diamonds; 2♦ is a transfer to hearts; 2♥ is a transfer to spades showing 3+ card support with 10+ working points (excluding honors in the opponent's suit); 2♠ shows a minimal raise. **Reuben raises are in effect when opener's partner either passes or makes a negative double.** If the overcall had been 1♥, then the bid of 1♠ is natural and forcing for one round (a jump to 2♠ is preemptive) since Reuben advances begin with 2♣ - the cheapest bid of opener's suit.

Summary of 1♣ - 1♠ - Pass (double)

1NT   balanced with a stopper
2♣   transfer to diamonds
2♦   transfer to hearts (over a pass only not a negative double)
2♥   3+ card support 10+ working points
2♠   shows minimal raise, poor defensive values
2NT   balanced with stopper and two card support for spades
3♣/♦ Western Cuebid, with a stopper bid 3NT
Over 1♣-1♥ - pass (double), 2♣ is a transfer to diamonds, and 2♦ is a transfer to hearts, showing a limit raise or better in hearts. After 1♦-2♣ - pass, 2♦ is a transfer to hearts, and 2♥ is a transfer to spades. Now 2♠ is natural.

Summary of 1♣ - 1♥ - Pass (double)

1♠   natural (over a pass only not a negative double)
1NT   balanced with a stopper
2♣   transfer to diamonds
2♦   transfer to hearts with 3+ card support (limit raise)
2♥   shows minimal raise, poor defensive values
2♠   natural and preemptive (over a pass only not a negative double)
2NT   balanced with stopper and two card support for hearts
3♣/♦   Western Cuebid, with a stopper bid 3NT

In both of these cases, a bid of 1NT would show a balanced hand with a stopper in opener's bid suit clubs and 2NT conveys two card support in the overcaller major.
Rueben advances are also in effect over the bidding sequence 1♦-1♠ - (pass). For this case, the bids are:

Summary of 1♦ - 1♠ - Pass (double)

1NT   balanced with a stopper
2♣   natural
2♦   transfer to hearts (over a pass only not a negative double)
2♥   3+ card support 10+ working points
2♠   shows minimal raise, poor defensive values
2NT   balanced with stopper and two card support for spades
3♣/♦   Western Cuebid, with a stopper bid 3NT

When the overcall involves two touching suits1♣-1♦, 1♦-1♥ or 1♠-2♣, Rueben advances do not apply. This is why they cannot be used with all overcalls. Now the cheapest bid of the opponent's suit shows a limit raise in overcaller's suit with 3+ card support.

How does the overcaller respond after the transfer?

Let's look at our last example where the bidding went: 1♦ - 1♠ - Pass - 2♦. The responses would be:

2♥   accept transfer with a minimum and 3 card support
2♠   deny support
3♣   deny support and shows second suit
3♥   accept transfer with 4+ card support
3♦   cuebid with 3+ card support and maximum
3♠   very good six card suit and maximum
3NT   stoppers in all suits but hearts

Montreal Relay Club Bids

In the first or second seat, one may open a short club (0-2) to find out whether or not partner has a five card major. A common system of bids is called the Montreal Relay Club bid which is used in the first or second seats are forcing; however in the third or fourth seats, the bid is non-forcing. The responses follow.

Open 1 Club with 11-19 starting points or **Double** if bid was stolen by the opening bidder.

High Card Points (HCP)	Responses	
		Opener's rebid 2♣ forcing
5/6-9 Points	1 ♦ 5+ Diamonds	Responder Re-Bid 6+ Major Suit
	1 ♥ 5+ Hearts	or Bid 4-card Suit
	1 ♠ 5+ Spades	or Bid 3-card Suit with A or K
	1 NT No 5-card Major	
10-12 Points	2♣ 5 Hearts	3♣ forcing, Next Level Responder Bids
	2♦ 5 Spades	4♦ - 1st Level Higher 10 Points
	2♥ 6+ Hearts	4♥ - 2nd Level Higher 11 Points
	2♠ 6+ Spades	4♠ - 3rd Level Higher 12 Points
	2NT No 5+ Major	
13+ Points	3♣ 5 Hearts	4♣ forcing, Next Level Responder Bids
	3♦ 5 Spades	13-14 4♦
	3♥ 6+ Hearts	15-16 4♥
	3♠ 6+ Spades	17-18 4♠
	3NT No 5+ Major	19+ 5NT

Note: With one or two four-card majors, may bid 2NT with 13+ points so that partner may bid their four card major suit if available. With no 4-card major, bid 3NT. With a larger hand bid 4NT Blackwood since no agreed upon suit.

*= Alert as Forcing Artificial Bid   @=announce Bid as Non-Forcing and maybe short

A less complicate system of bids played by some is called the Kennedy Club bids

Kennedy Club Bids

Open 1 Club with 11-19 starting points or **Double** if bid was stolen

High Card Points (HCP)	Responses	Opener's Rebids
5/6-10 Points	1 ♦ No 5-card Major	Bid four-card majors Up-the-line
	1 ♥ 5+ Hearts	jump with 15+
	1 ♠ 5+ Spades	Bid 1NT balanced minimum
	1NT No 4/5-card Major	Invite 2NT or bid best minor

The responder, holding neither a 4-card major suit nor a 5-card major suit, and no five-card support for opener's Minor suit, will bid No Trump on the appropriate level according to the number of working values: 2NT with values of 9/10 to 12, and 3NT with game values.

Montreal Relay Diamond Bids

In the first or second seat, one may open a diamond to find out whether or not partner has a four card major. A common system of bids is called the Montreal Relay Diamond bid which is used in the first or second seats is forcing; however in the third or fourth seats, the bid is non-forcing. The responses follow.

Open 1 Diamond with 11-19 starting points or **Double** if bid was stolen by the opening bidder.

High Card Points (HCP)	Responses	
6-9 Points	1 ♥ 4+ Spades	Opener rebid of 2♣ forcing
	1 ♠ 4+ Hearts	any other bid to play
	1 NT No Major	
10-12 Points	2♣ 4 Hearts	3♣ Forcing
	2♦ 4 Spades	any other bid to play
	2♥ 5+ Hearts	
	2♠ 5+ Spades	
	2NT No Major	
13+ Points	3♣ 4 Hearts	5♣ Forcing, Next Level Bids
	3♦ 4 Spades	13-14 5 Diamonds
	3♥ 5+ Hearts	15-16 5 Hearts
	3♠ 5+ Spades	17-18 5 Spades
	3NT No Major	19+ 5NT

*= Alert bid as Forcing and Artificial one or two four card majors

The Montreal Relay Club and Diamond bids are used to find major suit fits, either 5-3 or 4-4 in the majors. If you choose to use the "Montreal Bids", you cannot use the 2/1 inverted minor bids.

Multi Weak Two Bids

The opening bids of 2♦/2♥/2♠ usually show a hand with 5/6-10 HCP and a 6-card suit. Is there a better bidding strategy?

Yes, how about the multi-suit weak two bids.

The bids are defined:

2♦ - Single heart suit, or two suits: Diamonds and Clubs, or Diamonds and Spades
2♥ - Single spade suit, or two suits: Hearts and Clubs, or Hearts and Diamonds
2♠ - Single club suit, or two suits: Spades and Diamonds, or Spades and Hearts

Observe that the single suited hands are the next level suit (Diamonds implies Hearts, Hearts implies Spades and Spades implies Clubs), transfer like bids. Hence, responder bids the next suit up-the-line to play and opener passes if the hand is single suited. If opener has a two-suited hand (the hand includes the suit bid and two suits excluding the suit immediately above the suit bid), he refuses the two level bids and bids three clubs (after 2♦-2♥-3♣) or three diamonds (after 2♥-2♠-3♦ or 2♠-3♣-3♦), the lower ranking suit of a two suited hand. Partner now knows both suits and either passes or bids the second suit at the three level.

With game interest, responder does not use the relay bids of hearts, spades and clubs, but instead bids 2NT.

Now, opener bids his suit if single suited (Hearts, Spades or Clubs) at the three level. If two suited, he again bids three clubs or three diamonds, the lower ranking suit, with minimal values (5-7 HCP).

With 8-10 HCP, opener bids 3NT if single suited or the higher ranking suit at the three level if holding a two suited hand, for example the bids would be: after 2♦-2NT-3♠, after 2♥-2NT-3♥, and after 2♠ - 2NT - 3♠.

Let's look at three examples.

Example (1)

Opener: ♠ 6 ♥ A Q 8 7 6 5 ♦ 6 5 3 ♣ 10 7 6
Responder: ♠ A Q 7 8 ♥ J 10 ♦ J 10 4 ♣ A 2

In (1), opener bids 2♦*. Responder with only 12 HCP, bids 2♥ and opener would pass.

Example (2)

Opener: ♠ 6 2 ♥ A Q 8 7 6 ♦ A 9 6 5 3 ♣ 7
Responder: ♠ A Q 7 8 ♥ J 10 ♦ J 10 4 ♣ A 2

In (2) opener bids 2♥ and when partner bids 2♠, he does not pass, but bids 3♦ to show hearts and diamonds. Partner would now pass with three diamonds.

Example (3)

Opener: ♠ 7 ♥ A Q 8 7 6 5 ♦ 6 5 3 ♣ 10 7 6
Responder: ♠ A K J 8 ♥ K J 10 9 ♦ A 10 4 ♣ 4 2

In (3), after opener's bid of 2♦* responder bids 2NT. With only six HCP, opener bids 3♥ to show a minimal single suited hand. Responder bids 4♥; however with fewer points and no fit, responder could pass.

Some may feel that the multi-suit weak two bidding structure defined above is too complicated. Because the bids are weak, the structure must be involved to differentiate between invitational hands and game going hands.

If one increases the value of "weak" bids to hands with more points, say 10-12, the bidding structure may be greatly simplified; however, you have now given up weak two bids. With weak bids increased in value one may perhaps adopt the following bidding structure. Instead of using transfer bids, one may define a structure of bids as follows:

2♦ = diamonds or diamonds and a lower ranking suit
2♥ = hearts or hearts and a lower ranking suit
2♠ = spades or spades and a lower ranking suit.

With a weak hand, responder may pass; there is no relay involved. With game interest, responder bids 2NT. Now the bid of 2NT becomes an asking bid, What is your second suit if two suited?

Not having a second suit, you would rebid your suit at the three level; however, with a two suited hand you would bid your lower ranking suit.

The revised bidding structure of 10-12 HCP is not arbitrary; it is identical to opening a weak notrump. Thus, if you play weak notrumps you might want to also consider the two-suited/ single suited "weak" bids. Just a thought!

Let's look at two more examples.

(1) ♠ 83 ♥ K J 10 9 8 ♦ J ♣ A Q 10 9 8

(2) ♠ J 10 9 4 ♥ Q J 10 7 ♦ J 10 3 ♣ A Q 10

Hand (1) has only 11 HCP, but you are 5-5 in hearts and clubs. Open the bidding 2♥.

Hand (2) also has 11 HCP, however, it is balanced.

Playing weak notrumps open the hand 1NT.

If you adopt the weak notrump bid and the weak two bids with 10-12 HCP, consider the following bidding structure after vulnerable or non-vulnerable.

10-12   open the bidding 1NT
13-15   open 1♣, rebid 1NT
16-17   open 1♦, rebid 1NT
18-19   open one of a suit, rebid 2NT
20-21   open the bidding 2NT

Burgay Responses to 15-17 NT Opening

I found this very interesting convention when playing strong notrumps. It incorporates Stayman, Transfers, Smolen, slamish hands and major suit voids. It was developed by **Leandro Burgay, a** leading Italian expert in the early 1970s.

1. 2♣ forces opener to bid 2♦, then

> pass with a weak hand and diamonds
>
> 2♥/2♠ invitational with a four card major
>
> 2NT standard 1NT-2NT invitational sequence
>
> 3♣/3♦ 5-4 distribution in the minor (5-cards in bid minor, 4-cards in the other)
>
> 3NT 2-2-5-4 or 2-2-4-5
>
> 3♥ Smolen five spades and four Hearts
>
> 3♠ Smolen four spades and five Hearts

2. 2♦ transfer to 2♥, (opener bids 3♥ with a four-card heart suit unless min with 3=4-3-3 distribution), then:

> 2♠ shows 4 Hearts without four Spades

2NT shows four Hearts and four Spades

3♣/3♦ shows four cards in bid minor and five Hearts

3NT shows five Hearts, balanced hand

3. 2♥ transfer to 2♠, (opener bids 3♠ with four Spades unless min with 4=3-3-3 distribution), then:

2NT shows four Spades without four Hearts

3♣/3♦ shows four cards in minor and five Spades

3NT shows a balanced hand with five Spades

4. Other responses to the strong 1NT opening:

2♠ transfer to Clubs

2NT transfer to Diamonds

3-level suit bid natural 6 + card suit and slamish

3NT to play

4♣ major two suited hand, longer Hearts

4♦ major two suited hand, longer Spades

4♥ minor two suited hand, Heart void

4♠ minor two suited hand, Spade void

Kaplan Interchange

After an opening bid of 1♥, there is an advantage to switching the 1♠ and 1NT (forcing) responses. This is called the Kaplan Interchange. Suppose responder does NOT have spades but does have a typical 1NT force. Playing standard responses, you cannot play in 1NT, because that bid is forcing. However if you play the Kaplan Interchange, responder bids 1♠ with those hands, and opener with most minimum 5332 hands can now rebid 1NT to play, if responder agrees that is a good spot.

The disadvantage is that when responder **DOES** have spades he must bid 1NT forcing, so the partnership cannot play 1NT (with normal methods they can, with opener rebidding 1NT - 1♥-1♠ - 1NT).

However the advantage outweighs the disadvantage, because responder will **NOT** have spades more often than he will have spades, so you will be able to settle in 1NT more often. The interchange is not needed if you play 1NT as semi-forcing.

Ekren 2♦ Convention

The weak two diamond bid has little utility in duplicate bridge. Instead, many bridge players use it as Flannery, Extra Shape Flannery, Mini Roman, Mexican Two diamonds, and many others.

Because it is important to find a major suit fit, another option is to employ the bid as the Ekren 2♦ bid suggest by Biørn Olav Ekren of Norway.

The bid of 2♦, playing the 2/1 Game Force System is defined as 4-4, 4-5, 5-4 or 5-5 in the majors with 5-10 HCP.

Responses to the bid are:

> Pass   to play (can be a tactical maneuver in the absence of a major suit fit and does not guarantee long diamonds)

> 2♥/♠   to play
> 2NT   Relay (invitational or stronger)
> 3♣   Natural, not forcing
> 3♦   Invitational with 3-3 in the majors
> 3♥/♠   preemptive to play
> 4♥/♠   to play

In responding to the 2NT relay, the opener indicates whether his holdings are a minimum (5-7 HCP) or a maximum (8-10 HCP) and something about his distribution.

> 3♣ = any minimum (responder's 3♥/♠ rebid now indicates an invite)
> 3♦ = 5-5 min or max (creates game force)
> 3♥ = 4-5 max (creates game force)
> 3♠ = 5-4 max (creates game force)
> 3NT = 4-4 max (creates game force)

Playing the Ekren two diamond convention, one may use the bid of 2♥ to indicate a hand with 11-15 HCP and exactly 4-4 in the majors. This treatment has the advantage that the left hand opponent of the opener can hardly gamble on the fact that he will get a second chance to bid.

The bid of 2♠ shows a 5+ spade hand with 5-10 HCP and two of the top three honors when vulnerable.

When the Opponents Show Weakness

Playing 2/1 Game Force, you often hear the following auctions: 1♣-1NT or 1♦ - 1NT and you are in the balancing seat, what do you bid?

Clearly the points are 20-20, do you double? And if you do, what is the meaning of the bid? Do you really have the other three suits? I don't think so.

I would recommend the following strategy.

When you are 4-4 in the majors, cuebid their suit as a delayed "Michaels" bid, to show partner that you are 4-4 in the majors. And use a double to show that you are 4-4 in the two lowest unbid suits, like an unusual 2NT bid (e.g. diamonds and hearts after the club bid, and clubs and hearts after the diamond bid). If you have spades, bid them at the one level, even with four and with two of the top three honors.

How does partner respond? With a fit, he bids the suit; however, without a fit partner must bid his own 5-card suit at the two level.

Try to never let the opponents play 1NT in a duplicate game when you have the majors or hearts and a minor.

What if the bidding goes 1♥ - 1♠ - 1NT?

Because the opponents have bid the majors, it is usually best to pass with this bidding sequence. Let them play in a notrump contract. Who wants to play in a minor suit partial?

Fast Arrival or Picture bids

Playing the 2/1 Game Force system, suppose the bidding goes 1♠ - 2♣; 2♠ - 4♠. What does the game bid mean?

Using the principle of "fast-arrival" some may interpret the bid as "I am not interested in bidding on;" since if I were, I would have bid 3♠. Or, does it show a specific holding?

Some bridge experts agree that it should show a specific holding called a "picture bid". The bid of 4♠ would show that partner's high card points are in clubs and spades with no controls or shortness in the unbid suits.

This concept was considered by Eric Rodwell in his March/April 2008 Two-Over-One article called the "Principle of Fast Arrival" on the website /www.betterbridge.com/articles/ Two-Over-One/09-200803.pdf.

Fast Arrival does not rule out the possibility of slam when partner has extra values. Let's look at Rodwell's first example.

WEST	EAST
♠ K Q 8 7 6 4 3	♠ A J 2
♥ K 3	♥ A Q J 6 2
♦ A 9	♦ 8 4 2
♣ K 7	♣ 9 5

WEST	EAST
1♠	2♥
2♠	4♠
4NT	5♥
6♠	Pass

With a minimum for the 2/1 response, East's jumps to game over the 2♠ rebid. That doesn't deter West from going to slam once East shows a fit for spades, along with enough strength for a 2/1 game forcing response. East jump to game is called a picture bid. It paints a nice picture of his hand: a minimum opening bid with most of the high cards in hearts and spades with no controls in diamonds or clubs. With extra values, or high cards in clubs and diamonds, East could raise to 3♥. With shortness in clubs or diamonds, East could make a *splinter* jump to 4♣ or 4♦.

Both partners can use the bid. Sometimes the opener may take a fast route to game: We look at Rodwell's second example.

WEST	EAST
♠ A K J 7 5	♠ 8 2
♥ K J 6 2	♥ A Q 10 7 4
♦ 8 4	♦ K Q 6
♣ 9 8	♣ Q 7 4

WEST	EAST
1♠	2♥
4♥	Pass

West likes East's 2♥ response, but has a minimum opening bid with no help outside of hearts and spades. West quickly takes the partnership to game. East knows that opener could have simply raised to 3♥ to leave more room for slam exploration West's jump to game is again a picture bid. It paints a nice picture of the West hand: a minimum opening bid with most of the high cards in hearts and spades.

Playing the 2/1 game force system, a jump to the four level in the bid suit may not mean stop. You must discuss this with your partner.

As another example, suppose the bidding goes 1NT - 2♣; 2♦ - 4♣; what is the bid of four clubs? Clearly, a picture bid showing a distributional hand (perhaps 6-4-2-1 or 6-4-3-0) with values in clubs and a major inviting partner to investigate slam in clubs.

The picture bid may also be played with Jacoby 2NT. What does the bidding sequence 1♠ - 2NT followed by the opener's bid of 4♠ imply?

Consider this set of bids, playing picture bids:

- **3♣, 3♦ or 3♥** = Singleton or void in that suit.
- **3♠** = good 14+ HCP with extra length in spades, no singleton.
- **3NT** = 15-18 pts., balanced (no singleton or void).
- **4♣, 4♦, 4♥** = Decent 5-card side suit (QJxxx or better).
- **4♠** = 19+ HCP with slam interest.

Without the concept of picture bids, most partnerships playing Jacoby use the bid of 4♠ with no slam interest. Then the bid of 3♠ is either semi—strong of real strong. With this sequence of bids, information is conveyed to the opponents.

Instead, one should consider the bidding structure proposed above to convey information to your partner; instead of the opponents.

Masked Mini-Splinters

A mini-splinter is a jump bid such as 1♣-1♠-3♦ Here 3♦ is the equivalent to raising spades to the 3-level, but shows a singleton diamond or a void. Since 2♦ would be a reverse, the bid cannot be misunderstood.

A mini-splinter shows a 15+ to 18 - points, and should not be confused with the regular splinter bid at the 4-level, such as 1♣-1♠-4♦, where you are showing something like 18+ to 20 points with a shortage in diamonds, or 1♦-1♠-4♦ shows 4 card spade support with a 6 card diamond suit.

You are limited in how you use a mini-splinter, since 1♦-1♠-3♣ would be a natural jump shift. You have to think twice about whether you are showing a natural bid or a mini-splinter.

How do you tell the difference? What you do, playing mini-splinters is to use the concept of "masked mini-splinters." Using this concept, the bid of three clubs is a mini-splinter that is a game force in some suit, and three diamonds is a mini-splinter in some suit that is not forcing to game.

If partner is interested in slam, one now bids 3NT, where is your singleton? Now you bid your controls up-the-line. 3NT is not natural showing duplication and offering a choice of contracts. After you have splintered, there is no choice of contracts as the major is preferred.

There are some RKCB rules in mini/maxi splinter auctions. If ***either player*** has splintered, a six level response to the Specific King Ask in the splinter suit shows the Spade King. It is wasteful for the responder to show the king of the splinter suit when hearts is the agreed suit, so why not use it for something useful? Showing the spade king is always *dangerous* as its rank virtually forces you to a grand. Do not splinter with stiff kings as it is a splinter distortion. Splintering with stiff Aces is also a no-no.

Ingberman Convention

This convention was named for **Mr. Monroe Ingberman** of New York, who was a mathematician and bridge player. He was also known for Splinter and the Three No Trump response as a forcing Major raise. T*he Ingberman convention is used t*o allow you to stop below game after opener's 2-level reverse bid. It is similar to Lebensohl in that bidding 2NT (relay to 3♣) then giving preference is weaker than an original preference. However, other bids are also defined so that it is more than Lebensohl after a reverse bid.

Definition of a Reverse: Any rebid by opener which forces preference of the opening suit to the three-level. If the initial bid and response were one of a suit, this bid is forcing one round (promises a rebid), but does not create a game force.

For example:

(1) 1♣ - pass - 1♠ - pass   (2) 1♦ - pass - 1♠ - pass

    2♦ - pass - ??   2♥ - pass -??

Reverses after 1♦ - 2♣ are forcing to game since responder has shown 13+ HCP in 2/1 or 10+ in Standard American and opener has extra values.

Even after a response of 1NT by responder, reverses should be forcing to game, since opener knows there is no fit in the higher suit. If you don't have a game force in this situation, just raise to 2NT.

Let's now look at the responses by partner in example (2) in more detail.

2♠   5+ spades, any stength, forcintg for one round. All other calls deny five spades except for raises in hearts

2NT   Denies the values for game opposite a minimum reverse. Asks partner to rebid 3♣, so responder can take preference at the three-level to play

3♣	Good hand (10+), with values in clubs
3♦	2+ diamonds, values for game; denies 5+ spades
3♥	4+ hearts, values for game: serious 3NT is on by both hands
3♠	Solid or semi-solid spades, can play opposite a small singleton
3NT	8-10 HCP, club stopper, denies 3 diamonds or 4 hearts
4♣	Splinter in support of hearts
4♦	Good hand (13+), with values in diamonds.
4♥	*Picture Bid*: 5 spades, 4 hearts, and no controls in the minors

Note: Do not play fast arrival. Observe that the 3♦ preference bid may be made with a doubleton. This would only happen if you had nothing in clubs, for example, ♠AQxx ♥Kxx ♦Qx ♣xxxx. You certainly have the values for game, but have no other bid. If we the contract belongs in 3NT, it must be played from partner's side.

If instead the bidding goes:

1♦ - Pass - 1♠ - Pass

2♥ - Pass - 2NT - Pass -??

Then opener's bids are:

3♣	Relay bid 17+ points
3♦	6+ diamonds, game forcing
3♥	5+ hearts, 6+ diamonds, game forcing
3♠	3 spades, game forcing
3NT	Probably 2=4=5=2, 20-21 HCP

The responses for the bidding sequence:

1♦ - pass - 1♥ - pass - 2♠ - pass - ??

Are similar.

We next consider (1) in more detail.

1♣ - pass - 1♠ - pass-2♦ - pass - ??

2♠   5+ spades, any stength, forcintg for one round. All other calls deny five spades except for raises in hearts

2NT   Denies the values for game opposite a minimum reverse. Asks partner to rebid 3♣, so responder can take preference at the three-level to play

3♦	Good hand (10+), with values in diamonds
3♣	2+ clubs, values for game; denies 5+ spades
3♥	4+ hearts, values for game: serious 3NT is on by both hands
3♠	Solid or semi-solid spades, can play opposite a small singleton
3NT	8-10 HCP, club stopper, denies 3 clubs or 4 hearts
4♣	Good hand (13+), with values in clubs.
5♦	*Picture Bid*: 5 spades, 4 diamonds, and no controls in hearts or clubs.

If instead the bidding goes:

1♣ - Pass - 1♠ - Pass

2♦ - Pass - 2NT - Pass

??

Then opener's bids are:

3♣	Relay bid 17+ points
3♦	5+ diamonds, game forcing
3♥	4 hearts, 6+ clubs, game forcing
3♠	3 spades, game forcing
3NT	Probably 2=2=4=5, 20-21 HCP

PING PONG CONVENTION

The origin of this convention is unknown. The concept is to assist the opener to further clarify his holding when the first rebid by the opener is 1 NT, which can signify various hand types. The following diagram contains the various auctions whereby this conventional method may be employed:

North	East	South	West	Meaning
1♣/1♦/1♥	Pass	1♥ / 1♠	Pass	May only show a 4-card suit
1 NT	Pass	2♣		Forcing—the so-called Ping Pong action by responder (also known as a puppet bid)
2♦				An automatic rebid by opener

The 2♣ so-called Ping Pong is employed by the responder to show one of the following three holdings:

1.	To show weak holdings when the responder wishes to cease the auction in a part score in a Minor suit. If Diamonds is the Minor suit, then the responder passes the automatic rebid by opener. If Clubs is the intended suit, then the responder will correct to 3♣.
2.	To show balanced holdings of 5-3-3-2 or 4-3-3-3 and at least 10 high card points. Once the transfer (Ping Pong) has been completed and opener has rebid 2♦, then the responder rebids: <table><tr><td></td><td>2NT:</td><td>Shows a holding with 10-12 points.</td></tr><tr><td></td><td>3NT:</td><td>Shows a holding with 12-16 points.</td></tr><tr><td></td><td>4NT:</td><td>Shows a holding with 17-18 points.</td></tr></table> and the opener becomes the captain and establishes the final contract.
3.	To show limited, balanced holding with a range of 11-13 points. The holding also contains at least a 5-card suit in the first suit bid by the responder. Continuances are then considered natural sequences, but they are generally considered invitational and not forcing.

When the Ping Pong Conventional method is the partnership agreement, then all other responses by the responder to a 1 No Trump rebid by the opener has the following meanings:

1.	Bids at the lowest level are discouraging, particularly the raise of a 1♥ opening by partner.
2.	Any reverse bids or jump bids are considered natural and semi-invitational.
3.	A 2 NT rebid is natural, invitational, and denies a 5-card suit in any original Major suit bid by the responder.
4.	A 2♣ first response to a 1♣ opening is natural. A 2♣ first response to a 1♦ opening is natural and one-round forcing.

Marvin Two Spades Convention

The popular "Gambling 3NT" opening shows a solid seven-card minor with little outside strength. Besides being rather restrictive as to suit quality, the notrump contract is played from the wrong side. Not only is the lead through dummy's strength, but the exposure of that hand lets the opponents put up a "double dummy" defense. If responder can't support a 3NT contract, the bidding ends up at the dangerous four level.

Marvin 2♠ shows the same sort of hand, or (nine times as frequent) a semi-solid (KQJ or AQJ) seven-card minor with one ace or king outside. The hand must contain at least one ace, so responder can count on seven playing tricks. Besides a solid minor, opener could have:

♠32 ♥A7 ♦KQJ10876 ♣J2

or   ♠K3 ♥9 ♦962 ♣AQJ9432

or   ♠75 ♥92 ♦AQJ7652 ♣A

A third-seat bidder might cheat with an eight-card suit or regard an AKJ10 suit as solid.

Responder bids 3♣ to sign off, whereupon opener will pass with clubs, or rebid 3♦ with diamonds. If responder would raise clubs but not diamonds, she responds 3♦. If she would raise diamonds but not clubs, she bids 3♣. Opener can correct if responder bids the wrong suit.

A response of 3♥ or 3♠ is forcing. Opener bids 3NT to show Qx, xxx, or better support, so responder (perhaps fishing for a notrump contract) need not have a real suit (e.g., respond 3♥ with ♠A7532 ♥J76 ♦A87 ♣K2). Although this response must be alerted ("That is an asking bid, not a telling bid."), its ambiguous nature can make it useful as a lead inhibitor or as a complete psych when an opposing game is feared.

A 2NT response asks for clarification. Opener bids 3NT with a solid minor, or indicates where the outside high card is located when the minor is only semi-solid:

Opener	Responder
2♠	2NT

3NT - solid minor suit
3♣ - club suit, high card in diamonds
3♦ - diamond suit, high card in clubs
3♥ - high card in spades, may have either minor
3♠ - high card in hearts, may have either minor

Opener's rebid will usually give responder the information she needs to place the contract. These bids are designed so that opener's LHO cannot double to direct a lead through the high card (perhaps an unguarded king).

A 4♣ response asks opener to show a short suit:

Opener	Responder
2♠	4♣

4♦/4♥/4♠/5♣—short suit
4NT—no short suit

A 4♦ response asks for a major suit preference ("Ripstra"), and 4NT is Blackwood (5♣ or 5♦ with one ace—must have one—5♥ with two).

A game response is a signoff, but a jump to 5♣ is "pass or correct" (to 5♦).

When the Opponents Intervene

If the 2♠ opening gets doubled, presumably showing a spade suit, responder may choose to make a forcing pass. She would pass, for instance, with ♠972 ♥QJ543 ♦A2 ♣A53, giving opener a chance to bid notrump if he has spades stopped:

South West North East
2♠ Dbl Pass Pass

2NT - spade stopper
3♣/3♦ - no spade stopper

Suppose there is an overcall and responder cue bids:

South West North
2♠ 3♦ 4♦

South now bids 4♦ with solid diamonds, 4♥ with a high card in spades, 4♠ with a high card in hearts, 4NT with a high card in clubs, and 5♣ with a solid club suit! (Maybe 3♣ was meant as Michaels). Similarly:

South	West	North	East
2♠	3♦	4♦	Pass

4♥ - high card in spades
4♠ - high card in hearts

4NT - high card in diamonds, club suit
5♣/5♦ - solid suit

When the cue bid is in a major, opener has less room to show his hand and responder may have to guess opener's minor:

    South   West   North   East
    2♠   3♥   4♥   Pass
    4♠ - high card in spades, unknown minor
    4NT - high card in hearts, unknown minor
    5♣/5♦ - natural

The 5♣/5♦ bids show either a solid suit or a high card in the unbid minor.

    South   West   North   East
    2♠   3♠   4♠   Pass
    4NT - high card in spades, unknown minor
    5♣/5♦ - natural

The bidding here is so crowded that opener can show an outside high card in spades only.

Summarizing the advantages of Marvin 2♠ over Gambling 3NT:

1) It gives an accurate picture of more hard-to-describe hands.
2) It comes up ten times as often.
3) Notrump is played from the right side.
4) Responder can bail out at the three level.
5) Responder can inquire about a major at the three level.
6) Responder can ask for a short suit.
7) It frees the 3NT opening for another purpose (e.g., a nine-trick notrump hand, also hard to describe).

The above bidding sequence was developed by Marvin L. French (www.marvinfrench.com).

Ripstra Convention

Ripstra is a convention, developed by J. G. Ripstra, is used the opponents have opened 1NT. It is a variation of the Landy convention, using not only a 2♣ overcall to show the major suits (at least 4-4), but a 2♦ overcall as well. The difference between overcalling 2 2♣ and 2♦ lies in the strength of overcaller's minor suits. With better clubs he overcalls 2♣ and with better diamonds, 2♦. With equal length in the minors, overcaller bids 2♣. The purpose of Ripstra is to allow partner to pass 2♣/2♦ when he can see no major-suit fit but has a lot of cards in the minor suit that overcaller has bid.

Top and Bottom Cuebids

The origins of these cuebids are unknown. They are employed after a suit opening of any opponent and not after any No Trump opening by the opponents. The direct cuebid of the suit of the opponent may be employed in direct seat or in the balancing seat. The concept behind this method is to show that the two suits of the cuebidder are known to be the highest unbid suit and lowest unbid suit of the suit of the opener. The two-suiter of the overcaller should contain either a 5-4 distribution by favorable vulnerability; otherwise a distribution of at least 5-5 should be the norm by non-favorable vulnerability. The following chart indicates the possible suits following a suit opening by the opponents.

Opener		Overcaller		Meaning
1♣		2♣		Shows both the Spade suit and the Diamond suit.
1♦		1♦		Shows both the Spades suit and the Club suit.
1♥		2♥		Shows both the Spade suit and the Club suit.
1♠		2♠		Shows both the Heart suit and the Club suit.

As can be noticed by closer inspection, the main disadvantage of this concept is that the overcaller is unable to show a two-suited holding with both Major suits after a Minor suit opening by the opener.

In order to overcome this disadvantage, many partnerships have come to the understanding that the **Michaels Cuebid** should be used to show both Major suits if the opening has been in a **Minor suit** and restrict the **Top and Bottom Cuebids** to an opening by the opponent in either **Major suit**. Again, this understanding includes the disadvantage that the Diamond suit could not be shown by either cuebid, neither Michaels Cuebid nor Top and Bottom Cuebids. This particular flaw contained in this concept has led to a certain unpopularity of this conventional method. However, the partnership can come to an understanding by certain continuance rebids to show the Diamond suit as the second suit, but this is left up to the partnership to decide.

A Notrump Convention

In the 2/1 game force system, one usually employs the 15-17 HCP notrump range. An alternative suggested to me by Val Jakubowitch is to use a double barrel range for all notrump openings. This allows one to use 2NT openings and overcalls as preemptive.

The basic system assumes no 5-card major and no more than one doubleton. The advantage of the approach is that it prevents the opponents from overcalling at the one level. It goes as follows.

1NT: 12-14 or 15-17

2NT: 18-20 or 24-16

3NT: 21-23 or 27+

The specific bids are:

12 to 14 HCP	Open 1NT
15 to 17 HCP	Open 1♣ (partner announces "could be short") and bids 1♦. Opener is waiting and bids 1NT.
18 to 20 HCP	Bid 1♣ followed by 2NT
21 to 23 HCP	Bid 1♣ followed by 3NT
24 to 26 HCP	Open 2♣ followed by 2NT
27+ HCP	Open 2♣ followed by 3NT

When opening a weak notrump (12-14 HCP), and your LHO doubles, you must have an escape plan. Val recommends the following which allows the partnership to play in a 7-card or better fit at the two level or let the opponents have the contract. It works as follows.

If partner has a 5-card suit, he bids it and opener passes.

If partner is 4-3-3-3, he redoubles. Opener either bids his 4-card suit if your RHO passes or passes if your RHO bids.

If partner is either 4-4-3-2 or 4-4-4-1, he redoubles (which you must alert). If your RHO passes, you bid your 4-card suit. If your bid is your partner's one or two card suit, he will bid his next higher 4-card suits which allows for a 7-card fit which may be at the three level. A redouble by responder is for penalty.

What if the opponents interfere over 1♣?

One usually employs a negative double or with values bids a 5-card suit. However, a pass over interference does not necessarily mean a bust because the opener will usually get a chance to bid.

Responses to all notrump level bids, including an overcall are the same. Lebensohl, Smolen, 4-way transfers (yes, for weak notrump too) which apply over a double or 2♣ are the same. With the weak notrump bid, Crawling Stayman is popular.

When using the notrump convention, one now uses 2NT as 5-5 in the minors with 5-10 HCP non-vulnerable and 11-15 HCP vulnerable, similar to some versions of Precision.

For the notrump convention, all overcalls show 7-15 HCP and a double shows 16+. When responding to a major, 1NT is forcing and shows 9-12 HCP and a stopper if the opponents have bid a suit. Two notrump promises 2+ stoppers and 13+ HCP.

The Forcing Pass

A **Forcing Pass** in a competitive auction, is a pass that allows partner to choose the most profitable option between a rebid in agreed suit, doubling opponents' for penalty, allowing partner to redouble a makeable contract, showing a stronger hand than a simple competitive overcall, providing partner a conventional response and the like.

As a background, partnerships should decide on one of these methods:**METHOD 1**	**METHOD 2**
Bid shows a good offensive hand	Bid shows good offensive hand
Double shows good defensive hand	Pass shows a fairly good offensive hand
Pass implies neither of these hands	Double implies neither of the above

While many players employ METHOD 1, some partnerships (notably Mechkstroth-Rodwell) prefer METHOD 2.

Fundamentally, as summarized in bridgehands.com, we find partnership agreements fall in two camps: Industrialists and the Scientists. While Industrialist methods vary, a typical agreement might include: After we open, responder bids at the 2 level and opponents bid 3 Notrump or above, either partner's pass is forcing. Additionally, the Forcing Pass is the strongest action showing slam interest and at least a second round control.

A.	Forcing passes apply when your side bids a game or higher and the other side sacrifices
	1. You bid a vulnerable game
	2. You bid a non vulnerable game voluntarily
	3. The opponents have preempted
B.	There are five options at the 5 level:
	1. Cuebid is a slam try—strongest action
	2. Pass and pull partners double—also a slam try

	3. Bid 5 level—extra values but no slam interest
	4. Pass—offers partner to bid five with extra values
	5. Double—worst hand based on auction
C.	Cuebid with an outstanding hand, showing first round control and interest in slam.
D.	"Pass and pull" is uncommon. Be aware when you pass, partner doubles, you need to pass unless you have slam interest

On the side of the Scientists, in the Okbridge "Spectator" Marc Smith featured a series of Forcing Pass articles (6/01, 12/01, 1/02). Another Scientist, Eddie Kantar authored the definitive "Forcing Pass" book and wrote a series of articles in "Bridge Today" (2/05, 3/05, 5/05)

Naturally, Scientists methods for Forcing Pass bids vary considerably, possibly including:

1.	Opponents have made an obvious sacrifice bid
2.	Your side has voluntarily bid game based on strength, not merely distributional values. This is particularly true when partner's pass allows you to evaluate the tradeoffs of doubling for penalty, especially when opponents are vulnerable, as opposed to bidding at a higher level—perhaps exploring slam
3.	After 3 or 4 level opening preempt by Left Hand Opponent in first or second seat, double by partner, game raise by Right Hand Opponent, our pass is forcing except when opponents are vulnerable (assuming a sane RHO has values)
4.	Your side has established a baseline contract level exploring game or slam, but not yet reached that threshold and opponents have interceded in the auction
5.	A pass over opponents' high level obstructive bid typically shows a first round control (Ace or void). The threshold for "high level" may be the 5 or 6 level, depending on agreements
6.	Opponents have doubled a cuebid on your side
7.	Opponents are retreating by bidding multiple suits (usually up the line), where your partnership has repeatedly doubled
8.	Pulling partner's penalty double shows strong interest in slam

Scientists have more scenarios (and memory work) with less catch-all guidelines such as a universal "whenever opponents bid above our 3 Spade call and our bids are constructive, our subsequent pass is forcing." Regardless of your approach, consider Environmental Factors—particularly vulnerability, freak distribution, and offensive/defensive tricks.

Here are several common situations:

    2♣ - (any) - P - (any);
     P

When opener has near-game values such as a strong **2 Club** opener showing 22+ points, many play a subsequent pass is a Forcing Bid; lacking a better bid, responder can double to keep the auction alive. However, when opener begins with a **2 Notrump** bid showing 20-21 point, subsequent passes are not forcing.

    1♠ - (P) - 2N - (3♦)
     P

Responder's **2NT** bid is game-forcing so opener's pass is forcing.

    1♦ - (1♥) - 1♠ - (P);
    3♦ - (3♥) - 3♠ - (4♥);
     P

Assuming you recognize responder's **3♠** rebid as establishing a game force (opener jumps, responder rebids own suit), opener is making a Forcing Pass inviting responder to **double** or bid **4♠** with great Spades.

    1♦ - (1♠) - 2♦ - (2♠);
    1♥ - (2♦) - 2♥ - (3♦);

Here, opener can make a forcing bid by cuebidding opponents' suit or calling a new suit. When opener (the stronger hand) bids a new suit at the 3 level, the call is invitational. Jumping in a new suit at the 4 level subsequently establishes a Forcing Pass if necessary. Opener's jump to game has the same effect. Note: some play this treatment only with adverse vulnerability based on the risk-reward differential. At any rate, if opener takes another path, as rebidding at the 3 level, belated opener passes are not forcing. Note: many also playMaximal Doubles at the 3 level.

Yet rules like this one should not be thought of as iron-clad. Contrast these bids:

    W   N   E   S

    1♥ - (1♠) - 2♥ - (2♠);
    4♥ - (P) - P - (4♠);
     P

> 1♥ - (2♣) - 2♥ - (3♣);
> 4♥ - (P) - P - (5♣);
>   P

It is unlikely South is "walking the dog" with extra values on the above auctions. Apparently South is making a sacrifice bid so opener's pass is definitely a Forcing Bid in these auctions. However, south may indeed be walking the dog on this auction:

> **W   N   E   S**
>
> 1♥ - (P) - 2♥ - (2♠);
> 3♦ - (P) - 4♥ - (4♠);
>   P

The responder may be bidding game based on an anticipated double fit in the red suits after opener's Help Suit Game Try Realizing this, opponent South may upgrade a two-suited black hand and solely bid game. Thus, the meaning of opener's pass will vary by partnership agreement (again, some play forcing only with adverse vulnerability). As an aside, when your side bids a lower suit rank as Hearts over their Spades, it may not be wise to "advertise" a possible double fit—smart opponents certainly enjoy such useful information.

In some situations, the Scientists liberalize their conventional gadgets to replace the meaning of the Forcing Pass or even the double. Consider this auction:

> **W   N   E   S**
>
> --   --   (P) - P
> (1♦) - 1♥ - (2♥) - P
> (3♣) - 4♥ - (P) - P
> (5♦) - ?

Should a double be purely for penalty here, or is it a cooperative (optional) double asking partner to consider a 5♥ sacrifice with an offensive hand? Scientists point out the 1♣ overcall shows defensive values, not immediately making a preemptive jump to 4♥. So a common treatment is "DSI", asking partner to Do Something Intelligent! That is, "Partner, with defensive values of your own, let the double ride, otherwise think strongly about supporting my suit."

So we've seen the Forcing Pass agreements can have many subtleties, particularly for the Scientists. Regardless of your approach, be sure your partnerships have clear agreements.

Finally, here's what the Bridge World Standard says about the Forcing Pass:

1.	If a two-club opening is overcalled, responder's pass is forcing at every level—responder's double shows double-negative strength
2.	When a forcing bid is doubled and there is no contrary explicit system agreement or logic from the auction, a pass is forcing and a redouble is to play (suggests a contract)
3.	After a negative response to two clubs and an overcall, opener's pass is forcing
4.	After 1any—(X)—XX—(bid); opener's (or responder's) pass is forcing everywhere

Splimit

The Splimit, the combination of two bridge terms SPlinter andLIMIT, is a convention inspire by the Splinter family and defined by *Pier Massimo Fornaro*, author of the bidding system *'Quinta Maggiore Milano'*.

They may be integrated into any five card major bidding system, provided you do not play Bergen Raises.

After a major suit opening, the bids show 4-card support for the major and a singleton/void and are defined:

Openings: 1♥

2♠   Splimit. hearts fit, 7-10HCP spades singleton/void
3♣   Splimit. hearts fit, 7-10HCP clubs singleton/void
3♦   Splimit. hearts fit, 7-10HCP diamonds singleton/void

Openings: 1♠

3♣   Splimit. spades fit, 7-10HCP clubs singleton/void
3♦   Splimit. spades fit, 7-10HCP diamonds singleton/void
3♥   Splimit. spades fit, 7-10HCP hearts singleton/void

Jump-reverses (Mini-splinters)

They are also used over a minor suit opening when responder bids a major at the one level. To show a fit, responder with 15/16+ points and a singleton or void bids at the three level below the major into a higher ranking suit than the minor bid, a jump-reverse:

Here are the only four splimit response bids:

1♣ - 1♠; 3♦ singleton/void in diamonds

1♣ - 1♠; 3♥ singleton/void in hearts

1♣ - 1♥; 3♦ singleton/void in diamonds

1♦ - 1♠; 3♥ singleton/void in hearts

If you were not making a jump-reverse, a jump to the three level in a lower-ranking suit (for example, 1♦ - 1♠; 3♣), this would be considered a strong-jump shift showing 19+ points, and therefore is not a splimt bid.

Bluhmer bids

This not so well known convention has something similar to the Splinter and is due to the American player Lou Bluhm. When the rare opportunity comes it may be really very useful.

The convention may be adopted when the Opener shows a three suits hand, in a clear misfit situation stated by the responder with a NT bid: the convention takes place using an unusual jump done by the responder in the first suit answered

Two common sequences are used by the Bluhmer:

South	North
1♦	1♥
1♠	1NT
2♣	3♥

South	North
1♣	1♥
1♠	1NT
2♦	3♥

In the two sequences, responder's jump cannot show a strong hand or a long hearts suit, as these two possibilities have been both excluded by his previous bid of 1NT that could have been passed by the Opener. The jump in delayed repetition shows, instead, a great fit in the last suit of the Opener and almost total absence of values in his first suit.

South   North

♠KJ32   ♠Q104
♥   ♥8752
♦A9853   ♦K2

♣KQ106   ♣AJ1026

The bidding would go:

| 1♦ | 1♥ |
| 2♣ | 3♥ (bad hearts, great clubs) |

With these cards 3NT would be a very bad contract, easily beatable by one or more tricks. A c lub game or even slam, instead, shows sensible possibilities. A Bluhmer bid by North is really very effective as it shows to the Opener there are no wasted HCP in hearts.

Chapter 16

Wrap-Up

A common remark made by many bridge players is those computers dealt hands are more skewed than hands dealt manually. **THIS IS NOT TRUE.** The following analysis compares computer dealt hands with manual dealt hands using 100,000 deals. This was provided by Chuck Deal in The Villages.

Hand Distributions

Probability of Hand Distributions—The a priori probability of holding a certain hand pattern is based on mathematical odds. Aspiring bridge players make mental references to the hand distribution when bidding or determining the best line of play, particularly the *most probable* distribution. Among the thirty-nine possible hand patterns, five hand patterns comprise 70 percent of the possible hands based upon 100,000 deals and they follow a Normal Distribution. Manual deals DO NOT follow a Normal Distribution. The results follow.

Longest Suit	Distribution Pattern	Computer Dealt %/(Manual Dealt %)
4	4-4-3-2	21.6/(22.1)
	4-3-3-3	10.5/(10.8)
	4-4-4-1	3.0/(3.0)
		35.10/(26.90)
5	5-3-3-2	15.5/(15.7)
	5-4-3-1	12.9/(12.8)
	5-4-2-2	10.6/(10.5)
	5-5-2-1	3.2/(3.1)
	5-4-4-0	1.2/(1.2)
	5-5-3-0	0.90/(0.88)
		44.34/(42.98)

	6-3-2-2	5.6/(5.6)
	6-4-2-1	4.7/(4.6)
	6-3-3-1	3.5/(3.4)
6	6-4-3-0	1.3/(1.3)
	6-5-1-1	0.71/(0.65)
	6-5-2-0	0.65/(0.60)
		16.55/(16.15)
	7-3-2-1	1.9/(1.8)
	7-2-2-2	0.51/(0.48)
	7-4-1-1	0.39/(0.38)
7	7-4-2-0	0.36/(0.33)
	7-3-3-0	0.27/(0.24)
	7-5-1-0	0.1/(0.98)
		3.90/(4.21)
Others		**0.50/(0.98)**

Based upon 100,000 deals, the computer dealt hands follow a Normal Distribution almost exactly where the probability of acceptance for a "Normal" curve is 99.78 percent, using a Chi-square goodness-of-fit test. The corresponding probability of fit for manually dealt hands is <0.1 percent. **WOW!**

How do they break?—Handy Chart for easy reference

Cards Missing	Break	%
2	1-1	52.0
	2-0	48.0
3	2-1	78.0
	3-0	22.0
4	3-1	49.7
	2-2	40.7
	4-0	9.6
5	3-2	67.8
	4-1	28.3
	5-0	3.9
6	4-2	48.5
	3-3	35.5
	5-1	14.5
	6-0	1.5
7	4-3	62.2
	5-2	30.5
	6-1	6.8
	7-0	0.5
8	5-3	47.1
	4-4	32.7
	6-2	17.1
	7-1	2.9
	8-0	0.2

Note: With 5/6 Cards, use ratio 2/3 or 1/4 and 2/4 or 1/5 as approximations!

Probabilities and Odds in Bridge

Probability that either partnership will have enough to bid game, assuming a 26+ point game = **25.29%** (1 in 3.95 deals)

Probability that either partnership will have enough to bid slam, assuming a 33+ point slam = **.70%** (1 in 143.5 deals)

Probability that either partnership will have enough to bid grand slam, assuming a 37+ point grand slam = **.02%** (about 1 in 5,848 deals)

Number of different hands a named player can receive = **635,013,559,600=52! / (39! x 13!)**

Number of different hands a second player can receive = **8,122,425,444 = 39! /26! x 13!)**

Number of different hands the third and fourth players can receive = **10,400,600 = 26! / 13! x 13!)**

Number of possible deals = [52! /13!]**4 = **53,644,737,765,488,792,839,237,440,000**

Number of possible auctions with north as dealer, assuming that east and west pass throughout = 2**36 - 1 = **68,719,476,735**

Number of possible auctions with north as dealer, assuming that east and west do not pass throughout =
128,745,650,347,030,683,120,231,926,111,609,371,363,122,697,55

Odds against being dealt at least one singleton = **2 to 1**
Odds against receiving a hand with 37 HCP (4 aces, 4 kings, 4 queens, and 1 jack) = **158,753,389,899 to 1**
Odds against receiving a perfect hand (13 cards in one suit) = **169,066,442 to 1**
Odds against a Yarborough = **1827 to 1**
Odds against both members of a partnership receiving a Yarborough = **546,000,000 to 1**
Odds against a hand with no card higher than 10 = **274 to 1**
Odds against a hand with no card higher than jack = **52 to 1**
Odds against a hand with no card higher than queen = **11 to 1**
Odds against a hand with no aces = **2 to 1**
Odds against being dealt four aces = **378 to 1**
Odds against being dealt four honors in one suit = **22 to 1**
Odds against being dealt five honors in one suit = **500 to 1**
Odds against having at least one void = **19 to 1**
Odds that two partners will be dealt 26 named cards between them = 495,918,532,918,103 **to 1**
Odds that no players will be dealt a singleton or void = **4 to 1**

Reference: Antonio Vivaldi & Gianni Barracho (2003), "Probabilities and Alternatives in Bridge."

Final Note: Using combination notation, nCr, and probability theory, the total number of bridge hands is shown to be

52C13 X 39C13 X 26C13 X 1 = **52! / (39! x 13!) X 39! / (26! x 13!) X 26! / (13! x 13!) X 1**

=**53,644,737,765,488,792,839,237,440,000** or 53 decnillion bridge hands.

Now, what are the odds of each person receiving a complete suit (13 spades, 13 hearts, 13 diamonds, and 13 clubs, for example)? There are four! Or twenty-four ways for each player to obtain a complete suit; dividing the number of bridge hands by twenty-four yields the odds are 2,235,197,406,895,366,368,301,559,999 (2 decnillion) to 1 against receiving a complete suit. Or, if the entire adult population of the WORLD were to play bridge in every waking moment for ten million years, it would still be ten million to one against one of these perfect deals to turn up!

So, Duplicate Bridge Players, DO NOT EXPECT THIS TO OCCUR THE NEXT TIME YOU PLAY!

Good luck and Have a Great Game!

Chapter 17
Transfer Precision

Overview

Precison is an important bidding convention played by many pairs. To compete against pairs that play Precision, it is essential that you understand the bidding structure of the convention used. In this vesion of Precision one uses transfer bids over 1♣ and the Transfer Stayman Convention.

Basic Opening bids

1♣*	Artificial 16/17+ HCP—MUST ALERT with unbalanced/balanced Hand
1♦*	11-15 HCP may be short (at least 2) MUST ANNOUNCE
1♥/1♠	11-15 HCP 5+ Majors with Reverse Bergen Bidding Structure
1NT	13-15 HCP
2♣*	11-15 HCP 5/6+ Clubs (with 5 must have a 4-card major)—MUST ALERT
2♦*	11-15 HCP **4=3-1-5, 3=4-1-5, 4=4-1-4, or 4=4-0-5** MUST ALERT **Singleton Diamond or Void**
2♥/2♠	5-10 HCP 6+ Cards (Weak 2-bids Vulnerable with Ogust/Feature
2NT*	5-5 in the minors 5-10 HCP (NV) and 11-15 HCP (VUL)
3X	5-10 must have 2/3 of top 3 Honors in the Bid Suit Vulnerable and one if Non-vulnerable

3NT* GAMBLING solid 7+ minor suits (AKQJxxx)
* Indicates forcing bids and alerts

Responses to 1♦* Opening

Responses to 1♦* Opening (11-15 HCP diamonds may be short) strong Jump Shifts

1♥/1♠ 4+ Cards in suit with 6+ HCP (to show weak hand rebid majors since using strong jump shifts)

Rebids by Opener

	1♠	4+ spades ov 1♥
	1NT	11-15 HCP ov 1♥/1♠
	2♣	5+ clubs
	2♦	5+diamonds
	2M	**13-16 Dummy Points**
	3M	**17-18 Dummy Points**

1NT	6-10 HCP, balanced hand
2NT	11 - 12 HCP, balanced hand
3NT	13-15 HCP, balanced hand
2♣	13+ HCP forcing one round
2♦*	13+ 6/7+ diamonds (Criss-Cross)
2♥/2♠	16+ HCP strong jump shift in Major 5+ cards, game force
3♣*	10-12 HCP 6/7+ diamonds (Criss-Cross)
3♦*	less than 10 HCP, Weak, preemptive raise 6+♦
3♥/3♠	Splinter bid in support of diamonds (slam interest 16+)
4♣	Splinter bid in support of diamonds (slam interest 16+)
4♦	Minorwood 1430 Keycard for diamonds
4♥/4♠	Single suited hand to play

Over a major suit interference bid, the bid of 1NT by responder shows 6-10 HCP and diamonds.

Getting to notrump (Criss-Cross)

After an inverted minor raise 1♦* - pass - 2♦* (13+ HCP)

1. Show major suit stoppers 2♥ or 2♠, bid up the line. No extra values
2. Bid **2NT** with a minimum and both majors are stopped.
3. Bid **3♣** to show club stopper, neither hearts of spades stopped
4. Bid **3♦** with a minimum without major stoppers.
5. Bid **3♥** or **3NT**, showing ♥ stopped, over **2♠** with minimum values

After a weak raise 1♦* - pass - 3♣* (less than 10 HCP)

a. Pass with all minimum and almost all intermediate sized hands
b. A new suit is forcing one round and shows a very strong hand
c. **3NT** is to play regardless what partner had for his pre-emptive raise
d. **4 of the minor** is invitational (may be used as RKC Blackwood).

Responses to 1M Opening Reverse Bergen Bids over MAJOR

1NT	7-12, Forcing
1NT	followed by 3M with 10-12 HCP (limit raise with 3)
2M	8-10, 3 card support (constructive)

BROMAD (Reverse) Bids over a double of a major

XX A redouble is not part of BROMAD per se, but is worth mentioning. It shows 10+ points and denies 3+ card support.

2♦ A 3-card "Constructive" raise, showing 7-10 points and exactly 3-card trump support.

2♣ A 3-card Limit raise or better, showing 10-12 points and exactly 3-card trump support.

2♥/♠ A 3-card "Preemptive" raise, showing 0-6 points and exactly 3-card trump support.

2NT A preempt in clubs or diamonds (i.e. a hand that would normally make a 3♣ or 3♦ weak jump shift).

3♦ A 4-card "Constructive" raise, showing 7-10 points and exactly 4-card trump support.

3 ♣ A 4-card Limit Raise, showing 10-12 points and exactly 4-card trump support.

3♥/3♠ A 4-card "Preemptive" raise, showing 0-6 points and exactly 4-card trump support.

Responses to 1M Opening (Open 1♥/1♠ with 11-15 HCP)

2M 8-10 Dummy Points 3 cards support (constructive raise)

<u>Short Suit Game Try (SSGT) over 1♥-2♥ or 1♠-2♠</u>

Any three level suit bid by opener shows shortness in the suit 0-2.

Otherwise relay bids are used by the Opener and responder shows SHORTNESS

	1♥-2♥ 2♠	or	1♠-2♠ 2NT
Club Shortness	3♣		3♣
Diamonds Shortness	3♦		3♦
Heart Shortness 3♥			
Spade Shortness	2NT		
4333 min 8-9	3♥		3♠
4333 max 10-11	3NT		3NT
4333 with 4S amd Max 10-11	3♠		
5 to KQ+	4m		4m
Stiff Other Major	4♥		4♠

After SSGT, responder re-evaluates his hand with A=3 and K=1
With 9 or 10/11 responder bids game or cue bids minor with 4 of other majors
With 7 or 8 make last train bid if possible
With 6 or less sign-off

2NT   13+ with 4 trumps (Jacoby)

3♣	10-12 with 4 trumps
3♦	7-9 with 4 trumps
3M	0-6 weak with 4 trumps
2/3 other M	Ambiguous Splinter with 4-card support, 13+ Dummy Points
3NT	13-15 with three card support
4♣	16+ balanced with 3+ card support in the major
4♦	12-15 points with 5 trumps in the major bid

With Interference at the 2-level

Cue bid is Limit Raise with 3+ trumps

2NT	**Limit raise with 4+ trumps**
3♣/3♦	**Fit Jump Bids 3/4+ trumps with 4+ clubs /Diamonds**
3other M	**Fit Bid with 3/4+ trumps and 4+ cards in other Major**
3M	**Weak raise—0-6 Dummy Points with 4-card support for bid major**
4M/5m	**To-Play**
4m	**Splinter-Jump 4-card support with singleton**
4other M	**To-Play**

With Interference at the 3-level

X	**Trump Double (Western Cue)**
3X	**Invitational to game in a major**

4-level Cue bid Forcing raise to game in Major bid
3M weak with major fit
4X Fit jumps bids below major bid
4M peemptive

Ambiguous Splinter Bids (Simple)

Opener Responder Opener Explanation

1♥	2♠		Game Force with a singleton
		2NT	Opener asks responder to bid suit of singleton (4♥=♠)
	3♠		Game Force with a void
		3NT	Opener asks responder to bid void suit (4♥=♠)
1♠	3♥		Game Force with a singleton/void
		3♠	Relay bid
			Responder bids singleton suit
			With a VOID responder bid 3NT; Opener relays again 4♣
			Responder bids 4♦=♦, 4♥=♥, 4♠=♣

This method is simple and works well when opening a major. To investigate slam one may use 4NT or 4♠ if the agreed upon suit is hearts. The method is simple and always allows one to stop short of game, if necessary. It was suggested to me by Ted Deflippo.

Responses to 1NT Opening (With Double Barrel Stayman)

Responses to 1NT (13-15 HCP)

2♣	**NF Stayman**	**10-12 HCP**
	Opener Rebids	
	2♦ = 15 HCP	
	Responder Rebids	
	2♥ shows spades	
	2♠ shows hearts	
	2NT show both majors	
2♦	**Forcing Stayman**	**13+ HCP**
2♥/2♠	**to Play**	**0-8 HCP**
3♣/3♦	**6+ Card suit 2 of top 3**	**9-11 HCP**
3♥	**5-5 in the majors**	**11-12 HCP**
3♠	**5-5 in the majors**	**13+ HCP**

Responses to 1NT Opening (If you Prefer Transfer Bids)

Responses to 1NT (13-15 HCP)

2♣	**Stayman (may not have a 4-card major)/Smolen**
2♦/2♥	**Transfer hearts/spades**
2♠	**MSS bid minors up the line (3♣/3♦ shows 3+ card suit)**
	2NT denies a 4+ minor suit

After hearing the bid of 2NT responder next bids 3♣ says both minors and 3♦ says long diamond denies clubs while 3NT says 2245 or 2254 interest in slam. Cue bid of major shows a singleon with slam interest.

2NT	**Weak club suit (opener bids 3clubs)**
3♣/3♦/3♥/3♠	<u>**6 card suit with 2 of top 3 honors 9-11**</u>
3♥	**5-5 in majors (11-12 HCP)**
3♠	**5-5 in majos (13+)**
4♦/4♥	**Texas Transfer**

Over a double of 1NT we employ Helvic Notrump Runouts

Redouble shows a single suited hand (partner bids 2♣)
And bidding shows a two-suited hand

> **2♣=clubs and diamonds**
> **2♦=diamond and hearts**
> **2♥=hearts and spades**
> **2♠=spades and clubs**

If you pass the double you have a two-suited hand with two non-touching suits or you want to play 1NT for penalty—<u>partner must re-double or bid 5-card suit</u>. Opener may leave double in or bid the anchor suit.

Responses to 1NT Opening (If you Prefer Minor Suit Stayman)

2♣	**Stayman (may not have a 4-card major)/Smolen**
2♦/2♥	**Transfer hearts/spades**
2♠/2NT	<u>**Minor-Suit Stayman (mss)**</u>

Minor-Suit Stayman is just what its name implies: a device that allows a partnership to look for a **minor**-suit fit after an opening bid of 1NT (and over 2NT/3NT see note 2 below). Presupposing the use of **Jacoby Transfers**, the 2♠ response to 1NT is no longer needed to show **spades** and can be used to ask opener to bid a 4-card **minor** suit. The **OKB 2/1 card** uses a specific variant of **MSS**, which also includes weak hands with a long **diamond** suit, hence the notation "**MSS** or correct to or 3♦ with **diamond** bust". This is a treatment that is part of the Walsh system. Other **MSS** variants may not include the weak hands that Walsh does, and have different response structures, so it may be best to avoid this bid in a new partnership.

2♠ response to 1NT (strong NT) shows one of three types of hands. It is either a weak hand with long (6+) **diamonds**, a weak hand with both **minors** (5-5), or a strong hand at least 5-4 or 4-5 **minors** with **slam** interest.(With both **minors** and only minimum values for game, bid 3NT. 9 tricks in NT is usually easier than 11 in a **minor**. Using **MSS** may pinpoint a weak **major** for the opponents to lead)

The 1NT opener should rebid:

1. 2NT = denies a 4 card or longer **minor**
2. 3♣ or 3♦ = at least 4 cards in the **minor** bid, bid the better one with both.

After using **MSS** and hearing any of the above rebids, responder's available rebids are:

1. 3♣ over 2NT = weak both **minors**, opener may pass or correct to 3♦ (e.g. xx x KJxxx QTxxx)
2. 3♦ over 2NT/3♣ = weak with long **diamonds** (x xx QJxxxxx Qxx
3. Pass over 3♣/3♦ = content with contract, weak hand
4. 3NT = 2245 or 2254, slam invitational, non-forcing (xx Ax AKxxx KJxx)
5. Any **major** suit bid (!) = single/void in that suit, slam interest (3♠! with x Ax AKxxx KJxx)
6. 4NT = **Roman Key Card Blackwood** if **minor** suit has been agreed but natural otherwise

Note : The use of **MSS** over 2NT, or 2♣-2♦-(2NT/3NT) is easily defined in that, if **Jacoby** applies, so does **MSS**, i.e., if a **diamond** or **heart** bid is **Jacoby**, then a **spade** bid is **MSS**. The use of **MSS** over 2/3NT **always** shows slam interest. If a **minor** suit has been agreed, then a later bid of 4NT is **RKC**, otherwise natural.

2NT followed by 3♣ = club signoff, or 4441

Over opener's 1NT, a direct response of 2NT is a puppet(relay) to 3♣ which responder can pass with **clubs** and a bust, or show a game forcing 3-suited hand, either 4441 or 4450 with a 5 card **minor**. With the strong hand rebid the suit containing your singleton/void. With short **clubs**, either rebid 3NT, non-forcing, or bid 4♣ with slam interest to force opener to bid.

Examples: after 1NT-2NT-3♣-?

5. Pass (x xxx Kxx QT9xxxx)
6. 3♥ (AJxx x AKxx Qxxx)
7. 3NT (AJxx AKxx Qxxx x)
8. 4♣ (AJxx AKxx AQxx x)

After the strong shortness showing bids, opener picks a suit or rebids in NT with the short suit well-stopped (and hence wasted values for a suit slam). Over suit agreement, 4NT is RKC. Over 3NT, 4NT by responder is natural and invitational.

When playing a direct 2NT to 1NT as artificial, one must start with 2♣ **Stayman** to invite game in NT.

5. Opener with both **hearts** and **spades** bids 2♥
6. The sequence 1NT-2♣-2♥-2♠ shows exactly 4 **spades** and is invitational to game. Opener may pass, bid 2NT, 3NT, or 4♠
7. The sequence 1NT-2♣-2♥-2NT is invitational to game and denies 4 **spades**
8. Other sequences that start 1NT-2♣-2any-2NT do not promise or deny a 4 card **major**. This should be explained at the time of the 2NT rebid.

Over 13-15 notrump bids

3♣/3♦	6 card suit with 2 of top 3 honors
	And 9-11 invite to 3NT
3♥	5-5 in majors (11-12 HCP)
3♠	5-5 in majors (13+)
4♦/4♥	Texas Transfer

Over a penalty double or 2♣ over 1NT Systems are ON

Transfer Lebensohl over notrump

We open 1NT, and they overcall. Remember, if they bid 2♣, you just ignore it (so if you bid 2NT after their 2♣ overcall, you should treat the auction as if it went 1NT PASS 2NT—however you play it). If they bid 2♦, 2♥, or 2♠ we use TRANSFER Lebensohl. Recall that if we bid a suit on the 2-level, it is natural, NF. Using Transfer Lebensohl, if we bid a suit on the 3-level, starting with 3♣, it is a transfer to the "next" suit. (I'll explain the quote marks in a moment). By transferring, we are showing the suit (5+) transferred to with *invitational or better* values. (With less than an invitation, we either sign-off on the 2-level, or bid 2NT to relay to 3♣ to sign-off—the old fashioned-Lebensohl way). When we show invitational or better, partner can sign-off (just bid the suit transferred to), or he can accept the game try (by doing many things, including 3NT if he wishes). If partner "signs off" and you have the "or better," of course you just bid again (naturally). Some examples:

1NT (2♥) 3♣ = Diamonds, invitational or better (to sign off in ♦, responder would have bid 2NT to relay to 3♣, then bid 3♦)
1NT (2♠) 3♦ = Hearts, invitational or better. (If opener bids 3♥, he rejects your invitation, but you bid again with a GF.)

Remember, to sign off, you either bid on the 2-level, or use 2NT to relay to sign off on the 3-level. Using the transfer promises at least a game invite.

Now, what about the "quote marks?" When transferring to your suit on the 3-level, you have to take their suit into account. For example, if 2♥ showed ♥ and a minor, it wouldn't make much sense for you to transfer (via 3♦) into ♥. Accordingly, this is what we do: Transferring into "their suit" (such as 3♦ into their ♥) shows the next higher suit—i.e., ♠. Are you ready to kill me by now? Sorry, but if you want to be prepared, there is no shortcut. You simply must devote a little time to study and practice this. So, transferring "into their suit," is like transferring "through" their suit. What if you actually bid their suit? (Example, they bid 2♦ to show ♦+ whatever, and you bid 3♦). Cue-bidding their suit means what it means with regular lebensohl, typically "Stayman, no stopper." This assumes "FADS—Fast Always Denies Stopper." If you want to Stayman with a stopper, you go through the 2NT relay, then cue-bid 3♦. OK, no doubt you are ready to just scrap this and wing it, but maybe some examples will help:

1NT (2♠ = ♠+ whatever, or just ♠) :

2NT = Relay to 3♣ (either to play 3♣, or as a prelude to sign-off in 3♦ or 3♥, or to follow with 3♠ to show Stayman and a ♠ stopper, or to follow with 3NT to just show a ♠ stopper-no Stayman)

3♣ = ♦ Invitational+ (Opener rejects by bidding 3♦, but responder bids on naturally with a GF. Opener accepts by bidding above 3♦)

3♦ = ♥ Invitational+ (Opener rejects by bidding 3♥, but responder bids on naturally with a GF. Opener accepts by bidding above 3♥)

3♥ = ♣ Invitational+—This was tricky, but remember: Transfer to "their" suit is "through" their suit to the next highest suit, ♣ in this case.

3♠ = Cue-bid showing "Stayman, no ♠stopper"

3NT = To play, but no ♠stopper (Fast Denies)

Responses to 2M Opening

Responses to 2♥/ 2♠ (Open 5-10 6+ card suit)—Same as 2/1

Over 2NT asks for Feature/Ogust (per agreement)

The weak major 2-level bid is a "normal" weak two and typically shows between 5-10 points and at least a 6-card suit. The optimum hand for a weak-2 has most of its points in the long suit although it is recognized that this is not always possible and sometimes (particularly 3rd hand at favorable vulnerability) you have to go with what you've got.

4♣ is RKCB [used with weak two bids (2♥/2♠)].

The responses are:

4♦   first step 0 keycards in the agreed suit
4♥   second step, 1 keycard without the Queen
4♠   third step, 1 keycard with the Queen
4NT   fourth step, 2 keycards without the Queen
5♣   fifth step, 2 keycards with the Queen

The only step in which the queen is not known is the first-step. The next bid of 4♥ is the Queen ask - 4♠ = no and 4NT = yes. A jump over the four hearts bid (5♣/5♦/5♥/5♠) is the Specific Suit Ask (SSA).

When they Double Weak two-bid Mc Cabe Adjunct

2♥ - X then   Redouble show a stong hand
                 2♠ = to play
                 2NT =Clubs (partner bids clubs)
                 3♣ =shows A/K in suit bid
                 3♦ =shows A/K in suit bid

3♥ =shows an A/K of Hearts

2♠ - X then   Redouble shows a strong hand
                    2NT =Clubs (partner bids clubs)
                    3♣ =shows A/K in suit bid
                    3♦ =shows A/K in suit bid
                    3♥ = to play
                    3♠ =shows an A/K of Spades

Responses to 2♣* Opening

Responses to 2♣ Opening (Open 11-15 HCP, 6+ Clubs or 5/6clubs and 4 card major, must have two of the top three honors - 5+ in third seat.

Partner responses

2♦* 11+ HCP, conventional and forcing for one round

Opener Rebids

2♥   11-15 HCP, 4-card ♥ suit
2♠   11-15 HCP, 4-card ♠ suit
2NT   11-15 HCP, 6-3-2-2 BAL hand, 6-card club suit with a major stopper

         3♦* requests opener to clarify stoppers

Opener Bids

3♥*   ♥ stopper
3♠*   ♠ stopper
3NT   ♥ and ♠ stoppers

3♦   14-15 HCP 6+ clubs and 4+ diamonds
3♣   14-15 HCP non-forcing and unbalanced hand (1-3-3-6)
3♥   14-15 HCP, 5+card ♥ suit
3♠   14-15 HCP, relay back to ♣'s, solid club suit AKJ109x allows responder to bid 3NT
3NT   14-15 HCP, 5+spades and 6+ clubs

2♥/2♠   Natural with 5+cards, 8-10 HCP
2NT*   **Lebensohl (for two-suited hands)**

         Partner Bids 3♣
         Responder next bids

3♦	=	5-5 diamonds and hearts
3♥	=	5-5 hearts and spades
3♠	=	5-5 spades and diamonds

3♣	**10-12 Invitional**
3♦/3♥/3♠	6+ card suit, 12 HCP openers raises or bids 3NT **(Opener May Not Pass)**
4♣	Invitational to game in clubs
4♥/4♠	Natural and to play
4♦	RKCB for clubs

With interference

Negative double through 3♠	
Redouble	10+ HCP
Cuebid	13+ HCP

Responses to 2♦* Opening (Singleton/void in Diamonds)

Responses to 2♦* Opening (11-15 HCP)

Partner Response to 2♦*

3♦	Asks for controls
2♥/2♠	To play in hearts/spades
3♣	To play in clubs
2NT*	ASK

Opener Rebids

3♣*   any minimum 11-13, 3♦ ASK

3♥= four hearts
3♠ = four spades
3NT=4-4-1-4 or 4-4-0-5

3♦=4-4-**1**-4, maximum with singleton diamond
3♥=3-4-1-5, maximum with four hearts
3♠=**4**-3-1-5, maximum with four spades
3NT=4-4-0-5, maximum with five clubs

Responses to 2NT* Opening

Responses to 2NT* 5-5 in the minors 5-10 HCP NV and 11-15 HCP VUL

3♣ or 3♦ is to play
3♥* is an asking bid

Opener Rebids

3♠	5-5 minimum (5-10 NV; 11-15 VUL)
3NT	maximum
4♣	6-5 (clubs, diamonds), minimum
4♦	6-5 (diamonds, clubs), minimum
4♥	6-5 (clubs, diamonds), maximum
4♠	6-5 (diamonds, clubs), maximum
4NT	6-6 in the minors.

3♠	to play
3NT	o play
4♣/4♦	pre-emptive bids and to play
4♥/4♠	to play
5♣/5♦	to play

Over interference (Game force)

4NT === I prefer diamonds
4♣ === I prefer clubs

Gambling 3NT*------------Same as 2/1

Namyats-------------------Same as 2/1

Shows a hand with 8-8 ½ trick in hearts (Open 4♣*), in spades open 4♦*. Refuse transfer by bidding the step in between (4♦ over 4♣ and 4♥ over 4♦), requesting that partner bid an ace if he has one or to sign off in his long suit. 4NT is RKCB.

Responses to 3X Openings

Responses to 3X bids by OPENER (always ensures 2 of the top 3 honors Vulnerable) and 5-10 HCP plus distribution.

4♣	RKCB [over three level (3♦/3♥/3♠) bids]
4♦	Asks for outside controls first step 0-2 controls (A=2; K=1), second step = 3, etc.

The bid of 4NT should not be used since it may get the auction too high.

The responses for 4♣ RKCB are:

4♦	first step 0 keycards in the agreed suit
4♥	second step, 1 keycard without the Queen
4♠	third step, 1 keycard with the Queen

4NT   fourth step, 2 keycards without the Queen

5♣   fifth step, 2 keycards with the Queen

The only step in which the queen is not known is the first-step. The next bid of 4♥ is the Queen ask - 4♠ = no and 4NT = yes. A jump over the four hearts bid (5♣/5♦/5♥/5♠) is the Specific Suit Ask (SSA).

After the premptive bid of 3♣, the bid of 4♣ is natural and advances the preempt; a jump to 4♦ is RKCB for clubs.

Responses to 1♣* Opening

Responses to 1♣* OPENING (16+ HCP)

(1) Negative: 1♦* 0-7 HCP

Opener Rebids after 1♦*:

Non-forcing bids: 1♠/2♣/2♦ (minimum unbalanced hands with 5/6-card suits, 16-21 HCP).

1NT* 16-19 HCP Balanced May have a 5-Card Major

> **Partner Responses**
> Pass   0-6 HCP
> 2♣   6-7 HCP, Stayman
> 2♦/2♥   Jacoby Transfer
> 2NT   7HCP, inviting 3NT
> 3♣3♦   5-5 in the Minors Min/Max (0-5/6-7)
> 3♥/3♠   5-5 in the Majors Min/Max (0-5/6-7)
> 3NT   8-10 HCP to play

2♥   shows 22+ balanced hand or 5+ heart hand

> **Partner must bid 2♠**

> **Opener Responses**

> **3♥ 22+ with hearts**

> **2NT   22-23 with notrump hand**

> **3NT   24-26 with notrump hand**

2♠ shows 5+cards and 22+HCP—equivalent of Standard bidders 2♣

2NT* 20-21 HCP balanced may have 5-card major (no relay bid)

    Partner   **Responses**

    Pass   0-3/4 HCP

    Other bids same as 2/1 (e.g. 3♠ is transfer to 3NT)

    4♣= Gerber
    4♦=transfer to hearts
    4♥=transfer to spades
    4♠=transfer to clubs
    5♣-=transfer to diamonds
    4NT=invite 6NT

    Other bids same as 2/1 (e.g. 3♠ is transfer to 3NT)

3♣/3♦ shows very strong unbalanced minor suit hand 6+ cards (19+ HCP)

3♥/3♠ shows a solid major suit with 9 tricks

    Requires responder to cue bid ace or void

3NT 27+ HCP balanced may have a 5-card major

    Partner Rebids

    0-3 HCP   **pass OR**
                           4♣= Gerber
                           4♦=transfer to hearts
                           4♥=transfer to spades
                           4♠=transfer to clubs
                           5♣ - transfer to diamonds

    4-7 HCP and balanced   **4NT invite 6NT**

4♥/4♠ shows a hand stronger than a Namtats opener

(2) Tranfer Bids (Opener must have 3+ card support to accept transfer)

Transfer Positive Responses to 1 are all 5+ card suits except the transfer to 1NT. We use Transfer Positives to suits and 1NT.

    1.   1♣-1♥ shows 5+ spades.

2. 1♣-1♠ shows balanced 8-13 (Opener bids 1NT)
3. 1♣-1NT shows 5+ clubs.
4. 1♣-2♣ shows 5+ diamonds.
5. 1♣-2♦ shows 5+ hearts.

Positive 1NT Responses

1♠ is a transfer that shows 8-13 HCP, no good 5-card minor, no 5-card major. 1NT accepts the transfer and asks for further information. It uses a Transfer Stayman system that shows 4-card majors and splits the point ranges into 8-10 and 11-13.

Any other bid by opener is natural and at least 5-cards.

Responses to the 1NT acceptance are:

1. 2♣=8-10, **both** 4-card majors.
2. 2♦=8-10, 4 hearts.
3. 2♥=8-10, 4 spades.
4. 2♠=8-10, **no** 4-card major only one minor.
5. 2NT=8-10, **both** minors, at least 4-4.

6. 3♣=11-13, **both** 4-card majors.
7. 3♦=11-13, 4 hearts.
8. 3♥=11-13, 4 spades.
9. 3♠=11-13, **no** 4-card major only one minor.
10. 3NT=11-13, **both** minors, at least 4-4.

Note: Opener may accept the transfer even though he has a 5-card major, thus if you show no major if he bids a major it shows 5-cards in the suit.

After accepting the transfer (spades/clubs/diamonds/hearts)
Responder next tells about his controls
First Step 0-2 controls (A=2, K=1), next step = 3, etc.

TAB bid the Trump suit at any level

1ˢᵗ step	**Five or more trumps with no top honor (A, K, Q)**
2ⁿᵈ step	**Five with one top honor**
3ʳᵈ step	**Five with two top honors**
4ᵗʰ step	**Six or more with one honor**
5ᵗʰ step	**Six or more with two honors**
6ᵗʰ step	**Six or more with three top honors**

CAB bid a none-trump suit ASK

1st step	**No Controls (Jxx or worse)**
2nd step	**Second round Control (K/singleton)**
3rd step	**First round Control (A/void)**

Responding with Balanced Hands and no suit fit.

1/2NT*	**16-19 HCP**
2/3NT*	**20-21 HCP**
3/4NT*	**22-23 HCP**
4/5NT	**24+ HCP**

(3) 2♥/2♠ 4-6 HCP 6+card

(Weak Jump Shift with all values in the suit—with 7+ scattered values bid 1♦)

Opener Rebids

Pass	Game unlikely
4♥/4♠/3NT	20+ HCP
New suit	5+ cards without support for the majors

Partners Rebids

Raise	3+ support (or Qx)
Rebid ♥/♠	minimum no support
Cue-bid under 3NT	singleton or void

3♥/3♠   Minimal hand with support (16-18 HCP)

Partners Rebids

Pass or bid game

2NT	Feature
3NT	Natural
4NT	RKCB

(4) 2NT* 14+HCP, balanced no 5-card major (May not stop short of 4NT)

Opener Rebids

3♦/3♥/3♠	Natural bids
3♣*	Baron asking bid (Not Muppet)

Partner Bids

Bid 4-card suits up the line (3♦/3♥/3♠)
3NT show clubs

3NT   **ASK BID**
Responder bids
4♣ 14-15 points
4♦ 16-17 points

After 4 clubs and 4 diamonds, Opener bids 4-card suits up-the—line or bis 4NT sign-off or 6/7 NT

4♥ 18-19 points

4♠ 20-21 points

After 4 heartrs and 4 spades, Opener may bid 4NT ACE ASKING or bids 6/7 NT

4NT   **Blackwood Ace ask**

(5) 3♣* 1444/4441 Black Singleton Lacking 4 controls (8-13 HCP)

Opener Rebids after 3♣

3♦*   where is the singleton?

         3♥*   club singleton
         3♠*   spade singleton

3NT   to play
4♥/4♠ to play
4NT   Blackwood ace asking

Cue bid by Opener of singleton (4♣*/4♠*) is the CAB
         1st step 0-2 (at most one ace or two kings)
         2nd step 3 (ace and king)
         3rd step 4 (two aces)

(6) 3♦* 4144/4414 Red Singleton Lacking 4 controls (8-13 HCP)

Rebids after 3♦

3♥*   where is singleton?
         3♠* diamond singleton

           3NT* heart singleton

4♥/4♠ to play

4NT   Blackwood ace asking

Cue bid by Opener of singleton (4♦*/4♥*) is the CAB

        1st step 0-2 (at most one ace or two kings)
        2nd step 3 (ace and king)
        3rd step 4 (two aces)

(7) (Submarine Strong Singleton Responses after 1♣ bids)

3♥* specifically 1444 with 4+ controls, usually 14+ HCP
3NT* specifically 4441 with 4+ controls, usually 14+HCP
4♣* specifically 4414 with 4+ controls, usually 14+HCP
4♦* specifically 4144 with 4+ controls, usually 14+HCP

Next level bids BY OPENER are CAB (3♠*, 4♣*, 4♦* and 4♥*, respectively)
The responses to the CAB (3♠*/4♣*/4♦*/4♥*) are:

        1st step - 4 controls (two aces or ace and two kings)
        2nd step - 5 controls (two aces and one king/ ace + three kings)
        3rd step - 6 controls (three aces/ two aces and two kings)

(8) 3♠* a solid 7+ card suit (AKQxxxx), 9 + HCP with or without side controls

Opener Rebids

3NT   to play
4♥/4♠   natural showing at least 5-cards with no slam interest

Opener bids (if he knows the suit)

4♣*   CAB - Asks about outside suit controls
        Reponses to CAB
        4♦*   0-2 outside controls
        4♥*   3
        4♠*   4
        4NT*   5

Opener bids (if suit is unknown)

4♦*   asking for suit

Responses to suit ask

4♥*/4♠*/5♣* hearts, spades, clubs

4NT* diamonds

Opener may also bid 4NT which is Blackwood

SUMMARY—INTERFERENCE BIDS OVER 1♣* OPENING

Direct Seat Interference

Double—Mathe which shows Majors

Pass	0-4 HCP
1♦	5-7 HCP
Redouble	8+
1♥	8-10 HCP no stopper in hearts
1♠	8-10 HCP no stopper in spades
1NT	8-10 HCP stoppers in the majors
2♣	8-13 HCP and 6+ cards
2♦	8-13 HCP and 6+ diamonds
2♥	11+ spade stopper (no heart stopper)
2♠	11+ heart stopper (no spade stopper)
2NT	11+ both majors stopped

At 1 level—(natural)

Pass	0-4 HCP
Double	5-7 HCP
Suit	8+ HCP, 5+ card suit, Game Force
Jump in suit	SYSTEMS ON 3♣/3♦/3♥/3♠
1NT	8-13 HCP, with stopper
2NT	10+ HCP, with 1/2 stopper
Cuebid	10+ Game force no stopper

1NT—(natural)

Pass	0-4 HCP
Double	5-7 HCP
Suit	8+ HCP, 5+ card suit

1NT—Mathe which shows Minors

Pass	0-4 HCP
Double	5-7 HCP
2♣	5+ hearts, GF
2♦	5+ spades GF
2♥	5+ HCP, natural and non-forcing

| 2♠ | 5+ HCP, natural and non-forcing |
| 3NT | 10+ HCP, both minors stopped |

At 2 level—(natural)

Pass	0-4 HCP
Double	5-7 HCP
Suit bid	8+ HCP, natural
Cue bid	9+ Flat with no stopper
2NT	9-13 HCP with stopper
3NT	14+ with stoppers

At 3 level—(natural)

Pass	0-7 HCP
Double	8+ HCP
Suit bid	8+ HCP, and 5+ card suit

At 4 level—(natural)

| Pass | 0-7 HCP |
| Double | 8+ HCP, takeout or penalty |

Balancing Seat Interference

After 1♣* - (Pass) - 1♦ - (1♥/♠)

Pass	balance minimum no 5-card suit
Double	support for the other three suits
Suit Bid	Natural, non-forcing
1NT	shows stopper with (16-21 HCP)
2NT	shows stopper with (22+ HCP)
Cuebid	20 + HCP no stopper

After 1♣* - (Pass) - 1♦ - (1NT for Minors)

Pass	balanced minimum no 5-card suit
Double	support for the both majors
2♣/2♦	unusual extra values shows ♥/♠
2♥/2♠	Natural non-forcing
2NT	shows stopper with (22+ HCP)

After 1♣* - (Pass) - 1♦ - (Double = Majors)

Pass	balanced minimum no 5-card suit
Double	support for the both minors
2♣/2♦	natural 5+ card suit.
2♥/2♠	unusual extra values shows ♣/♦

2NT   shows stopper with (22+ HCP)

INTERFERENCE OVER 1NT by OPPONENTS

Direct Seat = Modified Cappelletti
Bal Seat = Modified DONT
Over Weak NT = Landy where 2♣ is for the majors and all other bids are natural and Double is for Penalty with 13+

OTHER CONVENTIONAL CALLS

Over a Major Bid Play Leaping Michaels, Unusual vs. Michaels
Unusual over Unusual, SSGT
Overcalls Michaels and 2nt=two—lowest unbid suits
3X level bids over the opponents bid are pre-emptive

4ᵗʰ Suit Forcing at the two levels is forcing one round - 3 level shows

Western Que

1♣ X is a power double 16+ and 1♦/1♥/1♠ X is take-out
1NT 15-18 Systems Off
LEADS - 4ᵗʰ Best leads No Trumps and 3/5 against Suits
A/Q ASKS FOR Attitude and King=count
Upside-down COUNT AND ATTITUDE (Suit and Notrump) Trump Suit Preference

Chapter 18

Meckwell Precison Bids

In this chapter we review the Precision bids used by Eric Rodwell and Jeff Meckstroth as summarized by **Luke Gillespie and Jim Streisand,** with their kind permission, often called the Meckwell Lite System.

Meckwell Lite is a simplifed version of the Precision system used by Jeff Meckstroth and Eric Rodwell (aka "Meckwell"). All balanced hands with 17+ HCP (except for hands that open 2NT) and all unbalanced hands with 16+ HCP open 1♣. Other opening bids are limited to a maximum of 15 HCP.

Their basic style is very aggressive. If not vulnerable, they almost always open 11-HCP hands and may respond with very weak hands (even yarboroughs!). They open many light distributional hands with only 9 or 10 HCP. They upgrade aggressively, BUT ALWAYS WITH A REASON. "I felt like it" is NOT a reason.

Keep in mind that these notes are guidelines, not a rigid set of rules. We may deviate when logic or inspiration so dictates, but we try to keep partner happy.

Notation (for this Chapter)

NT = No Trump
M = Major, OM = other Major m = minor, om = other minor
R = red suit, x = any suit
Nat = natural, Artif = artificial
Bal = balanced, Unbal = unbalanced
Spl = splinter
F = forcing, GF = game force, F1 = forcing one round
INV = invitational
P/C = Pass or Correct
COG = Choice of Games
RKC = Roman Keycard (0314)
NV = non-vulnerable, V or vul = vulnerable, FAV = NV vs. V, UNFAV = V vs. NV
HCP = High-Card Points (4321)
DNE = DOES NOT EXIST
Mulberry (Bush) = RKC variant used on 3-suited relay auctions
Opponents' bids shown in parenthesis
Distributional notation:
  4=4=3=2 means 4♠, 4♥, 3♦, 2♣ exactly
  4=4= (3-2) means 4♠, 4♥, 3 cards in either minor and two cards in the other

4-4-3-2 (or 4432) means 4-4 in any two suits and 3 in any third suit.

Table of Opening Bids

1♣   16+ unbalanced, 17+ balanced; upgrades allowed
1♦   10-15, 2+ diamonds; often a balanced 11-13
1M   10-15, 5+ cards in the major
1NT 14-16 (1ˢᵗ all, 2ⁿᵈ all, 3ʳᵈ NV), 15-17 (3ʳᵈ vul, 4ᵗʰ all)
2♣   10-15, 6+ clubs
2♦   10-15, three suited with short diamonds
2M   4-9, usually 6 cards, suit quality varies, especially NV
2NT 19-20 usually, but 20-21 when opening 1NT is 15-17
3x   Natural, wide range based on position/vulnerability
3NT Gambling, solid minor suit with no side ace or king; looser in 3ʳᵈ/4ᵗʰ
4x   Natural
4NT Blackwood (0123 responses)

Balanced Hand Ladder

11 to 13	Open 1♦ (or 1M with 5)
14 to 16	Open 1NT (5M, 6m, 5422 OK)
17 to 18	Open 1♣ and rebid 1NT
19 to 20	Open 2NT
21 to 23	Open 1♣ and rebid 2NT over 1♦, or rebid 1NT over 1M
24 to 26	Open 1♣ and rebid 2♥ (Kokish, GF) over 1♦, or rebid 2NT over 1♥. Over 1♠ must rebid 1NT and catch up later

In 4ᵗʰ seat, or vulnerable in 3ʳᵈ seat, 1NT is 15-17 with corresponding adjustments to all of the stronger sequences.

1♣ Opening Bid

All 16+ unbalanced.
All 17+ balanced except those that fall into the range for a 2NT opening.
Upgrade with extra playing strength or prime values, e.g., AKQxxx-AQx-xxx-x

Responses:

1♣	1♦	0-7 (almost) any—(see 3 level responses)
	1♥	8-11, any shape except primary spades
	1♠	8+ HCP, 5+ ♠
	1NT	12+ HCP, 5+ ♥
	2m	12+ HCP, 5+ m
	2♥	12-13 balanced (then 2♠ nat; also 2NT nat w/4-card suits up the line)

2♠	12+, 4441 (then 2NT asks short)	
2NT	14+ balanced (then 3♣ = Baron or nat, other = nat)	
3 any	natural, 7+ suit, <8 HCP—KJ10xxxx is typical	
3NT	DNE	
4 any	natural, 8-card suit (?)	

1♦ Response

1♣-1♦	1M	Nat, F1, may be 4 cards if unbalanced
	1NT	17-18 (18-19 when opening NT = 15-17)
	2m	Nat, 5+, NF, DENIES 4M
	2♥	Kokish—bal GF (24+), or nat very strong—**GF**
	2♠	Nat very strong, **GF**
	2NT	21-23 (22-24 when opening NT = 15-17)
	3♣	Nat GF, may have major
	3♦	Nat GF, DENIES MAJOR
	3M	GF, 4M and 5+ ♦
	3NT	To play—probably unbalanced
	4m	Demands cue ace
	4M	To play

1M Rebid

1♣-1♦-1M	1♠/1♥	F1, 4+ spades, 0-7, <4 ♥ (with 3♥, 4+♠ and 5-7, bid 1♠)
	1NT	0-4(5), <4M - over 1♥ denies 4♠
	2♣	Artif, 5+-7, <3M - over 1♥ denies 4♠
	2♦	Artif, 5+-7, exactly 3M, over 1♥ denies 4♠
		With 5 HCP can judge between 1NT and 2m.
	2M	0-4(5), 4+M
	2♥/1♠	(4)5-7, 6 hearts (weaker than 1♣-1♦-1♠-3♥)
	2♠/1♥	(4)5-7, 6 spades (wider range than 2♥/1♠)
	2NT	Artif, 4-7, exactly 4M w/some short (or super 5+M no short)
	3m	5+-7, nat, good 6+-card suit (also 1♣-1♦-1♠-3♥)
	3M	5+-7, 4M, no short
	3M+1	5+-7, 5M, some void (then relay asks, LMH)
	3M+2	thru 3M+4 5+-7, 5M, singleton (3NT=♠ spl/1♥)
	4M	5+-7, 5M, no short (or very weak w/short)

1♣-1♦-1♥-1♠ or		
1♣-1♦-1M-1NT	1NT	Nat, NF—may be unbalanced
	2m	Nat, NF, ambig lengths, may be 5-4 either way
	2♥/1♠	Nat, NF—at least 5♠, 4♥
	2M	Nat, NF, 6+M
	2♠/1♥	Nat, F1

2NT	Artif, some 6+m, exactly 4M
	3♣/3♦/4♣/4♦ P/C, 3♥/1♠ natural 0-4
3m	Nat, at least 5-5, strong but NF
3♥/1♠	Nat, at least 5-5, strong but NF
	AKQxx of both suits would qualify.
3M	Strong but NF
4m	6-6—Also 1♣-1♦-1S-1NT-4♥

Natural continuations over all of the above except as noted.

1♣-1♦-1M-2♣	5+-7, <3M, denies 4♠ over 1♥
	2♦ "Semi-artif", F1
	2♥/1♠ Exactly 5
	2♠/1♥ Artif, 5-5 minors
	2M Exactly 2
	2NT "Nat", <2M, default if no other call applies
	3m 6 bad (5 good?)—With 6 good bid 3m immed/1M
	Higher Undefined
	If opener does not place contract he implies real diamonds.
	If opener next bids 3♣ he implies 5+♣, 4(5)M, minimum.
	2♥/1♠ Nat F1
	2M Nat NF
	2NT Artif GF, some 6+m, exactly 4M
	3♣ asks m (3♦=♦, higher=♣), 3♥/1♠ natural
	3m Nat, at least 5-5, GF (also 1♣-1♦-1♠-2♣-3♥)
	3M GF
	3NT To play

1♣-1♦-1M-2♦	5+-7, 3M, denies 4♠ over 1♥
	2M To play, often with only 4M—responder bids at his peril.
	This is the ONLY signoff.
	2♥/1♠ Nat, F1, looking for second fit
	2NT Artif GF, asking—usually slammish in M
	3 new Natural (except 3♠/1♥)
	3M Punt, does not qualify for a different call
	3NT 4333
	4 new Short, also 3♠/1♥
	4M Good trumps (2 of top 3 or AJx or KJx)
	3m Nat 5+, implies only 4M, GF

NOTE: 2NT/3m is DIFFERENT over 2♦ than over 1♠/1NT/2♣.

	3M Nat invite (only way to invite in M)

1♣-1♦-1M-2NT	4-7, exactly 4M and some short (or supermax 5+M no short)
	3♣ asks
	3♦ Minimum

        3♥   Asks

                3♠ Some void, then 3NT asks (LMH)

                3NT/4♣/4♦ Singleton, LMH

        3♥   Max, some void, then 3♠ asks (LMH)

        3♠/3NT/4♣ Max, singleton, LMH

        4M   Supermax, 5+M, no short

1♣-1♦-2♥-2♠ GF, Kokish, 2♠=normal (can bid 3m with weak 6+ m)

        2NT   24+ balanced, GF—use 2NT structure

        3♣   Heart one-suiter

        3♦   Primary hearts, secondary diamonds

        3♥   Primary hearts, secondary clubs

        3♠   Primary hearts, secondary spades

        3NT   Primary hearts, natural, COG

1♣-1♦-2♠   3♣ 2ⁿᵈ neg—Then 3M is forcing (2♠=GF)

1♣-1♦-2NT   21-23 balanced, use 2NT structure

1♣-1♦-3m   3♦ Neutral—Opener bids 4-card M if he has one (3m=GF)

                   3M Nat, 5+M

1♣-1♦-3M   GF, 4M and (5)6+♦

1♣-1♦-3NT   100% to play

1♥ Response

The 1♥ response shows 8-11 with any shape except primary spades.

1♣-1♥   1♠   Nat, 5+♠

                1NT Bal, usually 17-18 but possibly 21-22

                        With 23+ bid 2NT.

                2m, 2♥ Nat, 5+ cards

                2♠   Artif, some 4441 (then 2NT asks, bid short at 3-level)

                2NT 23+, then use 2NT structure

                3x   Nat, sets trumps, asks for cue ace

                3NT To play—rare, e.g., Kx-K-QJx-AKQJxxx

1♠ Rebid

1♣-1♥-1♠   2♠   Usually 3 trumps, then 2NT asks

                2NT Asks, slam interest

                      3♣   5+ clubs

                      3♦   5+ diamonds

                      3♥   5+ hearts

                      3♠   4=3=3=3

                      3NT 3M, no feature

4x	**Splinter**	
4M	3M, 2 of top 3, no feature	
3X	Nat, strong suit	

2NT   Strongest raise, 4+♠

     3♣   Asks

         3♦   Some shortness (3♥ asks, LMH)

         3♥   Some 2nd 5+ suit (3♠ asks, LMH)

         3♠   4+♠, no short, better than 4♠

         3NT   4+♠, some void, relay asks (LMH)

         4m,4♥   4+♠, singleton, weaker than 2NT

         4♠   4+♠, no short, weakest raise

3x   **Natural, strong 6+ card suit (KQxxxx)**

1NT Rebid

1♣-1♥-1NT	2♣	Stayman—promises at least one major
	2♦	Transfer
	2♥	**Some 4441 (1♥ response denies primary spades)**
	2♠	Clubs (don't need size ask)—then 3♣ = likes clubs
	2NT	**Puppet Stayman (does not include 4441s with 4♥)**
	3♣	Diamonds
	3♦	5-5 minors
	3M	3=1=(5-4)
	3NT	8-11—Opener keeps bidding with big range
	4 Level	As in opening 1NT structure

1♣-1♥-1NT-2♣-2♦

     2M   Smolen

     2NT   Clubs

         3♣   Asks

              3♦   2=4=2=5 or 4=2=2=5

                    3♥   Asks, then 3♠=2425, 3NT=4225

              3♥, 3♠, 3NT   LMH short

         3♣   Diamonds with some shortness

              3♦   Asks

              3♥, 3♠, 3NT   LMH short

On both of these auctions 4♣ instead of 3NT shows same type with extras.

             3♦   2=4=5=2 or 4=2=5=2

                    3♥   Asks, then 3♠=2452, 3NT=4252

         3M   Shortness, implies 4441 (5440 w/weak 5-card m possible)

         3NT   8-11—Opener keeps bidding with big range

1♣-1♥-1NT-2♣-2M

     2♠/2♥   4♠, 6m—2NT asks, then 3m=nat

     2NT   Clubs, implies 4OM

         3♣   Asks, then 3♦, 3♥, 3♠=Bal,LH

3♣	Diamonds, implies 4OM		
	3♦	Asks, then 3♥, 3♠, 3NT=Bal,LH	
3♦	Min raise of M, some short (stiff if M=♠), relay LMH		
3♥/2♠	Spade raise, some void, relay asks (LMH)		
3♠/2♥	Max heart raise, short spades		
3M	Max raise of M, balanced		
3NT	8-11—Opener keeps bidding with big range (4m = 5)		
4m	Max raise of M, short m (also 4♥/2♠ = max ♥ spl)		
4M	Minimum, usually no shortness		

1♣-1♥-1NT-2♦-2♥

2♠	Clubs	
	2NT	Asks
		3♣ 5 clubs
		3♦, 3♠ FRAGMENT, then Mulberry (esp. over 3♠)
		3♥ 0=5=4=4, then Mulberry
		3NT 2524: 4♣ or 4♥ nat, **4♦ 6RKC**, 4♠ RKC ♥
2NT	Natural, maximum (bid 3NT w/min)	
3♣	Diamonds, then 3♦ asks (Bal, LH)	
3♦	Retran, 6+, minimum, unbal, relay asks (LMH)	
3♥	6+♥, slam try, no short (usually 6322, with 2722 bid 4♥)	
3♠, 4m	6+♥, maximum, shortness	
3NT	Natural, COG, minimum (bid 2NT w/max)	
4♥	2722	

1♣-1♥-1NT-2♥

2♠	**4 spades**	
	2NT 1=4=4=4	
	3x shortness	
2NT	**Asks for shape**	
	3x shortness	

1♣-1♥-2♣

2♦	Waiting, opener shows major if he has one
2♥	Nat, 5+ hearts
2♠	Artif, 5+ diamonds

1♣-1♥-2♦

2♥	Nat, 5+ hearts
2♠	Waiting

1♣-1♥-2m-3M 4M, fit for m, then first new suit sets M as trumps

1♣-1♥-2♥

3♥	3+♥, better than 4♥
3♠	4+♥, some void, relay asks (LMH)
3NT	4+♥, singleton ♠
4m	4+♥, singleton m
4♥	3+♥, weakest raise

1♣-1♥-2♠-2NT	3m	Can set any suit trumps below game (4M = weaker)
	3M	3♠ Sets spades
		3NT To play
THIS IS		4♣ Relay to 4♦, then NF nat slam try
"MULBERRY"		4♦ Relay to 4♥ for signoff in game
(BUSH).		**IF OPENER IS BIG HE BIDS > 4♥ (USUALLY 4♠)**
	4♥, 4♠, 4NT	RKC in LMH of opener's suits
	Higher	RKC RESPONSES for the SHORT suit

1♠ Response

Some versions of Meckwell Lite treat all positive responses other than 1♥ to show 12+ HCP. We use the "traditional" Precision treatment in that the 1♠ response doesn't promise more than GF values (ie, 8+ HCP). Most continuations after opener's rebid allow responder to immediately differentiate minimums (8-11) from maximums (12+).

1♣-1♠	1NT	Control asking bid
	2x	Nat, 5+ cards, support asking bid
	2♠	Trump asking bid
	2NT	???
	3x	Nat, sets trumps, asks for cue ace
	3♠	??? Balanced 17-18, 4 trumps
	3NT	To play—rare, e.g.,x-Kx-QJx-AKQJxxx

1NT Response (Hearts)

| 1♣-1NT-2♣ | Clubs or balanced—natural continuations |

Higher Responses

1♣-2m	5+m, 12+HCP, natural continuations
1♣-2♠-2NT	2♠=Some 4441, 12+HCP, use same structure as 1♣-1♥-2♠ (above)
1♣-2♠-3 suit	5-steps: 1=low stiff(2-10), 2=hi stiff(J-A), 3,4,5=4 support (LMH stiff)

Asking Bids

Tradition Precision systems feature extensive use of asking bids. We use some of these asking bids in limited circumstances, usually when responder bids 1M naturally. This can occur when an unpassed hand responds 1♠, when a passed hand responds 1M or when the opponents either double 1♣ or overcall 1♦.

Note that asking bids are not used if fourth hand intervenes over 1M; we then revert to natural bidding

Beta (Control Ask)

Beta asks responder to show his controls, counting Ace as two and King as one. The control responses stop at 2NT (6+) and three level responses show extra suit quality.

After 1♣-1M-1NT:

2♣	0-2 controls; 2♦ asks for clarification (see below)
2♦	3 controls
2♥	4 controls
2♠	5 controls
2NT	6+ controls
3x	5+ cards with 2/3 top honors in both suits
3M	6+ cards with 2/3 top honors plus the Jack

After 1♣-1♠-1NT-2♣-2♦:

2♥	0 or 1 control
2♠	Two controls
2♠	An Ace (all bids show two Kings)
2NT	5332, Two Kings
3x	4+cards, 2 Kings
3M	6+ cards, 2 Kings
3NT	5332, 2 Kings, 2 Queens

If responder is a passed hand, his maximum number of controls is four. Also, it's very unlikely that a passed hand would have two ♥♥xxx suits (one a major) and impossible for a passed hand to have ♥♥Jxxx in a major, so responses above 2♥ have different meanings.

After P-1♣-1M-1NT:

2♣/2♦/2♥	as above
2♠	5-5 with 2/3 top honors in the M; 2NT asks for side suit
2NT	???
3x	5-5 with 2/3 top honors in the second suit

Alpha (Support Ask)

Alpha asks for responder's general strength (in controls) and degree of support for opener's primary suit. Responder answers in steps.

After 1♣-1M-2x:

Step 1	0-3 controls, no support (less than ♥xx or xxxx)
Step 2	4+ controls, no support
Step 3	0-3 controls, support (♥xx or xxxx)
Step 4	4+ controls, support

Step 5	4 control, good suppor (♥xxx or better)
Step 6	5 controls, good support
Step 7	6 control, good support (etc.)

If responder bids the first or second step, opener's new suit is natural. If the responder bids the third step or higher then opener's suit is agreed and a new suit asks for specific controls.

Gamma (Suit Quality Ask)

Gamma agrees responder's suit and asks for suit length and quality. Responder answers in steps:

After 1♣-1M-2M:

Step 1	no top honor
Step 2	5 cards with one top honor
Step 3	5 cards with two top honors
Step 4	6 cards with one top honor
Step 5	6 cards with two top honors
Step 6	all three top honors

After the Gamma response, a new suit asks for specific controls

Epsilon (Specific Control Ask)

After a trump suit has been agreed following Alpha or Gamma, a new suit asks for first or second round control in that suit. Responder answers in steps:

Step 1	no control
Step 2	second round control (King or singleton)
Step 3	first round control (Ace or void)
Step 4	Ace and King

A repeat ask in the same suit asks for third round control:

Step 1	no control
Step 2	third round control (Queen or doubleton)

INTERFERENCE AFTER 1♣ OPENING

1♣-(DBL)	P	0-4(5)
	1♦	5+-7
	RDBL	GF, no good bid, usually bal or 4441, **then first DBL = TO**
	1M, 2m	Nat 5+ cards, GF

	1NT	Nat, 8-11 or 14+
	2NT	Nat, 12-13
	3 any	Nat, NF, 7-card suit

1♣-(bid)	P	0-4(5)
	DBL	(5)6-7 any, F through 2♠
	New suit	Natural, 5+ cards, GF
	Cheapest NT	Natural, 8-11 or 14+
	Jump in NT	Natural, 12-13
	Cue	8+, bal, no stop (2 level) - 3-suited (3 level)
	Jump Cue	4441, short in opponent's suit
1♣-(1 any)	3 new	Nat, NF, 7-card suit

Over 2♠ or higher Double includes 8+ with no convenient bid. **(Then 2NT=F)**
Over 3 any or higher any positive action is GF.

Over Fourth-hand Interference:

When responder has not shown a suit, opener's double is TAKEOUT.
The first double on either side is TAKEOUT. Subsequent doubles are business.
If responder has bid 2♥ or 2NT, opener's double is PENALTY.
Opener's cuebid is MICHAELS. Opener's jump cuebid = NATURAL.

Pass-Double Inversion:

1. Applies only after 1♣ opening.
2. Applies only in GF auctions.
3. Applies only at high levels (3♠ and up)

THEN: Pass requests Double, either (1) for penalty, or (2) to show a flexible hand (more than one place to play), or (3) to show extras with a fit.

> Double = would have passed partner's penalty double, but encourages a bid
> Bid = (1) single-suited if no fit found yet, or (2) weakest action with fit

EXAMPLES: 1♣-1♥-(3♠)-Pass and Pull = multi-suited, Direct Bid = 1-suited, Double = "you decide whether to defend"1♣-(1♥)-1♠-(4♥)-Pass and Pull to 4NT implies clubs + longer diamonds, pull to 5♣ implies diamonds + longer clubs, pull to 5♦ implies diamonds with spade tolerance, pull to 4♠ = slam try, immediate bids show one-suiters, immediate 4NT = RKC spades, Double = "you decide"

PASSED HAND RESPONSES TO 1♣

We revert to natural responses above 1♦.

1♦	0-7
1♥	GF, 5+♥
1♠	GF, 5+♠
1NT	GF, 8-10(11) balanced, may include a weak 5-card minor
2m	GF, 5+m
2♥	DNE??
2♠	GF, some 4441

1♦ Opening Bid

2+ diamonds, (10)11-15 HCP

If balanced 11-13 (or 14 when 1NT = 15-17)

Balanced includes hands with 5 clubs: 4=2=2=5, 2=4=2=5, 2=2=4=5 and (332)=5.

Unbalanced possibilities include:

> Primary diamonds
>
> 5 clubs: 4=1=3=5 or 1=4=3=5 or 3=1=4=5 or 1=3=4=5
>
> 4441 pattern including diamonds
>
> 5440 with 5m and void M

11-13 balanced is the most frequent and worst for offense. Thus, many auctions cater to not getting overboard with this type. When opener is unbalanced he must often take aggressive action to disclose his hand type.

Responses:

1♥	Occasionally 3 (Bart will usually have 4)
1♠	Assume 4+
1NT	Wide range, up to bad 11
2♣	Nat, F1, 5+—**DENIES MAJOR UNLESS GF AND 6+ CARDS**
2♦	Nat, F1, 5+—**DENIES MAJOR UNLESS GF AND 6+ CARDS**
2♥	5+♠, 4+♥, less than invitational values opposite 11-13 bal
2♠	5+♠, 4+♥, invitational opposite 11-13 bal
2NT	11+ to 13, bal, invitational
3♣	Preemptive/Mixed, BOTH MINORS, usually 5+ in both
3♦	Nat, preemptive/mixed, usually 6 diamonds
3M	Nat, preemptive
3NT	Nat, 13-15
4♣	BOTH MINORS, usually 11+ cards
4♦	Lots of diamonds
4M	Nat, to play
4NT	Blackwood (0123, since no "suit" shown)

1♥ Response

1♦-1♥ 1♠   Must show spades if held, even with balanced hand—1NT denies 4♠

1NT 11-13(14) bal, no singleton (Normal rebid w/3=1=(54) is 2♣)
2♣ Both minors, at least 5-4, ambig lengths, can be 5-4 either way, **NOT 6-4**
2♦ Nat, 6+♦, minimum, may have 4 clubs
2♥ Shows 4
2♠ Either 5♠ and 6♦ with some extras, OR minisplinter for hearts
2NT 6+♦ and 3♥, not minimum (with min bid 2♦)
3♣ 55 minors, maximum but NF
3♦ 6+♦, maximum, denies 3♥
3♥ Strongest invite (stronger than 2♠), some short (then 3♠ asks, LH)
3♠ 4♥, some void—3NT asks (LH)
3NT Offer to play with good long diamonds, usually 7
4♣/4♦ Artif, 4♥, splinter (LH), exactly a singleton (with void bid 3S) - 6♦
4♥ 5♥, 6♦

1♦-1♥-1♠-2♣ GF
    2♦ 5+♦, denies 3♥—Natural continuations
    2♥ All hands with 3♥, then: 2S=relay without 4♠, 2NT=relay w/4♠
        2♠ Relay, denies 4♠
            2NT Balanced
                3♣ Relay
                    3♦ 4♣, exactly 4=3=2=4
                    3♥ 4♦, exactly 4=3=4=2
                    3♠ 4=3=3=3 minimum
                    3NT 4=3=3=3 maximum
            3♣ 4=3=5=1 These two are the only possible
            3♦ 4=3=6=0 unbalanced shapes
        2NT Relay, shows 4♠, agrees Spades (see exception below)
            3♣ Balanced
                3♦ Relay
                    3♥ 4=3=2=4
                    3♠ 4=3=4=2
                    3NT 4=3=3=3, no min-max step here
                3♥ SETS HEARTS—changing horses
             3♦ 4=3=5=1
             3♥ 4=3=6=0
        2♠ Either 5♠ and 6♦, or 5♣ and a max
        2NT Asks
            3♣ 5♣, max
            Higher 5♠, 6♦—Specific meanings undefined
        2NT No 5m, no 3♥, thus 4234, 4243, or 4144
            3♣ Asks
                3♦ 4♣ balanced, exactly 4=2=3=4
                3♥ 4♦ balanced, exactly 4=2=4=3
                3♠ 4=1=4=4 minimum

3NT   4=1=4=4 maximum

3♣   5♣, minimum, either 4225 or 4135

1♦-1♥-1♠-2♦   F1, game invite with 5 hearts or 4 spades

    2♥   minimum, 2 or 3 hearts (then 2♠=nat inv)
    2♠   reject, 0 or 1 heart
    2NT   accept, 0 or 1 heart

Over any of the above 3m by responder shows 5♥, 4+m, invite

    3m   Does not exist?
    3♥   accept w/3♥
    3♠   5♠, 6♦?
    3NT   accept w/3♥ AND ♣ stop?

NOTE: With 4♥, 5+m and invite, jump directly to 3m over 1♠.

1♦-1♥-1♠-2NT   Nat invite
1♦-1♥-1♠-3m   Canape invite, 4♥, 5+m
1♦-1♥-1♠-3♥   GF—Slam try
1♦-1♥-1♠-3♠   GF—Slam try

1♦-1♥-2♣-2♠   Artif, GF

    2NT   3=1=(54), then 3m = 4 supp, then step 1 = 4m, other = 5m
    3♣   5-5m
    3♦   2=2=(54), then 3H asks HJx or more (**3NT=no**), and 3♠ asks ♠Qx or more (**3NT=yes**)
    3♥   1=3=4=5, then Mulberry
    3♠   1=3=5=4, then Mulberry
    3NT   0=3=5=5 minimum, then Mulberry
    4♣   0=3=5=5 maximum, then mod. Mulberry (can't make nat slam try)

1♦-1♥-2♠   Either 5♠-6♦ OR a heart mini-splinter (2.5 Heart raise)

    2NT   Asks and shows some values
        3♣ Low splinter (clubs)
        3♦ 5♠ and 6+♦
        3♥ High splinter (spades)
    3♣   Undefined as yet
    3♦   Bad hand, only bailout—opener should pass or correct to 3♥
    3♥   GF, natural, 6+♥

1♠ Response

1♦-1♠ 1NT   As over 1♥ (complete structure a couple of pages down)
    2♣   "Natural", can be 1=4=4=4 or 1=4=(53)—with 6♦-4♣ bid 2♦
    2♦   Natural, 6+♦ - THEN 2♥ = GF (ambiguous about hearts)

2♥		Artif, 4♠, not the pits, some short OR 5♥, 6♦ minimum
2♠		Shows 4 (unless 3=4=5=1)—shapely min or balanced
2NT/3m		As over 1♥
3♥		Natural, 5♥ and 6♦, maximum
3♠		Strongest invite, some short (then 3NT asks, LH)
3NT		As over 1♥ (to play with long diamonds)
4♣		Artif, 4♠, some void, then 4♦ asks (LH)
4♦/4♥		Artif, splinter (LH)—exactly a singleton (with void bid 4♣)
4♠		5♠, 6♦

1♦-1♠-2♣-2♦-2♥   1=4=3=5—Avoid 6-card ♦ fit, hope for some 8-card fit

1♦-1♠-2♣-2♥ Artif, GF

2♠		Artif: (a)1=4=4=4, (b) 1=4=(5-3), (c) Spade support			
	2NT	Asks			
		3♣	NOT spade support		
			3♦	Asks	
				3♥	1=4=4=4, Mulberry?
				3S	1=4=3=5, Mulberry?
				3NT	1=4=5=3, Mulberry?
			3♥	Sets hearts	
		3♦	3=1=4=5, then Mulberry		
		3♥	3=1=5=4, then Mulberry		
		3♠	3=0=5=5 min, then Mulberry		
		3NT	3=0=5=5 max, then Mulberry		
2NT		1=3=(54), then 3m = 4 support, then step 1 = 4m, other = 5m			
3♣		5-5m			
3♦		2=2=(54), then 3♥ asks ♥Qx or more **(3NT=yes)**, and 3♠ asks ♠Jx or more **(3NT=no)**			
3♥		0=4=4=5, Mulberry applies			
3♠		0=4=5=4 minimum, Mulberry applies			
3NT		0=4=5=4 maximum, Mulberry applies			

1♦-1♠-2♥   Artif ♠ raise w/short OR 5♥,6♦ minimum (bid immed. 3♥ w/max)

2♠		Signoff (then 3♦ = 5♥,6♦)
2NT		Asks
	3♣	Low splinter (clubs)
	3♦	5♥, 6♦ minimum—then Mulberry?
	3♥	High splinter (hearts)

1♦-1♠-2♣

3♣/3♦/3♠	Natural invite
3♥	5-5 GF

1♦-1M-1NT   2♣   Relay to 2♦, either to play or some invite or certain slam tries

             2♦   Forced

                    2♥/1♠ 4=1=4=4 inv+, resp can pass 2NT or 3m w/min

                           2♠ = NF, should be 3=4=3=3 w/weak hearts

                           3M = max w/corresponding m, 3NT = max no fit

                    2♠/1♥ 1=4=4=4 inv+, continue as above

                    2M   Nat, invite

                    2NT   Nat, invite (raising 1NT directly to 2NT is artif)

                    3m   ?? Nat, 5M, 5+m,invite?? (w/canape bid 2OM)

                    3♥/1♠ 5-5M—strong inv w/good hearts (else 2S over 1♦)

                    3M   Nat, 6+M, strong inv (w/6♠-4♥ bid 2♠/1♦, or this)

                    3♠/1♥ Self-splinter, singleton or void

                    3NT   5M, COG

                    4♣   Self-splinter, singleton or void

                    4R   Self-splinter, VOID

        2♦   Artif GF

                2♥   Artif, 3M, no 5-card minor

                2♠   Artif, <3M, some 5-card minor, then 2NT asks

                2NT   <3M, no 5-card minor

                3m   3M AND 5m

                1♦-1♥-1NT-2♦-3♦-4♥ = 6RKC (resp usually has 5♥). To sign off in 4♥

                must bid 3♥ first.

        2♥/1♠ Artificial, some canape inv+

                2♠   ♥♥x spade support

                2NT   Less than ♥♥x spade support

                    3m   Invite, 4♠ and 5+m (usually 6)

                    3M   GF, 4♠ and 5 (exactly) of corresponding m

        2♠/1♥ Artificial, some canape inv+

                2NT   Forced

                    3m   Invite, 4♥ and 5+m (usually 6)

                    3M   GF, 4♥ and 5 (exactly) of corresponding m

        2M   To play

        2NT   Artif, relay to 3♣ to play, or show various 5-5 hands

                3♣   Forced (This is how we escape to 3♣.)

                    3♦ ??

                    3♥ ??

                    3♠ ??

                    3NT ??

        3 lower Slam try, 5♠

        3M   Slam try, natural

        3♠/1♥ GF, 5♠ and 6♥

        3NT   The End

        4♣   RKC in M

        4♦/4♥   Splinter (exactly singleton—with void bid 2♣-2♦-4R)

4M		The End

1♦-1♥-2♥   2♠   Artif, asks
                        2NT   3=4=3=3
                        3♣   5 clubs, then 3♦ asks: BAL-LH
                        3♦   5 diamonds, unbalanced, then 3♥ asks, LH
                        3♥   minimum
                        3♠   minimum, 4♥, 6♦
                        3NT   2=4=5=2
                        4♣   Stiff club, implies 4=4=4=1, else bid 3♦
                        4♦   Stiff spade, implies 1=4=4=4, else bid 3m
                        4♥   Max bal

1♦-1♠-2♠   2NT   Artif, asks
                        3♣   5 clubs, then 3♦ asks: BAL-LH
                        3♦   3=4=5=1
                        3♥   5 diamonds, unbalanced, then 3S asks, LH
                        3♠   minimum
                        3NT   minimum, 4♠, 6♦
                        4♣   4=2=5=2
                        4♦   Stiff club, implies 4=4=4=1, else bid 3♥
                        4♥   Stiff heart, implies 4=1=4=4, else bid 3♣/3♥
                        4♠   Max bal

1♦-1M-2M   Jump in new suit = short, slam try

1♦-1M-2NT   6+♦, 3M, some extra (else bid 2♦)
                        3♣   "Wolffis♥", forces 3♦
                                    3♦   Forced
                                                P   To play (duh!)
                                                3M   To play
                                                3OM   Short with diamond support (2+)—NOT LH
                                                3NT   Short clubs with diamond support—NOT LH
                                                4♣   Short clubs, ♦ support, stronger than 3NT
                        3♦   GF, some slam interest (denies shortness, didn't bid 3♣)
                        3M   GF, natural, some slam interest
                        3OM   GF, 4M, 6(5)Clubs

1♦-1M-3♦   6+♦, denies (or unwilling to show) 3M
1♦-2♣ 2♦   5+♦, not NT type, 5422 or more shapely
                        2M   GF, (semi)natural, nat continuations
                        2NT   GF, natural
                                    3m nat, some interest in contracts other than 3NT
                                    3M short

		3NT	To play, regressive
	3♣		NF, nat invite
	3♦		GF, then 3M="naturalish" (looking for 3NT)
	3M		Short with ♦ support (expect 4)
	3NT		** To play **
	4♣		Natural, requests cue (but 4♦ by opener is RKC clubs)
	4♦		RKC Clubs
	4♥		RKC Diamonds

2♥   Artif, 11-13 balanced

       2♠   Relay to 2NT

            2NT   Forced

                  Pass   Possible but unlikely—save this for matchpoints

                  3♣   GF, nat, balanced, slam interest

                  3other   GF, short, 6+♣

                  3NT   To play

       2NT   GF, nat, want to declare, interest above 3NT, then 3M=nat w/♣ fit

       3♣   Natural, NOT FORCING

       3♦   GF, nat, presumably 4♦, 5+♣

       3M   GF, NATURAL, 4(5)M, 6+♣(with short M start w/2♠)

       3NT   The End

       4♣/4♦   As over 1♦-2♣-2♦

2♠   Artif, 4♣ (5 with crap) and some stiff

       2NT   Asks, then 3♣/♦=short ♥/♠

       3♣   NF opposite min, then 3♦/♥=short ♥/♠ max

       3♦   ??

       3M   GF, nat, then OM sets M

2NT   10-13, 4=4=4=1

       3♣   To play

       3other   GF, nat

3♣   5(4) clubs, balanced, don't want to declare NT, then stoppers

3♦   GF, 6+ solid diamonds, no 4M, not min

3M   GF, 5♣, short M (with 5 clubs and crap bid 2♠)

3NT   14-15, 4=4=4=1, then Mulberry applies

4♣   DNE

4♦   RKC Clubs (unlikely but possible with big fit)

4M   Natural, 5M, 6♦

If 4th hand overcalls M, then double = short M.

If 4th hand overcalls ♦ (any meaning), then double = real diamonds (usually 5+)

If 2♣ bidder is passed hand:

P-1♦-2♣   2♦   Nat, corrective

               2♥   Artif, good hand, forces 2♠, usually no club fit

                    2♠   Forced

	2NT	4=4=4=1		
	3♣	Nat, no short		
	3♦	Nat, suit not as good as P-1♦-2♣-3♦		
	3M	5M, 6♦		
2♠	4♣, some stiff, as above			
2NT	Nat, shows 2+ fit (with bal and no fit just pass)			
3♣	Nat—Weaker than 2♥-2S-3♣			
3♦	Nat—Good suit			
3M	GF, 5♣, short M			

1♦-2♦ 2♥   11-13 balanced (12+ or 13 if Jx or worse in ♦—with 12—bid 2NT immed)

- 2♠   Relay to 2NT
  - 2NT   Forced
    - 3♣   GF, Nat, ♦+♣
      - 3♦   Sets ♦, then 3M=short
      - 3M   Sets ♣, values in M, looking for 3NT
    - 3♦   GF, bal or short ♣
      - 3♥   Asks
        - 3♠   Short ♣
        - 3NT and higher   Balanced
    - 3M   GF, short M, slam interest
    - 3NT   To play
- 2NT   GF, nat, some interest above 3NT
- 3m   NF, nat
- 3M   GF, NATURAL, 4(5)M, 6+ diamonds (with short M start w/2♠)
- 3NT   The End
- 4♣   Void
- 4♦   Natural, requests (begs?) partner to bid RKC
- 4♥   RKC Diamonds

- 2♠   Artif, 4♦ and some stiff (or 5♦ with crap)
  - 2NT   Asks (LMH)
  - 3♣   DNE
  - 3♦   NF opposite min, then 3♥/3♠/3NT=short ♣/♥/♠ max
- 2NT   10 to bad 12 bal, Jx or worse in ♦ (with 12+ or 13 bid 2♥)
- 3m NF, nat
- 3M GF, short
- 3♣   (41)=3=5
  - 3♦   NF opposite min, then 3M=short max
  - **3M   Stopper, does not preclude 4-6 GF**
- 3♦ NF, bal, not "no-trumpy", 5(4)♦, then semi-natural (stoppers)
- 3M/4♣ GF, 5+♦, short M/♣

1♦-2♦ 3NT   DNE

If fourth hand overcalls, then double=short.

If 2♦ bidder is passed hand:

P-1♦-2♦	2♥	Artif, good hand, forces 2♠		
		2♠	Forced	
			2NT	Max, bad diamonds
			3♣	5♣, bal, usually looking for best partscore
			3♦	Stronger than 3♦ direct
			3M	5M, 6♦, looking for M fit
	2♠	4♦, some short, as above		
	2NT	Nat, ♦ fit		
	3♣	**Nat**		
	3♦	Weaker than 2♥-2♠-3♦		
	3M	GF, 5♦, short M		

Interference over 1♦

1♦-(DBL)	RDBL	4+ Hearts, then 1♥=3, 2♥=4, other=fewer and natural
	1♥	4+ Spades, then 1♠=3, 2♠=4, other=fewer and natural

After RDBL or 1♥ and any 1-level rebid by opener, 2♣ forces 2♦, 2♦=GF, 3♣=nat weak.

	1♠	Requests 1NT, no interest in major suit fit
	1NT	Clubs, F1 (NOTE: may wrong-side NT)
	2♣	Clubs, NF, good suit (else bid 1NT)
	2♦	Diamonds, NF
	2M	As w/o interference
	2NT	Diamonds, Lim+
	3m	As w/o interference
	3M	Nat preempt
1♦-(1♥)	DBL	Standard, usually exactly 4 spades
	1♠	5+ spades, F1 (with 6+ spades and GF, bid 2♠)
	1NT	Nat, NF—sometimes no stop if nothing else fits
	2♣	**Nat, NF (if followed by 2♥, forcing only to 3♣)**
	2♦	Nat, F1, 5+ cards—Nat continuations—**3♣ next = NF**
	2♥	GF, Clubs (possibly only 4)
	2♠	Nat, 6+ spades, GF
	2NT	Nat, NF
	3♣	Mixed with BOTH minors
	3♦	Mixed/pre with 6+(5) diamonds
	3♥	Transfer to 3NT
	3♠	Nat preempt
	3NT	To play, wishes to declare
	4m	As without interference
	4♥	RKC diamonds
	4♠	To play

1♦-(1♠) DBL Negative, normal OR GF w/exactly 5 hearts

1NT/2m	As over 1♥ (2♣=neg. free bid, 2♦=F1)
2♥	**Nat, 5+, NF—Negative Free Bid**
2♠	GF, Clubs (possibly only 4)
2NT/3♣/3♦	As over 1♥
3♥	GF, 6+ hearts
3♠	Transfer to 3NT
3NT/4m	As over 1♥
4♥	To play
4♠	RKC diamonds

1♦-(1NT) We play 2♣ as both majors plus transfers

DBL	Penalty, forcing through 2♦
2♣	Both majors
2♥/2♦	Transfer to major
2♠	Natural
2NT	Both minors, stronger than 3♣
3♣	Natural

1♦-(2♣/3♣) Min ♦=Hearts   **ALL OF THESE APPLY BY UPH ONLY.**
Min ♥=Spades Then cue=good raise, also DBL if 4ᵗʰ hand raises
Min ♠=Diamonds

1♦-(2♣)

2NT	Nat invite
3♣	5-5+ Majors, INV+
3♦	5+♦, Mixed/Pre
3M	GF, Nat, Strong Suit

Double then M is NF and implies 4OM (else immed transfer).

1♦-(2♠)

2NT	Nat invite	
3♣/3♦/3♥	Show ♦/♥/♣ respectively	**UPH ONLY**
3♠	Requests opener to bid 3NT ??	

1♦-(2♦ natural)

DBL	Neg or GF w/exactly 5M
2M	**Nat, NF—Negative Free Bid**
3♦	Asks Stop
3♠	Nat, GF, 6+

1♦-(2♦ Michaels)

DBL	Cards
2♥	Clubs, invite+
2♠	Diamonds, invite+
2NT	Both minors
3m	Nat, NF
3M	Short M, diamonds

1♦-(2♥ Michaels) As above, except 3♣ = Forcing

1♦-(2♥ Natural)   2♠=Neg. Free Bid, 3♠=GF, 6+

Over Fourth-Seat Interference

Support Doubles and Redoubles:

When responder shows a major at the one-level and 4th hand overcalls below 2 of responder's suit, we play Support Doubles, including when 4th hand overcalls 1NT, strong and natural. This applies whether or not 2nd hand has acted. We also play Support Redoubles if 4th hand doubles.

General Rules for Competing Over 2M by Fourth Hand

Many different auctions fall under this category. Second hand may or may not have acted. If he has acted, he could have doubled or overcalled 1M or overcalled in a different suit. Third hand also could have acted in one of several ways: Pass, 1NT, Negative Double, Negative Free Bid, Transfer or a Natural F1 Bid.

In the most general case:

Double	Extra values, invite+, often the strongest call available
2NT	Looking for a minor-suit fit on many auctions, but nat on others
3♣	Usually both minors—on a few specific auctions clubs only
3♦	Natural
Cue	??

1♥/1♠ Opening Bids

Style: 5 cards expected in 1st/2nd seat. 4 more often in 3rd/4th, but with a full opener we try to make the normal opening bid. Very aggressive, but we pay attention to vulnerability and suit quality. With 14/16 HCP and no singleton we tend to open 1NT, even with many 5422 patterns. Therefore, our Jacoby structure does not cater to showing such hands.

1♥	1♠	Expected on most hands with 4+ spades—with GF may start with 2/1
	1NT	Semi-forcing
	2♣	GF, nat or balanced
	2♦	GF, usually 5+
	2♥	Raise, not the pits, usually 3 trumps (with 4 can make mixed raise)
	2♠	**Weak, 6+ spades**
	2NT	GF, 4+M, bal or too strong to splinter
	3♣	**Limit raise; 3♦ asks:**
		3M B al, 4+ trumps
		3OM Unbal, 3 trumps, some singleton; 3NT asks (LMH)
		3NT Spade void

	4m	Void	
3♦	Mixed raise, 4+ trumps		
3♥	Preemptive raise, 4+ trumps		
3♠	Artif raise, some singleton—then 3NT asks (LMH)		
3NT	Spade void-10-12 HCP		
4m	Void-10-12 HCP		
4♥	Many hand types possible opposite limited opening		
4♠	RKC HEARTS (With a natural 4♠ bid must bid 1♠ first)		
4NT	Aces (0,1,2 . . .)		

1♠	1NT Semi-forcing	
	2♣	GF, nat or balanced
	2♦	GF, usually 5+♦
	2♥	GF, Nat, 5+♥
	2♠	Raise, not the pits, usually 3 trumps (with 4 can make mixed raise)
	2NT	GF, 4+M, bal or too strong to splinter
	3♣	**Limit raise; 3♦ asks (see above)**
	3♦	**Mixed raise, 4+ trumps**
	3♥	Natural, invitational
	3♠	**Preemptive raise, 4+ trumps**
	3NT	**Artif raise, some singleton; 4♣ asks (LMH)**
	4m	**Void - 10-12 HCP**
	4♥	**Void - 10-12 HCP (With a natural 4♥ bid must bid 2♥ first)**
	4♠	Many hand types possible opposite limited opening
	4NT	RKC SPADES

1♠ Response

1♥-1♠-1NT	2♣	Forces 2♦ to start invitational sequences		
		2♦	Forced	
			2M	Inv
			2NT	Nat invite
	2♦	Artif, GF		
		2♥	Strong suit (2 of top 3), denies 3 spades	
		2♠	3 spades	
		2NT	Neither	
		3m	2=5=(42), 4m, stopper in om	
	2M	To play		
	2NT	Relay to 3♣—then P=to play, 3x = ?? (not needed yet)		
	3m	GF, 5-5		
	3♥	Nat, slam try		
	3♠	Nat, slam try		

1♥-1♠-2♣	3♠	Natural, invite

1♥-1♠-2♥   **3♣**   **Artif, GF**

              3♦/♥/♠ Invite

1♥-1♠-2♠   **Shows 4 trumps, or 3 trumps plus weak m; 2NT asks:**

              3♣   **3 trumps, minimum (could be 3=5=(3-2)**

              3♦   **3 trumps, maximum, unbal (if bal open 1NT)**

              3♥   **4 trumps, minimum**

              3♠   **4 trumps, maximum**

              3NT   4=5=2=2, maximum, stuff in minors (?)

              4m   Splinter, 6 GOOD hearts

1♥-1♠-3m   Natural, 5-5, extras but NF

              3♦=NF, 3♥=NF, 3♠=F, 4m=F, 4om=RKC m, 4♠=RKC ♥

We have no force in hearts except 4♠ (=RKC)

1♥-1♠-3NT 4 spades, 7 hearts

1NT Response

1♥-1NT-2♣   Possibly as few as 2 (4=5=2=2), but assume 3+ with semi-forcing NT

1♥-1NT-2m   2♠   Artif, strongest raise of m

              3m   Courtesy raise, but some game interest

1♥-1NT-2♥   2♠   Artif, both minors, assume 5-5, indeterminate strength

1♥-1NT-3m   Nat, 5-5, extras but NF

              3♥=NF, 3♠=3-card LR, 4m=F, 4om=RKC m

1♥-1NT-2♠   5♠, 6♥—weakish

1♥-1NT-3♠   5♠, 6♥—strong

1♠-1NT-2m   Opposite SF NT this will be 4+ more often than 3, especially 2♦

1♠-1NT-2♣   2♦   5+ Hearts—With stiff opener must judge—Nat continuations

                        Responder can show 2♠,5♥ by bidding . . . 2♦-2♥-2♠

              2♥   Artif, Mod Bart: (a)♠ signoff, (b)good ♣ raise, or(c)♦ invite

                      2♠   Forced unless unusually good opposite ♠ signoff

                      P   To play—Weak with doubleton or bad with 3(4)

                      2NT   Max invite, 4 clubs

                      3♣   Max invite, 5+ clubs

                      3♦   Natural invite

                      Higher Undefined but show CLUBS

              2♠   Doubleton S, 9+ to 11

               2NT   Nat, 11-12

               3♣   Courtesy raise

               3♦   TO PLAY (Start with 2♥ to show ♦ invite)

               3♥   5♥, 5♣ (with 5♥, 4♣ start with 2♦)

               3♠   3-card limit raise

1♠-1NT-3m   Nat, 5-5, extra♠ but NF
                        3♥=Nat NF, 3♠=NF, 4m=F, 4om=RKC m, 4♥=3-card LR
1♠-1NT-3♥   Nat, 5-5, extras but NF
                        3♠=NF, 4m=artif, slammish in corresponding M, 4M=to play

1M-1NT-2NT Nat with 6 strong M, offering NT
1M-1NT-3M Nat, "strong", but limited by failure to open 1♣
1M-1NT-3NT Solid suit, offer to play
1M-1NT-4 lower   6-6

1M-2M	New suit	"Natural" game try
	2NT	**Natural try for 3NT, 6322 with side stoppers**
	4 new	Nat slam try, 6-5 or 6-6

2-over-1

Over a major-suit opening we play 2/1 game forcing.
2♣ over 1M is either natural or balanced.
If opener rebids 2M he shows 6+M.
Therefore, opener may have to make some ugly 2NT bids, either offshape or missing stopper(s), or both. **2NT is our punt; other bids should retain their integrity. Try NOT to rebid in a 3-card suit.**
A high reverse (e.g., 1S-2H-3♣) shows 5 of the second suit.
After a 2/1 opener's jump in a new suit is a SPLINTER.
Unlike many standard systems, we play FAST ARRIVAL on most auctions. This is a logical extension of the limited opening-bid style. But beware that sometimes we cannot use fast arrival when that would be RKC for the suit immediately below, a danger most frequent when we are bidding diamonds and hearts, e.g., 1H-2♦-3♦-4♥ is RKC for diamonds.

Modified Non-Serious 3NT

If we are in a game force, AND we have established a major-suit fit (8+ cards), AND the last bid was 3M (our fit), AND we still have potential slam interest, THEN we play Modified Non-Serious 3NT (with exceptions noted below).

Typical Auctions: 1M-2x-2M-3M, or 1M-2x-2y-2M-3M

Over 3♠:	3NT	Non-Serious slam try—partner cooperates with interest himself
	4m/4♥	Cue, serious slam try—partner must cooperate below game
Over 3♥:	**3♠**	**Cue, strength unspecified**
		3NT Artif, non-serious slam try
	3NT	**Artif, no spade control, non-serious slam try**
	4m	**Cue, no spade control, serious slam try**

EXCEPTION:

1♠-2♥-3♥   3♠   Nat, some slam interest, establishes 6RKC
            3NT   Non-Serious slam try
            4m   Serious slam try

NOTE: Non-Serious 3NT does NOT apply on the auction 1M-2x-2NT-3M. Opener's 3NT is an offer to play. With slam interest he should cuebid. His 2NT bid has already limited the slam potential of his hand.

Strong Raise

1M-2NT   Artif, GF, 4+M, bal or too strong to splinter
    3♣   All minimums except 6322 or 7222 garbage (bid 4M immed)
        3♦   Asks
            3♥   No shortness, exactly 5M, then 3S=still hoping
            3♠   Some void, then 3NT asks (LMH)
            3NT/4♣/4♦   LMH singletons
            4M   6322 or 7222—min but not crap (else immed 4M)
        3♥   Some void, too strong to splinter, forces 3S (LMH)
        3♠/3NT/4♣   LMH singletons, too strong to splinter
    3♦   Extras with some shortness
        3♥   Asks
            3♠   Some void, then 3NT asks (LMH)
            3NT/4♣/4♦ LMH singletons
    3♥   Extras, some 5422, then 3♠ asks (LMH 4-card suit)
    3♠   Extras, some 6-4, then 3NT asks (LMH 4-card suit)
    3NT   Extras, 6+M, balanced—nat (cue) continuations
    4x   Extras, nat, 5-5
    4M   6322 or 7222 garbage—We have THREE ranges with this shape.

Responder can break the relay only over 3♣.
With 5-5 show 2nd suit only with **2 of top 3**. With **6-4** show 2nd suit only with **A or K**.
With 5332 opener is limited to 13 HCP, else would have opened 1NT.

After Interference Over Jacoby 2NT

If RHO bids a new suit over 2NT, a pass by opener denies a control in the opponent's suit. Double shows shortness in the opponent's suit, and a four level cue bid shows a void. Any bid by opener promises a high-card control in the opponent's suit. A new suit shows shortness in the bid suit, 3M shows 6 cards with extra values, 3NT shows 6 cards with minimum values and 4M shows 5 cards with minimum values.

Passed Hand Responses

P-1♥   2♣   Drury (see below)

	2♦	Nat (often a weak 2♦ opener)
	2♥	Normal
	2♠	**Mixed raise, some shortness; 2NT asks (LMH)**
	2NT	Both minors (5-5)
	3♣	Nat, invite
	3♦	Fit-showing, 6♦, 3♥
	3♥	**Limit raise, 5 trumps; 3S asks for shortness (LMH/none)**
	3NT	Spade void, 4+ trumps
	4m	Void, 4+ trumps
P-1♠	2♣	Drury (see below)
	2♦	Nat (often a weak 2♦ opener)
	2♥	Nat
	2♠	Normal
	2NT	**Mixed raise, some shortness; 3♣ asks (LMH)**
	3♣	Nat, invite
	3♦	Fit-showing, 6♦, 3♠
	3♥	Fit-showing, 6♥, 3♠
	3♠	**Limit raise, 5 trumps; 3NT asks for shortness (LMH/none)**
	4x	Void, 4+ trumps

After P-1M-2♣:

2♦	Real opener, no immed game interest, nat continuations
2♥/1♠	Nat, F1
2M	Worst, min opener or less
2NT	**Slam interest**
3x	Slam try, length in x (also 2♠/1♥)
3M	**Solid 6 card suit plus side card**
3NT	**6322, side stoppers**
4x	Slam try, short in x (also 3♠/1♥)

If 2♣ gets doubled:

Pass	Worst w/4M
2M	Worst w/5M
RDBL	Clubs
Other	Ignore the double

INTERFERENCE OVER 1M

Over Unusual 2NT and "Standard" Michaels

1M-(DBL)	RDBL Bal, 8+, exactly 2 card support for M
	1♠/1♥ Nat, F1
	1NT Clubs, length or strength or both

	2♣	Diamonds, length or strength or both
	2♦/1♠	Hearts, length or strength or both
	2M-1	Artif, constructive raise of M
	2M	Weakest raise of M
	2♠/1♥	Nat, preemptive
	2NT	4+M, inv+, then 3♣=artif game try, 3M=NF, other=slam try
	3♣	Nat, preemptive
	3♦/1♠	Nat, preemptive
	3M-1	Artif, mixed raise
	3M	Preemptive
	3♠/1♥	**SPLINTER**
	3NT	Artif, raise to 4M with defense, lets opener participate
	4x	**SPLINTER, including 1S-(DBL)-4♥**
	4M	Wide range, opener is on his own
	4♠/1♥	Natural
	4NT	RKC M

1♥-(1♠)	1NT	Nat, NF, may be heavy because 2NT is artif
	DBL	Neg, then cue by either side = GF
	2m	Nat, F1
	2♥	Nat, normal raise
	2♠	Support, exactly a limit raise
	2NT	Artif raise, GF, like Jacoby 2NT, some extra (else 4♥ immed)
	3m	Nat, pre
	3♥	Nat, MIXED
	3♠/4m	Splinter
	3NT	Nat
	4♥	Nat, wide range, no slam interest if balanced
	4♠	RKC for hearts
	4NT	Blackwood aces only (0123)—rare exception to "always RKC"

1♥-(2m)	DBL	Neg
	2♥	Nat, normal raise
	New suit non-jump = Nat, F1	
	2NT	Artif, support, GF, like Jacoby 2NT
	3m	Support, exactly a limit raise
	3♦/2♣	Natural, preemptive
	3♥	Nat, MIXED
	3♠	Nat, preemptive
	3NT	Nat
	4m	Splinter
	4om	Splinter
	4♥	Nat, wide range
	4♠	Nat

	4NT	RKC Hearts
1♥-(2♠)	2NT	Exactly a limit raise—this auction differs from lower overcalls
	3m	Nat, F1 only
	3♥	Nat, NF
	3♠	Support, establishes force over 4♠
	4m	Splinter
	4♥	Nat, wide range
	4♠	RKC Hearts
	4NT	Blackwood aces only (0123)—rare exception to "always RKC"
1♠-(2x)	DBL	Neg, then cue by either side = GF
	New suit non-jump = Nat, F1	
	2NT	Artif, support, GF, like Jacoby 2NT
	3x	Support, exactly a limit raise
	New suit single jump at 3-level = preemptive	
	3♠	Nat, **MIXED**
	4x	Splinter
	New minor jump at 4-level = Splinter	
	4♥/2m Nat	
	4♠	Nat, wide range
	4NT	RKC Spades

If we have established a Major-Suit fit, then 3NT in comp is artificial and sets up a force. Cuebid at 4 level = VOID but does NOT establish a force. New suit = natural, also does not establish a force.

1M-1NT-(2x) Double is takeout, including 1♥-1NT-(2♠)-DBL. With a singleton need just a "normal" opener. Over 2♠ need some extras. If opener passes then double by responder is PENALTY, since opener usually has a balanced hand.

1♥-1♠-(2m)	DBL	Support double, shows 3 spades
	2♠	Shows 4 spades
1♥-1♠-(DBL)	RDBL	Support redouble, shows 3 spades
	2♠	Shows 4 spades

Over Unusual 2NT and "Standard" Michaels

1M-(2NT)	Minors	
	DBL	Negative (4 of OM)
	3♣	**Shows the other major**
	3♦	**Shows support for the opening suit**

In either case, the bid that shows opener's suit is a limit raise EXACTLY. The bid that shows the other major is GAME FORCING.

3M Nat, NF, from a sound single raise to just below a limit raise
3OM Nat, NF

With weak hands and either support or the other major, responder should pass and hope to balance with 3M or 3OM later. Thus, 3M or 3OM immediately shows some values.

3NT Artif, GF raise of M, creates force
4m Splinter—creates a force
4M To play, wide range
4OM To play
4NT RKC in M

1M-(2M) Michaels, OM and an unknown minor
DBL Cards, penalty interest
2♠2/♥ Support, limit raise exactly
2NT Clubs
3♣ Diamonds
3♦ Mixed Raise
3M Nat, NF (often 3)
3♥/♠ Support, limit raise exactly
3♠/♥ Splinter
3NT Artif, GF raise, creates force
4m SPLINTER
4M To play, wide range
4♥/♠ Splinter
4♠/♥ RKC in hearts

Over other 2-suited interference

If both suits are known:

Cheapest available cue shows the lower-ranking of "our" suits. Other cue shows the higher-ranking. For example, over 1♥-(2♥) showing spades and clubs, 2♠ shows DIAMONDS. Over 1♠-(3♣) showing hearts and clubs, 3♥ shows DIAMONDS. This may not always be best, but it should avoid screwups. A bid of the fourth suit is natural and non-forcing.

If only one suit is known:

Cuebid shows support. If 2NT is available it shows a GF raise. New suits are natural and FORCING. With a weak hand and a long suit pass and hope to get your suit in later. The Michaels defense above is a specific exception to this default defense.

1NT Opening Bid

1NT   14-16 in 1st seat, 2nd seat, and NV 3rd seat - 5M, 6m, 5422 OK
         15-17 in 4th seat and Vul 3rd seat

2NT   19-20 when 1NT = 14-16
         20-21 when 1NT = 15-17

With less than a 1NT opening, open 1♦ (or 1M with 5). We open most 11 HCP in 1st/2nd.
With the range between 1NT and 2NT, open 1♣ and rebid 1NT.
With the range above 2NT, open 1♣ and rebid 2NT over 1♦, or rebid 1NT over 1M.
With TWO ranges above 2NT, open 1♣ and rebid 2H (Kokish, GF) over 1♦, or rebi♦ 2NT
over 1♥. Over 1S must rebi♦ 1NT an♦ catch up later.

1NT	2♣	Stayman, promises a major
	2♥/2♦	Transfer, shows 5+ cards
	2♠	Size ask or clubs; opener bids 3♣ with a max FOR NOTRUMP
	2NT	**Puppet Stayman**
	3♣	**Diamonds, signoff or GF (we don't have an invite)**
		GF, 5-5m, then 3M=Flag corres. m, 4m=Nat w/<u>Optional</u> KC Responses
	3M	Stiff M, 3OM, (54)m, then 3♠ Nat, 4m Nat w/Optional KC Responses
	3NT	The End
	4♣	Gerber, aces only (0123)
	4♥/4♦	Transfer, then 4M+1 = RKC, higher = VOID (1NT-4♦-4♥-4NT = ♠ void)
	4♠	Artif, "Weak" raise to 4NT (since 1NT is relatively wide range)
	4NT	"Strong" raise to 4NT, then 5m=4 card, 6m=5(6) cards
	5m	To play
	5M	(23)=4=4, M=Fragment, Forcing to Slam
	5NT	Forcing

1NT-2♣-2♦		No major
	2♥	Garbage Stayman—opener may correct with 3=2 in majors
	2♠	Nat, shows 5♠, invite—only way to invite with 5♠
	2NT	Nat, invite, implies major(s)
	3m	Nat, GF, implies major—no special continuations YET
	3M	Smolen, shows 5OM, 4M—see below
	3NT	The End
	4♣	Gerber (0123)
	4♥/4♦	Transfer
	4♠	Artif, "weak" raise to 4NT
	4NT	"Strong" raise to 4NT—Opener's 5m = 4 cards, 6m = 5(6) cards

1NT-2♣-2♦-3M-3NT No support for OM

       4m   **Fragment, slam interest**

       4M   **Four cards in corresponding m, void om, slam interest**

1NT-2♣-2♥	2♠	Nat, shows 5♠, invite—only way to invite with 5♠
	2NT	Nat, implies 4♠, then opener's 3♠ is to play
	3m	Nat, GF, implies 4S—Anything special here?
	3♥	Nat, invite
	3♠	Artif, distro slam try in ♥, then 3NT asks short (LMH)
	3NT	To play, but implies 4♠S—opener may correct
	4♣	Artif, balanced slam try in hearts, then 4♦ = last train
	4♦	RKC in hearts
	4♥	To play
	4♠	Spade void
	4NT	Nat, implies 4♠

1NT-2♣-2♠	2NT	Nat, implies 4♥
	3m	Nat, GF, implies 4♥—Anything special here?
	3♥	Artif, distro slam try in ♥, then 3♠ asks short (VOID, LMH)
		With **spades** trump we have enough room to show exact voids.
	3♠	Nat, invite
	3NT	To play
	4♣	Artif, bal slam try in spades, then 4♦ = cue, 4♥ = last train
	4♦	RKC in spades
	4H	Heart void
	4NT	Nat, implies 4♥

1NT-2♦-2♥   2♠   Artif, all invites with hearts

		2NT	Reject without three hearts
			3m Nat, NF, invite, 5♥ and 5m
			3♥ 5-5 MAJORS, invite
		3♣	Max, only 2♥
		3♦	Max, 3+♥, may be COG
		3♥	Reject with 3(4) hearts
	2NT		4+Clubs, GF
	3♣		4+Diamonds, GF
	3♦		**Slam try w/some short**
	3♥		COG, must choose ♥ w/3
	3♠/4m		Void, slam try
	3NT		COG
	4♥		Nat, slam try, no short

1NT-2♥/2♦	**2NT**	**Super accept with 4 trumps**
	3M	**Super accept with 5 trumps**

After 2NT responder shows hand type with a slam try.
See August, 2009 Bridge World article by Henry Sun for details.

Responder, if making a slam try, can show any shortness (or bal), and any side 4+card side suit (or none). Cannot distinguish singletons/voids.

1NT-2♥-2♠	2NT	4+Clubs, GF
	3♣	4+Diamonds, GF
	3♦	5-5+ Majors, GF (with 5S,4♥ use Smolen)
	3♥	Slam try w/some short OR 6♠,4♥
	3♠	COG, must choose ♠ w/3
	3NT	COG
	4m/4♥	Void, slam try in spades
	4♠	Nat, balanced slam try

1NT-2♠   Size ask or clubs
            2NT   Rejects NT try
                    3♣   To play
                    3♦   Clubs, slam try, balanced or short diamonds
                            3♥   Asks
                                    3♠   Singleton diamond exactly
                                    3NT Balanced
                                    4♣   Balanced, stronger than 3NT
                                    4♦   Void
                    3M   Clubs, short M, then 4♣=**OPTIONAL** RKC
                    3NT To play—implies clubs but no longer interested opp. min.
                    4♣   ??
                    4♦   RKC in clubs
                    4M   VOID
            3♣   Accepts NT try
                  Pass To play
                  Other As above—3NT does not imply clubs opposite acceptance.

1NT-2NT   **Puppet Stayman**
            3♣   **DNE (??)**
            3♦   **No five card major**
                    3M 4 cards in the other major
            3M   **Five cards**

1NT-3♣   **Transfer to diamonds, after opener's 3♦ (forced):**
          Pass **To play**
          3M   **Shortness, 6+ ♦**
          3NT **Bal, slam interest**

INTERFERENCE OVER 1NT

System on over non-penalty doubles (any meaning) or 2♣ (any meaning except majors).

Meckwell runouts over penalty doubles:

P	To play—we can't redouble for penalty
RDBL	Artif, one minor or both majors
2m	Two suits, m + higher suit (slight mod to Meckwell, catering to both m)
2M	Nat

1NT-(2♣)	Both majors	
	DBL	Penalty interest
	2♦	Nat, NF
	2♥	Artif, competitive with both minors
	2♠	Artif, GF, one or both minors
	2NT	Relay to 3♣, usually to play, **but 3R=Transfer, F, shows R+1**
	3m	Nat, GF, 6+m
	3M	Short
	3NT	To Play
1NT-(2♦)	Both majors	
	As over 2♣, but 2NT relays to 3♣ to get out in **either** minor, and 3M=Nat.	
	3M direct = Short	
1NT-(2♦)	Nat or other artif meaning (not both majors)	
	DBL	Neg, usually like Stayman
	2M	Nat, NF, to play
	2NT	Relay to 3♣, to play in 3♣ (or in 3♦ if logical)
	3 of opponent's suit (if known) = short	
	3 of any other suit = nat, GF	
	3NT	To play
1NT-(2♥)	Both majors	
	DBL	Penalty
	2NT	Leb, relay to 3♣ to get out in 3♣ or 3♦, or 3M=Nat F
	3m	Nat, GF
	3M	GF, short
1NT-(2M)	Nat, or nat with another (unknown) suit	
	DBL	Neg, Staymanish—try to avoid with shortness
	2♠/2♥	Nat, NF
	2NT	Leb, either (1) to get out in a suit below M, or (2) GF with clubs
		3♣ Then P or 3 lower = to play (opener's 3♦ = good clubs)
		3M Clubs, unbalanced, slammish
		3♠/2♥ 4♠, primary clubs, GF
		3NT Clubs, bal, slammish (NOT stopper show/ask)
	3♣	Diamonds, inv+, then OM by responder = nat, 2nd suit
	3♦	Artif, OM (5+), inv+
	3♥	GF, short M—NOTE: 3♥ is same over EITHER major. **3♠ Four cards in OM**
	3♠	F, both minors—NOTE: 3♠ is same over EITHER major.

3NT   To play—we do <u>NOT</u> have a way to <u>ASK for</u> (or <u>show</u>) a <u>stopper</u>.

If opponents show two specific suits, then cheaper cue = competitive with the other suits, and higher cue = GF with at least one (often both) of the other suits.

1NT-(3♣)	DBL	Neg
	3♥/3♦	Transfer, then raise = slam try
	3♠	Diamonds, then 3NT by opener shows stop and lack of interest
	4♣	Short
	4♥/4♦	Transfer, then 4M+1 = RKC
1NT-(3♦)	DBL	Neg
	3♥	**Spades**
	3♠	**Hearts**
	4♣	Nat, GF
	4♦	Short ♦
	4M	Natural—No 4-level transfers over 3♦ or higher.
	4NT	Nat
1NT-(3M)	DBL	Neg

New suit below game is forcing.

4NT asks aces (0123), then 5NT asks kings (# of) and other is to play.

1NT-(4x)	??

INTERFERENCE BY FOURTH HAND

1NT-2♣-(DBL)	RDBL	4+ clubs, attempt to play
	Pass	**Denies club stopper**
		RDBL Re-Stayman, opener's rebid is transfer
		2♦ Garbage Stayman
		2♥ 4♠, 5♥ invite
		2♠ 5+♠, invite
		Higher As if opener bid 2♦, except No Smolen
	2x	**Shows stopper, then system on**
1NT-2♣-(2NT/3♣/3♦)	SMOLEN STILL APPLIES	
1NT-2♣-(bid)	Double by either side is penalty	

1NT-2R-(DBL)	Pass	Denies 3M
		RDBL Re-transfer, then 2NT SHOWS stop, new suit = F
		2M Light invite w/6M
		2NT Nat, DENIES stop
		New suit = Nat, NF (including 2♠ = 5-5 inv)
		RDBL Shows 3(4)M and will accept game try (then 3R = re-tran)
		2M Shows 3(4)M and will reject game try
		Higher As without the double

2NT Opening Bid

This structure applies over opening 2NT, 1♣-1♦-2NT, 1♣-1♥-2NT and 1♣-1♦-2♥-2♠-2NT. The 2NT class of openings or rebids shows at least 19 HCP. 2NT does not by itself establish a force unless we are in a game force. However, if responder bids Stayman that DOES establish a force. 3-level transfers do NOT establish a force, but 4-level bids do.

2NT	3♣	Stayman, implies at least one major
	3♦/3♥	Transfer, promises 5+cards
	3♠	Relay to 3NT preparatory to slam try in one or both minors (or wk both m)
	3NT	To play (bitter experience has taught us to play this natural)
	4♣	Gerber (0123)
	4♦/4♥	Transfer, then 4M = RKC, other = void (2NT-4♦-4♥-4NT = ♠ void)
	4♠	Raise to 4NT with (32)=4=4, but over Kokish = "weak" raise to 4NT
	4NT	Nat, implies 4333 or possibly 5332 with a minor (over Kok = "strong")
	5m	To play
	5M	(23)=4=4, M = Fragment, Forcing to Slam
	5NT	Forcing

2NT-3♣	3♦	No major	
		3M	Smolen—use same structure as over 1NT
		3NT	To play
		4m	Nat, 5+m, GF, implies a major
			4NT Signoff
			4m+1, etc. RKC **RESPONSES** for m
		4M	NATURAL, to play (no delayed Texas over 2NT)
		4NT	Nat, invite, then opener bids minors naturally if accepting
	3♥	**Shows hearts, DOES NOT DENY SPADES**	
		3♠	Artif, slam try in hearts
		3NT	To play
		4m	Nat, 5+m, implies 4 spades
			4♠ Nat
			4NT Signoff
			4M+1, etc. RKC RESPONSES for m
		4♥	To play
		4♠	RKC for hearts (don't need 2-range invite over 2NT)
		4NT	Nat, invite, then opener bids minors naturally if accepting
	3♠	Shows spades, DENIES HEARTS	
		3NT	To play
		4m	Nat, 5+m, implies 4 hearts
			4NT Signoff
			4m+1,etc. RKE RESPONSES for m
		4♥	Artif, slam try in spades
		4♠	To play

		4NT	Nat, invite, then opener bids minors naturally if accepting
		5m	To play (To bid RKC in Spades must bid 4♥ first)
2NT-3♣	**3NT**	**DNE**	
	4♣	**DNE**	

2NT-3♦-3♥	3♠	5-5M, slammish
		3NT Regressive
		4m Slam try in corresponding M, stronger than 4M
		4M Weaker than 4m
	3NT	COG
	4m	Nat, GF, at least mild slam interest
		4♥ Signoff
		4NT Signoff
		Cheapest unbid 6RKC for m
		Next unbid 5RKC for M
	4♥	Nat, slam try
	4♠	Splinter, then 5♥ = signoff, other = RKC RESPONSES
	4NT	Nat, NF, slam try with 5♥
	5m	Splinter, then 5♥ = signoff, other = RKC RESPONSES

2NT-3♦	3♠	Artif, max super-accept (typically decent trumps, good controls)
	3NT	REJECTS HEARTS, wants to play NT
	4♥	Minimum super-accept (typically good trumps, bad controls)
	4m	**Undefined**—we want to save space with the big one

2NT-3♥-3♠	3NT	COG
	4m	Nat, GF, at least mild slam interest
		4♠ Signoff
		4NT Signoff
		Cheapest unbid 6RKC for m
		Next unbid 5RKC for M
	4♥	5-5M, game only
	4♠	Nat, slam try
	4NT	Nat, NF, slam try with 5♠
	5x	Splinter, then 5S = signoff, other = RKC RESPONSES

2NT-3♥	3NT	REJECTS SPADES, wants to play NT
	4♣	Artif, max super-accept (typically decent trumps, good controls)
	4♠	Minimum super-accept (typically good trumps, bad controls)
	4♦/♥	**Undefined**—we want to save space with the big one

2NT-3♠-3NT	**4♣**	**Slam try in ♣, then 4NT=signoff, other=RKC responses**
	4♦	**Slam try in ♦, then 4NT=signoff, other=RKC responses**
	4M	**Shortness, 5-4 or 5-5**

      4NT   2=2=(5-4)

      5♣   6+-5+ minors (either way), WEAK

      5♦   5-5m, FORCING, then 5H = 6RKC

2♣ Opening Bid

The 2♣ opening bid shows 6+ clubs and 10-15 HCP. Opener may have a side suit including a five card major.

2♣	2♦	Artif ask, at least constructive values
	2M	Nat, NF, 5+M—raise w/3M, bail with <2, judge whether to bid with 2
	2NT	Artif, relay to 3♣ to play there or show GF non-fit 2-suiter (5-5)
	3♣/3♦/3♥	Transfers, invite+, show 6+ in next higher suit
	3♠	GF, 6+♠ and 4♥, then 4♦=slammish for S
	3NT	To Play
	4♣	Nat, NF, preemptive
	4♦	RKC for clubs
	4M	To Play
	4NT	Aces only (0123)

2♣-2♦	2♥	Artif, shows EITHER 4♥ or 4♠

          2♠   Asks

                2NT/3♣   Hearts/Spades

                        3♣/P   To play

                        3♦   Artif, club slam try

                        3M   Nat invite

                        3OM Artif, slam try in M

          2NT   Asks with positional considerations (usually to right-side NT)

                3♣/3♦   Hearts/Spades

                      As above, where possible—don't bid 2NT if can't cope

          3♣   Constructive raise, no M interest

          3♦   Artif, club slam try

          3M   Natural, 5M, GF

          3NT   DNE—with a nat 4NT bid, use 2♣-2NT-3♣-3NT

          2♠   Artif, no major (nor 5♦), useful hand, do not want to bid NT

              2NT   F1, ask

                    3♣   Reject in context, then 3♦ ask M short (LHN)

                    3♦/3♥/3♠   Accept, short in bid suit

                    3NT   Accept, no short

               3♣   Mainly to play after not finding M fit

               3♦   Artif, club slam try

                3M   Nat, GF, exactly 5M

               3NT   To Play

          2NT   Natural, F1, non-minimum, usually bal with Qx or better in 2+ side suits

	3♣	Mainly to play after not finding M fit
		Other as over 2♠
3♣	Worst	
3♦	Nat, 5-card side suit	
	3♥	GF, agrees clubs
	3♠	GF, agrees diamonds
	4♣	NF
	4♦	NF
	4M/4NT	DNE

2♣-2♦ 3♥/3♠ Nat, 5-card side suit

3♠/4♥	Artif, agrees ♥/♠, slammish
4♣	NF
4♦	Artif, club slam try—**?**
4♥/4♠	To Play
4NT	DNE over 3♥, RKC S over 3♠?

2♣-2NT-3♣

Pass	To play, non-constructive
3♦	Artif, GF, 5-5M, then 3M agrees M
3♥	GF, 5♥+5♦, then 3S agrees ♥
3♠	GF, 5♠+5♦, then 4♥ agrees ♠
3NT	Quant raise to 4NT

2♣-3♣/3♦/3♥ Transfers, 6+ suit, inv+

Accept transfer is weakest, may have no support

4♣	Good suit, no support—**NF**
4♦	GF, strong raise of suit shown
3♠/3♦ or 4♥/3♥	Nat, 5♠/♥ and 6♣

2♣-3♠ GF, 6+♠, 4♥

3NT	No M interest, ♦ stop
4♣	No M interest, no ♦ stop (or no NT interest)
4♦	Artif, S fit, slammish
4♥	♥ support, wide range
4♠	No slam interest, stiff honor possible, limited by failure to bid 4♦

2♣-3NT The End

INTERFERENCE AFTER 2♣ OPENING

2♣-(DBL) RDBL Penalty interest, establishes force at 2-level, not higher

2♦	Artif, asks for M, opener shows NATURALLY
2M	Nat, NF, as without interference
2NT/3x A	RTIF, SYSTEM ON

2♣-(overcall) DBL Neg, asks for major, opener shows naturally
             New suit   Nat, F1
             2NT   Nat, NF

2♣-2♦-(DBL)   Bid=Nat, P=Min, RDBL=Max
2♣-2♦-(2M)   DBL=4OM
2♣-2♦-(3♦)   DBL=TAKEOUT, bid=nat (no penalty interest)

PASSED HAND BIDDING

P-2♣   2NT/3♣   Natural
       3 other   Fit-showing with 5 of bid suit

2♦ Opening Bid

The 2♦ opening bid shows a three suited hand, short diamonds and 10-15 HCP. Acceptable hand patterns are 4=4=1=4, 4=4=0=5 and (4-3)=1=5; a five card major is not allowed.

2♦   P   To play
      2M   To play, but see below
      2NT   Artif, inv+, asking
      3♣   To play
      3♦   Natural, invitational
      3M   Nat, NF, shape-based, need super-max to raise with 3
      3NT   To play
      4♣   Preemptive, raise only if prime
      4♦   RKC in clubs
      4M   To play, wide range

2♦-2♥ To play   **Over 2♥ opener BAILS with just 3.**
      2♠   4=3=1=5, any strength
      2NT   Max, 4=4=0=5
      3♣   Max, 4=3=1=5
      With 4=4=1=4 max must <u>pass</u>.

2♦-2♠ To play   **Over 2♠ opener MUST PASS WITH 3.**
      2NT   Max, 4=4=0=5
      3♣   Max, 4=3=1=5
      With 3=4=1=5 any strength just pass.
      With 4=4=1=4 max must <u>pass</u>.

2NT Response

The 2NT response asks for opener's strength (min/max) and exact pattern. Mulberry applies after opener has completed the description. Note that opener's 3M, either directly or after a 3♣ rebid and 3♦ re-ask, shows 3 cards in the M and four cards in the OM.

2♦-2NT	Asking		
	3♣	All minimums	
		3♦	Asks
			3M 4OM-3M=1=5, then 3♠ (over 3♥) = invite
			3NT 4=4=1=4
			4♣ 4=4=0=5
		3M	Nat, invite
	3♦	Max, 4=4=1=4, GF, **then 3M = F**	
	3M	Max, 4OM-3M=1=5, GF, then 3♠ (over 3♥) = FORCING	
	3NT	Max, 4=4=0=5, GF	

By passed hand 2NT is <u>system on</u>, asking with game interest.

INTERFERENCE AFTER 2♦

2♦-(DBL)	P	To play
	RDBL	Request for 4-card major
	Other	System on, but 2M=To Play

2♦-(overcall)	DBL	PENALTY
	Bid	Nat, NF

2♦-(2NT)   3♦   Request for 4 card major

2♦-(3♣)   If 3♣ is artificial, DBL = Clubs

2♦-2NT-(3♣) DBL=penalty, P=neutral

2♦-2NT-(3♦)	P	Minimum (but NOT 4=4=0=5)
	DBL	Max, 4=4=1=4
	3M	Max, 4OM-3M=1=5
	3NT	4=4=0=5 any strength

2♦-2NT-(3M)	P	Minimum (or neutral)
	DBL	4M, good trumps
	Other	"Naturalish"

WEAK TWO BIDS

Style: 6-card suits expected. 5 possible at fav, or in 3rd seat. 7 rare. Suit quality may be suspect NV, especially fav. Vul we expect high honors or internal solidity or both. Strength defined as 4 to 9 HCP, but QJ10xxx and out qualifies at fav. Many hands that are max weak twos in "standard" are one-bids for us, e.g., KQxxxx-x-AJx-xxx, although we can go either way in certain seats and vulnerabilities with that hand.

2M	2NT	Asks feature—Show a feature unless you have the pits.	
		3♣	Club feature or maximum without feature, like AKJxxx-xx-Jxx-xx
		3 other	Feature, Q or better, preferably A or K
		3M	Minimum
		3NT	**Artif, 4OM, then 4♣=mini-RKC in M, 4♦ sets OM, slammish**
		4x	6M and 5x
2M-2NT-3♣	3♦	Artif, asks	
		3♥	No club feature
			3♠ Asks short (Bal-LMH)
		3♠+	Artif, club feature and shape (Bal-LMH)

2M-2NT-3♦/3♥/3♠   Cheapest suit (including 3M) asks shape (Bal-LMH)

2M-2NT-3♣/3♦/3♥/3NT   4♣ Mini-RKC (still on after feature ask)

2M-2NT-3♠   4♣ Shape ask (Bal-LMH)

                            4♦ Mini-RKC <u>over 3S response only</u>

After feature ask & shape ask, mini-RKC is the cheapest 4-level call other than 4M. If the mini-RKC ask gets doubled, IGNORE THE DOUBLE.

2♥	2♠	Nat, F1	
		2NT	Artif, doubleton spade with interest
		3m	"Nat" without ♠ support
		3♥	No fit, no minor feature
		3♠	Shows 3
		3NT	Nat with stuff in both minors (not recommended)
		4m	Splinter with 3♠
		4♥	To play, semi-solid suit
2M	3m	Nat, F1	
	3♥/♠	Nat, F1, then 4m = nat	
	3M	Nat, not constructive, but opener can bid game with a twist (6-5 or void)	
	3NT	To play—if you pull you better be right	
	4♣	Mini-RKC, then 4♦=0, 4♥=1, 4♠=1+Q, 4NT=2 no Q, 5♣=2+Q	
	4♦	DNE	
	4M	To play	
	4OM	To play	

Mini-RKC does <u>NOT</u> apply after auctions that start 2M-new suit.

OVER INTERFERENCE

2M-(DBL) RDBL Penalty-oriented (but pass then double = penalty)
               2♠   Nat, NF
               2NT through 3M-1 are transfers, either own suit or lead-direct.
               3M-1   Transfer AND suggests lead of M
               3M   Does NOT suggest lead of M
               Higher Fit-showing
2M-(overcall) New suits nat, NON-FORCING—This includes, e.g., 2♠-(3♥)-4♣

We do NOT play Mini-RKC in comp.

2M-2NT-(DBL)	P	Minimum, bad shape (usually no singleton)
	RDBL	High-card max
	3x	Feature
	3M	Minimum, but with some shape (usually a singleton)
2M-2NT-(overcall)	DBL	High-card max, at least 2 of their suit
	Bid	Feature
	Cue	Short
	4M	Allowed after interference over 2NT

HIGHER PREEMPTS

Style: Aggressive but not insane (except occasionally at favorable). NV we may have six-card suits at the 3-level, but we try to have seven. Vul we usually have seven and some texture, especially at unfav.

New suits forcing if no overcall, but NF after overcall. **3x-(DBL): RDBL thru 4x-1 = transfer (3S=clubs, 3NT=nat). Transfer to our suit invites opener to compete. (??) 4♣ Mini-RKC applies over 3♦/3♥/3♠. 4♦ is Mini-RKC over 3♣. Same responses as above.**

Opening 3NT is Gambling. Over 3NT: 4♣/5♣/6♣ is P/C, 4♦ asks short (4M=short, 4NT=no short, 5m=<u>short om</u>), 4M is natural to play, 4NT asks for an eight card suit.

4m is **NATURAL**—WE DO **NOT** PLAY NAMYATS.

4M is natural and wide-ranging. We like to open 4M, despite the wide range and potential guessing for partner. After all, there are two opponents to guess wrong.

4♥-4♠ is NATURAL, TO PLAY. Over 4M we must bid 4NT to ask for keycards.

Over 4M or 5m opening, 5 of a new suit ASKS FOR CONTROL.

NOTE: Opening 4NT is BLACKWOOD

SLAM BIDDING

Our usual cuebidding style is "American": First-round controls before second-round controls, and length (first cuebid) before shortness. However, we may vary to help pinpoint a key control efficiently when we can handle the later auction.

Roman Keycard (RKC-0314)

Our main slam tool is Blackwood, usually Keycard. RKC has its detractors, but we are not among them. Often RKC is the only sensible way to get concrete information when the level gets high.

IF IT'S ACE-ASKING, THEN its <u>KEYCARD, AS LONG AS WE HAVE SHOWN AT LEAST ONE SUIT</u>. THE ONLY EXCEPTIONS (<u>AND ONLY WHERE EXPLICITLY NOTED</u>) ARE WHEN WE USE ONE CALL (USUALLY "1-OVER") AS A KEYCARD ASK AND HAVE 4NT AVAILABLE TO ASK FOR ACES-ONLY.

WE DO NOT PLAY EXCLUSION BLACKWOOD. EVER! If we make a funny jump to the 5-level that you might play as Exclusion with your other partners, it may well show a void, but we do NOT play RKC responses to it.

We have several possible response structures, but we should have little difficulty figuring out which one applies, or in figuring out which suit (or suits) is key. Our first step always includes ZERO ("old-guy responses"):

1. Normal: First step   0 or 3 out of FIVE keycards (4 aces plus trump king)
                 Second step   1 or 4 KC
                 Third step   2 KC, no trump queen
                 Fourth step   2 KC plus trump queen
                 Fifth step, etc. Same as first step, etc., PLUS A VOID

Don't show a void unless (a) the void suit is "obvious", AND (b) you know it's safe, AND (c) you are confident that you're not spoiling partner's plans.

"Normal" RKC applies whenever our side has shown at least one suit naturally. This includes specifically 1M-4NT, which is RKC for M. Bart likes it this way. Humor him.

2. Mini-RKC First step   0 KC
                 Second step   1 KC, no trump queen
                 Third step   1 KC plus trump queen
                 Fourth step   2 KC, no trump queen
                 Fifth step   2 KC plus trump queen

Mini-RKC applies over weak 2-bids and weak 3-bids. It is a bid of 4♣, usually directly, but after a weak 2-bid, responder can inquire with 2NT and then bid 4♣. Over an opening 3♣ bid, 4♦ is Mini-RKC. Over other 3-level preempts 4♣ is Mini-RKC.

3. Non-RKC	First step	0 or 4 Aces
	Second step	1 Ace
	Third step	2 Aces
	Fourth step	3 Aces

Grandma's Blackwood. It applies when we have shown NO SUITS naturally. Examples: 4NT opening or 4NT overcall over a suit opening of 3♠ or lower, Gerber directly over a 1NT or 2NT opening, or after a "no-major" response to Stayman. We use old-fashioned responses because there may still be ambiguity between 0 and 3. (Imagine 10 solid and 3 singletons for example.)

4. 6-RKC	First step	0 or 3 of 6 keycards (4 aces plus kings of TWO key suits)
	Second step	1 or 4 KC
	Third step	2 (or 5) KC plus NEITHER key queen
	Fourth step	2 KC plus the LOWER key queen
	Fifth step	2 KC plus the HIGHER key queen
	Sixth step+	2 KC plus BOTH key queens

If there is enough room below one of our trump suits, use additional steps to show or deny specific side kings. For example, if both majors are key, then over 4NT bid 6♣ to show both major-suit queens and the club king, bid 6♦ to deny the club king and show the diamond king, and bid 6♥ to deny both minor kings. WE CANNOT SHOW VOIDS WHEN USING 6-RKC.

6-RKC applies in two main situations: a. Two suits bid and raised immediately, e.g., 1S-2♥-3♥-3♠ establishes 6-RKC. b. Two-suiter opposite a known balanced hand, AND the second suit is known to be 5+ cards long. For example, 1NT-2♥-2♠-3♥-3♠-4NT is 6-RKC because responder showed 5-5 in the majors.

WHAT BIDS ARE ACE-ASKING?

1. "One-over" the trump suit. This is the most common bid we use as RKC. **It applies even if not a jump.** "Trump suit" usually means a bid-and-raised suit. Occasionally we can IMPLY a fit by jumping into the "one-over" suit, e.g., 1♠-2♦-4♥ is RKC for diamonds (opener can have AKxxxx-x-KQxxx-x or the like). **RKC TAKES PRECEDENCE OVER SPLINTERS.**

Ambiguities can arise if the "one-over" suit has previously been bid naturally. Our default is that RKC APPLIES unless we have also established a fit in the "one-over" suit. For example, 1H-2♦-3♦-3S-4♣-4♥ is RKC for diamonds. 1♥-2♦-3♦-4♥ is RKC, because a natural 3♥ is available. Similarly for 1♥-2♦-3♦-3S-4♥. Generally, if 3 of the 1-over suit is forcing, then 4 of the 1-over suit is RKC.

If the "one-over" suit would clearly be natural, then the RKC bid is the next highest call that is clearly NOT natural. **DISCUSS.**

If the rules for 6-RKC indicate that it applies, then it's still on even if the ace-asking bid is something other than 4NT, e.g., 1H-2♦-3♦-3♥-4♣-4♠ is 6-RKC for both red suits.

2. 4♣ over weak two-bids and three-bids (except 3♣), and 4♦ over 3♣. Also, 4♣ after responding 2NT over a weak two-bid. These bids are Mini-RKC, discussed above.

3. Opening 4NT, and 4NT overcalls immediately over opening natural suit bids through 3S. These ask for aces only, with old-fashioned replies (0/4, 1, 2, 3).

4. 1NT-4♣, 1NT-2♣-2♦-4♣ and 2NT-4♣ are ace-asking for ACES ONLY (0/4, 1, 2, 3).

5. 1NT-2♣-2M-4♦ is RKC for M. (4♣ would be a balanced slam try for M.)

WHAT BIDS ARE <u>NOT</u> ACE-ASKING?

1. In general, when 4 of some suit is ace-asking, then 4NT is something else:
If 4NT is NOT a jump, then it is a substitute cuebid in the suit that WOULD be RKC. For example, 1♥-2♦-2♥-3♥-4♣-4NT is a SPADE cuebid, since 4♠ would be RKC. (This is an unlikely sequence, but you get the idea.)
If 4NT IS a jump, then it should be a natural slam try. For example, 1H-2♦-3♦-4NT is a power slam try, not forcing, because 4♥ is RKC. (4S is NOT 6-RKC; bid 3H first. 4♠ shows a VOID. Eddie)

2. If CLUBS is the agreed trump suit, then 4♦ is the ONLY RKC available. If we cuebid above 4♦, then 4NT is a further slam try, but it is NOT RKC.

3. A "weak" hand cannot ask for aces. This applies to a 1♦ responder to 1♣, but even then certain big jumps would "obviously" be RKC.

WHAT IS THE KEY SUIT OR SUITS?

A bid and raised suit is key. **Two suits bid and raised early are BOTH key. A bid and raised suit along with a second suit known to be 5+ opposite a balanced hand makes BOTH suits key.**

If no suit has been raised, the default is the last bid suit: 1S-4NT is RKC for spades. 1S-2H-4NT is RKC for hearts (4♠ would be natural). Sometimes the logic of the auction makes it clear that some other (strongly bid) suit should be key, even if it was not the last bid suit: 1♦-1♠-3♦-3♥-4♣-4NT should be RKC for diamonds (both 4♥ and 4S would be natural).

INTERFERENCE IN RKC AUCTIONS

1. If opponents BID over RKC BELOW our trump suit, then we play DOPI:

> Double = 0 or 3
> Pass = 1 or 4
> First step = 2, no Q
> Second step = 2 + Q

In the specific case where they interfere directly below our trump suit, we don't bid the second step (=5T+1) unless we are confident that we have enough keycards for slam.

2. If opponents BID over RKC AT OR ABOVE our trump suit, then we play DEPO:

> Double = 0 or 2 or 4 (even)
> Pass = 1 or 3 or 5 (odd)
> Bid is undefined, but logically shows an even number that does not want to defend.
> The mnemonic when the opponents bid is that double always shows 0 (possibly) and

pass always shows 1 (possibly). If you have more than one you have to figure it out.

3. If opponents DOUBLE the RKC ASK:

> Pass denies a control in the doubled suit, then redouble is "Re-RKC".
> Bid shows a control and is a normal RKC response.
> Redouble shows a control and TAKES CONTROL, i.e., responder is now asking for

keycards (!).

4. If opponents double the RKC RESPONSE:

> Pass asks for control, then redouble shows control.
> Redouble is to play (very rare).
> Bid shows control and continues the RKC sequence as if no double.

RKC CONTINUATIONS

Queen Ask: If the RKC response did not clarify the trump queen (step 1 or step 2), then the queen ask is the cheapest call that is not to play AND is not the king ask. (K ask is usually a repeat of the RKC suit 1 level higher—see below.) Over the queen ask, the cheapest bid in the trump suit denies the queen, and anything else shows the queen. A response in a new suit also shows that king. When the queen ask is below 5 of the trump suit, then 5NT shows THE KING OF THE QUEEN-ASK SUIT. (And 6 of the queen-ask suit shows some non-K plus value.) In this case a jump to 6 of the trump suit shows the queen and nothing else noteworthy. When the queen ask is above 5 of the trump suit, 6 of the trump suit denies the queen, and 5NT shows the queen with no biddable side king. **In 6RKC queen-ask auctions we use coded responses: Step 1=no Q, Step 2=lower Q, Step 3=higher Q, Step 4 and higher=both Qs.**

King ask: If the RKC ask was "4x", then the king ask is "5x", which takes precedence over the queen ask. (Usually we avoid the problem of "not enough room" by using "one-over" RKC.) The "King Ask" SHOWS that we own all of the key cards and INVITES A GRAND SLAM. Responder is allowed to bid a grand right now. If he does not, then he is **obligated** to cuebid a king **below the trump suit**. (The only exception to this obligation is when asker is limited and responder knows that the grand is impossible. For example, if a 1NT opener bids RKC and then shows all of the keycards via the king ask, he is merely giving an unlimited responder the chance to bid 7. If responder DOES show a king, then he is also announcing grand slam potential opposite a 1NT opening.) If 5NT is available, then it shows the king of the "king-ask" suit. Responder is NOT obligated to show a king above the trump suit, which is tantamount to forcing to 7.

Other tries: If asker bids something other than the queen ask or king ask, it is a grand slam try with emphasis on the bid suit, usually seeking third-round control. If only one such suit is available, then it MAY be a general grand slam try, kind of like a "Last Train" try for 7. If more than one such suit is available, any suit other than the highest is a specific try with emphasis on the bid suit. The highest suit MAY focus on that suit, or may be a general try; responder has to figure it out. Note that the failure to use the "king ask" affords inferences about what the asker needs.

If asker uses the king ask, gets a king-showing response, and then makes another call between there and the trump suit, the same conditions apply. This time the asker may need a DIFFERENT king than the one already shown, or he may need some other kind of extra value. Again, responder has to figure it out.

Mulberry

Mulberry is a special RKC on certain relay auctions that end with 3♥ or higher and where the trump suit can be one of several. This applies after auctions that specifically show a three-suited pattern such as 1♣-2♠, 1♣-1♥-2♠, 1♦-2♣-3NT, 2♦-2NT and a few other well-defined sequences. On these auctions, if the last call by the multi-suited hand is 3♥, 3♠ or 3NT, then:

> 4♣   Artif, puppet to 4♦, then next bid = nat slam try, NF.
> 4♦   Artif, puppet to 4♥, then next bid (or pass) is TO PLAY.
> 4♥/4♠/4NT are RKC in the lowest/middle/highest of multi-suiter's three suits.
> 5♣+ are RKC RESPONSES in multi-suiter's SHORT SUIT.

If the last call by the multi-suited is hand is 4♣ then the NF slam try is no longer available, but the other bids remain unchanged.

We call this method "Mulberry Bush", or just "Mulberry". **(Thanks, Chris Compton)**

JUMPS TO 5NT—CHOICE OF SLAMS or GRAND SLAM FORCE?

Our <u>default</u> for jumps to 5NT is <u>"choice of slams"</u>. This applies when we do NOT have a clearly defined trump suit.

If trumps are well-defined, then a jump to 5NT is the Grand Slam Force. Our response structure, regardless of how many steps are available, is <u>"the more you bid, the more you have."</u> **In all cases responder should jump to 7 with 2 of the top 3 honors.** A jump to 7 of a new suit normally shows extra strength in that suit and is offering 7NT as a contract. (We try to avoid this kind of torture.) Details:

Spades trump—four steps

6♣	No A, K or Q—then 6♦ asks for extra length
6♦	Q exactly—then 6H asks for extra length
6♥	A or K <u>without</u> extra length
6♠	A or K <u>with</u> extra length

Hearts trump—three steps

6♣	Q or none—then 6♦ asks for the queen
6♦	A or K <u>without</u> extra length
6♥	A or K <u>with</u> extra length

Diamonds trump—two steps

6♣	Q or none
6♦	A or K

Clubs trump—one step

6♣	Fewer than 2 of the top 3

Don't sweat the details. If you remember "more = more" you'll usually be close enough.

NON-JUMP BIDS OF 5NT

On those rare occasions when we haven't bid RKC and we are cuebidding at the 5-level and someone bids 5NT, the default is still choice of slams. However, if the trump suit is obvious and we are clearly trying for 7, then 5NT is the try that emphasizes TRUMPS. It is NOT the GSF, but it suggests needing help in trumps. Side-suit tries suggest needing help outside of trumps.

NON-SERIOUS 3NT

When we are in a game force with an 8+ major-suit fit and the last bid is 3M (our fit), and we have slam potential, then (usually) we have two degrees of slam try available. 3M+1 is a non-serious try, and a cuebid is a serious try. (3NT over 3♥ is a serious spade cuebid.) **A raise from 3M to 4M denies any slam interest.** Over the non-serious try you can sign off or cooperate. When hearts are trump and the last bid was a non-serious 3S, then 3NT is a spade cuebid.

Applies: 1M-2x-2M-3M, or 1S-2m-2♥-2♠-3♠, or 1♠-2♥-3m-3♠ (assume ♠-card fit here even though not quite assured)

Does NOT apply: 1M-2x-2NT-3M Here 3NT is still a possible contract, and opener is somewhat limited. He can bid 3NT to play, cuebid with slam interest, or raise to game with no slam interest.

1♠-2♣-2♥-3♣-3♥-3♠ Probable 7-card fit, so 3NT is natural.

Wrinkle: 1♠-2♥-3♥ 3♠ is natural and wide-range. It establishes 6-RKC. Then 3NT BY OPENER is a non-serious try.

> 3NT is a non-serious try and denies spade support.
> 4m is a serious try.

LAST TRAIN

On cramped auctions the bid just below game in our trump suit is often an artificial slam try, showing interest but not willingness to bid above game. Bart suggests that we don't get hung up worrying about whether we actually have a control in that suit; in a pinch, assume we do.

DEFENSIVE BIDDING

Definition: Defensive auctions are those in which the opponents initiate the bidding.

Overcalls

Our style is aggressive but not insane, with special attention to the vulnerability. We do NOT overcall aggressively with 4-card suits. Not vul we will try to show any decent 5-bagger at the one level.

If the opening bid of 1-of-a-minor could be a **doubleton or shorter**, then:

(1♣)	2♣	Natural
	2♦	Michaels
	3♣	More clubs—preemptive
	3♦	Natural and preemptive—lowest ♦ preempt available
(1♦)	2♦	Natural
	2♥	"Weak" Michaels
	3♦	"Strong" Michaels

Advancing 1-level overcalls: Cuebids ALWAYS show support. 3-card support is expected, but Hx is allowable in a pinch. Overcaller is allowed to jump to game with a 5-bagger. After cue-bidding, a new suit or NT by advancer is natural, but STILL SHOWS SUPPORT. Simple new suits are not forcing and "semi-constructive" (whatever that means). If you have a good suit, BID IT. If third hand passes, NEW SUIT JUMPS ARE STRONG AND FORCING. This should cover the (rare) strong misfit. If third hand **acts**, then jumps are preemptive and 2NT shows a 4-card LR. If third hand PASSES, then 2NT is NATURAL. In either case, Jump cue = mixed raise.

If we overcall 1M and third hand doubles, then we play TRANSFERS, starting with 1NT and through 2M-1. The direct raise is weaker than the transfer raise. A transfer into the opening bid suit (if it showed 3+) is equivalent to a cuebid in support. But if the opening suit can be 2 or fewer (e.g. Precision 1♦, Polish 1♣), then a transfer into that suit is <u>natural,</u> 2M-1 = limit raise (usually 3M), and a raise to 2M has a wider range.

Advancing 2-level overcalls: Again, cuebids show support. If third hand passes, new suits are FORCING. (1♠)-2♥-(2♠)-2NT is an artificial heart raise. (1♠)-2♥-(3♠)-3NT is an artificial heart raise **AND creates a force**.

Fourth-seat overcalls: After (1x)-P-(1y) both 2x and 2y are NATURAL. **3x and 3y are also natural.**

Tackout Doubles

We make takeout doubles very aggressively. We strain to get in when we have unbid majors or when we have 12 HCP or more. We prefer to make immediate balanced doubles than to have to guess later whether to back into the auction.

Advancing takeout doubles: Jumps are invitational. Cuebid is forcing to game or suit agreement. Cuebid by doubler over a minimum advance does not promise another call unless advancer bids ABOVE his original suit. Cuebid by doubler followed by a new suit by doubler is FORCING. Cuebid by doubler over a non-minimum advance is GF. New suit by doubler over a non-minimum advance is F1. **CUEBID BY A PASSED HAND ADVANCER PROMISES ANOTHER CALL.** (Doubler can thus keep it low with a good hand and get info without using up a lot of room.)

Special cases: (1♠)-DBL-(2♠)-2NT is NATURAL and Double is Responsive. Double followed by 3♥ is invitational. **(1♥)-DBL-(2♥)-DBL SHOWS SPADES. (1♥)-DBL-(2♥)-2♠ IS EQUIVALENT TO A RESPONSIVE DOUBLE. (1♥)-DBL-(2♥)-2NT is NATURAL.**

Michaels (and other) Cuebids

We play wide-range Michaels. We like to show our two-suiters and sort out the strength issues later. When we are 6-5 (in that order) we try to bid the 6-bagger first and show the 5-bagger later, since advancer to Michaels will bid the lower suit with equal length. However, there are still many 6-5 hands where that approach is untenable and we bid Michaels anyway. We play (1M)-2M shows the other major and an unknown minor.

Advancing over Michaels: After (1m)-2m jumps are invitational, 3m shows high cards, **4C=slammish in hearts and 4D=slammish in spades.**

(1♥)-2♥-(P)	2♠	To play
	2NT	Artif, inv+, asking
	3m	Nat, minimum
	3♥	Artif, CLUBS, maximum
	3S	Artif, DIAMONDS, maximum
	3NT	6M, maximum, minor still unknown
	4m	Nat, 6+m, extras
	3♣	Pass-or-correct-to-3♦, regressive
	3♦	Artif, invitational in spades
	3♥	Slammish
	3♠	Nat, preemptive
	3NT	To play
(1♠)-2♠-(P)	2NT	Artif, inv+, asking, then continue as above
	3♣	Pass-or-correct-to-3♦, regressive
	3♦	Artif, invitational in hearts
	3♥	Nat, wide range—cannot distinguish preemptive from bailing
	3♠	Slammish
	3NT	To play
(1M)-2M-P	4♣	**?? P/C, pre in both m??**
	4♦	**Constructive bid of 4OM (establishes force?)**
(1M)-2M-(3M)	DBL	Minors, better than 4♣
	3NT	Natural
	4♣	P/♣, weaker than double
	4♦	Constructive bid of 4OM

(1m)-3m is natural, EXCEPT when 1♦ could be 2 or fewer then 3♦ is "Strong" Michaels.

(1M)-3M shows a strong one-suiter and is asking for a stopper. The strong suit is allowed to be THE OTHER MAJOR (rare). If advancer is weak with no stopper he must bail to 4♣. If he is strong enough to think about slam he can ignore his stopper and cuebid in return (?). **4♦ is P/C.**

Unusual Notrump Overcalls

(1x)-2NT shows the two lower unbid suits. **This is still true even if the opening bid does not guarantee length in the bid suit, for example, over Polish Club.**

Natural Notrump Overcalls

We're aggressive here, too, nominally 15-18, but we are not obligated with 15 bad, especially with a passed partner. Our sandwich notrump is also natural at the one level. We play "System On" after a direct 1NT overcall (including the Sandwich type), **except** on the specific auction (1x)-1NT-(2y) we play PENALTY DOUBLES, since x and y are different and the opponents may be in trouble. On this auction a raise to 2NT is NATURAL. If third hand <u>RAISES</u> opener we play <u>System On</u>.

Our balancing 1NT shows (10)11-15(16). We play "3-Range Size-Ask" Stayman here:

(1x)-P-(P)-1NT-2♣	2♦	Minimum, no major
	2M	Minimum, 4M (bid hearts with both—rare)
	2NT	Middle range, then 3♣ = "ReStayman"
	3x	Maximum, "natural" (M if possible, else better m)

On the auctions (2M)-2NT, (2M)-P-(P)-2NT, and (1M)-P-(P)-2NT (the last of these shows about 19 HCP) we play:

3♣	Relay to 3♦, with diamonds <u>or</u> both minors <u>or</u> signoff in OM	
	3♦	Forced
		P — To play
		3OM — To play
		3M — Short M, both minors
		3NT — Diamonds, slammish
3♦	Transfer to OM, inv+ (then 4M=weakest accept, 3OM=strongest accept, then 4♦=retransfer)	
3M	Stayman	
3OM	Clubs	

If we overcall 2NT over a <u>minor</u> we play our "front-of-the-card" 2NT system on.

If we overcall 3NT over a weak 2-bid or a 3-level preempt, we play a version of TONTO:

4♣/4♦/4♥	Transfers to H/S/♣/♦, skipping opponent's suit
	Then accept xfer=weakest, first step=strongest (mid=mid if avail.)
	Then 4NT by resp.=quantitative, cheapest new suit = RKC
4♠	BLACKWOOD, ACES ONLY (0123)
4NT	Nat invite

Over Preempts: We play Leaping Michaels over weak two-bids, with a modification over 2♦.

(2♦)	3♦	Majors
	4♣	Clubs and Hearts, forcing
	4♦	Clubs and Spades
	4M	Nat
	4NT	BLACKWOOD (Aces only, 0123)

(2M)	3M	Strong one-suiter, stopper ask
	4m	Two-suiter, m and OM, forcing
	4M	BOTH MINORS
	4NT	BLACKWOOD (Aces only, 0123)

We play takeout doubles to the moon, including over 4♠ and (to a lesser extent) 5m. **We play lebensohl only after a DIRECT double of a weak two-bid.**

(2♥)-DBL	2NT	lebensohl, relay to 3♣		
		3♣	Normal, may bid more with extras	
			P/3♦	To play
			3♥	GF with ♥ stop
			3♠	Natural invite, NF
			3NT	Stop, suggests other contracts
	3m	Nat, NF, constructive		
	3♥	GF, no H stop		
	3♠	**FORCING**		
	3NT	To play, no interest in other contracts (else 2NT-3♣-3NT)		

Also:	(3m)	4m	Majors
		4♦/3♣	Diamonds and a major
		4NT	BLACKWOOD
	(3♥)	4♥	5♠ and 5m
	(3♠)	4♠	5-5 minors
	(3M)	**4NT**	**BLACKWOOD**
	(4m)	**4NT**	**??**
	(4M)	DBL	**Takeout**, then 4NT shows 2 places to play
	(4♥)	4NT	Minors
	(4♠)	4NT	2 suits, may include hearts

Over 1NT Opening Bids

We play two defenses, one for "Strong" NT and one for "Weak" NT. **"Strong"** is defined as **any range that includes 15 HCP**, regardless of the lower limit. **"Weak"** is defined as any range with a **maximum of 14 HCP** or less. The "Strong" defense also is used by a passed hand vs. any range NT.

"Strong" NT defense (Meckwell), vs. range that includes 15 HCP or more:

(1NT) DBL	Either one minor or BOTH majors
	2m	Pass or correct
	2M	Natural, shows own suit
	2NT	Good hand, F1

If third hand acts, DBL by advancer is competitive, implying some fit.

| | 2m | Two suits, m + some major, relative lengths ambiguous |

2♦ over 2♣ is artif, asking for major.
If 2m is doubled: P=To play, RDBL=Asks Major, 2 any=Own Suit
2M   Natural

"Weak" NT defense (Pen DBLs and Transfers), vs. range that is max of 14 HCP:
(1NT) DBL Penalty, tricks or good 14+ HCP—Natural continuations.

We are forced through 2♦, but not higher. Doubles of 2m are takeout in direct seat. In balancing seat we need more latitude, since we're in a force. Doubles above 2M are more "card-showing"/takeout; again, we need more latitude, since we're NOT in a force, especially advancer, who has not yet shown values.

2♣   Both majors, then 2♦ = "you pick"
       If 2♣ is doubled: P=To play, RDBL="You pick M", 2D=Natural
2♦   5+ Hearts
2♥   5+ Spades
2♠   4♠ and a longer minor
2NT   4♥ and a longer minor

Over Multi 2♦

We play the defense where bids are natural and double shows up to about 15 HCP or a very strong hand, and 2NT is about 16-18. Use the ACBL defense if we can. **If we can't use ACBL defense, DISCUSS BEFORE WE PLAY.**

Over Flannery 2♦

DBL = 13+ to 16, 2♥ = Minors, 2♠ = Nat, 2NT = (16)17-19 (then use 2NT overcall defense with opp's suit = Hearts), 3m = Nat, 3H = Ask stop, 3♠ = Nat.

Over Flannery 2♥: Same except DBL = Minors, and 2NT = wider range.

Over Transfer Responses to 1♣

Over a response of 1R (showing a major), double is takeout with OM and DIAMONDS. Bidding their major is Michaels, with OM and CLUBS. 2 of their major is NATURAL. Over an artificial response of 1S double SHOWS SPADES.

Over Artificial Bids

Generally, a double of an artificial bid shows that suit. Unfortunately, we have numerous exceptions. If the artificial bid is a raise AND is at the 3-level (Bergen Raises), then our meaning depends on the strength shown. If the bid shows INVITATIONAL STRENGTH OR MORE, then our double shows that suit. If the bid shows a WEAKER hand, then our double is **takeout** of the anchor suit. At the TWO LEVEL, our doubles of artificial raises are **takeout**, e.g., **a double of Drury is takeout**.

Over Kaplan Inversion

Kaplan Inversion switches the meaning of the 1♠ and 1NT responses to an opening bid of 1♥. Note that some practitioners revert to "natural" if responder is a passed hand.

After (1♥)-P-(1♠), which shows a forcing NT but which may contain 4 spades, double is takeout of hearts and 1NT is natural. **QUESTION: what does the 1NT overcall mean when intervenor is a passed hand?**

After (1♥)-P-(1NT), which shows five or more spades and is forcing for one round, double is takeout for the minors.

LEADS

Versus Suits

Honor Leads:
Rusinow (2nd of touching honors). Applies down to the 8. That is, from 98x or 87x we lead the 8 (but try to lead low if you must lead the suit). Rusinow does NOT apply in partner's suit. "Partner's suit" is defined as any naturally bid suit (including a 1D opening bid), or any unbid major shown by a takeout double, or any 4+ card implied suit, e.g., after (1♣)-P-(1♥)-DBL, the doubler "owns" both spades and diamonds. We also lead standard honors if we preempt showing a long suit and lead a different suit, and when leading DUMMY'S suit(s).

We do not lead differently versus high-level contracts, although for tactical reasons we will vary more often from the "correct" lead, especially from AK(x).

Spot-card Leads:
3rd from even and lowest from odd, but from a 7-card suit we lead FIFTH, preserving seventh for oddball purposes. If we have raised we will often lead high from small cards; otherwise usually 3rd.

Shifting:
We lead **standard** honors when shifting, **except 10/9 = 0/2 higher.** We lead 3/5 when shifting **if we are trying to give count**, but often we shift to an "attitude" card.

Versus Notrump

Honor Leads:
King is the "power lead" (asks for unblock or count). Other honors are Rusinow. We lead Rusinow from holdings of 4 cards or more. 3-card suits are considered "short" for NT

purposes, so we lead standard honors from 3-card or shorter holdings (except Q from KQx and A from AKx).

The Ace asks for attitude. Lead Ace from AKJx; lead King from AKJ10. Lead Q from KQJx; lead K from KQJxx (usually).

Spot-card Leads:
4th best is normal. We MAY lead a higher card from a bad holding, but we do so less often than most players (Bart speaking). If we are leading high, we lead the second best from a disconnected holding (86xx) but MAY lead top from a connected holding (876x).
We lead 3rd best in PARTNER'S SUIT, even from four.

Shifting:
We lead **standard** honors when shifting, **except 10/9 = 0/2 higher.** We lead 4th **if we are trying to give count,** but often we shift to an "attitude" card.

SIGNALS

We are NOT compulsive signallers. Our theory of signals is to make them on a "need-to-know" basis, not on an "every-card-tells-a-story" basis. Nevertheless, we signal often enough to get the job done. We will signal more against weak opposition than strong.

We play **UPSIDE-DOWN COUNT AND ATTITUDE**, vs. both suits and notrump. Our top priority is attitude, with count a close second. Suit preference is third.
EXCEPTION: Vs. SUITS, on a lead that shows ACE-KING, we play a STANDARD signal at TRICK ONE.

At trick one vs. suits, when dummy has a singleton and 3rd hand is known to have sufficient length, very high or low cards are suit preference and middle is neutral or encouraging.

We play suit-preference in trumps, but sometimes will echo in ruff situations.

We play Smith Echo only when 3rd hand plays the JACK (if Bart remembers).

Chapter 19
Precision Simplified Overview

In this Chapter we review the bids of the Precison System developed by Timm (2011) in his book "Precision Simplified", Second Edition, published by Trafford Press. While many of the bids are similar to Transfer Precison, it employs the 1♥ and 2♥ relay bids.

Basic Opening bids

1♣*   Artificial 16+ HCP—MUST ALERT

1♦*   11-15 HCP may be short **NV** (at least 2) MUST ANNOUNCE May be short **VUL no annoucement since have 4+ Diamonds**

1♥/1♠   11-15 HCP 5+ Majors with Meckwell Bidding Structure

1NT   **12-15 HCP Vul or 4ᵗʰ Seat 10-12 HCP NV (Transfers On)**

2♣*   11-15 HCP 5/6+ Clubs (with 5 must have a 4-card major)—MUST ALERT

2♦*   11-15 HCP **4=3-1-5, 3=4-1-5, 4=4-1-4, or 4=4-0-5** MUST ALERT **Singleton Diamond or Void**

2♥/2♠   7-11 HCP 5/6+ Cards (Weak 2-bids Vulnerable with **Modified Ogust 5-5-6-6**)

2NT*   5-5 in the minors 5-10 HCP (NV) and 11-15 HCP (VUL)

3X   5-10 must have 2/3 of top 3 Honors in the Bid Suit Vulnerable and 1 if Non—vulnerable

3NT* GAMBLING solid 7+ minor suits (AKQJxxx)
* Indicates forcing bids and alerts

Responses to 1♦* Opening

Responses to 1♦* Opening (11-15 HCP diamonds may be short) strong Jump Shifts

1♥/1♠ 4+ Cards in suit with 6+ HCP (to show weak hand rebid majors since using strong jump shifts)

Rebids by Opener

1♠	4+ spades ov 1♥
1NT	11-15 HCP ov 1♥/1♠
2♣	5+ clubs
2♦	5+diamonds
2M	**13-16 Dummy Points**
3M	**17-18 Dummy Points**

1NT	6-10 HCP, balanced hand
2NT	11-12 HCP, balanced hand
3NT	13-15 HCP, balanced hand
2♣	13+ HCP forcing
2♦*	10-12 HCP 5/6+ diamonds (Rev-Crisscross)
2♥/2♠	16+ HCP strong jump shift in Major 5+ cards, game force
3♣*	13+ Dimond raise 5/6+ diamonds
3♦*	less than 10 HCP, Weak, preemptive raise 5/6+♦
3♥/3♠	Splinter bid in support of diamonds (slam interest 16+)
4♣	Splinter bid in support of diamonds (slam interest 16+)
4♦	Minorwood 1430 Keycard for diamonds
4♥/4♠	Single suited hand to play

Getting to notrump (Rev-crisscross)

After an inverted minor raise 1♦*-pass - 3♣* (13+ HCP)

1. Show major suit stoppers 2♥ or 2♠, bid up the line. No extra values
2. Bid **2NT** with a minimum and both majors are stopped.
3. Bid **3♣** to show club stopper, neither hearts of spades stopped
4. Bid **3♦** with a minimum without major stoppers.
5. Bid **3♥** or **3NT**, showing ♥ stopped, over **2♠** with minimum values

After a weak raise 1♦* - pass - 3♦* (less than 10 HCP)

a. Pass with all minimum and almost all intermediate sized hands
b. A new suit is forcing one round and shows a very strong hand
c. **3NT** is to play regardless what partner had for his pre-emptive raise
d. **4 of the minor** is invitational (may be used as RKC Blackwood).

Responses to 1M Opening Meckwell Bids over MAJOR

Responses to 1M Opening (Open 1♥/1♠ with 11-15 HCP)

2M 8-10/11 Dummy Points 3 cards support (constructive raise)

Short Suit Game Try (SSGT) over 1♥-2♥ or 1♠-2♠

Any three level suit bid by opener shows shortness in the suit 0-2.
Otherwise relay bids are used by the Opener and responder shows SHORTNESS

	1♥-2♥ 2♠	or	1♠-2♠ 2NT
Club Shortness	3♣		3♣
Diamonds Shortness	3♦		3♦
Heart Shortness			3♥
Spade Shortness	2NT		
4333 min 8-9	3♥		3♠
4333 max 10-11	3NT		3NT
4333 with 4S amd Max 10-11	3♠		
5 to KQ+	4m		4m
Stiff Other Major	4♥		4♠

After SSGT, responder re-evaluates his hand with A=3 and K=1
With 9 or 10/11 responder bids game or cue bids minor with 4 of other majors
With 7 or 8 make last train bid if possible
With 6 or less sign-off

3M 0-6 Dummy Points 4 card support (weak raise)

1NT   7-12 Dummy Points 0-2/3 card support
        After partner bids at the 2-level, a jump to 3M shows 10-12 with 3-cards

2NT   12+ Dummy Points 4+ card support

Ambiguous Splinter with 4-card support = 3 level bid of other major 13+ Dummy Points

3NT	13-15 with three card support
3♣/3♦	Weak 6+ clubs/diamonds less than 7 points
4♣	16+ balanced with 3+ card support in the major
4♦	12-15 points with 5 trumps in the major bid

With Interference at the 2-level

Cue bid is Limit Raise with 3+ trumps

2NT	Limit raise with 4+ trumps
3♣/3♦	Fit Jump Bids 3/4+ trumps with 4+ clubs /Diamonds
3other M	Fit Bid with 3/4+ trumps and 4+ cards in other Major
3M	Weak raise - 0-6 Dummy Points with 4-card support for bid major

4M/5m	To-Play
4m	Splinter-Jump 4-card support with singleton
4other M	To-Play

With Interference at the 3-level

X	Trump Double (Western Cue)
3X	Invitational to game in a major

4-level Cue bid Forcing raise to game in Major bid

3M weak with major fit

4X Fit jumps bids below major bid

4M peemptive

Scroll Bids (Modified)

To locate the singleton, the opener uses scroll asking bids. Thus, the bidding goes: 1♥ - 3♠, 3NT or 1♠ - 3♥, 3♠. The responses after the 3NT scroll asks are: 4♣, 4♦, 4♥, which shows singletons in either clubs, diamonds, or spades, respectively; and the corresponding responses after bidding 3♠ are: 3NT=♥, 4♣=♣, and 4♦=♦.

To determine a void, one continues with a scroll bid. Then up-the-line bids are used to show a singleton or VOID and simultaneously provides one with information about keycards for the agreed upon suit. After hearing the response to the asking scroll bids (3NT or 3♠), one uses the next sequential up-the-line bid to determine the nature of the shortage. The responses are: Step 1 (the next cheapest bid) says it is a singleton, and Steps 2-5, the next four bids, indicate that one has a void and simultaneously shows keycards (e.g. 1/4 or 0/3 or 2 or 2 with Queen).

Responses to 1NT Opening

Responses to 1NT (13-15 HCP VUL and 10-12 HCP NV)

2♣	Stayman/Smolen
2♦/2♥	Transfer hearts/spades
2♠	Transfer to the minor (2NT by opener says he prefers diamonds and 3♣ says he prefers clubs)
2NT	Iinvitational in notrump (11+ Vul and 13+NV)
3♣/3♦/3♥/3♠	<u>6 card suit with 2 of top 3 honors 9-11 Strong (12-14 Weak) HCP</u>
4♦/4♥	Texas Transfer

If NV and 13-15 HCP Open 1D ==== the bid of 1NT = 13-15 ov heart or spade (ALERT)

<u>**Over a double of 1NT (weak or Strong) we employ Helvic Notrump Runouts**</u>

Redouble shows a single suited hand (partner bids 2♣)
And bidding shows a two-suited hand

     2♣=clubs and diamonds
     2♦=diamond and hearts
     2♥=hearts and spades
     2♠=spades and clubs

If you pass the double you have a two-suited hand with two non-touching suits or you want to play 1NT for penalty—<u>partner must re-double or bid 5-card suit</u>. Opener may leave double in or bid the anchor suit.

Transfer Lebensohl over notrump.

After (1) 1NT (2X)?

(a) X = Diamonds/Hearts/Spades.

     Double = Penalty/negative (ov 2♠ or higher)
     2Y to play where Y is not equal to X.
     2NT: Puppet to 3♣
          -> Pass /Lower Suit: To play.
          3X cuebid Stayman with stopper GF
          Over X=H, 3♠=both minors
          3NT Slammish with stopper.
     3♣: Transfer to diamonds, INV or better. *
     3♦: Transfer to hearts, INV or better. *
     3♥: Transfer to spades, INV or better. *
     * If transfer to opponents—> Stayman w/o stopper
     3♠: Transfer to clubs no stopper
     3NT: To play, but no stopper
     4m: Leaping Michaels. 5-5 up.
          (X=M: 4♣=C+OM. 4♦=D+OM.
          X=D: 4♣=C+One major. 4♦=H+S.)
     4M: Unbid: NAT. with stopper.
          Jump Cue: Minors. Strong.
     4NT: Minors. (Weak if X=M.)

(b) X = Clubs.
          Double = Cuebid Stayman w/o stopper
     2Y where Y is not equal to X: To play.
     2NT transfer to diamonds no stopper.
          -> 3♦=Accept. 3♣=Decline.
     3♣: Stayman with a stopper GF

3♦: Transfer to hearts, INV or better.
3♥: Transfer to spades, INV or better.
3♠: Transfer to diamonds no stopper
3NT: To play but no stopper
4m: Leaping Michaels.
4M: NAT. with stopper.

Over 2♦/2♥/2♠ - Transfer Lebensohl if 3-level but neg double over the majors

Responses to 2M Opening

Responses to 2♥/ 2♠ (Open 5-10 6+ card suit)—Same as 2/1

Over 2NT asks for Feature

The weak major 2-leve bid is a "normal" weak two and typically shows between 5-10 points and at least a 6-card suit. The optimum hand for a weak-2 has most of its points in the long suit although it is recognized that this is not always possible and sometimes (particularly 3rd hand at favorable vulnerability) you have to go with what you've got.

4♣ is RKCB [used with weak two bids (2♥/2♠)].

The responses are:

4♦   first step 0 keycards in the agreed suit
4♥   second step, 1 keycard without the Queen
4♠   third step, 1 keycard with the Queen
4NT   fourth step, 2 keycards without the Queen
5♣   fifth step, 2 keycards with the Queen

The only step in which the queen is not known is the first-step. The next bid of 4♥ is the Queen ask - 4♠ = no and 4NT = yes. A jump over the four hearts bid (5♣/5♦/5♥/5♠) is the Specific Suit Ask (SSA).

When they Double Weak bid—Reverse Mc Cabe

2♥—X then   Redouble shows a strong hand
              2♠ =Spades
              2NT =Clubs (partner bids clubs)
              3♦ =transfer into suit shows A/K of Hearts
              3♥ =No A/K of Hearts

2♠—X then   Redouble shows a strong hand
              2NT =Clubs (partner bids clubs)

3♥ =transfer into suit show A/K of Spades
3♠ =No A/K of Spades

Responses to 2♣* Opening

Responses to 2♣ Opening (Open 11-15 HCP, 6+ Clubs or 5/6clubs and 4 card major, must have two of the top three honors - 5+ in third seat.

Partner responses
2♦*   11+ HCP, conventional and forcing for one round

    Opener Rebids

    2♥   11-15 HCP, 4-card ♥ suit
    2♠   11-15 HCP, 4-card ♠ suit
    2NT   11-15 HCP, 6-3-2-2 BAL hand, 6-card club suit with a major stopper

        3♦*   requests opener to clarify stoppers

    Opener Bids

        3♥*   ♥ stopper
        3♠*   ♠ stopper
        3NT   ♥ and ♠ stoppers

    3♣   14-15 HCP non-forcing and unbalanced hand (1-3-3-6)
    3♥   14-15 HCP, 5+card ♥ suit
    3♠   14-15 HCP, relay back to ♣'s, solid club suit AKJ109x allows responder to bid 3NT
    3NT   14-15 HCP, 5+spades and 6+ clubs
2♥/2♠   Natural with 5+cards, 8-10 HCP

2NT*   **Lebensohl (for two-suited hands)**

    Partner Bids 3♣
    Responder next bids
        3♦ =   5-5 diamonds and hearts
        3♥ =   5-5 hearts and spades
        3♠ =   5-5 spades and diamonds

3♣   **10-12 Invitional**
3♦/3♥/3♠   6+ card suit, 12 HCP openers raises or bids 3NT **(Opener May Not Pass)**
4♣   Invitational to game in clubs
4♥/4♠   Natural and to play

4♦   RKCB for clubs

With interference

    Negative double through 3♠
    Redouble   10+ HCP
    Cuebid   13+ HCP

Responses to 2♦* Opening (Singleton/void in Diamonds)

Responses to 2♦* Opening (11-15 HCP)
Partner Response to 2♦*

2♥/2♠   To play in bid majorr
3♣   To play in clubs
2NT*   ASK

    Opener Rebids

    3♣*any minimum 11-13,

        3♦ ASK (by responder)

        3♥= four hearts
        3♠ = four spades
        3NT=4-4-1-4 or 4-4-0-5

    3♦=4-4-**1**-4, maximum with singleton diamond
    3♥=3-4-1-5, maximum with four hearts
    3♠=**4**-3-1-5, maximum with four spades
    3NT=4-4-0-5, maximum with five clubs

Responses to 2NT* Opening

Responses to 2NT* 5-5 in the minors 5-10 HCP NV and 11-15 HCP VUL

3♣ or 3♦ is to play
3♥* is an asking bid

    Opener Rebids

    3♠   5-5 minimum (5-10 NV; 11-15 VUL)
    3NT   maximum
    4♣   6-5 (clubs, diamonds), minimum

4♦   6-5 (diamonds, clubs), minimum
4♥   6-5 (clubs, diamonds), maximum
4♠   6-5 (diamonds, clubs), maximum
4NT   6-6 in the minors.

3♠   to play
3NT   to play
4♣/4♦ pre-emptive bids and to play
4♥/4♠ to play
5♣/5♦ to play
Over interference (Game force)

4NT === I prefer diamonds
4♣ === I prefer clubs
Gambling 3NT*----------------Same as 2/1

Namyats----------------------Same as 2/1

Shows a hand with 8-8 ½ trick in hearts (Open 4♣*), in spades open 4♦*. Refuse transfer by bidding the step in between (4♦ over 4♣ and 4♥ over 4♦), requesting that partner bid an ace if he has one or to sign off in his long suit. 4NT is RKCB.

Responses to 3X Openings

Responses to 3X bids by OPENER (always ensures 2 of the top 3 honors Vulnerable) and 5-10 HCP plus distribution; Non-vulnerable at least ONE top Honor.

4♣   **RKCB [over three level (3♦/3♥/3♠) bids]**
4♦   **Asks for outside controls first step 0-2 controls (A=2; K=1), second step = 3, etc.**

The bid of 4NT should not be used since it may get the auction too high.

The responses for 4♣ RKCB are:

4♦   first step 0 keycards in the agreed suit
4♥   second step, 1 keycard without the Queen
4♠   third step, 1 keycard with the Queen
4NT   fourth step, 2 keycards without the Queen
5♣   fifth step, 2 keycards with the Queen

The only step in which the queen is not known is the first-step. The next bid of 4♥ is the Queen ask - 4♠ = no and 4NT = yes. A jump over the four hearts bid (5♣/5♦/5♥/5♠) is the Specific Suit Ask (SSA).

After the premptive bid of 3♣, the bid of 4♣ is natural and advances the preempt; a jump to 4♦ is RKCB for clubs.

Responses to 1♣* Opening

Responses to 1♣* OPENING (16+ HCP, but 17 + HCP for a balanced hand and a 4 card major)

(1) Negative: 1♦* 0-7 HCP

Opener Rebids after 1♦*:

Non-forcing bids: 1♠/2♣/2♦ (minimum unbalanced hands with 5/6-card suits, 16-21 HCP).

1NT* 16-19 HCP Balanced May have a 5-Card Major (NO MUPPET)

> **Partner Responses**
> Pass   0-6 HCP
> 2♣   6-7 HCP, Stayman
> 2♦/2♥   Jacoby Transfer
> 2NT   7HCP, inviting 3NT
> 3♣3♦   5-5 in the Minors Min/Max (0-5/6-7)
> 3♥/3♠   5-5 in the Majors Min/Max (0-5/6-7)

2NT* 22-23 HCP balanced may have 5-card major (no relay bid)

> **Partner Responses**
>
> Pass   0-2 HCP

> **Other bids same as 2/1 (e.g. 3♠ is transfer to 3NT)**

> **3♣—Muppet Stayman**

> **3NT*** shows 5 hearts. Responder can either pass if he has spades, or if responder wants to play it in hearts, bids 4♦* as a transfer to hearts which allows the strong hand to play the contract in 4 hearts

> **3♠*** shows 5 spades

> **3♦*** **has 1 or 2 four-card majors**

3♥*   shows no 4-card major or no 5-card major, but may have a 3-card spade suit. Responder will usually now bid 3NT. But, if responder has 5 spades and 4/3 hearts, he can now bid 3♠, looking for the 5-3 major spade fit.

When opener bids 3♦*, responder makes the following rebids.

3♥*   Responder bids the major he does not have (like Smolen). This sequence shows 4 spades and denies 4 hearts. Opener either bids spades or 3NT.

3♠*   Responder bids the major he does not have. This sequence shows 4 hearts and denies 4 spades; opener either bids hearts or 3NT.

4♣*   **Responder has both majors, it asks partner to pick the major.**

4♦*   **Most p**artnerships play the bid of 4♦ to show slam interest, pick a slam.

* Alert (Do not use Muppet if 4-5 in spades-hearts, Transfer to Hearts and Bid spades)

4♣= Gerber
4♦=transfer to hearts
4♥=transfer to spades
4♠=transfer to clubs
5♣-=transfer to diamonds
5NT=invite Grand Slam

Other bids same as 2/1 (e.g. 3♠ is transfer to 3NT)

1♥* relay responder must respond 1♠*

Opener Rebids after 1♥*

1NT 20-21 HCP balanced may have a 5-card major **(May Use Muppet and the same bids reviewed over the bid of 1♣-2NT)**

2♣   5+ hearts, 4+ clubs. Non-forcing
2♦   5+hearts, 4+ diamonds Non-forcing
2♥   5+ heart suit, no extras
2♠   5+hearts, 4+ spades, non forcing

2NT 24-25 HCP balanced **(May Use Muppet and the same bids reviewed over the bid of 1♣-2NT)**

3♣/3♦ Forcing, possibly 5-5 in hearts and the suit bid (clubs/diamonds)

3♥	5/6-card suit, invitational over the 1♦ response
3♠	5+ hearts, 4+ spades with extras.
3NT	to play
4♣ 6	clubs, 5+ diamonds, forcing
4♦ 6	diamonds, 5+ clubs, forcing
4♥/4♠	to play
4NT	Blackwood ace ask

Exceptions—Do not relay hearts to spades if the following conditions apply.

After 1♥* responder bids:

1NT	5-5 or better in the majors, very weak (0-4 HCP)
2♣/2♦/2♥/2♠	modest 6+ card suit, very weak
2NT	5-5 or better in the minors, very weak (0-4 HCP)
3♣/3♦/3♥/3♠	modest 7+ card suit, very weak

After 2♥* responder bids:

| 2NT | two suited 5-5 or better, extremely weak (0-2) |
| 3♣/3♦/3♥/3♠ | modest 7+ card suit, extremely weak |

2♥* relay responder must bid 2♠*

Opener Rebids and Corresponding Partner Rebids
2NT 26-27 HCP balanced hand may have a 4 card major
(May Use Muppet and the same bids reviewed over the bid of 1♣-2NT)

3♥ - 5/6+hearts—equivalent of 2/1 bidders 2♣ 22+ HCP (forcing)

| 3NT | 0-4 HCP, minimum and no support |
| 4♥ | 0-4 HCP, minimum and 2-card support |

3♣/3♦—unbalanced very strong 7+ minor hand (game force, 22+ PTS)

New suit	shows king/void/ace
3NT	no king or void
4♣/4♦	with singleton
Raise to game	denies K, singleton, or void

3NT - 5-5 in the minors with 22+ HCP

4♣/4♦ - 6-5 clubs-diamonds/6-5 diamonds-clubs 22+ HCP

New suit	shows king/void/ace
4NT	no king or void
Raise to game	denies K, singleton, or void

2♠/3♣/3♦ without relay shows 5+cards and 22+HCP—equivalent of Standard bidders 2♣ (no-relay)

Bids follow 2/1 structure

3NT 28+ HCP balanced may have a 5-card major
Partner Rebids

0-3 HCP	pass OR
	4♣= Gerber
	4♦=transfer to hearts
	4♥=transfer to spades
	4♠=transfer to clubs
	5♣ - transfer to diamonds
4-7 HCP and balanced	4NT invite sslam

(2) Transfers to MAJORS Positive Bids

1♥#	5+ spades opener bids 1♠ 12+ points
2♦#	5+ hearts opener bids 2♥, 12+ points
1♠#	8+ points balanced/unbalanced hand may be 5-5 in major-minor, 5-5 in majors or 5-5 in the minors

announced as a transfer

Opener (Only accepts Transfer if he has a fit by bidding 1♠/2♥ with three card support). After the bid of 1NT, Stayman/ Smolen and transfers are again used.

3♥/3♠	Shows a 3-3-3-4 hand - 3-card support for the major (16-17 HCP)
4♥/4♠	Show a hand with exactly 16 HCP and 4-card support

Responder uses (Gamma) control bids to show length after Opener ACCEPTS showing 17+ HCP.

3♣* by responder says I have 5
3♦* by responder says I have 6+

Next level bids of the MAJOR by Opener at the 3 level after Gamma bids are 1430 RKCB asking bids.

3♥*/3♠*
3♠/3NT   **show 1 or 4**
3NT/4♣   **show 0 or 3**
4♣/4♦   **show 2 keycards**
4♦/4♥   **show 2 with Queen**

Over the 1/4 or 1/3 level bids, next bid up is Queen ask.

Over the bids of 2 keycards with the Queen the next level bid is the specfic King (4♥/4♠ respectively—last bid in chain).

An important adjunct to Gamma length bids (when one has 6+ trumps) is the CAB which is initiated by bidding the SUIT! Note that this is used for the investigation of SLAM in a suit and NOT Notrump.

Responses to CAB (abbrevated) are for the suit bid, step after queen ask:

> 1st step no controls
> 2nd step second round control—king/singleton
> 3rd step first round control—ace/void

When responder is 5-5 in spades and a minor

Bid 1♥ as a transfer to spades ==== after the relay bid of 1♠ one bids:

> 2♣* = 5-5 in spades and club
> 2♦* = 5-5 in spades and diamonds
> 3♣* = 5 spades and no 5-card minor
> 3♦* = 6+ spades and no 5-card minor

Opener next bids 3♠* is 1430 for spades and then 4♠ is the spec king ask.
Furthermore, 3♣* and 3♦* are Minorwood bids.

When responder is 5-5 in hearts and a minor

Bid 2♦ as a transfer to hearts ==== after the relay bid of 2♥ one bids:

> 2♠* = 5-5 in hearts and clubs
> 2NT =5-5 in hearts and diamonds
> 3♣* = 5 hearts and no 5-card minor
> 3♦* = 6+ hearts and no 5-card minor

If opener next bids 3♥*=1430 for hearts where last train bid is the spec king ask Over 2♠/2NT then the bids of and 3♣*/3♦* are Minorwood asks.

When responder is 5-5 in the majors

If responder is 5-5 in the majors after 1NT, he next bids 3♥/3♠.

3♥*=5-5 and 12+ HCP
3♠*=5-5 and 8-11 HCP

The next bid up by opener is DRKCB (e.g. 3♠*/3NT*), Game bids are to play.

3NT/4♣	1or 4
4♣/4♦	0or 3
4♦/4♥	2 with neither queen
4♥/4♠	2 with one queen
4♠/4NT	2 with both queens

Note that in the second step (4♦/4♥), you do not know which queen. However, if partner makes a first or second step response to a DRKCB asks, unless the asker has both of the agreed-upon suit queens, the queen situation is unknown.

To now ask about queens, the asker uses the next available "free bid" step (4♥/4♠).

The four-response steps now become:

1st step	no queen
2nd step	lower-ranking queen only
3rd step	higher-ranking queen only
4th step	both queens

When responder is 5-5 in the minors

If responder is 5-5 in the minors after 1NT, he next bids

3♣*=5-5 and 12+ HCP
3♦*=5-5 and 8-11 HCP

Next step 3♦*/3♥* (**next step bids are DRKCB for the minor** and 3NT is to play

5♣/5♦ is to play game in the minor

DRKCB Minorwood for clubs (Example—similar for hearts)

Over 3♦

3♥   1 or 4 keycards (the 14 step)   1st step

3♠	0 or 3 keycards (the 03 step)	2nd step	
3NT	2 with neither Queen	3rd step	
4♣	2 with one Queen	4th step	
4♦	2 with both Queens	5th step	

Note that in the second step (3♥/3♠), you do not know which queen. However, if partner makes a first or second step response to a DRKCB asks, unless the asker has both of the agreed-upon suit queens, the queen situation is unknown.

To now ask about queens, the asker uses the next available "free bid" step.

The four-response steps now become:

1st step	no queen
2nd step	lower-ranking queen only
3rd step	higher-ranking queen only
4th step	both queens

Last Train bids are the specific King asks.

When responder has 8-11 HCP ====1♣-1♠-1NT

Responder Bids

2♦ transfer to Hearts with 5+
2♥ transfer to Diamonds with 5+
2♠ transfer to Minors with 5+

> **2NT by opener says he prefers diamonds**
> **3♣ says he prefers clubs**

2NT 8-9
3NT 10-11

When responder has one long minor

The bid of 2♣* by responder says he has a long minor (8-13 HCP) and the bid of 1NT* shows a balanced hand (with 12-13 HCP) details (3) and (4) below.

NON-TRANSFER BIDS by OPENER -5+card suit of his own denying a fit in the transfer major. Or one may bid 1NT showing balanced hand with 16-19 HCP.

Responding with Balanced Hands and no major suit fit.

1/2NT*	16-19 HCP
2/3NT*	20-21 HCP
3/4NT*	22-23 HCP
4/5NT	24+ HCP

(3) 1NT* 12-13 HCP and no 5-card Major (1♣-Pass - 1NT—?)

Opener Bids

2♣	**Stayman**
2♦/2♥/2♠	Shows 5-card suit 16/17 HCP
2NT	Show Clubs with 16/17 HCP
3♣/3♦/3♥/3♠	Strong Hand with 18+ HCP and 5/6 card suit
3NT	16/17 HCP and no 4-card major

(4) 2♣* 8+ HCP 6-cards in a Minor

Opener Rebids (after 1♣* - 2♣*)—Summary

2♥/2♠	Shows a 5-card major suit

> **Partner Rebids**
> Raise major with support or bid minor

2♦ (Ask)	**Asking partner for Minor**

> **Partner Rebids**

2♥	**shows CLUBS**
2♠	**Shows DIAMONDS**

> **Opener Bids**

2NT	**1430 for the MINOR**

2NT	**Forcing with Major stoppers**
3NT	No interest in slam or the minor
4NT	Blackwood Ace Asking

(5) 2♥/2♠ 4-6 HCP 6+card

(Weak Jump Shift with all values in the suit—with 7+ scatterd values bid 1♦)

Opener Rebids

Pass	Game unlikely
4♥/4♠/3NT	20+ HCP
New suit	5+ cards without support for the majors

Partners Rebids

Raise	3+ support (or Qx)
Rebid ♥/♠	minimum no support
Cue-bid under 3NT	singleton or void

3♥/3♠	Minimal hand with support (16-18 HCP)

Partners Rebids

Pass or bid game

2NT	Feature
3NT	Natural
4NT	RKCB

(6) 2NT* 14+HCP, balanced no 5-card major (May not stop short of 4NT)

Opener Rebids

3♦/3♥/3♠	Naturl bids
3♣*	Baron asking bid (Not Muppet)

Partner Bids
Bid 4-card suits up the line (3♦/3♥/3♠)
3NT show clubs

3NT	**ASK BID**

Responder bids
4♣ 14-15 points
4♦ 16-17 points

After 4 clubs and 4 diamonds, Opener bids 4-card suits up-the—line or bis 4NT sign-off or 6/7 NT

4♥ 18-19 points

4♠ 20-21 points

After 4 heartrs and 4 spades, Opener may bid 4NT ACE ASKING or bids 6/7 NT

4NT   **Blackwood Ace ask**

(7) 3♣* 1444/4441 Black Singleton Lacking 4 controls (8 - 13 HCP)

Opener Rebids after 3♣

3♦*   where is the singleton?

                3♥* club singleton
                3♠* spade singleton

3NT   to play
4♥/4♠   to play
4NT   Blackwood ace asking

Cue bid by Opener of singleton (4♣*/4♠*) is the CAB

            1st step 0-2 (at most one ace or two kings)
            2nd step 3 (ace and king)
            3rd step 4 (two aces)

(8) 3♦* 4144/4414 Red Singleton Lacking 4 controls (8-13 HCP)

Rebids after 3♦

3♥*   where is singleton?
              3♠* diamond singleton
              3NT* heart singleton
4♥/4♠   to play
4NT   Blackwood ace asking

Cue bid by Opener of singleton (4♦*/4♥*) is the CAB

            1st step 0-2 (at most one ace or two kings)
            2nd step 3 (ace and king)
            3rd step 4 (two aces)

(9) (Submarine Strong Singleton Responses after 1♣ bids)

3♥* specifically 1444 with 4+ controls, usually 14+ HCP
3NT* specifically 4441 with 4+ controls, usually 14+HCP
4♣* specifically 4414 with 4+ controls, usually 14+HCP
4♦* specifically 4144 with 4+ controls, usually 14+HCP

Next level bids BY OPENER are CAB (3♠*, 4♣*, 4♦* and 4♥*, respectively)
The responses to the CAB (3♠*/4♣*/4♦*/4♥*) are:

1st step - 4 controls (two aces or ace and two kings)
2nd step - 5 controls (two aces and one king/ ace + three kings)
3rd step - 6 controls (three aces/ two aces and two kings)

(10) 3♠* a solid 7+ card suit (AKQxxxx), 9 + HCP with or without side controls

Opener Rebids

3NT   to play
4♥/4♠   natural showing at least 5-cards with no slam interest

Opener bids (if he knows the suit)

4♣*   **CAB—Asks about outside suit controls**
           Reponses to CAB
           4♦*   no outside controls
           4♥*   outside king
           4♠*   outside ace or 2 kings
           4NT*   Ace/2-3 kings

Opener bids (if suit is unknown)

4♦*   **asking for suit**

           Responses to suit ask
           4♥*/4♠*/5♣*   hearts, spades, clubs
           4NT*   diamonds

Opener may also bid 4NT which is Blackwood

SUMMARY—INTERFERENCE BIDS OVER 1♣* OPENING

Direct Seat Interference

Double—Mathe which shows Majors

Pass	0-4 HCP
1♦	5-7 HCP
Redouble	8+
1♥	8-10 HCP no stopper in hearts
1♠	8-10 HCP no stopper in spades
1NT	8-10 HCP stoppers in the majors
2♣	8-13 HCP and 6+ cards
2♦	8-13 HCP and 6+ diamonds
2♥	11+ spade stopper (no heart stopper)
2♠	11+ heart stopper (no spade stopper)
2NT	11+ both majors stopped

At 1 level—(natural)

Pass	0-4 HCP
Double	5-7 HCP
Suit	8+ HCP, 5+ card suit, Game Force
Jump in suit	SYSTEMS ON 3♣/3♦/3♥/3♠
1NT	8-13 HCP, with stopper
2NT	10+ HCP, with 1/2 stopper
Cuebid	10+ Game force no stopper

1NT—(natural)

Pass	0-4 HCP
Double	5-7 HCP
Suit	8+ HCP, 5+ card suit

1NT—Mathe which shows Minors

Pass	0-4 HCP
Double	5-7 HCP
2♣	5+ hearts, GF
2♦	5+ spades GF
2♥	5+ HCP, natural and non-forcing
2♠	5+ HCP, natural and non-forcing
3NT	10+ HCP, both minors stopped

At 2 level—(natural)

Pass	0-4 HCP
Double	5-7 HCP
Suit bid	8+ HCP, natural
Cue bid	9+ Flat with no stopper
2NT	9-13 HCP with stopper
3NT	14+ with stoppers

At 3 level—(natural)

Pass	0-7 HCP
Double	8+ HCP
Suit bid	8+ HCP, and 5+ card suit

At 4 level—(natural)

Pass	0-7 HCP
Double	8+ HCP, takeout or penalty

Balancing Seat Interference

After 1♣* - (Pass) - 1♦ - (1♥/♠)

Pass	balance minimum no 5-card suit
Double	support for the other three suits
Suit Bid	Natural, non-forcing
1NT	shows stopper with (16-21 HCP)
2NT	shows stopper with (22+ HCP)
Cuebid	20 + HCP no stopper

After 1♣* - (Pass) - 1♦ - (1NT for Minors)

Pass	balanced minimum no 5-card suit
Double	support for the both majors
2♣/2♦	unusual extra values shows ♥/♠
2♥/2♠	Natural non-forcing
2NT	shows stopper with (22+ HCP)

After 1♣* - (Pass) - 1♦ - (Double = Majors)

Pass	balanced minimum no 5-card suit
Double	support for the both minors
2♣/2♦	natural 5+ card suit.

| 2♥/2♠ | unusual extra values shows ♣/♦ |
| 2NT | shows stopper with (22+ HCP) |

INTERFERENCE OVER 1NT by OPPONENTS

Direct Seat or Balance SEAT over Strong NO TRUMPS

Double:	♣♦♥ or ♦♥ or ♥ (weak or strong)
2♣	♦♥♠ or ♥♠ or strong ♠
2♦	♥♠♣ or ♠♣ or strong ♣
2♥	♠♣♦ or ♣♦ or strong ♦
2♠	♠ + minor
2NT	one or two minors
3♣	♣♥ (non-forcing)
3♦	♦♠ (non-forcing)

Over Weak (10-12) NT

Direct Seat DOUBLE = Penalty with 13+ and Landy where 2♣= majors and all other bids are natural

OTHER CONVENTIONAL CALLS

Over a Major Bid Play Leaping Michaels, Unusual vs. Michaels
Unusual over Unusual, SSGT
Overcalls Michaels and 2nt=two - lowest unbid suits
3X level bids over the opponents bid are pre-emptive

4th Suit Forcing at the two levels is forcing one round - **3 level shows**

Western Que
Rosencrantz Doubles over a Major/Minor Overcalls

1♣ X is a power double 16+ and 1♦/1♥/1♠ X is take-out
1NT 15-18 Systems Off

LEADS - 4th Best both suits and notrump
A/Q ASKS FOR Attitude and King=count
Upside-down COUNT AND ATTITUDE (Suit and Notrump)
Trump Suit Preference

Chapter 20

Interfering over Precision

Interfering over Precison players is similar to interfering over the 2/1 15-17 HCP strong notrump pairs. In this final Chapter we review several conventions. Interference comes in many flavors. There are natural bids, artificial bids, and two-suited bids among others that are designed to interfere in the direct or balancing seat.

Overview of Interference Systems used over the Precision 1♣* bid

Mathe

The most popular system is called Mathe, developed by Lewis L. Mathe from California. It is popular because of its simplicity. It goes:

Over 1♣*, bids in the direct seat are:

Double*	4-4 or better in the majors
1NT*	4-4 or better in the minors
2NT*	5-5 or better in the minors

All one-level bids are natural (diamonds, hearts, and spades) and the bid of 2♣ shows a club suit. The system is also used in the balancing seat over the sequence: 1♣* - Pass - 1♦* - (?)

Because both bids are artificial, all Mathe responses remain the same; however, now two clubs and two diamonds are natural. Higher two-level bids usually show a distributional hand. A disadvantage of Mathe is that the double does not interfere significantly over the strong club bid.

An alternate is the system Bill Amason and I call SPAM, which says **SP**ades **A**nd **M**ore, to be used against other Precision players. The advantage of spam is that it employs the bid of one spade as a takeout bid making it more difficult for Precision player. However, the most destructive bid is 3♠.

SPAM (played in the direct seat only)

Double	the majors (4-4 or 5-4)
1♠*	takeout with an unspecified long suit 5+ cards
1NT*	the minors (5-5)
2♣*	the majors (5-5)
2♦*	diamonds and a major (5-5)

2NT*	strong notrump 15-17 HCP
3X	Natural suit 6+ cards

CRASH

Another convention used by some partnerships is called CRASH, representing **C**olor **RA**nk and **Sh**ape. The system was developed by Kit Woolsey and Steve Robinson. The basic bids are:

Double*	2 suits of the same color (red or black)
1♦*	2 suits of the same rank (majors or minors)
1NT*	2 suits of the same shape (rounded ♣ ♥ or pointed ♦ ♠)
1♥/1♠/2♣/2♦	shows natural 5+ card suits

CRASH, like Mathe, may also be employed in the balancing seat.

Mathe and CRASH are probably the most widely used systems to interfere over the Precision club.

Because many 2/1 Game Force partnerships play some version of DONT or Weber (Transfer bids), I have modified the bids to make them consistent with Modified DONT (Meckwell). The system is similar to DONT+T (ON), developed by Tony Melucci in cooperation with Neill Currie. The bids follow. I call the system MDONT +T.

MDONT + T (played in the direct seat only)

1♦*	Transfer to hearts with 5+ hearts
1♥*	Transfer to spades with 5+ spades
1♠*	Transfer to clubs
1NT*	Transfer to diamonds

2♣*	Clubs + Major
2♦*	Diamonds + Major
2♥*	Hearts + Spades (the majors are at least 4-4)
2NT*	Clubs + Diamond (the minors are at least 5-5)

Higher level bids are natural.

Another system developed by Tony Melucci and Neill Currie is called MACE. Because some feel that coping with the MACE bids is difficult, I have included their system of bids.

MACE

Double*	4-4 in the Minors

1♦*	shows 3-3 or 4-3 in the Majors
1♥/1♠	Natural 5+ card suit
1NT*	Rounded or Points Suits (4-4 or better)
2NT*	Both Majors or Both Minors (5-5 or better)

Suit bids at the two - or three-levels are natural

SUCTION

This convention was developed by **Harold Feldheim** of Hamden, Connecticut, United States. The overcall of any suit shows the next-higher suit, or the other two suits. This is known as a *transfer overcall* since the overcaller is actually transferring his partner to the desired suit. The objective and advantage of this *transfer overcall* is that the 1♣ bidder is then forced to lead the first card as opposed to being in third seat.

2♣:	Shows a one-suiter in Diamonds, or a two-suited holding with Spades and Hearts.
2♦:	Shows a one-suiter in Hearts, or a two-suited holding with Spades and Clubs, or both black suits.
2♥:	Shows a one-suiter in Spades, or a two-suited holding with Clubs and Diamonds, or both Minor suits.
2♠:	Shows a one-suiter in Clubs, or a two-suited holding with Diamonds and Hearts, or both red suits.
2 NT:	Shows non-touching suits, either Clubs and Hearts or Diamonds and Spades.
Double:	*Optional:* Shows non-touching pointed suits, Diamonds and Spades, as opposed to an overcall of 2 No Trump.

When should you interfere over Precision and what is the best system?

The guidelines for interference over the strong club follow those you used when playing 2/1 Game Force. In the direct seat, you need a distributional hand and in the balancing seat you need shortness. Again, the rules of 8 and 2 apply.

Rule of 2

You should interfere over the bid of 1♣* in the balancing seat if you have at least two shortness points. Otherwise, do not interfere.

Rule of 8

Provided you have at least 6 HCP, you should interfere over 1♣* in the direct seat if the number of cards in your two longest suits minus the number of losers in your hand is two or more. Otherwise, do not interfere.

The best system to play over Precision is the one you remember. The simplest are SPAM and Mathe. Even though MDONT +T address the most hand combinations, SPAM is simple and provides adequate interference over the strong club opening; more importantly, it is easily remembered.

INDEX